Making Things Valuable

Making Things Valuable

Edited by
Martin Kornberger, Lise Justesen,
Anders Koed Madsen, and Jan Mouritsen

OXFORD
UNIVERSITY PRESS

OXFORD
UNIVERSITY PRESS

Great Clarendon Street, Oxford, OX2 6DP,
United Kingdom

Oxford University Press is a department of the University of Oxford.
It furthers the University's objective of excellence in research, scholarship,
and education by publishing worldwide. Oxford is a registered trade mark of
Oxford University Press in the UK and in certain other countries

First published 2015

Published in the United States of America by Oxford University Press
198 Madison Avenue, New York, NY 10016, United States of America

British Library Cataloguing in Publication Data
Data available

ISBN 978–0–19–871228–2

Contents

List of Figures

List of Tables

List of Contributors

Laure Cabantous, Senior Lecturer, Cass Business School, City University London.

Gian Marco Campagnolo, Lecturer, Science, Techology & Innovation Studies, University of Edinburgh.

Liliana Doganova, Associate Professor, Centre de Sociologie de l'Innovation, Mines ParisTech.

Théodora Dupont-Courtade, Paris School of Economics, University Paris 1 Panthéon-Sorbonne.

Wendy Nelson Espeland, Professor of Sociology, Department of Sociology, Northwestern University.

Lise Justesen, Associate Professor, Department of Organization, Copenhagen Business School.

Martin Kornberger, Professor, Department of Organization, Copenhagen Business School; Professorial Fellow, University of Edinburgh School of Business, and Research Fellow, Research Institute for Urban Management and Governance WU Wien.

Stacy E. Lom, Assistant Professor, Department of Sociology, University of Central Arkansas.

Celia Lury, Professor, Centre for Interdisciplinary Methodologies, University of Warwick.

Anders Koed Madsen, Assistant Professor, Techno-Anthropology Research Group, Department of Education, Learning and Philosophy, Aalborg University Copenhagen.

Noortje Marres, Senior Lecturer, Centre for the Study of Invention and Social Process, Department of Sociology, Goldsmiths University of London.

Jan Mouritsen, Professor, Department of Operations Management, Copenhagen Business School.

Fabian Muniesa, Centre de Sociologie de l'Innovation, Mines ParisTech.

José Ossandón, Assistant Professor, Department of Organization, Copenhagen Business School & Associate Researcher, Instituto de Investigación en Ciencias Sociales, Universidad Diego Portales, Chile.

Trine Pallesen, Assistant Professor, Department of Organization, Copenhagen Business School.

Pierre Pénet, PhD in sociology from Northwestern University & Sciences Po Paris/OSC and postdoctoral fellow at the Graduate Institute of International and Development Studies in Geneva.

Neil Pollock, Professor, University of Edinburgh School of Business, University of Edinburgh.

Paolo Quattrone, Professor, University of Edinburgh School of Business, University of Edinburgh.

Juliane Reinecke, Associate Professor, Warwick Business School.

Sabina Du Rietz, Assistant Professor, Department of Accounting, Auditing and Law, Norwegian School of Economics.

Introduction

Making Things Valuable

Martin Kornberger, Lise Justesen, Anders Koed Madsen, and Jan Mouritsen

This introductory chapter pursues two objectives. First, it offers a critique of some of the assumptions that structure the debate between economic sociologists, anthropologists of markets, and economists; and second, following Dewey's flank movement, the chapter suggests understanding valuation as an activity. Rather than focusing on values and arguing about their relative significance, this introduction as well as the following chapters, investigate the practices, processes, and technologies through which things are made valuable in the first place. Empirically, this calls for a focus on rankings, ratings, reviews, standards, classifications, categorizations, and myriad other practices and devices that calculate, make commensurable, and evaluate objects. In so doing, this volume contributes to our understanding of how valuation is accomplished. This introduction is structured as follows. First, we outline the contours of the valuation debate by focusing on two distinct arguments, one involving an economics reading of value that collapses the plurality of values into one principle—that of utility; and one comprising an economic sociology reading that argues for distinct orders of worth that maintain the plurality of intersecting values. Then we will argue how *Making Things Valuable* departs from this discussion by shifting the focus onto the valuation devices and practices that constitute values in the first place. We conclude with an overview of the chapters and how they advance our understanding of how things are made valuable.

Economizing Values

The economy enjoys a reputation as the origin and arbiter of value. In almost all domains of life, it is the economist who is called upon to (e-)valuate benefits and costs and provide the basis for decision-making. Why do we entrust the economy with such a difficult task? The writings of Jeremy Bentham are a fruitful place to begin looking for an answer. Bentham was a man of many talents. His well-known sketches of the panopticon represented an architectural answer to the problem of social order. His lesser-known writings on government and morals outlined an approach to the question of how to deal with values. In his *Principles of Morals and Legislation*, Bentham introduces the guiding principle of utility: 'Nature has placed mankind under the governance of two sovereign masters, *pain* and *pleasure*. It is for them alone to point out what we ought to do, as well as determine what we shall do' (Bentham 1789/1823, 1). For Bentham, this principle of utility is 'the sole and all-sufficient reason for every point of practice whatsoever' (Bentham 1776/1988, 59). Pain and pleasure are sufficient guiding principles for all action and it is overall happiness that provides the yardstick for any decision: '*the greatest happiness of the greatest number is the measure between right and wrong*' (Bentham 1776/1988, 3). This principle of utility is the philosophical centre of Bentham's philosophy and, as such, beyond proof: 'for that which is used to prove everything else, cannot itself be proved: a chain of proofs must have their commencement somewhere. To give such proof is as impossible as it is needless' (Bentham 1789/1823, 4). For Bentham there is nothing behind, beyond utility—even the critique of utility falls under its spell: 'When a man attempts to combat the principle of utility, it is with reasons drawn, without his being aware of it, from that very principle itself' (Bentham 1789/1823, 4–5).

Bentham's argument takes an important turn when it translates the philosophical principle of utility into a political programme; if the panopticon was moral theory set in stone, then his work on utility is moral theory made calculable. Bentham stresses the idea of quantification: only if utility can be calculated can it guide action. Bentham offers the example of two people arguing over the merits of a proposed law. Their arguments, so Bentham claims, are nothing but 'womanish scolding' and

> childish altercation which is sure to irritate, and which can never persuade.—'*I* say, the legislature can*not* do this—*I* say, that it *can*. *I* say, that to do this, *exceeds* the bounds of its *authority*—*I* say, it does *not*.' It is evident, that a pair of disputants setting out in this manner, may go on irritating and perplexing one another for everlasting, without the smallest chance of ever coming to an agreement. (Bentham 1776/1988, 104)

Bentham's solution to avoid these childish altercations is to quantify pain and pleasure and to use them as inputs in a calculation of utility that results in a clear guidance for decision-makers. In the reframed discussion, calculation replaces the judge, and numbers substitute arguments: '*I* say, that the mischiefs of the measure in question are to *such* an amount—*I* say, *not* so, but to a *less*.—*I* say, the benefits of it are only to *such* an amount.—*I* say, *not* so, but to a *greater*.—This, we see, is a ground of controversy very different from the former' (Bentham 1776/1988, 104).

What Bentham proposed, and what the economist would put into action, is a new way of thinking and arguing—a new rhetoric (McCloskey 1994)—in which to articulate and justify political ideas. Bentham's political philosophy—his moral panopticon—can be seen as an implicit critique of justifications of social order, such as Rousseau's social contract or Hobbes' imaginary Leviathan. For Bentham, they were nothing but metaphysical niceties that put a form of theatre, an abstract representation, at the heart of society. Bentham replaced this spectacle, which he viewed as corrupt, with a calculation of pain and pleasure. Consequently, the debate shifts from the issue of representations, contracts, and principles to a calculation of grades and degrees. Bentham's shift poses a costly challenge; it requires an evaluative infrastructure that is able to (or at least can claim to) measure and quantify pain and pleasure adequately. Chapter IV of *The Principles of Morals and Legislation* is tasked with exactly that challenge: how to measure pain and pleasure? The objective of the legislator is to increase the happiness of the lot: 'Pleasures and pains are the instruments he [the legislator] has to work with: it behoves him therefore to understand their force, which is again, in other words, their value' (Bentham 1789/1823, 29). Bentham provides criteria to account for the value of pain and pleasure, such as intensity, duration, certainty or uncertainty, and so on. Based on these indicators, Bentham suggests making an *exact account* of the sum total of pains and pleasures: 'Sum up all the values of all the pleasures on the one side, and those of all the pains on the other. The balance, if it to be on the side of pleasure, will give the good tendency of the act upon the whole' (Bentham 1789/1823, 31).

Bentham's thinking is important because it introduces a twofold translation of the problem of value. First, the question of 'how much?' has to be investigated and summed up in an account or an overall 'balance' as a guide for decision-making and action; second, the pragmatic concern with the technical questions of how to measure pain and pleasure requires calculative practices able to deliver numbers as material for utility calculations. If the world consists of nothing but pain and pleasure, then the calculation of pain and pleasure is the most adequate measure of progress. What is right and wrong is not a matter of the difference between truth and false, just and unjust, or beautiful and ugly; rather, the only relevant question is that of profit and loss expressing the balance and concluding the account. The truth is in numbers. Consequently, Bentham's system allows for a novum in moral philosophy, the possibility of calculating evil. In Bentham's world, values are quantified and are made commensurable on a scale (including negative numbers for pain/evil). Following utility theory, engaging in evil is morally acceptable if the profits (pleasure) outweigh the losses (pain).

Of course, Bentham realized the formidable challenge involved in quantifying personal preferences, sentiments, emotions, etc. Does the pleasure I gain from smoking a cigarette outweigh the pain the smoke inflicts on you as a non-smoker? Addressing these difficulties, Bentham suggests focusing only on what he described as material values: 'It is to be observed, that here, as well as henceforward, wherever consequences are spoken of, such only are meant as *material*. Of the consequences of any act, the multitude and variety needs must be infinite: but such of them only as are material are worth regarding' (Bentham 1789/1823, 70).

What counts and what does not is defined by the materiality of an act's consequences. This means that if an act is not empirically observable, difficult to represent, or hard to attribute, then it is discarded from the pain/pleasure equation as immaterial. Of course, this is a problematic categorization of events because the invisible or distant consequences (externalities) of acts continuously trouble utility calculations. Perhaps more critically, Bentham's own guiding principles, pain and pleasure, have an immaterial element at their core: how else could the pleasure of the masochist be his pain? But, Bentham's utility calculation requires a world in which only the material that is counted, counts. The melancholy of economists from Smith onwards stems from this focus on material improvements and the insight into the dissatisfaction that ultimately results from the material world. Von Mises provides a fine example of the economist's nihilistic tendencies when he writes:

> human action must be called inane even when judged merely with regard to its immediate goals. It can never bring full satisfaction; it merely gives for an evanescent instant a partial removal of uneasiness. As soon as one want is satisfied, new wants spring up and ask for satisfaction. Civilization, it is said, makes people poorer, because it multiplies their wishes and does not soothe, but kindles, desires. All the busy doings and dealings of hard-working men, their hurrying, pushing, and bustling are nonsensical, for they provide neither happiness nor quiet. Peace of mind and serenity cannot be won by action and secular ambition, but only by renunciation and resignation. The only kind of conduct proper to the sage is escape into the inactivity of a purely contemplative existence. (von Mises 1949/2007, 881)

But, even if what von Mises argues is correct, human beings cannot help pursuing wealth and happiness: 'in every living being there works an inexplicable and nonanalyzable *Id*. [...] Human reason [and the economist] serves this vital impulse' (von Mises 1949/2007, 882). Von Mises accepts the overall irrationality of life. Economics can still be a science of optimizing the means to the ends that remain an unintelligible *Id*.[1] Economics becomes a rational science of the pursuit of the irrational. The economist is Captain Ahab's right-hand man.

Economists usually gloss over this rather dark side of their discipline and work on its periphery instead. They call for more accurate, more widespread, and a greater diversity of measurements, tools, and accounting techniques that render the immaterial material visible. In so doing, they economize the world. The expansive nature of the economist's project can be illustrated by the work of Gary Becker, a Nobel Prize-winning economist. Building on von Mises and Hayek, he took economics as an explanation of life (Becker 1993). This includes issues about discrimination, crime, punishment, education (human capital), gender, family matters, drug addiction, and altruism. Understanding economics as the rational choice approach, Becker claims that people attempt to maximize welfare as they understand it. This is a forward-looking activity where people forecast the pros and cons of decisions about their entire lives. One important illustration is his concern with the family (Becker 1991). The claim is that when deciding about marriage and having children, people make choices based on utility maximization comparing benefits and costs. People marry because they expect to be better off than if they stayed single, while divorce is also intended to increase their welfare. The calculus involved understands life decisions as costs and benefits. Consequently, the rich tend to divorce less often than poorer people, whose spouses may not have economic prospects due to chronic unemployment. Becker also explains why family size tends to decline as income rises. The wealth of parents is an indication of the market value of their time and the higher this value, the lower the inclination to allocate time to having children. Likewise, when wealth is high, the cost of childcare rises and the inclination to have children decreases. Among the wealthy, large families are relatively rare. Last, the investment families put into their children's schooling in modern societies is likely to be a burden on large families and therefore more attention is put on quality as opposed to the quantity of education. Such an investment calculus is likely to reduce the size of modern, rich families. Poor families, in contrast, may pursue opposite strategies because time is less valuable to them. They can supervise their children with only little opportunity cost and they will not invest in schooling. Rather, they may seek to spread the burden of their old age on many children, any of whom may decline to perform this role. Many children are therefore a risk management strategy for retirement purposes. In short, according to Becker's reasoning, issues related to family and other types of social decisions, including crime and drug addiction, are the effects of rational, forward-looking cost–benefit calculations. The personal value of decisions, like the one to marry or to commit a crime, is seen as the result of a balance between costs and benefits—or pains and gains (pleasure). Therefore, this value can—in principle—be quantified and calculated.

In Defence of the Plurality of Values

Economic sociologists and anthropologists of markets challenge this dominant regime of economic valuation. They argue that there are non-commensurable values that elude economic calculation, and perhaps even more fundamentally, that economic calculation itself is based on non-economic values that transcend its own rationality. Early social theorists, including Weber, Veblen, Simmel, and Sombart, describe the non-economic basis of economic action as religious, cultural, metaphysical, and historical forces that shape the objects that only afterwards could be made conducive to economic analysis. Inspired by Weber's notion of value spheres (Weber 1915–20/1989) and Polanyi (1944/2001), economic sociologists posit that market exchange is a 'form of social interaction that cannot be explained by a "natural propensity to truck, barter and exchange" (Smith, 1776/1976, 17), but only by the institutional structures, social networks, and horizons of meaning within which market actors meet' (Beckert 2009, 247). This claim challenges the hegemony of economics: markets need to be understood as shaped by political (Fligstein 1996), cultural (Zelizer 1979), and social (Granovetter 1973, 1985) processes. Granovetter's embeddedness thesis (1985) has become one of the most used analytical tools to counter the explanatory imperialism of economics. Essentially, Granovetter posits that the structure of social networks (the strength of ties) determines access to information, and hence it also improves the ability to search for new ideas and the quality of decision-making. There is disagreement as to whether strong ties (Powell et al. 1996) or the lack thereof (Burt 1992) are more beneficial; what matters is the shared assumption that the position within social networks is the key to understanding economic action. Of course, the thesis that the social position in a network determines economic performance reinforces sociology's claim to be able to account for economic realities—and not the other way round. But, the assumption of *post hoc ergo propter hoc* is a fallacy; maybe the network positions are a result of superior economic performance, which would mean that economic sociologists and economists agree on the same 'facts' but disagree on the attribution of causality. Nevertheless, both share the desire to identify a perhaps utopian first mover (the market, the social) that structures what follows. This makes the embeddedness thesis difficult to defend; as Latour (2013, 426) points out: 'because there is no such thing as "Society" that could serve as a duvet, a canopy, a hotel room where The Economy could be tucked into bed', the idea of embeddedness is misleading.

Boltanski and Thévenot (2006) develop an alternative position in *On Justification*, whose subtitle, *Economies of Worth*, signals the plurality thesis the book proposes. On the one hand, Boltanski and Thévenot agree with economic sociologists that some values are incommensurable, and hence, cannot be internally compared by applying a common metric. They argue that if one pays attention to everyday situations, it soon becomes clear that worth and the attribution of value are both a disputed and a multiple phenomenon. When people evaluate things, they draw on very different principles of worth depending on the given situation. Boltanski and Thévenot set out to reconstruct these principles, which they identify in classical works by political philosophers, to develop a polity model of worth and suggest six different orders of worth: the inspired world; the domestic world; the world of fame; the civic world; the market world; and the industrial world. The list is not final, however. Boltanski and Chiappello (2005), for instance, have identified the projective world as yet another order of worth. Each world has its own distinct principles for evaluating people and things, its own principle of equivalence. The worthy person in the inspired world embodies a set of values, such as uniqueness and originality, which differs from the world of fame, where worth derives from the opinion of many others, and so on. On the other hand, even though Boltanski and Thévenot propose a plurality of orders, their position is not relativist. The different worlds do not designate separate spheres that different groups of people are attached to:

> Thus we have to give up the idea of associating worlds with groups; we can attach worlds only to arrangements of objects that qualify the various situations in which persons are acting when they attribute value to these objects. However, in a differentiated society, each person regularly has to confront situations stemming from distinct worlds, has to recognize such situations and prove capable of adjusting to them. (Boltanski and Thévenot 2006, 216)

Rather than being separate spheres, the worlds are different grammars of worth invoked in situations that call for judgement and justification and where people attribute value to things. This means that several orders of worth may be present in the same situation and that people will adjust to the situation and may shift between different principles when they try to reach agreement.

Stark (2009) argues that Boltanski and Thévenot's theoretical framework escapes a sharp distinction that has haunted discussions about value for a long time, namely, Parson's legendary pact, where economists study value, compared to sociologists, who study values, in the plural. According to Stark, Boltanski and Thévenot go beyond this distinction because they fuse value and values in the concept of worth. In their work, 'orders of worth are not values counterposed to value but are constitutive of value. Orders of worth are the very fabric of calculation, of rationality, of value' (Stark 2009, 11). In that sense, they reject the dichotomies between value and values, economy and society, calculation and judgement. They avoid what Zelizer calls the separate spheres view, the hostile worlds view, and the nothing-but view (Zelizer 2010). The separate spheres view holds that economy and society are distinct spheres with distinct principles that operate relatively harmoniously, but that are incomparable because they work according to different rules. This perspective is reflected in Parson's pact. The hostile spheres view is also based on the premise of two different spheres, but here the purity of the spheres is under threat. Cold calculation may jeopardize the moral sentiments of social life or, conversely, emotions may contaminate the sphere where efficiency is supposed to prevail. An example of the hostile worlds view is found in Sandel's (2012) book, *What Money Can't Buy: The Moral Limits of Markets*. Sandel laments the fact that '[t]he reach of markets, and market-oriented thinking, into aspects of life traditionally governed by nonmarket norms is one of the most significant developments of our time' (Sandel 2012, 7). The nothing-but view is a reductivist perspective that tells us that basically everything can be reduced to the same principle, whether it is utility, culture, or power. Bentham's utilitarian approach is an example of this view.

While Boltanski and Thévenot escape these pitfalls, they remain surprisingly abstract in their work. On the one hand, they call for attention to everyday situations, disputes between people, and tests. On the other hand, detailed analysis of the mechanisms of valuation is not part of their project. In the world of Boltanski and Thévenot, there *are* orders of worth. The scholar's task is to study their coexistence and occasional collisions. Like Bentham, they are in search of principles. But, *how* that which we value has become valuable remains inside a black box. This insight marks the point of departure of this edited volume: *Making Things Valuable* is not concerned with principles, but practices. It asks the (Nietzschean) question of how values have become valuable in the first place.

Making Things Valuable

Pragmatically, *Making Things Valuable* follows Dewey's flank movement, which avoids the pitfalls of an economic and sociological reading of values (Dewey 1939; Muniesa 2011). For Dewey, the question What is value? is the wrong one to pose. Rather than defining value, he suggests looking at practices of valuation through which objects are made valuable in the first place. He argues for a processual view, studying valuation as an 'activity of ranking, an act that involves comparison' (Dewey 1939, 5). His approach suggests focusing on the concrete mechanisms and the everyday practices of valuation, and analysing how they constitute values as their corollary. For instance, if we want to understand the value of university education, Dewey's analytical strategy would suggest not looking for utility or (perhaps contradicting) orders of worth but studying university rankings, government-led research assessments, global teaching programme ratings, and other valuation mechanisms that conduct the mundane work of bestowing value upon education. This is a fundamentally different analytical strategy than trying to define the utility of a degree or attempting to describe the clash of orders of worth that trouble universities.

Dewey's flank movement proposes asking an altogether different question. Put metaphorically, to assume value to be an essential characteristic of an object would equate to 'calling the ball struck in baseball, a hit or a foul' (Dewey, quoted in Muniesa 2011, 25). It is not the ball, however, that is valued as a hit or a foul in itself. Rather, it is the apparatus around it that makes it one or the other. It is the players, referees, coaches, spectators, sponsors, media, and myriad other actors as well as the material and symbolic elements, such as the lines drawn on the playing field, conventions, rules, league performance tables, tournaments, etc.—all these elements conspire when the ball touches the ground and gives that in that serendipitous moment meaning beyond its occurrence. The flank movement shifts attention from the ball to the network of elements, the evaluative infrastructure, that make it valuable. The emphasis is on the process of *making things valuable*: through which practices, technologies, and devices are objects evaluated? How are things commensurated, compared, categorized, and classified? What accounts make some things count more than others? These questions are significant, for it is through valuation practices that the world is ordered, hierarchized, and ultimately valued. Perceived as real, valuations such as rankings, ratings, models, and other evaluation devices are real in their consequences (Thomas and Thomas 1928; Bowker and Star 2000). Epistemologically, the focus on valuation departs from a utilitarian approach because it argues for the constructed nature of utility, i.e. what is useful and what is not, what counts and what does not, has to be understood as a consequence of valuation practices. Picking up the baseball metaphor again, the epistemological position of *Making Things Valuable* can be illustrated as follows:

> The story goes that three umpires disagreed about the task of calling balls and strikes. The first one said, 'I calls them as they is.' The second one said, 'I calls them as I sees them.' The third and cleverest umpire said, 'They ain't nothin' till I calls them.' (Simons 1976, 29, as cited in Weick 1979, 1)

With Dewey, we would introduce a fourth umpire, who says 'You calls them nothin' till the lines have been drawn in the sand, the rules of the game agreed upon, the spectators in place, the sponsors in sight, etc.' This places the fourth umpire in an unusual position, as this umpire is more material than the first and second stressing the myriad ways in which the world intervenes in the game; but he is simultaneously more constructivist than the third umpire because he is aware of all the conventions and mechanisms that transform throwing a ball from a backyard game into a high-publicity event that pays the umpire's and many other people's bills. In other, perhaps more scholarly words, *Making Things Valuable* aims at redirecting attention towards the practices, mechanisms, and technologies through which value is bestowed upon objects, including balls. Following this movement, the task of researchers is to investigate the work of valuation through its constitutive elements. Each of the chapters in this book takes on this task in its own specific way.

Overview of Chapters

In the first chapter, Wendy Nelson Espeland and Stacy E. Lom do a comparative study of three calculative devices that have been used to create new visibilities in three distinct institutional spheres. In the sphere of public policy, the device in focus is environmental impact statements; in the context of education the case is university rankings; and in the context of sports the device studied is figure skating scores. A common finding across the three cases is that the creation of new evaluative infrastructures supports new forms of behaviours on the part of involved actors. This chapter shows how specific devices allow specific aspects of the world to become visible, quantifiable, and therefore comparable. For instance, Espeland and Lom show how practices of skating and university management changed with the introduction of calculative devices that brought new measures—and thereby new visibilities—to the fore. By making this link between commensuration, cognition, and practice visible, the authors provide a compelling argument for the need to sharpen the analytical focus on those aspects of the world that are hard to make visible and, by extension, valuable in dominant regimes of calculation.

Paolo Quattrone continues Espeland and Lom's focus on the consequences of calculative devices with a chapter that revolves around the impacts of such devices in quite a specific practice—accounting. In line with Espeland and Lom, he emphasizes the performativity of calculation and takes this as a stepping stone for arguing that accounting could be conceptualized as a maieutic machine that asks questions rather than a machine that provides answers, that is, a machine that can instil doubt about what is valuable and thereby bring wisdom back into valuation practices. Quattrone points out that this way of thinking about the rationale of accounting can be traced back to the Jesuits, who used accounting to stimulate reflection on the relationship between value and values. He uses the case of Parmalat to illustrate that the alternative approach—thinking about accounting as a neutral device—is utopian.

Pierre Pénet's contribution focuses on how things are figured out. He discusses how Moody's credit rating reports on Greek bonds in the context of the financial crisis can productively be conceptualized as 'figuring documents', that is, documents that were designed to create figures about—and figure out—the uncertainties and inconsistencies that arose around the Greek economy in the late 2000s. Pénet pinpoints three techniques that were constitutive of the way Moody's conferred meaning upon the financial uncertainties they were tasked with predicting. First, they worked hard on affirming the overall plausibility of their investment ratings and on positioning them as strong risk scenarios, even quite late in the process. Second, they resorted to backwards reasoning to maximize continuity between different ratings and thereby validate them. By inferring the meaning of new information in a way that vindicated former views, however, Moody's ended up in a rating inertia that ensured consistency among ratings. Finally, Moody's had to anticipate the likely consequences of their predictions as they were used in the financial world—a technique Pénet describes as reactivity. Through a discussion of these techniques, he concludes that a linear understanding of market infusion of ratings is inadequate. Rather, he paves the way for conceptualizing credit rating reports as figuring documents through which rating agencies 'see' uncertainties in less linear ways.

Neil Pollock and Gian Marco Campagnolo's contribution complements Pénet's discussion of figuring practices with insights into the way valuation processes are influenced by processes of framing. This chapter presents a study of the role played by the magic quadrant in the consultancy firm Gartner and it suggests an analytical vocabulary that can help make sense of the way such two-by-two matrices act as important frames in the business world. Pollock and Campagnolo show how such matrices establish the boundaries within which decision-makers in the business world act. The authors introduce the psychological concept of subitizing to capture a unique characteristic of the two-by-two matrix, namely that it provides a fast and immediate framing of decisions. The matrix builds on the human skill to immediately make rapid, accurate, and confident judgements about small numbers. The authors emphasize that not all framing devices have speed as their rationale and the chapter accordingly paves the way towards a theoretical vocabulary that can pinpoint the heterogeneity of framing devices.

Liliana Doganova and Fabian Muniesa's contribution illuminates the ways in which quite a specific model—the business model—works in adding value to future products. Through a study of two business successes,

Genetech and Google, this chapter argues that a successful business model is characterized by realizing quite specific encounters, i.e. encounters between the product and its users, the firm and its competitors, and—perhaps most importantly—encounters between the entrepreneur and her investors. The authors suggest that it is through its ability to establish these encounters that the business model can transform non-economic entities (such as key words in a search query) into capitalized entities that can generate cash flows (such as clicks). The chapter, in that sense, echoes Dewey's point that the value of entities, such as a click, is dependent on situated practices and the network of elements that comprises them. The chapter recasts the relationship between business models and valuation, and in doing so, offers a profound critique of functionalist interpretations of what business models are.

Trine Pallesen shifts the focus from successful business models to a historical analysis of the way a particular administered price—the feed-in tariff for wind power—was added into the French energy market in 2000. By making something previously invisible (the value of wind power) visible, this tariff became a central actor in the energy market. Pallesen's contribution illustrates how this specific tariff was realized when it knit together a distinct set of assemblages, including entities such as competing energy technologies, electricity system management, and calculations of 'fair' profitability. The chapter echoes some of the points made by Espeland and Lom as it argues that issues concerning the commensurability of wind and nuclear power were central to the controversies around the tariff. For instance, Pallesen shows that the comparison to nuclear power was especially important in establishing the final price that—once it was detached from the controversies around its definition—became an influential numeric representation of wind power's value.

Sabina Du Rietz's chapter explores the way Nordic investor analysts use devices to make decisions about the quality of companies' social and environmental work. Du Rietz focuses on the extent to which similarities and differences exist across the devices used for making assessments in this field. Her study shows that several similar, although slightly differently composed, valuation devices coexist. The reasons for these differences—the author argues—are not to be found in differences in the tasks at hand or in the thing to be valued. Rather, the study shows that the specific distribution of devices is better explained by the way they are oriented to each other in the field of social and environmental work assessment. One key finding is that the devices are oriented both to other pre-existing models in the field and to their own past incarnations and that there is a struggle to differentiate devices from other devices with which they unintentionally share features. In this way, Du Rietz indicates how dynamics of imitation and differentiation among devices ultimately influence decision-making and valuation practices.

Laure Cabantous and Théodora Dupont-Courtade continue Du Rietz's interest in understanding how the existence of a multiplicity of different models in a field influences decision-making. The empirical context, however, is no longer social and environmental work assessment but risk analysis in the context of catastrophes. The decisions in focus are risk analysts' evaluation of insurers' exposure to catastrophe risks. This chapter builds on a three-year participant observation among risk analysts in the INSUR Group, a European insurance company. Cabantous and Dupont-Courtade investigate how analysts in the group blend different risk models in their daily work, showing that a core competency of these analysts is to integrate risk evaluations of dissonant catastrophe models into evaluations of the quality of these models. It is from this basis that the analysts carry out the evaluation of an insurer's risk exposure and thereby fulfil their job function. The centrality of this specific competency leads the authors to conceptualize risk analysts as 'qualculators' who turn a multiplicity of quantitative inputs into qualitative valuations of risk exposure.

José Ossandón provides insights into the link between insurance and valuation by illustrating how economic objects are enacted and stabilized in three different ways in the private health insurance sector in Chile. This chapter focuses on those things that are sold, priced, and exchanged in this specific insurance market. One way of enacting such economic objects is through the practice of singularization, which is the creation of a calculative space in which a specific good can be connected and compared to a finite list of other products. While recognizing the importance of this form of enactment, Ossandón argues that it has been given too much attention in recent literature. He suggests the need to distinguish two other modes of enacting economic objects: the delimitation of property rights and commoditization. More specifically, he shows that valuation in the context of health insurance is not only achieved by singling out objects and making them comparable to each other. It also requires linking these objects to legal decisions about property rights and establishing risk as a commodity.

Juliane Reinecke's study turns to a classical institutionalized measure of value—namely gold. Previously the standard that the value of other currencies was measured against, gold had material qualities that made it highly fungible in the sense that one quantity of gold could be substituted with any other. Gold was gold, so to speak, and it was therefore a reliable standard. Reinecke shows, however, that this is no longer the case through an examination of the way states, non-governmental organizations (NGOs), and other civil society actors have worked to differentiate gold on social and ethical grounds. In other words, gold is no longer just gold. Reinecke's chapter focuses on the emergence of a distinction between conflict-free gold and conflict gold. She shows how the discussions around this distinction pose new and interesting questions about the relationship between value and values. This chapter thereby points to the importance of studying the politics of valuation and the political institutionalization of what and whose values matter in defining valuation criteria for objects like gold.

The two final chapters explore valuation as a form of visualizing and tracing. They share a focus on the way visualizations based on digital traces can be seen as valuation practices even though they aim at something else besides setting the prices of things. First, Celia Lury and Noortje Marres' chapter draws on the pragmatism of Dewey and Cooley to suggest ideas on the role digital objects can potentially play in practices of valuation. Valuation through digital objects must be seen as an environmental occasion, in the sense that an open-ended set of entities participate in the processes of selection that underpin the creation of, for instance, search results on Google. The authors argue that there is no need for an a priori distinction between the acts of selection and problematization when working with this type of objectual valuation. Rather, it is important to look at the way digital objects afford certain selections and problematizations and thereby specific modes of socialization and valuation. This leads to the authors' thesis that the determination of relevance and valuation is distributed among so many entities that transparency over the process is lost. This also means that valuation practices are open for reinterpretation. The authors conclude that analysing how digital objects acquire values is important because this process represents an act of politics.

Anders Koed Madsen's chapter continues some of the arguments made by Lury and Marres and presents a case study of the way visualizations of tweets are used to forecast crises for the UN. It suggests thinking about such visualizations as visions that prioritize a scarce resource on the part of the UN, namely attention. It indicates who is worthy of attention and who is not. The chapter provides insight into the distributed networks that make up these evaluative visions, discussing how the affordances of interfaces, categorical schemes, and other devices influence the way digital visualizations can assign meaning and value to the world. In the case of the UN's visualizations, the author shows how anomaly detection is an empirical technique that is central to the evaluative infrastructure that makes a certain crisis-prone country visible. By building on this particular technique, the visualizations come to enable a kind of fast decision-making similar to the one discussed by Pollock and Campagnolo earlier in the book. Koed Madsen's contribution suggests that Gibson's perceptual theory is a particularly useful theoretical resource with which to understand the characteristics of valuation devices that use pattern detection in real-time feeds of digital traces to quantify and visualize what Bentham would have called non-material values, such as sentiment.

Conclusion

What Bentham loathed was the theatre of representation that Hobbes' Leviathan and Rousseau's social contract put at the heart of social order. For Bentham, these were mere fictions that could neither explain the state of affairs nor provide guidance for decision-making. Bentham substituted these fictions with the calculation of pain and pleasure. Throughout his oeuvre, this struggle between the fiction of an original contract and the future-oriented utility maximization doctrine is embodied in the figure of the lawyer. Bentham saw the lawyer as a master of rhetoric who would use, and if necessary, invent fictions to defend the status quo. Bentham's utility maximizer does not argue based on fictions projected back onto history but based on future pleasure/pain calculation.

Today, any economic form of valuation follows Bentham's logic of 'How much?', which is designed to replace speculation with calculation. In reality, however, Bentham only trades one fiction with another: his principle of utility, pain, and pleasure, and the interest in maximizing one and minimizing the other, is also a fiction. Take the example of punishment. For Bentham, punishment is always mischief, and following the principle of utility, it should be deployed only to avoid greater evil (Bentham 1789/1823). For the sense of pleasure that a victim might experience seeing the offender being punished never outweighs the actual pain that the offender experiences; the only use of punishment is deterrence. Consequently, for Bentham, in order to maximize the utility of punishment, it has to be turned into a spectacle. He proposes that convicts wear masks, where 'guilt will thus be pilloried in the abstract, without the exposure of the guilty', and he continues: 'In a well composed penal law, I know not a more essential personage than the manager of the theatre' (Bentham 1791/1995, 100). Indeed, was not the whole idea of the panopticon a play with illusion, a mirage of perspective and lights that would fool prisoners into subordination? Bentham's thinking set out to show representations as necessarily dishonest and false; yet his own logic forces him to argue for a theatre, including a manager, to stage the spectacle of punishment's utility. What was meant to be precise, direct, and empirical turns out to be murky, mediated, and metaphysical.

In one of his later writings, 'A Fragment on Ontology', Bentham argues that fiction is not simply something that does not exist (if this were true, then it would not have to bother us). Rather, a fictitious entity is 'an entity to which, though by the grammatical form of the discourse employed in speaking of it, existence be ascribed, yet in truth and reality existence is not meant to be ascribed' (Bentham 1813–14/1995, 123). Fiction has its roots in language: 'To language, then—to language alone—it is, that fictitious entities owe their existence—their impossible, yet indispensible, existence' (Bentham 1813–14/1995, 125). For

Bentham, fictitious entities include, amongst many other words, also 'interest' by which he means the 'desire of pleasure and of exemption from pain, being, in some shape or other, the source of every thought, as well as the cause of every action [...] would be among the very earliest to which the faculty of discourse would give existence' (Bentham 1813–14/1995, 137). In other words, even what people call their own interest (the desire for pleasure and avoidance of pain) is a discursive accomplishment, a fiction, something that comes alive in staged events and theatrical performances.

Perhaps the study of making things valuable provides us with the necessary analytical tools to understand the theatre of valuing, including its practices and devices, technologies and visualizations. It recognizes the impossibility of accounting for values without resorting to fiction (even the seemingly simplest interest in pleasure and avoidance of pain is fictitious, as Bentham reminds us); it directs our attention towards the vocabulary and the grammar that constitutes values; it scrutinizes the networks through which values travel and are translated; and it investigates the struggles that occur as the often invisible work of making things valuable is performed.

Note

1. The *Id* alludes to the Freudian structuring of the human psyche into super-ego, ego, and id.

References

Becker, G. 1991. *A Treatise on the Family*. Chicago: University of Chicago Press.

Becker, G. 1993. 'Nobel Lecture: The Economic Way of Looking at Life'. *Journal of Political Economy* 101(3): 385–409.

Beckert, J. 2009. 'The Social Order of Markets'. *Theory and Society* 38(3): 245–69.

Bentham, J. 1776/1988. *A Fragment on Government*. Cambridge: Cambridge University Press.

Bentham, J. 1789/1823. *Principles of Morals and Legislation*. Oxford: Clarendon Press.

Bentham J. 1791/1995. 'Selections for Postscript I'. In *The Panopticon Writings*, ed. J. Bentham. London and New York: Verso.

Bentham J. 1813–14/1995. 'A Fragment on Ontology'. In *The Panopticon Writings*, ed. J. Bentham. London and New York: Verso.

Boltanski, L., and E. Chiapello. 2005. *The New Spirit of Capitalism*. London: Verso.

Boltanski, L., and L. Thévenot. 2006. *On Justification: Economies of Worth*. Princeton: Princeton University Press.

Bowker, G. C., and S. L. Star. 2000. *Sorting Things Out: Classification and Its Consequences*. Boston: MIT Press.

Burt, R. 1992. *Brokerage and Closure: An Introduction to Social Capital*. Oxford and New York: Oxford University Press.

Dewey, J. 1939. 'Theory of Valuation'. *International Encyclopedia of Unified Science* 2(4): 7–67.

Fligstein, N. 1996. 'Markets as Politics: A Political-Cultural Approach to Market Institutions'. *American Sociological Review* 61(4): 656–73.

Granovetter, M. 1973. 'The Strength of Weak Ties'. *American Journal of Sociology* 78(6): 1360–80.

Granovetter, M. 1985. 'Economic Action and Social Structure: The Problem of Embeddedness'. *American Journal of Sociology* 91(3): 481–510.

Latour, B. 2013. *An Inquiry into Modes* of *Existence: An Anthropology of the Moderns*. Cambridge, MA, and London: Harvard University Press.

McCloskey, D. 1994. *The Rhetorics of Economics*. Madison: University of Wisconsin Press.

Muniesa, F. 2011. 'A Flank Movement in the Understanding of Valuation'. *Sociological Review* 59(2): 24–38.

Polanyi, K. 1944/2001. *The Great Transformation: The Political and Economic Origins of Our Time*. Boston: Beacon Press.

Powell, W. W., K. W. Koput, and L. Smith-Doerr. 1996. 'Interorganizational Collaboration and the Locus of Innovation: Networks of Learning in Biotechnology'. *Administrative Science Quarterly* 41(1): 116–45.

Sandel, M. J. 2012. *What Money Can't Buy: The Moral Limits of Markets*. New York: Farrar, Straus & Giroux.

Simons, H. W. 1976. *Persuasion*. Reading, MA: Addison-Wesley.

Smith, A. 1776/1976. *The Wealth of Nations*. New York: Modern Library.

Stark, D. 2009. *The Sense of Dissonance: Accounts of Worth in Economic Life*. Princeton: Princeton University Press.

Thomas, W. I., and D. S. Thomas. 1928. *The Child in America: Behavior Problems and Programs*. New York: Knopf.

Von Mises, L. 1949/2007. *Human Action: A Treatise on Economics*. Indianapolis: Liberty Fund.

Weber, M. 1915–20/1989. *Die Wirtschaftsethik der Weltreligionen. Konfuzianisums und Taoismus*. Tübingen: J. C. B. Mohr (Paul Siebeck).

Weick, K. E. 1979. *The Social Psychology of Organizing* (2nd edition). New York: McGraw-Hill.

Zelizer, V. 1979. *Morals and Markets: The Development of Life Insurance in the United States*. New York: Columbia University Press.

Zelizer, V. 2010. *Economic Lives: How Culture Shapes the Economy*. Princeton, NJ: Princeton University Press.

1

Noticing Numbers

How Quantification Changes What We See and What We Don't

Wendy Nelson Espeland and Stacy E. Lom

Valuing is fundamental to social life. Consciously or not, we value when we make decisions, make judgements, or reflect on experience. What is worth doing, who or what has merit, how to recognize and reward excellence, and how best to distribute resources or people are all efforts to establish qualities. All cultures have multiple modes of defining quality. Valuing requires focus, discipline, and authority, and always involves the imposition of forms onto things, people, or relations.[1] Forms are always reductive, selectively compressing and framing life and ideas in patterned ways, guiding our attention towards some features and away from others. Whether this involves contemplating a painting, remembering a friend, or pricing an antique, forms of valuing are built upon layers of classifications that sort, siphon, and distinguish.[2] Valuing organizes attention in particular ways that can reflect the techniques, contexts, and motives of those doing the valuing, and valuing is saturated with power: What and how we notice has important implications for how power is maintained or challenged, when and how we intervene, and whose standards prevail.

Narrative is a familiar form for expressing values, one that edits and expresses information in well-known literary tropes. Quantification is another important form that we often use to value. Quantification entails imposing a shared metric on the objects or people to be valued. Common examples of values that are quantified include the prices we attach to commodities, the performance metrics we use to evaluate assets or people in accounting or management, and the standardized tests we use to assess merit or mastery. Increasingly, we use sophisticated quantitative techniques to quantify all kinds of relationships, and valuing is often at the heart of these. As Michael Power (1994, 1997), Marilyn Strathern (2000), and Kevin Davis et al. (2012) have argued, auditing, along with the standardization and quantification that undergird it, has become a hegemonic form of global culture, one that often renders other forms of evaluation suspect.

Quantification is so naturalized that we often don't notice what a subversive technology it is. By translating qualities into quantities with a common metric, quantification creates new forms of unity or coherence and precise distinctions and subverts pre-existing categories. Old forms of classification, qualitative distinctions, and similarities become irrelevant when we rely on numbers to express our values or order our decisions. Quantification produces comparability. Metrics make it almost impossible *not* to compare their objects, and comparison is a specific kind of visibility that creates sameness, unity, and distinction simultaneously.

Because we associate quantification with such desired qualities as rationality, transparency, and efficiency, and because we rely on it to enact some of our most cherished goals—assessing merit, practising democracy, or distributing fairly—we grant a unique and often privileged form of authority to it that we do not confer to other forms of value. 'Anecdotal' information is almost always perceived as inferior to 'metrics'. Quantitative authority rests, sometimes uneasily, on an infrastructure of attention that is determined by various technologies of rules and methods and modes of combining, separating, and comparing. The tremendous increase in the use of statistics, auditing, benchmarking, rankings, and performance measures in the past twenty-five years makes it all the more imperative that we examine what quantification makes obvious and obscure and to whom.[3]

Visibility is often a motive for quantification. As James Scott (1998) argues, state intervention requires that its targets be made visible, often to distant authorities. States have been enthusiastic producers and users of statistics, as the etymological link between the two suggests. For example, Laura Hein (2004) describes how Japanese intellectuals saw state statistics as a force for modernizing and democratizing following the Second World War. In some cases, the use of statistics is what produces a modern state, as Tong Lam (2011) shows in his analysis of the Qing Dynasty in China.

It is not only states that have an interest in making distant others visible. Part of the appeal of double-entry bookkeeping, which emerged in the late fourteenth century in what is now Italy, was that it made it possible for merchants to check on agents in far-flung places that they did not necessarily trust. We now routinely rely on accounting to let shareholders and regulators view and assess companies' performances. This capacity to 'see' people and monitor projects without the demands of proximity or a highly centralized authority is a crucial aspect of modern power that makes what Peter Miller and Nikolas Rose (1990) and their colleagues Rose et al. (2006) have called 'governing at a distance' or 'dispersed governmentality' possible. Especially at a time when pressures to integrate economies, financial instruments, and governance are so pronounced, and when the terms of proximity are being redefined and subverted at astonishing speeds, the terms of visibility and who gets to see what are crucial issues with often-simultaneous political, economic, and moral dimensions. And seeing is often done via numbers.

In this chapter, we analyse what might be termed 'relations of visibility' as they are made and expressed in three forms of quantification located in three institutional spheres: governmental decision-making, higher education, and high-stakes sport. In one case, quantification demanded a commensuration that subverted the boundaries around the sacred. In another, it imposed a harsh discipline on organizations, even as they rejected its legitimacy. In our final case, quantification was a response to scandal that threatened to undermine the legitimacy of an international sport. In each example, quantification changed power relations, the content of the object or action it measured, and how excellence or value was defined. The politics of visibility were central in each of these processes, as were the varying roles that media played in making, expressing, and circulating numbers.

Valuing Incommensurables

Beginning in the early 1940s, engineers in the US Bureau of Reclamation (hereafter, BR), part of the Interior Department in the executive branch of the federal government, began planning to build a dam, later known as Orme Dam, at the confluence of the Salt and Verde Rivers in central Arizona.[4] The dam was part of the Central Arizona Project, an elaborate project to bring more water from the Colorado River to central Arizona and the Sonoran desert of southern Arizona, home to Arizona's two largest cities, Phoenix and Tucson.[5]

The Colorado River plays a starring role in the politics and imagination of the American West. Best known for carving the Grand Canyon millions of years ago (how long ago is disputed by geologists, whose estimates range from 70 million to 6 million years), it drains the watershed of seven arid states in the US and two in Mexico. Its 2,330-kilometre trip begins with a trickle in the southern Rocky Mountains and is nourished by more than eighty tributaries, and thanks to plenty of conflict, massive civil engineering, and reckless watering, no river water has reached its natural outlet in the Sea of Cortez since around 1960. Instead, water from 'America's Nile' is stored, diverted, or evaporated via its twenty-nine dams, twelve tunnels, and hundreds of miles of canals that partition the West like highways.

Known regionally as 'water wars', fights over the use of the Colorado River are enduring and often lurid. They have been initiated and refereed by federal and state legislators, district and Supreme Court justices, a dozen or so federal agencies, private and quasi-private utilities, municipal governments, treaties (mostly broken), contracts, customs, the Army, various state militia, the National Guard, powerful Political Action Committees (PACs) (before and after they were called that), churches, and God only knows who else. The list of its 'water stakeholders' is even longer. The thirty-plus interest groups who share in BR water and power, however unevenly, include seven US and two Mexican states, dozens of federal and state agencies and cities, twenty-nine Native American Tribes, outdoor enthusiasts, businesses, farmers, and any entity concerned with reliable water, which includes everyone in arid climates, whether they know it or not.

The confluence dam proposed by the BR made for appealing hydrology because it would regulate two rivers, the Salt and Verde Rivers, with one structure located near many of its users.[6] It was economically appealing for the flush budgets that the BR would enjoy, along with the contractors, utilities, farmers, and proliferating food-chains that feed on the abundant, some say squandered, water and power it would supply.[7] But to focus on these utilitarian uses of dams would be to miss much of their meaning and drama. Like most of us, BR engineers become invested in their projects in ways that transcend our rational defences of them. Dams, like other cultural objects, can be infused with passion. They are tangible symbols—of ambition, political clout, technical prowess, and transformation—and like all symbols, they generate polymorphous meanings. The juxtaposition of dramatic architecture in remote and rugged canyons produces ritual sites of grand proportions, ones that photograph well. Moreover, the meaning of a dam (unlike its foundation) need not stand still. Even before it was built, Orme Dam became, for some, the emblem of their profession, the culmination of their careers; for others, it was their worst fear. But this semiotic view of dams did not sit comfortably in the offices of BR engineers or within the strictures of bureaucratic rationality.

The dream to build Orme Dam was delayed for decades as a result of the factious, litigious world of water politics in the arid West. After the protracted process of cultivating Congressional allies, epic court battles between California and Arizona over water rights, and inter-agency rivalry, conflicts that absorbed and frustrated the careers of numerous BR engineers, it seemed like Orme Dam was finally going to be authorized, funded, and built in the mid-1970s. Most of the political and economic leaders in Arizona were ardent supporters of the dam, and they assumed that residents felt like they did. Mostly, they did. But the costs of Orme Dam, once they were calculated more expansively than the conventional categories of the 'old' or 'real' Bureau, depending on your tenure and job description, were less benign than they had been in the 'old' days. These new 'costs' included the destruction of unique riparian habitat that sustained a range of threatened and endangered species, a reservoir that would fluctuate from lake to mud flats more than a boater would want, and, most importantly, the forced relocation of the Yavapai people from the last bit of what was once part of their ancestral land. These costs had begun to mobilize opponents to the dam, and it wasn't until after a disastrous public meeting that the agency realized that this dissent was real and possibly serious.

This surprise stemmed partly from the selective vision that gradually emerges anywhere where routines, specialized expertise, and homogeneous hiring occur. These blinders also reflected the cumulative experience of a powerful agency that had largely had its way. BR engineers had a hard time grasping that Arizonans might fail to support a water project. They had also blundered by assuming a mantle of expertise that they didn't legitimately possess. In preparing the first environmental impact statement (EIS) on the project in compliance with new environmental law, BR engineers wrote or edited much of the analyses themselves. In the EIS, the forced relocation of the Yavapai was portrayed as being beneficial to the Tribe, as a 'positive social impact' (US Bureau of Reclamation 1976). The preparers reasoned that having survived brutal, forced removals from their land several times in the nineteenth century, Yavapai culture possessed strong 'survival elements' that would ease their adjustments to yet another forced relocation; moreover, the recreational 'benefits' that would accrue from the dam—boating, fishing, and food concessions that might complement the new reservoir formed by the dam—would prove to be an economic boom to the impoverished Tribe. The distraught tribal leaders and impassioned speeches of Orme's opponents who attended the disastrous public meeting when this early EIS was made public provided a powerful, compelling counterpoint to the BR's upbeat analysis.

This headline-making political debacle eventually forced the agency to produce a new EIS, this time one prepared by people with credentials in the relevant areas. For practically the first time in its eighty-year history, the BR hired new kinds of specialists, including people with degrees in natural sciences, such as biology and wildlife management, or in social sciences (other than economics), such as psychology and sociology. These non-engineers replaced the former writers and managers of the relevant studies. As unconventional employees, they had a stake in expanding the constituencies of the agency beyond the carefully cultivated water 'elite' that had dominated public outreach to all groups that would experience the benefits and costs associated with water development, including Orme Dam.

With consequences that ranged from better flood protection to the destruction of an eagle habitat, how to commensurate and weigh the various impacts quickly became a pivotal concern for this group, which we have named the New Guard. Adapting ideas from cognitive psychology and economics, the New Guard's methods were based on a logic of quantitative trade-offs as a means of including the projected impacts of all groups, of treating them fairly by treating them formally. Commensuration would be the vehicle by which the values and preferences of all groups would be measured, integrated, and aligned with the water projects that the BR designed. For Orme Dam and the alternatives to it that environmental law and politics now required the BR to create, the 'qualities' of its projects would be measured by trained experts, the preferences of the 'public'—the groups with stakes in the decision—would be carefully measured, and a complex, multi-attribute trade-off computer program designed by a member of the New Guard would do the maths and tell groups which BR plan would best satisfy their values and preferences. For the New Guard, quantification was more than a measure. It was a rigorous, unbiased, defensible means of making visible and public what had been invisible in the past: the social and environmental impacts of Orme Dam and how members of the affected groups thought about them. Quantification was a vehicle for inclusion and fairness.

This was not how the Yavapai understood the New Guard's analysis. After more than 150 years of malevolent governmental strategies, most of which involved forced or attempted forced removal from their land, trust was hard won. The initial EIS made relations between the agency and the Yavapai community even worse, such that many people on the reservation believed that the BR would never prepare or endorse an unbiased study due to what one observer termed 'their will to build'. The reassurances from the New Guard about its commitment to inclusion and the virtues of its new methods were not reassuring to Yavapai residents who believed they had heard it all before. The social scientists hired by the BR as employees and consultants did produce new, more inclusive modes of analysis; even so, many Yavapai people believed that the logic behind these analyses did not accurately represent the stakes of the decision for them, but this was difficult for members of the New Guard to understand.[8]

The Yavapai's critique of the New Guard's approach emerged from their defence of their land and their efforts to explain their connections to it in ways that would help others understand why the dam would be so devastating for them. This required them to provide accounts of themselves and their culture to others who knew little about them or sometimes wilfully misunderstood them. Land, they explained, to reporters, bureaucrats, audiences at endless public meetings, and sociologists like us, is the core of who they are as individuals, as a people, as inheritors of a distinctive history and culture that is their duty to protect and pass on. They described this special relationship as 'participating with the land'. Land is the vehicle of continuity, for remembering—history, ancestors, biography—and for practising religion, making a living, and enjoying life. Not just any land can fulfil these roles. Only the land that one's ancestors lived on and fought to protect, land that was 'cared for' by generations of Yavapai people, is meaningful in this way. That is why offers to 'swap' land, pay a premium price, or relocate individuals or even the community were not understood as appropriate remediation. As one teenager put it, 'The land is our mother. You don't sell your mother.'

This way of understanding land and its inextricable links to culture, identity, and history was incompatible with the New Guard's methods of including the Yavapai in the Orme investigation and decision. Land, for the Yavapai, was sacred, incommensurable. Effort to make it commensurable through procedures of measuring social impacts and values was not just a simplified way of documenting the suffering that would come with losing their land; it was antithetical to the identity and the value it was representing. Being inclusive and rational, for the New Guard, demanded commensuration; being Yavapai meant a deep investment in the incommensurability of their land. While the New Guard was dedicated to showing how high the stakes of the decision were for the Yavapai, to show how devastating the 'social impacts' of the dam would be, they did not understand that their terms for doing so were fundamentally a misrepresentation, a contradiction, of what losing their land, of what being Yavapai, meant for nearly everyone on the reservation.

What does this have to do with visibility? For the New Guard, visibility was a motivation; they wanted to make the consequences of dam building visible and public for all parties seriously affected by the dam, including previously invisible ones. And they were successful in doing this. Procedures for explaining the decision and measuring public preferences included a vigorous 'public involvement' programme that created many public and semi-public forums where those who had formerly been excluded or marginalized, including the Yavapai, could express their views and learn what experts said about the projected effects of the projects. 'Nature', too, became a public 'stakeholder' in that activists and scientists could speak out about environmental harms.

But the techniques that the New Guard used for inclusion were not as neutral as they had hoped. By making commensurate the measures of economic, environmental, and social consequences, by making commensurate the various public responses to those impacts, and by making commensurate a synthesis of the two, the New Guard's procedures for integrating impacts were, by necessity, abstract and methodologically complicated representations that shaped what could be noticed and what was neglected, what was put together or pulled apart. First, these technologies constructed a formal set of simplifications and comparisons that were useful to decision-makers and to citizens who would otherwise be overwhelmed by the volume and complexity of the data and the analysis.

Comparisons, by their nature, highlight relations of similarity and difference. The cognitive scheme that makes the comparing seem sensible, the overarching relations that lend the quality of sameness to the objects being compared, and, as in this case, the decision and plans that comprise it make it sensible to compare what would otherwise seem like radically different projections. Comparisons also highlight differences. With commensuration, difference is rigorously restricted to intervals on a shared metric. Qualitative difference disappears and is replaced by quantitative difference, a formal, more reductive form. Comparisons make possible brief summaries of the impacts of projects that convey in seemingly clear terms how projects will perform and how people feel about that.

A second and more subtle kind of visibility has to do with which kinds of consequences, which aspects of context, and which evaluations of them were inexpressible within the terms of the New Guard's calculations of qualities and preferences. For example, the long history of broken promises about the right and security of Yavapai to their land could only be expressed as a strong weight attached to the effects of their removal. The morality of having broken promises also disappeared from the consequentialist logic of the New Guard's framework. Most importantly, the rejection of transitivity and the commodification of Yavapai land and culture, the mistranslation of singularity into relative relationships, the very processes that define them and their culture, were both violated and made invisible in the New Guard's techniques for inclusion and transparency. However, despite this fundamental misrepresentation, the forum for the decision that was created by the New Guard permitted the Tribe and their allies to voice their opposition and explain their reasons. In the end, much to their astonishment, they triumphed.

Rankings as Relative Vision

The relative relations created by the New Guard's technique could not accommodate just any kind of singularity.[9] The *significance* of the relativity that commensuration creates, of course, varies depending on its form and context.[10] For the Yavapai, the relativity of cost-benefit-like trade-offs subverted their defence of themselves in the terms that defined them, a relativity which seemed to them to hasten their doom. But the relativity constructed via commensuration in other forms, for other audiences, can shape relations in many ways. Rankings are one common example of a rigorous relativity that, like the decision techniques of the New Guard, prevents the expression of singularities, but rankings reveal distinctive patterns in their effects on what we notice and how we evaluate.

Consider the difference between ratings and rankings, two common ways to organize judgements about quality. Even if both are based on aggregations and calculations, a rating need not be an exclusive position, nor does it create as precise a relationship among the groups that are encompassed by it. For example, a restaurant might be judged as being worthy of 'two stars' according to some critic. The processes that result in this label, this *rating*, might entail a series of calculations of various aspects of dining: the service, ambience, wine list, creativity of preparation, and mastery of cooking technique. These components might be quantified and scaled and then, depending on their sum and established thresholds, assigned a rating. The rating is ordinal in that three stars are better than two, which are better than one.

But compare this with a *ranking* of restaurants in a particular city where similar calculations are then aggregated according to a standardized scale such that all restaurants are given a precise ranking on an interval scale. Unless there is a tie, each restaurant has its own distinctive number which indicates a precise relationship to every other restaurant. With ratings, many restaurants might earn the same one, and the rise of one restaurant would not affect others. In sharp contrast, the relationships among restaurants created by rankings are zero-sum so that a rise in one might affect the relative ranking of many, depending on how many were ranked above and below the restaurant that improved its rank. This form of relativity makes comparisons easy, as do ratings, but rankings also convey more information: a precise ordering that pits one against all, where one is always 'better' or 'worse' than all others. Needless to say, this encourages competition and closer scrutiny of 'neighbours' that the rankings create. Physical proximity is no longer the most salient factor of competition; metrical proximity powerfully creates who is defined as 'near' or 'alike'. Our second case illustrates some of the consequences of the forms of relativity and visibility that are imposed by rankings. These distinctions between ratings and rankings are also relevant to the judging changes in figure skating, which we discuss in the next section.

In 1983, *U.S. News and World Report* (*USN*), then a weekly news magazine, was looking to distinguish itself from its far more successful competitors, *Time* and *Newsweek*. This search for a new identity ended when Morton Zuckerman, the new owner of *USN*, selected the folksy slogan: 'news you can use'. It's unclear just where the idea for university rankings originated, but the decision to make them exemplified this new focus. Rankings could tell people which schools were best.

These rankings' origins were humble. They began as a simple survey sent to American university presidents asking them to name the ten best universities. The resulting list (with the top spots going to Stanford, Harvard, and Yale, in that order) attracted the attention of readers and reporters and was judged as promising. Before long, the magazine launched an expanded programme of rankings, using more sophisticated data to produce annual rankings of colleges and universities in 1987 and annual rankings of graduate programmes, including disciplinary programmes and professional programmes in law, medicine, and engineering, in 1990. It is hard to convey the power of these rankings today, but initially they were mainly ignored. Those who did notice them found them laughable, offensive, or both. But it didn't take long for deans of admissions to realize that prospective students were using rankings to decide which schools to apply to and attend. Once newspapers began reporting rankings annually, it was impossible to ignore them. Publicly, administrators now referred to them as 'Mickey Mouse', 'stupid', or 'deeply misguided'. Private responses, no doubt, were even more vivid.

Rankings did exactly what editors at *USN* hoped they would do. People bought them, as well as the university guidebooks that *USN* began publishing annually, in droves. Before long, *USN* became tantamount to rankings. Not wishing to miss out, other media soon followed suit, producing rankings of their own—with rankings in the UK, Canada, Germany, and Poland. In 2003, the first global ranking of universities was created by two Chinese educators, and two years later, two other world rankings were established. There has been no turning back.

The effects of rankings on universities and graduate programmes have been described in detail elsewhere (Monks and Ehrenberg 1999; Espeland and Sauder 2007; Salini and Saroyan 2007; Hazelkorn 2007, 2008), but a brief overview helps disclose their stakes. Rankings have catalysed broad changes in universities. Schools now admit students to boost their selectivity statistics, which means that students who do not score well on standardized tests—in the US, the less affluent, non-Asian minorities; older applicants; and people from the South—are more costly to admit. Schools redeploy resources in order to attract high-scoring students, so scholarships are diverted from the needy to those with high test scores. Millions of dollars are spent on marketing in an effort to boost results from surveys of reputations. Globally, some countries have shifted their educational policies from more egalitarian approaches to a star system; in the hopes of creating a 'world-class' university, science and technology are favoured over humanities and social sciences, so resources are shifted accordingly, and faculty are hired for their capacity to boost rankings. Administrators must now account for themselves annually in terms of rankings criteria to prospective students, current students, alumni, superiors, employers, and media. Schools with missions not captured in rankings are punished for their heterogeneity, and people think differently about these institutions.

Inside universities, administrators must keep their eyes on the numbers. Many have been creative in their efforts to boost rankings; some have been devious. With gaming that ranges from granting only spring leaves to faculty because faculty–student ratios are calculated in autumn, to flat-out lying about selectivity or placement statistics, the clarity and precision of the rankings obscure the machinations that underlie the production of those numbers. Like sausages, it is not always pleasant to see how statistics are made.

Rankings have redirected our attention in crucial ways. They have created a new status system in which every school has a specific location. Rankings have made winners and losers clearly visible. The whole world can know a school's ranking within minutes, and whether the results are the subject of celebration or hand-wringing, there is no opting out. Because of the precise relations that rankings create among schools, rankings also reveal 'differences' that may not have existed or may have been invisible. Tiny, insignificant differences, the 'noise' of measurement, may mean the difference between being in the first or second tier, a 'top 100' university or not. Moreover, small, meaningless shifts must now be explained in terms of rankings factors. The things that matter that are not reflected in the rankings become irrelevant.

These rankings have also changed relations of accountability. With highly visible numbers, anyone is qualified to demand an explanation. Deans now must meet with irate students, boards of visitors, regents, members of the press, or even ministers of education if rankings fall. The differences between what insiders and outsiders pay attention to have blurred. And because rankings are produced annually, they create clear trends, trajectories that are linked to the people who inhabit universities. A school may drop during someone's watch, or that administrator may be given credit for its rise.

Most importantly, qualitative differences have disappeared as this new means of sorting has taken hold. Qualities that could distinguish a school, like catering to poor or rural people, specializing in the arts, participating in an experiment to end segregation, or emphasizing teaching, are all back-stage to rankings, and the rankings punish schools for these kinds of innovations—or they are made invisible.

The Whole as the Sum of Its Parts

Messy, complicated decisions may require more of us cognitively than we are capable of giving.[11] That is why the quest for integration, for creating common denominators, is so appealing. For the New Guard, commensuration offered what seemed to be a fair way to simplify and include. For prospective students, commensuration through rankings reduced overwhelming choices into clear signals about what to want and what to do. But commensuration offers other alluring features. As historian Theodore Porter (1995) shows, in the face of conflict and scandal, quantification can be used to contain discretion and produce decisions that are defensible to outsiders.

The pairs competition during the 2002 Winter Olympics in Salt Lake City was tight. After the short programme, the Russian pair, Elena Berezhnaya and Anton Sikharulidze, led Canadians Jamie Salé and David Pelletier. The Russians made a small technical error in their long programme, but the Canadians delivered a flawless programme, and American and Canadian broadcasters projected their win on live television. When the scores were announced, contrary to expectations, the Russians came out on top. The result was quickly challenged, first by broadcasters, then by officials and by Canadian and American media. During an investigation, the French judge admitted to 'swapping votes' with the Russian judge. Media around the world denounced the cheating, and the resulting scandal threatened the legitimacy of competitive skating. The International Olympic Committee (IOC), which monitors all Olympic sports, threatened to eliminate figure skating from the Olympics if the International Skating Union (ISU) did not find a better way to measure the sport.

In response, the ISU, figure skating's international governing body, overhauled its judging system and ultimately how competitive skating performances are valued. The ISU had begun looking into changing its judging system even before 2002 as part of the IOC's examination of all subjectively-judged sports, but this threat sped up the process, and the ISU had a new system—known as the 'international judging system', or 'IJS' for short—in place in time for the next Olympics in 2006.

Figure skating judges have always used numbers in their evaluations, but there were two important changes in the new IJS procedures. One clear change was how complicated the new system is. The rules for how to judge are now so intricate that elaborate training is required to master them. Judges are certified only after they have passed a battery of difficult tests. A second important difference between the two systems is that the old 6.0 judging system was built around valuing whole programmes, while the IJS is based on valuing small parts. Under the 6.0 system, each judge used two marks to evaluate each skater's programme, one for technical merit and one for artistic presentation. Judges used these marks to compare and place skaters, so their placements were more important in determining competition outcomes than their actual marks. These marks were supposed to reflect the whole programme and were based on criteria that were loosely defined and gave judges a lot of freedom. The IJS, in contrast, is much more numerically precise and has very strict judging criteria, with both the technical and artistic aspects broken down into specific parts. Each technical element has a base value that is published in the IJS rulebook. After a new three-person technical panel identifies each element as the skater performs them, the judges evaluate them with a 'grade of execution' (GOE) score from –3 to +3. The old artistic mark has been divided into five separate programme components that the judges evaluate on a scale from 0.25 to 10 at the end of each programme. Competition outcomes are now determined based on point totals instead of judge placements.

This transition from valuing based on wholes to parts has changed skating in ways that were unanticipated. Because judges and technical panellists are now so focused on specific aspects of a skater's programme, they no longer have any sense of what the overall performance looked like, how well certain skaters did compared to others, or even how they evaluated a particular skater in relation to others. One judge reported that she could not even remember who won the most recent competition she had judged, and another explained that conversations in the judges' room following competitions have changed a lot as a result of the judging changes. After competitions that were judged using the 6.0 system, judges typically engaged in very intense discussions about their placements, and when the results were posted, 'everyone would flock over and look at it' to see the final results and how well their marks lined up with other judges' marks. None of this happens under the IJS because the judges 'have no idea' where they placed skaters (national-level judge).

This judge reported a common refrain: 'I've found myself under the new judging system not even looking to see who won. It no longer matters. I don't really feel like I'm playing a role in figuring out who won' (national-level judge). Part of this is due to the division of labour that the IJS has introduced with its separate technical and judging panels. In fact, the technical panellists are not even supposed to pay any attention to how well a skater does the elements they are busily identifying, so in theory, all they know at the end of each programme is which elements the skater performed and how difficult they were. A different judge summed up the thoughts of many skating insiders when he said, 'You feel completely detached from that process. You're just putting numbers on paper and letting the computer do the work' (international-level judge). All of this reflects how the value of the overall programme has disappeared and has been replaced by valuing the sum of a programme's parts.

These judging changes have also prompted skaters to perform similar elements. Just as the 6.0 system gave judges a lot of freedom in deciding which marks to give a certain programme, it gave skaters a lot of freedom in constructing their programmes. The IJS is so specific that skaters are essentially forced to do certain elements if they want to score well. The IJS rulebook lists base values for each element according to how difficult it is. Base values for jumps are fairly self-explanatory in the sense that triple jumps are more difficult than double jumps, and quadruple jumps are more difficult than triple jumps. For example, a skater receives 3.3 base points for a double Axel compared to 8.5 points for a triple Axel, the most difficult triple jump by far, and 4.1 points for a triple toe loop (considered the easiest triple jump) compared to 10.3 points for a quadruple toe loop. Base values for spins, footwork, and spirals are determined according to levels of difficulty, with level 4 being the most difficult and therefore worth the most points. A 'layback spin level 1' is worth 1.5 base points, for instance, whereas a 'layback spin level 4' is worth 2.7 points (International Skating Union 2010). These point differences make clear how important it is for skaters to perform more difficult elements.

For skaters to increase their levels of difficulty on these elements, they must incorporate a certain number of 'features' based on the criteria published in the rulebook: two features for level 2, three for level 3, and four for level 4. The features listed for spins include 'a difficult variation', 'another difficult variation in a basic position which must be significantly different from the first one', 'change of foot executed by jump', 'backward entrance', 'clear change of edge in sit (only from backward inside to forward outside) or camel', and 'at least 8 [revolutions] without changes in [position]/variation, foot, or edge' (International Skating Union 2010). If a skater wants to achieve a level 4 spin, he or she must conform to this list, which does allow for some flexibility but has encouraged skaters to perform very similar spins. During the 2010 Olympics, for instance, many of the combination spins in the top singles skaters' programmes had backward entrances followed by awkward-looking transitions to spinning on the other foot. This was very uncommon, if not nonexistent, under the 6.0 system. Some other elements or ways of performing them that were common in the past have virtually disappeared because they are not highly valued under the IJS. One former elite skater who competed under both judging systems explained that most skaters perform similar spin variations 'because those are the tried and tested ways that they're achieving the higher levels... You have to do it a certain way in order to get it' (former elite skater).

This also reveals what one judge called the 'uglification' of figure skating. There are only a few ways to achieve a 'difficult variation' in a spin or spiral sequence, and they often involve positions that are considered unattractive. Several skating insiders commented that pairs skating has been hit the hardest. One illustrated this point by describing how death spirals are now performed:

> In the death spiral, this ghastly position of the lady holding her heel, which we saw this year, and I found that absolutely, you know, abominable to watch because it was so unattractive, and in fact, it actually showed how not to do the death spiral. But those that thought it was a cool thing to add as a bullet point to get points, it actually ended up making skating not as attractive. (Olympic medallist and TV commentator)

Similarly, one of the features listed for layback spins is a 'Bielmann' position at the end of the spin, where the skater grabs her free leg and pulls it over her head, and many skaters try this position even though they cannot do it very well. The IJS now favours difficult elements over beautiful ones.

This compromise of technique over artistry has given rise to performances in which the composition of a programme is conceived of mainly as a vehicle for incorporating difficult elements—jumps, spins, and step sequences. This leaves less time for flowing movements, novel musical interpretations, or pure expressiveness. As one judge put it:

> We're seeing a lot of attempts at higher levels of difficulty, say for spins, and we, I think a lot of judges anyway, and I think a lot of spectators, miss just a plain, wonderful spin, and the way the system is right now it's not worth it to do a plain, beautiful spin, because you need that higher level of difficulty. (National-level judge)

Other judges lamented how it is rare to see a programme or even a particular element under the IJS that is 'simple and beautiful' (judge), such as 'a beautiful, simple, gorgeous, classic layback spin', which is 'only a level 1' (national-level technical panellist).

This is related to a bigger issue, which is that many skaters have given up on trying to tell a story within their programmes because they have to do so much to fulfil the IJS's strict technical requirements. A former skater explained this trend:

> One, because a lot of elements take longer, and two, because the grades of execution of jumps and spins are so important, there aren't any more stories... It's all about fitting in those points... So, I don't enjoy watching it as much, and I'm sure, I don't think a lot of other people do because that side is missing from the sport now, and it's very hard to find the right music, fit the right elements in the right places, and have space for choreography. The footwork is a perfect example. It's very, very hard to create footwork that hits all the bullet points to achieve a high level like a level 3 or level 4, and can also be choreographed to the music and look unique to fit the music, and also tell the story. (Former elite skater)

Skaters approach constructing their programmes differently now. Instead of beginning with a concept, music, and choreography, with the conjoining of technical and artistic aspects in service to the music, most skaters' main focus is on accumulating points, so they start with the technical elements and go from there. Many skating insiders think that skating has declined as a result.

Figure skating's transition from the 6.0 system to the IJS has fundamentally changed evaluation within the sport, from emphasizing wholes to parts. This has changed the experience of both judging and skating, relationships among skating insiders, and ultimately what competitive skating looks like.

The most visible aspect of a programme used to be the overall programme itself, but that has become invisible with respect to determining competition outcomes. No single mark under skating's current judging system takes the performance as a whole into account, and it is not uncommon for a flawed programme built around many difficult elements to accumulate more points than a beautiful, mistake-free programme with a story behind it. As a result, the most complete overall performance does not always win. More broadly, this illustrates how imposing numeric valuation systems can render what many people would describe as the most important quality of an object or activity—in this case, the artistic aspects of performance—invisible.

Now You See It, Now You Don't

As these three cases show, noticing is a complex cognitive, political, and professional process that is powerfully mediated by the form we give to valuation. Quantification solves many problems for its users. For busy people, it simplifies to make decisions easier. It is a strategy for reducing and organizing the avalanche of information that we confront each day. It is a means for including and integrating disparate things and people. It can be used to limit political or personal biases in decision-making.

But these virtues of quantification come at a price, one that is too easy to ignore. The trade-off techniques of the New Guard made the consequences of the forced relocation of the Yavapai unrepresentable. They compressed the historical and moral dimensions of the decision such that they were impossible to recover in the abstract language of quantification. The stakes of this decision for future generations of people who 'could not really be Yavapai' were impossible to show. And it was not just the Yavapai who felt misrepresented by the decision techniques. The substantive value that Orme Dam had become for the Old Guard could not be conveyed in a trade-off scheme that demanded a relative value. Unlike the Yavapai, they had no language to defend themselves. They could not claim to love a dam.

The power of rankings was to produce a relativity that pitted one against all in a ferocious status competition. No longer would claims to be a good law school be convincing when 'how good' was public. It became necessary for administrators to meticulously police the boundaries around volatile and meaningless distinctions—distinctions that did not exist before rankings. This form of evaluation introduced an unremitting anxiety about status, as well as an exacting discipline aimed at maintaining one's place in a stratification system that was fixed—but with fluid positions.

As the devaluation of artistry in skating shows, the loss of discretion that quantification brings may entail a great sacrifice. The need to curtail politics overwhelmed other considerations, including the beauty that many believed was skating's raison d'être. The lesson this example offers is that in art, as in life, the forms we create are irreducible, and taking them apart, even for worthy goals, is costly.

There are some general patterns in how commensuration shapes cognition. It unifies disparate objects or events by imposing a shared metric on them. This may be a shallow form of unity compared with other forms, such as a common identity or common language, but the effect can be profound. One only needs to consider the implications of pricing to appreciate the power of universalizing forms for social relations. But the truly generative aspect of commensuration is that it creates precise distinctions at the same time that it unifies. These distinctions may reflect pre-existing cultural understandings, but their precision is often something new. Precise distinctions force comparisons and stratification. It is impossible not to notice who or what is higher or lower. This attention to difference is fundamental to making judgements about quality, and as Anders Koed Madsen (this volume) suggests, visibility implicitly prioritizes by making entities, sometimes literally, objects of perception.

One other important pattern in quantification is that we are more likely to emphasize that which is easiest to measure. The algorithm *USN* used to create rankings included measures that schools routinely collected. For example, students' satisfaction with their school was operationalized as the percentage of students who donated to their university. This clearly benefits schools with wealthy students compared to those with poorer students. Rankings criteria also include the statistics that schools routinely collect, such as test scores and grade averages. The quality of libraries is measured by the number of their books. In skating, artistic merit is elusive compared to counting various technical feats, the focus of the new judging system. Because prices are so naturalized, in bureaucratic decision-making, it is common to use prices as a measure of value, and when prices are not available, we often create them using methods of contingent valuation. For example, in measuring the value of wilderness, it is common to create surveys of how much people are willing to pay to visit the wild.

It is important to consider the role of media in each of these cases. The New Guard's techniques required public forums for measuring people's public values and preferences. Had the Yavapai not had access to this public sphere, their efforts to explain their distinctiveness would have been witnessed by smaller and less powerful audiences. The fact that educational rankings are products of media which are experts at dissemination meant that *USN* could subvert the traditional guardians of institutional reputations and bring their product directly to their targeted consumers. The judging dispute in skating only became an international scandal because the predictions and comments of announcers were broadcast to enormous audiences, including other media that were primed for coverage. Not all quantitative judgements matter, so it is important to consider which factors influence their success or failure. Given the tremendous rise in rankings, auditing, benchmarking, and performance measures of all sorts, it is imperative that we analyse the power of quantification to direct our attention.

Noticing and ignoring are perhaps the most basic qualities of culture and of power. We cannot change what we do not see. We do not appreciate what we cannot represent. As Paul DiMaggio (1997) argues, in understanding cultural processes, it is crucial that we understand cognition. All valuation hinges on relations of visibility, and we must notice and explain these if we wish to understand how qualities are made and used.

Notes

1. For a review of work in the sociology of valuation and evaluation, see Lamont (2012).
2. What seems to be a rejection of form or formalism also implies form of some sort in that it reduces, edits, and shapes visibility and attention. For example, part of what makes John Cage's famous composition *4'33"* is that a formal structure is created by its temporal boundary which distinguishes the sounds and silences that occur during the duration of the piece, from the sounds and silences that it interrupts, as well as by other features of form, such as the performer's presence and actions and the expectations of the audience. This piece evokes an especially contingent visibility and invisibility in performers and audience members. Coughs, rustling, and perhaps a hyper-intense concentration on the presence or absence of sound, or the boundaries marking the beginning or ending of the piece, are likely features of how this particular form organizes attention.
3. For a few examples of work analysing the emergence and spread of quantification, see Hacking (1990); Power (1994, 1997); Porter (1995); Desrosières (1998); Carson (2007).
4. This section draws on Espeland (1998).
5. The Central Arizona Project is described by the BR, the main agency that built it, at <http://www.usbr.gov/projects/Project.jsp?proj_Name=Central+Arizona+Project>.
6. The Salt and Verde Rivers are tributaries of the Gila River, which is a tributary of the Colorado River.
7. For a glimpse of just how elaborate and specialized the projects affected by BR budgets are, consider that Hoover Dam, one of the agency's premier structures, maintains its own police force, which is formally part of the agency, and helps manage some 300 recreational sites that have 90 million 'visits' each year. And this is just a tiny part of an agency with employees. Like most successful organizations, 'the agency' is a vast, scattered series of organizations, and it is adept at finding new uses for itself as circumstances change.

8. Espeland was hired by the BR as a consultant to help prepare parts of the social impact assessment for the new investigation (known as the Central Arizona Water Control Study), so she participated in the implementation, if not the design, of these new procedures. Because of assurances of confidentiality, other participants are not named except when their names and statements are part of the public record.
9. This section relies on work done collaboratively with Michael Sauder. See, for example, Espeland and Sauder (2007) and Sauder and Espeland (2009).
10. For a theoretically sophisticated treatment of singularities and their judgements, see Karpik (2010).
11. This section draws on Lom (2013).

References

Carson, J. 2007. *The Measure of Merit: Talents, Intelligence, and Inequality in the French and American Republics, 1750–1940*. Princeton: Princeton University Press.

Davis, K., A. Fisher, B. Davis, and S. E. Merry. 2012. *Governance by Indicators: Global Power through Classification and Rankings*. Oxford: Oxford University Press.

Desrosières, A. 1998. *The Politics of Large Numbers: A History of Statistical Reasoning*. Cambridge, MA: Harvard University Press.

DiMaggio, P. 1997. 'Culture and Cognition'. *Annual Review of Sociology* 23: 263–87.

Espeland, W. 1998. *The Struggle for Water: Politics, Rationality and Identity in the Southwest*. Chicago: University of Chicago Press.

Espeland, W. and M. Sauder. 2007. 'Rankings and Reactivity: How Public Measures Recreate Social Worlds'. *American Journal of Sociology* 113(1): 1–40.

Hacking, I. 1990. *The Taming of Chance*. Cambridge: Cambridge University Press.

Hazelkorn, E. 2007. 'The Impact of League Tables and Ranking Systems on Higher Education Decision Making'. *Higher Education Management and Policy* 19(2): 87–110.

Hazelkorn, E. 2008. 'Learning to Live with League Tables and Rankings'. *Higher Education Policy* 21: 193–215.

Hein, L. 2004. *Reasonable Men, Powerful Words: Political Culture and Expertise in 20th Century Japan*. Berkeley and Washington, DC: University of California Press and Woodrow Wilson International Center for Scholars Press.

International Skating Union. 2010. 'Communication No. 1611: Scale of Values, Levels of Difficulty and Guidelines for Marking Grade of Execution for Single and Pair Skating'. <http://www.isu.org>.

Karpik, L. 2010. *Valuing the Unique: The Economics of Singularities*. Princeton: Princeton University Press.

Lam, T. 2011. *A Passion for Facts: Social Surveys and the Construction of the Chinese Nation-State, 1900–1948*. Berkeley: University of California Press.

Lamont, M. 2012. 'Toward a Comparative Sociology of Valuation and Evaluation'. *Annual Review of Sociology* 38: 201–21.

Lom, S. 2013. '"Sometimes Less Is More": The Development and Effects of Evaluative Cultures'. PhD dissertation, Northwestern University. Ann Arbor: ProQuest/UMI (Publication No. AAT 3563771).

Miller, P. and N. Rose. 1990. 'Governing Economic Life'. *Economy and Society* 19: 1–31.

Monks, J. and R. G. Ehrenberg. 1999. 'U.S. News and World Report's College Rankings: Why They Do Matter?' *Change* 31: 42–51.

Porter, T. 1995. *Trust in Numbers: The Pursuit of Objectivity in Science and Public Life*. Princeton: Princeton University Press.

Power, M. 1994. *The Audit Explosion*. London: Demos.

Power, M. 1997. *The Audit Society: Rituals of Verification*. Oxford: Oxford University Press.

Rose, N., P. O'Malley, and M. Valverde. 2006. 'Governmentality'. *Annual Review of Law and Social Science* 2: 83–104.

Salini, J. and A. Saroyan. 2007. 'League Tables as Policy Instruments: Uses and Misuses'. *Higher Education Policy and Management* 19(2): 31–68.

Sauder, M. and W. Espeland. 2009. 'The Discipline of Rankings: Tight Coupling and Organizational Change'. *American Sociological Review* 74(1): 63–82.

Scott, J. 1998. *Seeing Like a State: How Certain Schemes to Improve the Human Condition Have Failed*. New Haven: Yale University Press.

Strathern, M. 2000. *Audit Cultures: Anthropological Studies of Accountability, Ethics and the Academy*. London: Routledge.

US Bureau of Reclamation. 1976. 'Socioeconomic Study of the Fort McDowell Indian Reservation and Community With and Without the Development of Orme Dam and Reservoir'. Prepared by the Natelson Corp.

2

Value in the Age of Doubt

Accounting as a Maieutic Machine

Paolo Quattrone

The Parmalat Scandal, the Accounting Framework, and the Impossibility of Transparency[1]

Fourteen and a half billion euros. This is the hole that Parmalat left in the financial market when it became clear that it was insolvent in December 2003.

How could this happen? And whose fault is it? This is of course something that magistrates in Italy and elsewhere are still trying to understand but the picture is becoming clearer and clearer although, as often happens with scandals of this size, the whole truth will possibly never emerge. As an Italian comedian commented, Parmalat is in the dairy business and thus the truth at the end of the story will very likely be much skimmed.

The Parmalat scandal is an interesting case of failure of organizational, institutional, and social controls. It is a case of organizational controls failure because the whole top management of the multinational was implicated and leagued with shareholders to make sure that funds distractions could happen for years. It is a case of institutional controls failure as neither the market, nor the regulators, nor those institutionally devoted to check on Parmalat's financial robustness (auditors, rating agencies, and stock exchange authorities) managed to raise red flags to avoid misdoings. When they did it, it was too late. It is a case of social controls failure as there are many grey areas of connivance amongst all of those parties of the economy and society (in Italy and elsewhere) which should have maintained an ethical conduct, or checked upon that of firms, banks, auditors, accountants, and regulatory bodies. As I will argue later, the lack of effectiveness of controls in Parmalat is possibly a metaphor for the failure of an entire world-view, that is, the idea of financial markets as spaces where transparency should guarantee effective internal and external controls on managers' behaviours and the efficiency and fairness of the whole economy and society.

But how did Parmalat get there? How was it possible to dig a hole as big as 1 per cent of Italy's GDP?

What follows is a partial reconstruction of what happened. It is partial in a twofold sense. First because of space constrains. Second, dust has not settled yet, and trials are still taking place to ascertain the role of shareholders, auditors, banks, and regulators in the story. But let us proceed with order. And begin with a bit of history on the company.

Parmalat History

Parmalat was founded on 15 April 1961 as the result of the division of a family business dedicated to the production and commercialization of salami and tomato sauce. Calisto Tanzi (with other members of his family, the infamous Parmalat's main shareholder), saw an opportunity in the dairy industry, thanks to the existence of two Swedish inventions: the first, the existence of Tetra-Pak, the famous firm producing aseptic packs which contain all sorts of liquids. The second, the UHT (Ultra High Temperature) milk quasi-sterilization process, which allows milk to last for long periods and far longer than fresh milk. Mr Tanzi had the idea of combining these two things and this is how Parmalat began to grow, first by commercializing fresh milk in Tetra-Packs and then filling the packs with UHT milk. Parmalat's headquarters was, and still is, in Collecchio, near the city of Parma: hence Parmalat, as 'latte' is the Italian for 'milk'.

Things went extraordinarily well for the first two decades. Turnover grew at a rate of 50 per cent per year and jumped from 260 million lire (125,000 euros) in the 1960s to 635 billion lire (310 million euros) in 1984. Parmalat was growing fast both in economic terms and in terms of image. Its brand became famous all over the world with Parmalat sponsoring Formula One teams, and skiing champions. Like many Italian tycoons, Tanzi could not resist the attraction of soccer and TV and in the 1990s he bought Parma calcio, Parma's local football team which also managed to do a decent job in Serie A (the Italian Premier League), and Oden TV, with the idea, so they say, of competing with Mr Berlusconi's Mediaset group. By then Parmalat was already a big multinational, one of the few in the Italian milieu, with commercial subsidiaries all over the world, and large investments in Italy, Europe, Latin America, and elsewhere.

However, from the late 1970s, the fantastic growth in revenues and investments was accompanied by an equally extraordinary growth in debt. This is not bad per se. As Mr Tanzi himself stated when asked how he felt sitting on a mountain of debt, he replied that debt is a substantial part of the strategy of growth of a firm. It is then top management's role to make sure that this does not exceed a certain proportion of the equity and that interest expenses do not go over a certain percentage of the revenues: an answer that any professor of financial management would have given.

Let us therefore look at the Parmalat scandal through the eyes of an accounting framework (financial reporting in this case) to see how theory and practice may diverge quite substantially.

The Efficiency of Market and Institutional Controls: Theory

If you open a manual of financial reporting, the first chapter will very likely provide you with a representation similar to that shown in Figure 2.1.

Figure 2.1 enumerates various stakeholders who are interested in financial reporting information. Typically the manual will state that each of these categories (shareholders, investors, etc.) will have one very specific interest in reading financial statements:

- *Shareholders*, especially those who can exert control through majority of shares and given the growing separation between ownership and management, look at financial reports to understand how managers are performing, and whether they are creating shareholder value.
- *Managers* also want to get information on the company's performance to improve shareholder value and make sure that their performance is adequately rewarded.

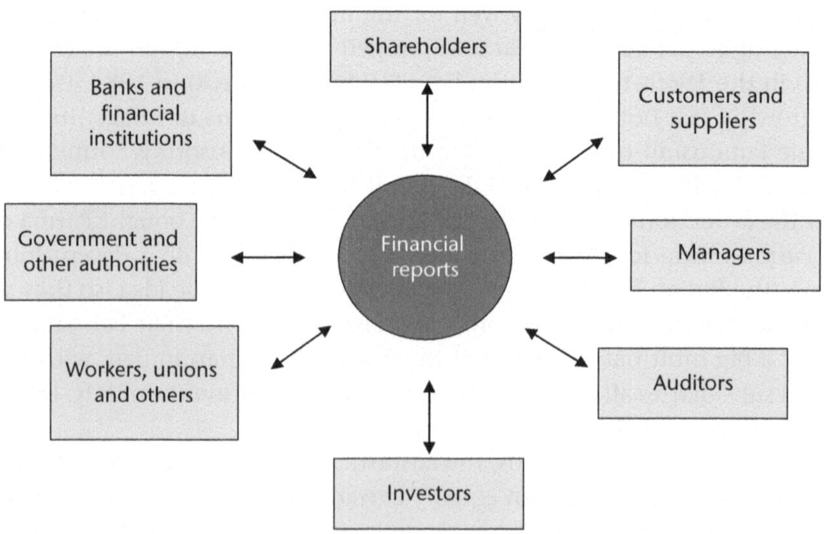

Figure 2.1. How the accounting framework frames social actors

- *Banks and financial institutions* want to know from financial statements whether the company is financially solvent and liquid to get capital back and interest paid at regular intervals.
- *Government and other authorities*, such as anti-trust, by looking at these reports want to ascertain whether companies are paying a fair amount of taxes, and whether profits are rising due to concentration and lack of competition in the industry and thus requiring intervention.
- *Customers and suppliers* will have a similar interest to banks and workers as they want to be sure that guarantees and payments are honoured, respectively.
- *Auditors and rating agencies* are there to check on the validity of these accounts and the financial reliability of the company.
- *Workers* want to know whether the company which employs them will be stable and healthy enough to pay their salary and do so for a theoretically undetermined period of time.
- *Other investors* share with majority shareholders a need for information on value creation and return on their investment.

In this picture financial reports contribute to the transparency required for the efficient and effective functioning of financial markets. This framework also indirectly guarantees internal controls and good manager/sharerholder relationships because, if managers do not perform well, the market will realize it and share prices will go down. Poor shares performance will force shareholders to intervene to put the situation back on track, possibly by firing managers and substituting them with better ones. The system also helps to regulate relationships with all of the stakeholders, as it works in the interest of shareholders, who though, by pursuing their own interest also, and magically, act in the interest of the whole economy and society.

Too good to be true. Let us look at what happened in practice with Parmalat.

The Efficiency of Market and Institutional Controls: Practice

Real life is always richer than simplified models. The Parmalat scandal, though, is a case of reality going beyond imagination. Let us look at the behaviour of the various agents involved, revisiting the various and familiar categories illustrated above, following the same order, but filling each box with some real personages.

- *Shareholders.* Parmalat's main shareholders were Calisto Tanzi and his family. Mr Tanzi had a dream which is difficult to fulfil without huge financial resources: to build a big multinational by buying and selling milk, a product with relatively low margins and returns. While Parmalat stayed within its core business (i.e. until the end of the 1970s) things were not going badly and margins were as high as 9 per cent. However, with the expansion in other non-core businesses such as bakery products (biscuits, snacks, etc.) and as far away from the core as TV, tourism, and sport, things begun to become problematic. One may interpret this expansion as a strategy of diversification and one may be right. However, Mr Tanzi was also driven by other objectives which would not strictly fall into the aseptic agency of a shareholder/entrepreneur as described in economics, finance, and accounting manuals. These will become clearer later but certainly Mr Tanzi has entertained close relationships with politicians, and members of the Opus Dei amongst others, and, so they say, has always displayed a tendency to please them all. We will see that Parmalat's expansion was possibly driven by, or somehow related to, these relationships more than a pure interest in profit. The objective of expansion also provided a rhetoric to sustain the growth of debt, for any expansion needs finances and Mr Tanzi had in his CFOs good collaborators with good ideas on how to raise these.

- *Managers*. The names of Parmalat's managers involved in the scandal are many. But one of them has become more famous given his key role in the expansion of Parmalat debt and in arranging the mechanism through which this debt could be sustained. His name is Fausto Tonna. Fausto Tonna became Parmalat's MD in 1987 and then CFO in 1991. Under his administration Parmalat's debt rose from 164.32 million euros, in 1987, to 6340.15 million euros in 2002. Interestingly, and this is the key of the whole scandal, cash and liquidity grew at a similar pace: from 8.95 million euros in 1987 to 3363.56 million in 2002. Cash and liquidity jumped substantially in 1990, when Parmalat was quoted at the *Borsa di Milano*, the Italian stock exchange market. The question that many analysts asked themselves in all of those years of growing debt was: why did Parmalat recur to financial markets (through the recurrent issue of various kinds of bonds) and pay an increasing interest rate when it could have slashed its debt by reducing this enormous liquidity? The answer was always that Parmalat wanted to be ready to take buying opportunities on the market and thus needed liquidity for these eventualities. This could have been a convincing answer in the first years of the expansion but not when the level of debt rose to unsustainable levels. Merrill Lynch analysts were the first and only ones who looked with suspicion at this liquidity and suspected that it was fictitious. Unfortunately, they were right but too late. Mr Tonna and his collaborators had devised a series of techniques to boost revenues (e.g. faking invoices of powder milk sales to Cuba), increase assets (e.g. through the sale of non-existent intellectual properties and technologies amongst offshore subsidiaries), and decrease losses and debt (e.g. by shifting uncollectable receivables sometimes artificially created to offshore subsidiaries in the Cayman Islands and other fiscal havens where accounting controls were virtually non-existent). But these are only a few examples as the list is much longer. Parmalat was growing debt to repay its debt: in the absence of a sufficient cash flow generated by genuine sales, the only way to repay the debt was generating other debt. This went on and on from the early 1990s with no one raising substantial doubts about the whole situation until the early 2000s. At one , though, and we are close to the end, a bond needed to be repaid and some cash was to be found. Mr Tonna turned once again to banks for help.

- *Banks and financial institutions*. Many of the most important world banks had business relationships with Parmalat (e.g. Citi group, Morgan Stanley, Deutsche Bank, Bank of America) and of course all of the main Italian ones (e.g. Banca Intesa, Capitalia, San Paolo-IMI, Unicredito). Some of these banks were overexposed and tried to reduce their credits towards Parmalat. In a sense, and this is why some of these banks have been brought to court by the new Parmalat administrator, they were not in a position to ignore Parmalat's situation and they must have been aware of the problems. Whatever the truth is (and some of these banks have been cleared of any misdoing), they endorsed Mr Tonna's idea to keep buying Parmalat bonds to then resell them to the public and small investors. Of course banks, like every organization, are a coalition of different agencies and it could therefore happen, for example, that the same bank was trying to reduce the exposure towards Parmalat in one office and buying Parmalat's bond in another. Some argue that Italian financial authorities should have intervened. Mr Tremonti, then Treasury Minister of the first Berlusconi government, fiercely attacked the then Governor of the Bank of Italy, Mr Fazio, for his lack of action on the whole matter. Some defended the Bank saying that its role was to invigilate on the banking system not firms and that the CONSOB, the Italian equivalent of the US Securities and Exchange Commission, should have intervened. For sure there were too many institutional (e.g. the Bank of Italy's equity was subscribed by the banks involved in the scandal) and personal overlaps (with the Governor later found guilty of entertaining personal friendship with most of the bankers in the institutions that he should have controlled... but that is another story) to allow Parmalat irregularities to emerge before it was too late. These relationships did not exclude politicians and members of the various governments in power throughout the Parmalat saga.

- *Government and other authorities*. Parmalat's expansion strategy went in many geographical directions. One amongst these is particularly exemplary of the other rationales underpinning the expansion: a factory in Nusco, a small village in Campania, a region in the south of Italy. The reason for that investment could be found in a rational economic decision but also in much more pragmatic issues of public relations, given that Nusco is the electoral district of Ciriaco De Mita, former Italian Prime Minister and high-profile member of the Christian Democrats (DC), politically close to Mr Tanzi. But other politicians also benefited from their closeness to Mr Tanzi. Apparently Mr Cossiga, Emeritus President of the Italian Republic, could travel on Parmalat's jet. Mr Tanzi was also close to Mr Alemanno (former Minister of the Agriculture and former Mayor of Rome) who was charged with having favoured Parmalat when allowing the commercialization of Parmalat's new high quality milk as 'fresh' even though it did not technically fall into the definition of 'fresh' (milk which is a maximum four days old; Lattefresco Parmalat could instead be as much as eight days old). Mr Alemanno has since been acquitted. Parmalat is also said to have supported Mr Massimo D'Alema (also former Prime Minister) through publicity in the magazine of his Foundation Italianieuropei, and Mr Romano Prodi (former Prime Minister and President of the European Commission). Both of them deny the charges or admit only those which have legally been recorded. In this respect, as noted by a magistrate investigating these relationships, sponsoring political parties is not illegal, if it is done transparently. And if politicians do not know of the illegal provenance of the money they receive, they are not responsible as far as this money is correctly accounted for on the receivers' books. Mr Tanzi also sponsored Forza Italia (Mr Berlusconi's party) and some argue that Parmalat diverted TV publicity to Mediaset preferring it to RAI and giving up the discount that that volume of ads would have generated. In summation, could the government, as an interested party in financial reporting information, solve this intricate nest of relationships and make things more transparent? Yes it could, if the Prime Minister were not a tycoon himself. But again this is another story...
- *Customers and suppliers*. The relationship with suppliers was not as clear as it should have been. Tetra-Pack, for instance, was officially paid by Parmalat at the full price for its supplies but in fact offered a discount based on volume. The difference between the price paid and the price recorded on Parmalat's books was a way of distracting money from Parmalat and accumulating it in a Swiss bank account held by Mr Tanzi, who apparently used it for his personal use and for financing Italian political parties.

- *Auditors and rating agencies*. Were the auditors (mainly Grant Thornton) aware of this situation? According to Mr Tonna's declaration to the magistrates not only did they know but they helped to orchestrate various offshore operations and offshore subsidiaries such as Bonlat which had the role of absorbing losses generated by the industrial divisions, and also incorporate two other companies which had played that role in previous years (Zilpa and Curcastle). Interestingly the two auditors involved (Mr Penca and Mr Bianchi) had worked also for Hodgson Landau Brands when this audited Parmalat's accounts and moved to Grant Thornton when they audited Parmalat. There is therefore a clear example of conflict of interest here, as in the whole story.
- *Workers and other investors*. Those who do not appear in this web of relationships are those in whose interest Figure 2.1 was drawn: unaware small investors. They, along with workers, are the only ones who do not appear in this scandalous story and will be those who pay the price for it. The forecast is that only four out of 100 small shareholders and bond holders will get a partial refund.

This incredible network of relationships and fraud was discovered in December 2003 when Mr Tanzi was forced to resign under the pressure of the CONSOB and various banks. Mr Bondi was appointed as administrator of Parmalat and soon discovered that, for example, the bank statement of an account held at the Bank of America worth 3.5 billion dollars was in fact faked in a small office with a colour printer. The entire paper castle constructed by Mr Tanzi & Co. collapsed in a matter of hours.

What the Parmalat scandal teaches us is that theory sheds some light on things (including financial transactions and relationships) but also and at the same time casts a shadow on many other relationships. What Figure 2.1 does is to assign a clear and unique agency to various economic and institutional actors. It black-boxes them and, in doing so, it makes invisible what is not contemplated by that theory. A shareholder is interested in his own return. But Mr Tanzi was interested in many other things such as possibly financing a great part of the Italian political apparatus, and this not only for economic self-interest. The result is that we do not imagine and thus expect what could instead happen in practice, where the boxes in Figure 2.1 are, in fact, networks of relationships.

Paradoxically, a model thought to create and ensure transparency of markets, institutions, and transactions ends up making these opaque. It is much better to believe that this transparency is not achievable and instead constantly seek to unveil what happens in practice, without relying on a tick-box mentality. And to design accounting systems that build on this impossibility rather than on its possibility.

The Challenge: Can Accounting be Positive without Being Positivist?

This recounting of the Parmalat scandal provides, if needed, further evidence of the pressing need for rethinking the role, functions, and workings of accounting in organizations, economy, and society.

Accounting, especially for those who trust its representational power too much (Porter 1995) and are trapped in that search for certainty that characterizes modern times (Schreiner 2011), is often associated with concepts such as 'transparency', 'true and fair', and, last but not least, 'fair value'. In making this association, accounting is believed to be able, at least in principle and as aspiration, to provide a positive knowledge of the value of financial transactions and entities with the aim of producing some kind of numerical calculation that would constitute the basis for investors' and managers' decisions (Burchell et al. 1980). The transparency of financial representations and the objectivity of the resulting valuations are often invoked for the sake of market efficiency.[2]

Accounting and valuations are two activities that have gone hand in hand for centuries. Reference to various forms of valuations was already made in early modern accounting treatises (e.g. Flori 1636) and still a few centuries later, and until very recently, accounting manuals spent hundreds of pages arguing in favour of (or against) various valuation and recognition methods for all kinds of assets, provisions, expenses, and revenues (e.g. D'Ippolito 1945; Amodeo 1970): all of that, very often, without showing a single number, almost as if these books' authors were worried about their power. However, the rise of beliefs in market efficiency has made central bankers, as well as the majority of men and women in the street, believe that the task of valuation can be delegated to markets, that it does not require judgement, that subjectivity should be reduced to the minimum, and that valuation practices are not linked to various kinds of institutional, social, and political influences and relationships. Borrowing from Bruno Latour, a 'great divide' between accounting and valuation has come into being, with market values becoming benchmarks to be matched or approximated when making accounting calculations.

It is possibly only thanks to the recent great financial crisis that doubts have been cast upon the market's functionality. Despite the recurrent attempts to solve market failures by reverting to market-oriented solutions, this time around it seems that faith in the self-regulating abilities of such an institution is vacillating. This breakdown sees the problem of values and valuing regaining central stage in academic, political, and public debates. There is no need therefore to perform any further critique of the realist assumptions which still inform accounting beliefs and regulations. From a theoretical point of view, years of research have laid new post-realist epistemological foundations to build an alternative understanding of how accounting works in valuation practices. From an empirical standpoint, the great financial crisis has provided unequivocal evidence to corroborate the critique of market-based views of valuation.

The analysis of the Parmalat scandal has offered a pretext to speculate on what principles should underpin the development of non-representationalist forms of accounting and therefore of valuation. In the Parmalat case the role played by the actors in the story simply does not fit with those assumed to be played by stakeholders as depicted by the accounting framework. This scandal seems a particularly interesting space to show how a search for transparency inevitably makes things opaque, to reflect on how the regulations that should help in avoiding accounting scandals create the conditions for such scandals to emerge, grow, and eventually explode. As Marilyn Strathern has illustrated so well (2000), a search for transparency presupposes what one wants to make transparent, and therefore this search can be deceptive, creates illusions of certainty, allows purposeful manipulation of accounting data, and, above all, makes accounting users blind and the practice of valuation go unquestioned. This tyranny of transparency is ubiquitous in contemporary societies. So we live in 'orgies of calculations' all directed to make our actions auditable and to make us accountable (Meyer 1986). All of these attempts work backwards, that is, they assume what needs to be represented and account only for this limited range of possibilities leaving the others at the margin, obscured by the light shed on something else.

Another example from the Parmalat case can illustrate this point. Mr Fausto Tonna, the accountant, was theoretically accountable to Mr Tanzi for the way in which he managed Parmalat's resources. In fact, he was accountable to much broader systems of interests which expanded beyond the borders of Parmalat. This is why accounting and finance are not theoretically (and epistemologically) equipped to deal with scandals such as Parmalat and Enron. These theories assign a specific role and functions to various stakeholders (and to shareholders in particular) and whatever deviates from this view is obscured and marginalized by the accounting framework, although it is ready to strike back at the first occasion. In a sense, the various accounting scandals that cyclically affect our economies and societies can be seen as a result of greater calls for accountabilities, as these always presuppose what needs to be accounted for and make us ignore other important and relevant issues. These calls have the arrogance of knowing what is 'right', what needs to be done to make financial markets efficient. This is why they cyclically fail. No one is God and it would be useful to be periodically reminded of this small detail.

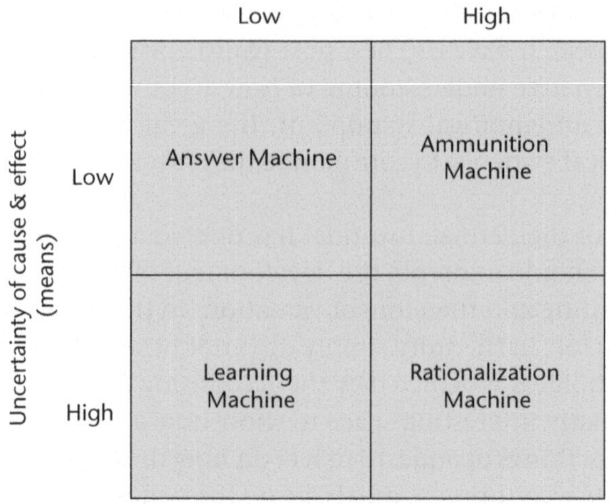

Figure 2.2. The four roles of accounting
Source: Burchell et al. (1980, 14).

Perhaps it is worthwhile to briefly recall the seminal study by Burchell et al. (1980) on the roles of accounting in organizations and societies to define the boundaries of the search for a positive role of accounting beyond positivism. That study proposed a two-by-two matrix that is still useful today to discuss issues of valuation in practice (see Figure 2.2). On the two axes we can place the degree of uncertainty of management's objectives and the means to achieve these objectives, respectively. This degree can be relatively 'certain' or 'uncertain'. Crossing these two dimensions you have four different roles that accounting plays in organizations and society. If degrees of uncertainty are low, a rare but possible event, then accounting works as an *answer machine*. It gives you answers, it tells you, for example, the 'right' cost of two production lines so you can understand whether to push production on one line or the other; it tells you whether managers are acting in the interest of shareholders by measuring variations in shareholder value, and so forth. This ideal and unrealistic situation, where knowledge is easily attainable (or is thought to be attainable), is the default situation assumed in many dominant views of what role accounting is supposed to serve in organizations and societies. It seems to be also the selling point of information technology packages (and the dream of those who purchase them) that automate the production of accounting numbers and make the process of valuation so smooth: one interrogates a screen on a PC and the Oracle gives the answer!

However, it seems obvious that this situation is quite rare if not impossible in reality. Most likely, there is a high degree of uncertainty in at least one of, if not both, these two dimensions. So accounting becomes an *ammunition machine* when there is uncertainty over the means to be used to achieve a given objective. It is then mobilized by different parties to promote their vested interests with valuation becoming a space of negotiation rather than of calculation. If instead there is uncertainty over the objectives, then accounting is used as a *rationalization machine*, as it can justify organizations' actions ex post, i.e. after these actions have taken place. Here numbers become rhetorical means of persuasion, arguments that do not have any relationship with an underlying financial reality. When instead objectives are pretty clear but no one is sure of how to get there, accounting plays the role of a *learning machine*. This is the case, for example, of budgets and how they are often used to explore the future, to understand what actions realize the yearly targets.

What Figure 2.2 and the research tradition initiated by Burchell et al.'s seminal article (1980) teach us is that accounting is not just about representations and true and fair views. Accounting rarely, if ever, works as an answer machine which truly represents the financial situation of a company. As has been noted, if representations could be a transparent image of the represented they would not be needed: representations exist (and can be conceived of) only if there is a gap between the represented and the representer, if the transparency which representation aims to achieve is, in fact, impossible to achieve. A true and fair representation of accounting transactions is impossible as accounting signs cannot represent the financial world: such inscriptions speak of this world in its absence (Latour 1988). This is why this world needs to be made present again through accounting inscriptions: it needs to be '*re*-presented' (paraphrasing a passage in Latour 1986).

The impossibility of the sign to construct a full reference to a supposedly objective financial reality positions all of us (researchers as well as accounting users) in that bottom-right quadrant of the matrix in Figure 2.2. This is also the quadrant inhabited by Parmalat's numbers: these numbers deceive, they fool the user. They construct an economic value which marginalizes and expunges other possible notions of value. The accounting framework underpinning Figure 2.1 allows an easier consumption of financial values, where the consumer of accounting numbers is technically and socially alienated from their production process. As much as the buyer of groceries in supermarkets does not know what he is buying when shopping, valuation and accounting practices are designed to make consumption of financials quicker, unreflective, and superficial. And even if labels tells us the quality of the food, they do not tell us whether this is the food we need, exactly as accounting standards and auditing certify adherence to generally accepted principles but do not warn us on whether these are the principles we need to understand financial worlds and why we have these and not others.

The response to the impossibility of escaping the conundrum posed by the bottom-right quadrant of the matrix in Figure 2.2 has generated a series of constructivist accounts of accounting and valuation. These accounts have often been qualified as the 'sociology *of* accounting', as the 'politics *of* accounting', as the 'history *of* accounting', or, more broadly, as 'interdisciplinary perspectives *on* accounting'. Similarly, the 'sociology *of* finance' has offered new vistas on finance as the discipline which has grown in importance at the same pace as the growing relevance of the market, which is seen as the valuation mechanism par excellence in contemporary market economies. In these various attempts, the use of the prepositions '*of*' and '*on*' denotes that the theoretical development which has shed new light on accounting and finance practices happened somewhere else (in sociology, in politics, in history or in science and technology studies) but not *in* one of the core spaces that especially accounting was used to occupy and monopolize: that of valuing things, people, and activities, where this valuation was more akin to a construction and mediation of different social interests rather than the preservation and praise of one amongst them. The very same title of the first accounting manual by Pacioli (1494, *Summa de arithmetica, geometria, proportioni et proportionalità*) points to the intrinsic morality of a calculation which is more about distribution of values (the proportion) that its crude measurement: more about reflection than representation.

The question therefore becomes: once we know that we cannot epistemologically escape the quandary of that bottom-right quadrant, unless we want to fool ourselves, is there any positive, not alienating, and reflective role that accounting valuations can play? And if so, what are the epistemological principles, the institutional arrangements, and the technical solutions that we have to devise to make it happen? How would we design an accounting and valuation system if we assume the impossibility of representation? And, if we hammer out these questions in our heads, what is then the role that accounting plays in organizations, economies, and societies beyond the naivety of representation and the amorality of legitimation and ex-post rationalization?

Sketching the contours of an answer to these questions, exploring the possibility for accounting to be positive outside positivism and clarifying what this exploration means and entails are the objectives of the remainder of this chapter.

Valuing in the Age of Doubt: Where to Begin?

Crisis is a word that denotes a turning point in a disease, a moment when judgement is needed. I think this financial crisis has created a space for judging what this great divide between accounting and valuation implies and whether it is time to overcome it. Valuing in the age of doubt, in my view, requires valuation and accounting to go back together but in new ways.

This difficult task has a multifaceted nature. It is an epistemological matter of how accounting produces knowledge on financial transactions in an economy (i.e. what principles underpin accounting frameworks). It is an institutional issue concerning how various bodies and actors govern this production (think of the role played by bodies such as the IASB and FASB and their related power networks). Finally, it is a question of how these complex issues are translated into technical financial reporting theories and principles, management accounting and control techniques, accountability and governance mechanisms (think of how different financial statements' formats define what counts as relevant and what does not in the context of financial information).

A difficult task, I said: from where to begin? Given that a picture is said to paint a thousand words, perhaps I could start with an example from Escher's works. These works show how often irreconcilable opposites and illogical patterns are made to appear real and logical in front of your eyes. *Print Gallery*[3] is one of these and may help us to find new principles for rethinking accounting valuations in 'socie-*ties*', that is, to speculate on how valuation is a relational issue which ties things together, where economic, moral, and social values are no longer deemed to be separable.[4] What one sees in the lithograph is a young man in a gallery. He is looking at a picture of a ship in a harbour of a town where there are various buildings, turrets, and finally a window where a woman is gazing out from her apartment. This apartment is above a picture gallery in which a young man is looking at a picture and... What?! He is within the picture he is observing!

This seems against all logic but, as will soon become clear, there is nothing truer than what this picture tells us. When one is observing something one is never neutral in making this observation: we are always *within* what we are observing, as we observe by carrying with us a baggage of experiences which are mediated by the various technologies and other material artefacts that we use in this observation. We are related to a network of artefacts (the gallery, the frame, the colours, the technology of lithography, etc.) that make that vision apparently clear in front of our eyes. *Print Gallery* also teaches us that every observation is incomplete. The hole in the middle of Escher's lithograph is unavoidable. You can move it around within the frame, and this will help you in seeing what the hole had previously made invisible, but it will modify the other parts of the picture. Although the hole can be reduced to the infinitely small, as with every dot, it can never be considered finite or closed: it cannot be filled (and Escher shows this mathematically) and the picture thus will never be complete as one can never have a full picture of reality. The way in which this hole has been filled in *Print Gallery* is by the imposition of the author's signature. That signature is Escher's statement that this is the way in which he views knowledge. It is the author's authority: an act of faith, if you like.

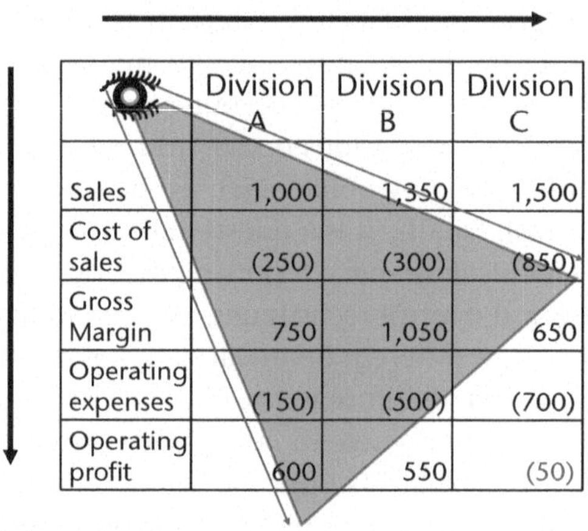

Figure 2.3. Accounting praising truth

Does this relate to accounting and valuation? The answer is a resounding 'yes'. It does, and a small example shows that. Look at Figure 2.3. 'What do you see?' I normally ask my students when showing these numbers which for me are a figure. Confident accountants would state without a doubt: 'a multi-divisional profit and loss account!', looking at each other bewildered, believing that an accounting professor could not ask such a trivial question. 'Yes, correct'. I would then urge them to reflect on this other question: 'And what is the most important box in this P&L?' Whatever the level of the class participants, from inexperienced undergraduates to mature executives, I rarely get the answer that I want to hear. Some state 'sales!', some others 'operating profit'!, some others 'the gross margin!' In a few minutes all the possible boxes will be named but one, the one I think is the most important to understand the information that this other matrix is providing us with: the top-left corner, which is indeed empty!

This box defines *what* is to be seen (i.e. the various divisions, which is only one amongst many different ways in which the vision of a corporation can be composed) and *how* (i.e. the structure of the P&L, organized according to business functions in this case, one amongst many possible alternatives). It also conceals *why* the statement has this format, obscuring the political agenda it brings with it, that is, the predominance of the shareholder who will eventually decide which of the functional managers are to be rewarded and which to be sacked in order to preserve the ultimate bottom line, net profit, on which basis dividends are distributed (with a plethora of accounting standards, and other technologies to reinforce this statement). Without reflecting on and questioning this empty box, without asking ourselves how the accounting gaze composes visions of a corporation, we would not understand how values are constructed, what they result from, and indeed why they are portrayed and what they do to us once they are transformed into apparently neutral numbers. We would look at the value of each divisional bottom line without really understanding what kind of values this representation portrays, constructs, and supports. This financial statement is a subtle political statement whose epistemology works silently, almost marginalized, relegated into a corner, an empty box which resembles the empty circle in the middle of Escher's lithography. It is this lack of reflection on accounting constructions that makes users forget that 'data' are not 'given' but attributed by the reference systems we use to construct them (as the Latin etymology of the word suggests, from *datum*, i.e. attributed). It is this unawareness of the power of representations and the perspective that they inevitably take that makes the very same users believe that these numbers are facts, incontestable values where the correctness of the calculation implies its justness, making people forget that facts are always made (again from Latin *factum*, indeed 'made'!).

Without making this empty box the centre of our accounting concerns there is no escape from the representationalist trap that the accounting perspective has set up for, and against, us in this symmetrical, ordered, and apparently insignificant system of calculation and valuation.[5] It is the absence in the top-left quadrant that reminds us of the importance of the hole in Escher's *Picture Gallery*. It exemplifies an impossibility of knowing and it is from this impossibility that the possibility of representation emerges, that the possibility of questioning valuation activities becomes real. It is thus from here that we need to depart for rethinking what accounting and valuation are all about. Making of this emptiness the departure point for the theorization and design of accounting and valuation systems allows us to explore a further role that accounting can play even in that bottom-right quadrant of Figure 2.2, where the epistemological impossibility of representing makes of accounting not only a tool to explain the invisible rather than the visible (Meyer 1986), but one that can play a positive role outside positivism by mediating amongst different members of that society that accounting ties together and tears apart.

Praising Doubt: Accounting as a Maieutic Machine

I remember well the day in September 2007 when Northern Rock, the UK based bank, was announced to be bankrupt. I was in Oxford and, as almost every day, I went to work at the Saïd Business School. I reached the corridor on the second floor and as I was heading to my office down a long corridor I saw a bunch of colleagues with financial statements of banks in their hands. I asked them: 'What are you doing?' They replied: 'What?! We are trying to understand where to put our savings!'

During the financial crisis, regular savers trying to find a safe harbour where to shelter their savings, stopped trusting rating agencies, auditors, and reassuring accounting standards and began to look at the statements of the banks directly (possibly making the wrong assumption that these could provide them with more reliable information!). The fear of losing money and the doubt cast on accounting numbers by the great financial crisis made them go deeper. They started to systematically ask questions. They no longer stopped at the superficial level of the indicator provided by rating agencies let alone were they driven by the attractiveness of the interest rate offered on now publicly recognized unsafe deposits. In order to know whether these banks were fundamentally solid (i.e. in terms of their accounting fundamentals, rather than their volatile market values), they began to question what was until then a taken for granted financial reality.

What lesson can we learn from this anecdote? The first one is that, when calculating values, accounting should embrace an uncomfortable doubt rather than searching for a reassuring certainty. Accounting, rather than giving answers and providing comforting values to be taken as the starting point of decision-making needs to prompt instead questions on what is not known, on the rationales and rationalities other than the economic one, which are obscured by their translation into the reductionist language of numbers.

This is by no means a new idea. Actually, this is what accounting has been doing for centuries, and until very recently. Another example can provide concreteness to this statement.

The Jesuits, for instance, knew only too well that accounting is a powerful tool in simplifying the complexity of businesses thus allowing action that would otherwise be paralysed by endless analysis.[6] But they did not want this simplification to go too far. This is why they devised a series of solutions to make those dealing with financial issues reflect on how financial value is intertwined with values that go beyond finance. The actual cash box of the Jesuit colleges had a padlock with two keys: one to be kept by the Procurator, i.e. the equivalent of today's CFO, in charge of financial matters; the other by the Rector, the equivalent of today's CEO, who was responsible for the college as a whole, with its missionary, pedagogical, and economic activities. This material solution forced the Procurator and the Rector to talk. It forced them to mediate amongst several and different purposes (e.g. pragmatic needs related to running the college, political matters related to the Jesuit influence on the local community, pedagogical and religious concerns) for which the Procurator and the Rector acted as spokespersons. It was the existence of this material padlock that forced these two figures to mediate amongst various and contrasting issues and to strike a balance amongst them. The padlock was thus an instrument to gain wisdom: rather than maximizing shareholders' value by cashing as much as possible, it made them to seek for a point of balance amongst various complex issues that did not have obvious solutions. It was an instrument to question the rationale of each cash transaction and instil doubt on what the right course of action could be so to make the whole organization more resilient. Reaching a balance was the key to Jesuit wisdom, and accounting was the instrument to achieve it. The knowledge informing the rationale of Jesuit decision-making was therefore contingent to the situation in specific times and spaces, which were all subject to scrutiny, interrogation, mediation, and discussion. Accounting prompted a reflection, not a pure representation. Its aim was a search for wisdom, not truth.

Praising doubt through accounting does not supplant the quest for knowledge and transparency altogether. It shows that knowledge is precarious and is intrinsically and inextricably a moral matter. Assuming the impossibility of representation (of the testimony: Agamben 1998; Levi 1986) is the only form through which a representation is thinkable, possible, and indeed sought and needed: paradoxically, the possibility of gaining knowledge emerges from questioning this very same possibility: transparency is more likely to happen when it is assumed to be impossible. More reality, not less, will be gained by praising doubt rather than certainty. This is why accounting is necessary and if you sneer at this claim and say 'this is going back to realism', yes it is. A little relativism takes one away from realism; a lot brings one back (Latour 1988, 173).

If accounting always refers to something which is intrinsically absent, to a lacuna, then this lacuna, this empty space, is a place for reflection in need of constant questioning not for representations to be mass produced. Interestingly, this reference to an absence, to the intrinsically 'other', will force a speculation, but in the Latin sense of the word, from *speculum*, i.e. a mirror. A mirror where we can reflect on our images to understand who we are and with what morals we inhabit our societies. It is from this empty space that one needs to begin to think of new forms of accounting and valuation: from the absence of a lacuna rather than from the presence of a fact. We move from positivism, and its search for knowledge as empirical truth, to what can be labelled 'pragmatic negativism', where the search for knowledge equates with a reflection on moral values.

This is why I propose, drawing on Escher's picture, to add a fourth role to Burchell et al.'s matrix (1980): accounting as a 'maieutic machine', where the role of accounting reports is to instil doubt in the users in order for this doubt to generate questions and open a debate.[7] We thus need to modify Figure 2.2 to insert Escher's hole at its core (see Figure 2.4). This hole testifies to and reminds us all of the impossibility of representation and for the need to always try to understand what is shadowed by preconceived notions of transparency, knowing that there is no ultimate truth that can be used as a benchmark. This benchmark is given by the debate amongst parties in the conversation which is governed by checks and balances (the key to medieval wisdom). If you like, this is a call for more critical knowledge and for a critical

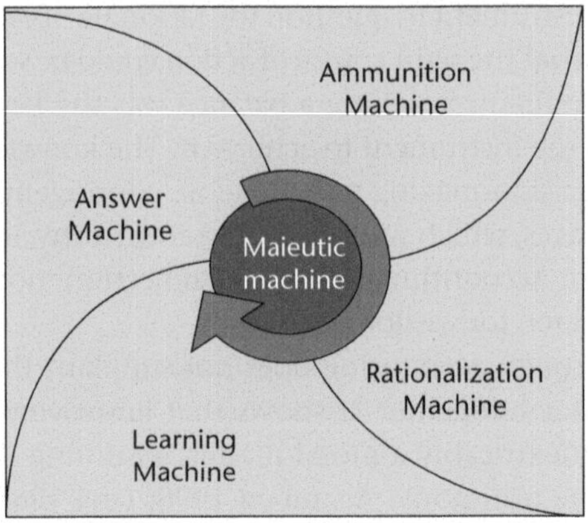

Figure 2.4. Praising doubt: redefining the role of accounting as a maieutic machine

role to be played not only by academics but also by managers, financial controllers, and experts on accountability and corporate governance. Someone needs to be responsible and accountable to those investors of Parmalat who could not speak, who could not be heard as they were not part of the network of power relations in which Calisto Tanzi swam as a fish in the water.

Why are these quasi-philosophical arguments of importance to accounting and valuation? What are the implications of this negative epistemology for accounting and valuation practices?

Because accounting as a maieutic machine, as the example of the Jesuit cash box suggests, is a form of accounting that opens up a discussion rather than closing it down. On the contrary, a reference to a 'true and fair view' (where accounting standards guard the validity of the accounts), or even a rhetorically more powerful reference to 'fair value' (with the market as the ultimate judge of the validity and morality of the valuation) are ways of reducing the possibility of knowledge rather than multiplying it. They do not leave room for diverse opinions and the 'other' to emerge, at least in theory. Praising doubt and questioning notions of value, their pragmatic meanings, their calculations, uses and effects have to become the key cornerstone of this renewed alliance between accounting and valuation. This approach at least coheres with what we see in practice, that is, the pragmatic impossibility of separating value from values. All the rest is hypocrisy.

This chapter aims to prompt a discussion on the implications of this shift from positivism to negativism, a conversation that needs to move from the relativist epistemological foundations I have outlined to the institutional and the technical levels, where accounting valuation is practised.

Institutionally, there is another hypocrisy to voice: the belief in the idea that accounting bodies, external non-executive directors, controllers, and various kinds of emerging agencies created to act in the name of some transparency are independent. Independence, as much as representation, transparency, accountability, and the like, is another utopian project (as utopian as mine, one could say) and the Parmalat case provided evidence of how utopian this dream is. Better to assume that independence and neutrality of views are not possible and seek to discover why certain bodies are not independent, and to whom they are linked, rather than assuming that they are. As a way of showing that my dream is less utopian than a belief in impartiality, one should think of the governance of the US Federal Reserve or the Italian financial system where a diffused ownership of the federal and central banks is thought to work better than the presence of a supposedly independent controlling body. The system fails when the concentration of banks is too high and therefore checks and balances disappear. The assumption of the independence of auditors, rating, ranking, and valuation agencies paralyzes our critical and alerting action as much as the presence on the board of non-executive directors renders small and unaware shareholders tranquil.

On a technical level, if reporting financial numbers cannot rest on the assumption that they are an expression of objectivity, much better to take the relativity of these numbers seriously and devise techniques which draw upon this relativity rather than pursuing the chimera of objectivity. Operationalizing doubt is not an impossible task. A great many of the Italian accounting theories from the 1930s until their defeat at the hands of the globalization movements (incarnated by the adoption of European Directive IV and later the global diffusion of International Financial Reporting Standards in the late twentieth century) made doubt the cornerstone of the design of accounting reports. In some of the Italian accounting tradition, for example, the income statement was designed in the form of a 'T' account, with each section organized in three bands, according to the reliability of the reported values (see Dagnino and Quattrone 2006). Income was conceived more as a buffer, as a matter of concern, rather than as a matter of fact (translating accounting in Latourian jargon).

Thus, praising doubt in accounting research also means thinking of the design of accounting reports, of the significance beyond the financial of technical solutions and how these technicalities embed and produce certain kinds of world-view and social interactions. An income statement that shows 'value added', for instance, is a completely different political statement if compared to one showing a 'net profit' (see the history of budgeting and planning techniques at IRI in the 1960s: Quattrone et al. 2015).

Going back to history, even only the most recent one, is a source of great inspiration to find alternative forms of valuation outside a market and neoliberal ideology. Design and history, arts and the humanities, not economics, are the fields that should inform not only accounting theory but also accounting techniques if the great divide between accounting and value is to be bridged wisely. Reasonable human beings are far better than rational ones as much as reasonable choices are more attainable than illusionary rational ones.

Some Concluding Remarks

The great financial crisis has prompted a series of initiatives in the area of valuation. Accounting has a long tradition of studies in this area, which has produced a wealth of publications in journals such as *Accounting, Auditing and Accountability, Accounting, Organizations and Society*, and *Critical Perspectives of Accounting*.[8] The work published there that cannot be ignored by anyone who ventures into the realm of financial calculations with the aim of investigating the non-financial implications of valuation practices. Questioning the role of accounting in organizations and societies has been one of the key features of the interdisciplinary movement of accounting studies in the last few decades. These studies have now the epistemological maturity to move beyond criticism and provide alternatives without losing the emancipatory power of being critical.

I want to draw on the advantages of constructivism but not to get to the point of deconstructing everything and ending up with nothing. We have already been alerted to this risk:

> Typically... the sociologist knows less than the natural scientist, while the sociologist of science knows still less. Those engaged from day to day with the problem of reflexivity would, if they could achieve their aims, know nothing at all. We might say that SSK [sociology of scientific knowledge] has opened up new ways of knowing nothing. (Collins and Yearley 1992, 302)

Going down a route to know nothing is not the route to go. Showing how values, numbers, and beliefs are constructed is important and useful. But, this deconstruction cannot create another 'great divide' between those who criticize and those who act, between those who speculate and those who practise, between those who propose alternatives and those who show how faulty those alternatives are.

As with Bruno Latour, in thinking about value and accounting in the age of doubt:

> we want to be at once *more* scientific than sciences—since we try to escape from their struggles—and much *less* scientific—since we do not wish to fight with their weapons. Our quandary is similar to that of a non-violent pacifist who still wishes to be 'stronger' than a violent militarist. We are looking for weaker, rather than stronger, explanations, but we still would like these weak accounts to defeat the strong ones. (Latour 1988, 165)

This afflatus is the only way in which we can overcome the general unease in academe on the possibility for constructivist approaches to accounting to have an impact, to make of accounting research one that can be constructivist and pro-positive (Ahrens et al. 2008). It is also the only way to counteract tendencies to leave the perilous waters of constructivism to navigate back to the comforting harbour of positivism, in forms which seem different but are in fact epistemologically very similar to those which have characterized (and still characterize) empirical and market-based valuation practices and accounting research.

Notes

1. This chapter expands the arguments in Macintosh and Quattrone (2010) where this account of the Parmalat scandal first appears. The description of this scandal draws on Capolino et al. (2004) and press articles.
2. Some research traditions have based their fortune on this too easily accepted relationship, either by praising its validity or by harshly criticizing it. The critique of Positive Accounting Theory (PAT, see Watts and Zimmerman 1979) operated by Tinker et al. (1982) is just one example of this diatribe. The establishment of journals such as the *Journal of Accounting and Economics*, on one side, and *Accounting, Organizations and Society*, on the other, is testimony to the broader issues at stake and the radical differences in conceiving accounting as a technique of valuation.
3. A reproduction of *Print Gallery* is available at: <http://www.mcescher.com/gallery/recognition-success/print-gallery/>. The picture is repoduced and commented on in Hofstadter (1979, 776, figure 142). Its relationships with accounting epistemology, theory, and practice are explored in Quattrone (2000).
4. See Latour's notion of 'societ-ies' in Latour (1993).
5. I am grateful to Keith Hoskin and his lectures in Manchester for having alerted me on the power of matrixes.
6. I have explored the features of Jesuit accounting in Quattrone (2004, 2009, forthcoming).
7. The term 'maieutic' comes from Socrates' maieutics, a practice of producing knowledge by asking questions rather than giving answers. I explore the notion of accounting as a rhetorical and maieutic machine in Quattrone (2009) and Busco and Quattrone (2014).
8. Giving a full account of the works that have inspired the arguments of this chapter and have contributed to unveiling the epistemological, social, and political dimensions of accounting practices more generally would be a work on its own.

References

Agamben, G. 1998. *Quel che resta di Auschwitz*. Turin: Bollati Boringhieri.

Ahrens, T., A. Becker, J. Burns, C. S. Chapman, M. Granlund, M. Habersam, A. Hansen, R. Khalifa, T. Malmi, A. Mennicken, A. Mikes, F. Panozzo, M. Piber, P. Quattrone,

and T. Scheytt. 2008. 'The Future of Interpretive Accounting Research: A Polyphonic Debate'. *Critical Perspectives on Accounting* 19(6): 840–66.
Amodeo, D. 1970. *Ragioneria generale delle imprese*. Naples: Giannini.
Burchell, S., C. Clubb, A. Hopwood, S. Hughes, and J. Nahapiet. 1980. 'The Roles of Accounting in Organizations and Society'. *Accounting, Organizations and Society* 5(1): 5–27.
Busco, C. and P. Quattrone. 2014. 'Exploring How the Balanced Scorecard Engages and Unfolds: Articulating the Visual Power of Accounting Inscriptions'. *Contemporary Accounting Research* (DOI: 10.1111/1911–3846.12105).
Capolino, G., F. Massaro, and P. Panerai. 2004. *La grande truffa*. Milan: Classeeditori.
Collins, H. M. and S. Yearley. 1992. 'Epistemological Chicken'. In *Science as Practice and Culture*, ed. A. Pickering. Chicago and London: University of Chicago Press, 301–26.
Dagnino, G. B. and P. Quattrone. 2006. 'Management and Business Research Italian Style: The Methodological Contribution of *Economia Aziendale* to Business Economics'. *Journal of Management History* 12(1): 36–52.
D'Ippolito, T. 1945. *La contabilità e il bilancio delle aziende di produzione*. Milan: Giuffrè.
Flori, L. 1636. *Trattato del modo di tenere il libro doppio domestico con suo essemplare composto dal P. Lodovico Flori della Compagnia di Gesù per uso delle case e dei collegi della medesima Compagnia nel Regno di Sicilia*. Palermo: Decio Cirillo.
Hofstadter, D. R. 1979. *Gödel, Escher, Bach: An Eternal Golden Braid*. New York: Basic Books.
Latour, B. 1986. 'Visualization and Cognition: Thinking with Eyes and Hands'. In *Knowledge and Society: Studies in the Sociology of Culture, Past and Present*, ed. H. Kuklick and E. Long. London: Jai Press, 1–40.
Latour, B. 1988. 'The Politics of Explanations: An Alternative'. In *Knowledge and Reflexivity: New Frontiers in the Sociology of Knowledge*, ed. S. Woolgar. London: Sage, 155–76.
Latour, B. 1993. *We Have Never Been Modern*. Cambridge, MA: Harvard University Press.
Latour, B. 1999. *Pandora's Hope: Essays on the Reality of Science Studies*. Cambridge, MA: Harvard University Press.
Levi, P. 1986. *I sommersi e i salvati*. Turin: Einaudi.
Macintosh, N. and P. Quattrone. 2010. *Management Accounting and Control Systems: An Organizational and Sociological Approach*. London and New York: John Wiley.
Meyer, J. W. 1986. 'Social Environments and Organizational Accounting'. *Accounting, Organizations and Society* 11(4–5): 345–56.
Porter, T. 1995. *Trust in Numbers: The Pursuit of Objectivity in Science and Public Life*. Princeton: Princeton University Press.
Quattrone, P. 2000. 'Constructivism and Accounting Research: Towards a Trans-Disciplinary Perspective'. *Accounting, Auditing and Accountability* 13(2): 130–55.
Quattrone, P. 2004. 'Accounting for God: Accounting and Accountability Practices in the Society of Jesus (Italy, XVI–XVII centuries)'. *Accounting, Organizations and Society* 29(7): 647–83.
Quattrone, P. 2006. 'The Possibility of the Testimony: A Case for Case Study Research'. *Organization* 13(1): 143–57.
Quattrone, P. 2009. 'Books to be Practiced: Memory, the Power of the Visual, and the Success of Accounting'. *Accounting, Organizations and Society* 34(1): 85–118.

Quattrone, P. forthcoming. A Procedural Approach to Institutional Logics: Unfolding Rationality in the Jesuit Order (*Administrative Science Quarterly*).

Quattrone, P., P. Monfardini, and P. Ruggiero. 2015. 'Le pratiche di programmazione e controllo nel Gruppo IRI. Tra contesti organizzativi, politica economica e cambiamenti globali', in *La storia dell'IRI*, vol. 5, ed. F. Russolillo. Bari: La Terza, 747–98.

Schreiner, S. E. 2011. *Are You Alone Wise? The Search for Certainty in the Early Modern Era*. Oxford: Oxford University Press.

Strathern, M. 2000. 'The Tyranny of Transparency'. *British Educational Research Journal* 26(3): 309–21.

Tinker, A. M., B. D. Merino, and M. Neimark. 1982. 'The Normative Origins of Positive Theories: Ideology and Accounting Thought'. *Accounting, Organizations and Society* 7(2): 167–200.

Watts, R. L. and J. L. Zimmerman. 1979. 'The Demand for and Supply of Accounting Theories: The Market for Excuses'. *Accounting Review* 54(2): 273–305.

3

Rating Reports as Figuring Documents

How Credit Rating Agencies Build Scenarios of the Future

Pierre Pénet

Introduction

For many, the 2008 financial crisis demonstrated the colossal failure of credit rating[1] agencies (hereafter: CRAs) to predict risk events.[2] This was especially true of their ability to predict the prospect that sovereign (country) issuers would default on their debt. Until 2008, investors and CRAs considered the sovereign bond market a safe haven for a wide range of reasons. From the years following the Second World War until the late 1990s, sovereign debt rescheduling and defaults remained quite low (Reinhart and Rogoff 2009).[3] And, although most advanced economies saw their credit positions erode in the 2000s due to a conjunction of factors (including higher public spending, lower capacity to tax, and low GDP growth), investors assumed the trend of trustworthiness would last, most specifically in the newly constituted European Monetary Union. But the 2008 financial crisis proved everyone wrong.

The 2012 Greek default—the largest sovereign default in recent history and the epicentre of the European debt crisis—spurred controversies about the role of CRAs and led investors, regulators, and public officials to blame CRAs for their lack of foresight in the months preceding the Greek sovereign crisis. For eighteen months, between September 2008 and spring 2010, CRAs displayed rating inertia before issuing multinotch downgrades of Greek sovereign bonds, a dramatic pattern of rating migration that significantly forced Greece out of international capital markets. Greece is not an isolated case, as evidenced by similar problem of valuation in the months leading up to the Asian sovereign crisis in the 1990s (Ferri et al. 1999). The valuation of risky credit derivatives in the US subprime market also presents a similar pattern of rating downgrades. Upon realizing that they had bestowed generous ratings to debt instruments that were defaulting at a much higher rate than anticipated, CRAs aggressively downgraded the ratings of billions of dollars' worth of securities. This wave of downgrades prompted global panic across capital markets, an event widely cited as one of the main causes of the subprime mortgage crisis and the 2008 financial meltdown (Carruthers 2010; Rona-Tas and Hiss 2011).

How CRAs 'See' Risk: Multinotch Rating Downgrades and the Problem of Sovereign Risk Valuation

CRAs are often accused of bestowing generous ratings to debt instruments that default at a much higher rate than anticipated (Reinhart 2002). This pattern of rating migration poses a problem of valuation and begs the question of how CRAs 'see' risk and produce risk knowledge. The European sovereign debt crisis beginning in 2009 presents three puzzling developments with regard to the valuation of financial risks.

First, in the months leading up to the European sovereign crisis, risk perceptions expressed in market prices and expert assessments significantly diverged as all three major CRAs had more optimistic risk views than the market-based perceptions embedded in market prices, notably CDS spreads.[4] Credit default swap (CDS) and government bond spreads suggested a much higher probability of Greek default than was encoded in the ratings of the three main CRAs, notably Moody's (Gaillard 2012).[5]

Second, as the market's risk perceptions diverged from those of CRAs, the ratings of the three main CRAs also varied substantially from one another. Standard & Poor's (S&P) and Fitch perceived Greece as more risky than did Moody's, until Moody's finally issued a four-notch downgrade on Greek sovereign ratings in June 2010 (see timeline in appendix). From 2008 to mid-2010, Moody's ratings sharply contrasted from the ratings of S&P and Fitch as well as from market indicators: until the first European bailout of Greece in May 2010, Moody's proceeded to only two downgrades against four and five for Fitch and S&P, respectively. Moody's ultimately issued a four-notch downgrade of Greek bonds on 14 June 2010, almost two years after the collapse of Lehman Brothers.

Finally, Moody's' four-notch downgrade of Greek sovereign bonds in June 2010 was, at the time of issuance, the sharpest downgrade a CRA had ever issued on a sovereign issuer. Overall, Moody's downgraded Greek bonds by six notches in just six months between December 2009 and June 2010, a rating pattern unprecedented in the recent history of sovereign ratings.[6] Never before the 2008 financial crisis had CRAs issued such sharp and repeated multinotch downgrades of sovereign bonds. Descriptive data show Moody's issued sixty-seven multinotch downgrades actions (MDAs) of sovereign bonds between 1987 and September 2013, thirty-three of them between 2008 and 2013. Among these thirty-three MDAs, twenty-six targeted European sovereigns (see Table 3.1 and Figure 3.1).[7]

Table 3.1. Multinotch Downgrade Actions (MDAs) by country (1987–September 2013)

MDAs/Country						No. of MDAs/Country	
Ireland	17/12/2010 Aa2–Baa1	5	Ecuador	14/9/1998 B1–B3	2	Cyprus	6
Greece	14/6/2010 A3–Ba1	4	Ecuador	5/10/1999 B3–Caa2	2	Greece	5
Portugal	5/7/2011 Baa1–Ba2	4	Fiji Islands	22/4/2009 Ba2–B1	2	India	4
Belize	26/10/2005 B3–Caa3	3	Greece	24/5/1994 Baa1–Baa3	2	Belize	3
Belize	1/6/2012 Caa1–Ca	3	Hungary	13/7/1990 Baa2–B1	2	Ecuador	3
Brazil	4/12/1987 Ba1–B1	3	Hungary	6/12/2010 Baa1–Baa3	2	Iceland	3
Cyprus	8/10/2012 Ba3–B3	3	Iceland	11/11/2009 Baa1–Baa3	2	Korea	3
Cyprus	10/1/2013 B3–Caa3	3	India	4/10/1990 A2–Baa1	2	Portugal	3
Ecuador	16/12/2008 Caa1–Ca	3	India	26/3/1991 Baa1–Ba2	2	Spain	3
Greece	7/3/2011 Ba1–B1	3	India	24/6/1991 Baa3–Ba2	2	Uruguay	3
Greece	1/6/2011 B1–Caa1	3	India	19/6/1998 Baa3–Ba2	2	Hungary	2
Greece	25/7/2011 Caa1–Ca	3	Ireland	5/4/2011 Baa1–Baa3	2	Ireland	2
Iceland	8/10/2008 Aa1–A1	3	Italy	13/8/1992 Aa1–Aa3	2	Italy	2
Iceland	4/12/2008 A1–Baa1	3	Jamaica	18/11/2009 B2–Caa1	2	Moldova	2
Indonesia	9/1/1998 Ba1–B2	3	Jordan	26/6/2013 Ba2–B1	2	Slovenia	2
Italy	4/10/2011 Aa2–A2	3	Korea	27/11/1997 A1–A3	2	Belgium	1
Japan	18/5/2009 Aaa–Aa2	3	Korea	10/12/1997 A3–Baa2	2	Bolivia	1
Malaysia	23/7/1998 A2–Baa2	3	Korea	21/12/1997 Baa1–Ba1	2	Brazil	1
Moldova	14/7/1998 Ba2–B2	3	Latvia	23/4/2009 Baa1–Baa3	2	Colombia	1
Moldova	11/7/2002 Caa1–Ca	3	Nicaragua	30/6/2003 B2–Caa1	2	Dominican Republic	1
Slovenia	2/8/2012 A2–Baa2	3	Paraguay	28/4/2003 B3–Caa1	2	Fiji Islands	1
Spain	13/6/2012 A3–Baa3	3	Philippines	5/2/2005 Ba2–B1	2	Indonesia	1

(continued)

Table 3.1. (Continued)

MDAs/Country						No. of MDAs/Country	
Argentina	4/12/1987 Ba3–B2	2	Portugal	13/7/2010 Aa2–A1	2	Jamaica	1
Argentina	12/10/2001 Caa1–Ca3	2	Portugal	15/3/2011 A1–A3	2	Japan	1
Belgium	16/12/2001 Aa1–Aa3	2	Romania	6/11/1998 B1–B3	2	Jordan	1
Belize	5/8/2004 Ba3–B2	2	Slovenia	30/4/2013 Baa2–Ba1	2	Latvia	1
Bolivia	16/4/2003 B1–B3	2	Spain	18/10/2011 Aa2–A1	2	Malaysia	1
Colombia	11/8/1999 Baa3–Ba2	2	Spain	13/2/2012 A1–A3	2	Nicaragua	1
Cyprus	24/2/2011 Aa3–A2	2	Thailand	27/11/1997 Baa1–Baa3	2	Paraguay	1
Cyprus	27/7/2011 A2–Baa1	2	Turkey	2/6/1994 Ba1–Ba3	2	Philippines	1
Cyprus	4/11/2011 Baa1–Baa3	2	Uruguay	3/5/2002 Baa3–Ba2	2	Romania	1
Cyprus	13/6/2012 Ba1–Ba3	2	Uruguay	10/7/2002 Ba2–B1	2	Thailand	1
Dominican Republic	7/10/2003 Ba2–B1	2	Uruguay	31/7/2002 B1–B3	2	Turkey	1
			Venezuela	22/7/1998 Ba2–B1	2	Venezuela	1

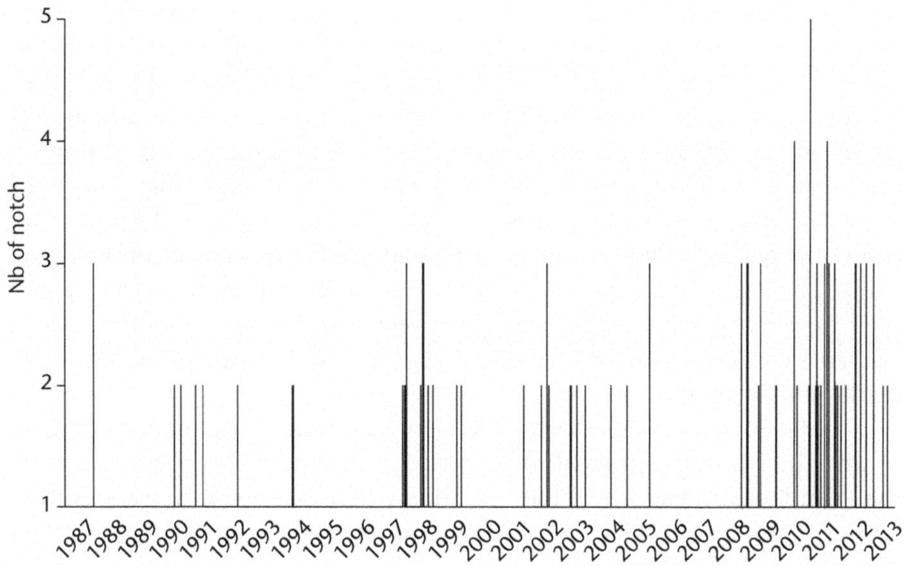

Figure 3.1 Multinotch Downgrade Actions (MDAs) by year (1987–September 2013)

At first, multinotch downgrades seem to indicate that ratings were too high and 'overtly optimistic' in the first place (Carruthers 2010). In this spirit, economists have pursued studies of rating criteria and ratings' informational content which seek to explain CRAs' poor predictive performance, thereby lending credence to the notion that CRAs 'missed' the crisis (Cantor et al. 1996; Ferri et al. 1999 ; Bhatia 2002). Classical studies of rating criteria typically conceive of ratings as mere compendia of information. Their informational approach suggests that CRAs' poor track record in predicting future outcomes originates in the failure to 'discover' market information, which results in inaccurate predictions. However, this purely informational approach to rating failure has limited explanatory value for the sovereign debt market because financial parties (including investors and CRAs) typically rely on similar credit information from public sources or governmental agencies. Therefore, information issues pertaining to access, quality, or asymmetry—to pick just a few—cannot alone explain the gap between ratings and market perceptions. Nor can an informational approach explain why CRAs maintained their ratings in spite of conspicuous evidence of a rapidly changing market environment.

The informational approach to ratings is also limited to explain rating practices during rapidly changing market environments typical of times of crisis. In this chapter, I posit a significant difference in anticipatory practices depending on whether agencies operate under 'settled' or 'unsettled' market times.[8] In settled market times, a sovereign rating action expresses the continuous and linear adjustment to changing risk information. In unsettled market times, in contrast, a rating action reflect changing informational components *and* the perceived strength of the ties that the rating analyst assumes link these components together at the aggregated rating level. Departing from a purely informational approach, I argue that in the sovereign sector, where information is public and available, the main problem facing CRAs during unsettled times is not the censored terms or the information their methodologies might have left aside. Drawing on a map-territory analogy, the 'territory' is well known and additional risk information will do little to improve the accuracy of the rating 'map'. The main challenge for CRAs rests on active rating maintenance and their capacity to achieve consistency between, on the one hand, the various elements composing the rating as an aggregate, and on the other, changing market environment.

In the face of ambiguous, contradictory, or fragmented information—typical of unsettled times—anticipatory knowledge producers like CRAs do more than simply collect additional information when they are unsure about their ratings. This chapter shows that CRAs resort to a set of constitutive practices by which they figure out and confer meaning upon the financial uncertainties they are tasked with predicting. Focusing on sovereign rating practices, this chapter shows that CRAs' failure to predict sovereign risk events was not entirely predicated on informational inconsistencies but also and predominantly on social (external) and cognitive (internal) processes at the level of the practices that CRAs use to produce anticipatory knowledge under high uncertainty. Centring on Moody's' ratings during the Greek sovereign debt crisis, this chapter analyses how Moody's minimized the uncertainties arising during the Greek sovereign debt crisis by resorting to three constitutive practices (plausibility, backward reasoning, and reactivity) by which they constituted the reality of those same financial threats they were tasked with predicting.

The Constitution of Financial Uncertainties during the Greek Sovereign Debt Crisis

Scholars in sociology of knowledge and science studies have recently begun to focus on the practices that anticipatory knowledge producers adopt and which condition their ability to predict likely outcomes. This research includes studies in banking and high finance (Beunza and Stark 2004; Muniesa and Callon 2007; Stark 2009), environmental policy (Dalmedico and Guillemot 2008), and food safety (Borraz and Besançon 2008). In this spirit, recent studies have located CRAs' failure to anticipate risk events in the organizational and cognitive practices that they adopt under conditions of uncertainty (Callon 1998; Callon and Muniesa 2005; Millo and MacKenzie 2009 ; Knorr Cetina 2011). For instance, MacKenzie (2011) shows how CRAs adapted to the problem of valuing ABS-CDOs by 'borrowing' (Stark 2009, 113) the techniques of calculation they used to rate other, less sophisticated, financial instruments.[9] Finding an endogenous solution within the cognitive and organizational realities of their existing evaluation practices both minimized uncertainty and made ABS-CDOs profitable. As the crisis revealed, however, this lateral borrowing had its own hidden problems. As a result of their methodological choices, CRAs underestimated correlation values, a central cause of the subprime market collapse.

While these studies adopt a much warranted practical focus in discussing the issue of rating failure, they are also keen to present failure of calculation devices to anticipate risk events as a disaster waiting to happen. The demise of calculative technologies occurs in linear and orderly fashion: complex procedures 'perform' markets until built-in errors resulting from dangerous assumptions and internal inconsistencies are revealed. This view fits with the 'performativity thesis' (Callon 1998; MacKenzie 2006, 2011; MacKenzie et al. 2007) developed by scholars in the social studies of finance. This non-contingent path to failure is also consistent with research on disaster events resulting from technical failure (Perrow 1984; Vaughan 1996). Here, the failure of instruments of calculation is invariably portrayed as an epiphany, a moment of collective lucidity during which market actors realize that everything was false. The programmatic delimitations of this 'technological turn' in new economic sociology and social studies of finance is, however, not always acknowledged (Miller 2002; Mennicken et al. 2008; Miller 2008a, 2008b). In the case of sovereign rating practices, these studies appear *over-socialized* to properly account for the non-technical (e.g. political, institutional, and legal) nature of rating inconsistencies in the sovereign sector. In turn, this research is also *under-socialized* for it adheres to a conventional—linear—framework in which producers of anticipatory knowledge work in the isolation of the laboratory, never having to acknowledge the consequences their predictions may bear on a future course of events.

This project proposes to adapt the practical focus of these studies to understand how CRAs *see* financial uncertainties in the sovereign risk sector. No research has yet focused on sovereign ratings, partly because the latter do not mobilize the highly formalized models that CRAs use to rate other classes of assets, most notably structured financial instruments. Indeed, CRAs use qualitative analytical techniques to formalize sovereign risk and arrive at a judgement about the *willingness* of a country to repay its debt on time and in full. Second, sovereign ratings combine information of fundamentally different nature. On the one hand, sovereign risk depends on continuously and gradually changing market information and macroeconomic factors. On the other, sovereign risk is also the by-product of unequivocal political events (e.g. a coup, a revolution) and categorical institutional decisions (e.g. the prospect that a central bank might refuse to extend external support). Therefore the computation of sovereign risk inevitably requires a significant cognitive effort to engineer commensuration between discontinuous threads of risk information at the aggregate rating level.

Documenting Finance: Rating Reports as Figuring Documents

My focus on financial documents served as the organizing principle of data collection for this project. This chapter takes as its main data previously unexamined rating reports and press releases issued by Moody's between November 2002 and June 2010 (available on the agency's website). In the event of a rating action, CRAs typically issue a rating report to subscribers via a press release. The rating industry is notoriously secretive and resistant to investigation by social scientists. As a result, little is known about the ways in which CRAs compute risk. Since the motivations behind rating actions are not always clear, especially in time of acute financial stress, rating reports deserve careful attention.

Rating reports are 'double' objects. First, rating reports establish a dialogue with investors by providing a wealth of details and figures and explanatory guidance about financial uncertainties that can be difficult to pass along in ratings alone. In doing so, rating reports provide informational insight into the considerations CRAs undertake and the choices they make when reflecting on the relevance of a rating action. Beyond these informational features, rating reports also reflect on the messy and highly ambiguous nature of the rating process by displaying the doubts, hesitations, and the occasional contradictions that rating practices invariably entail. Therefore, if these reports give prime access to the rationale behind rating actions, they also indicate how, under high uncertainty, CRAs do more than simply collect additional information when they are unsure about their ratings. In reports, CRAs also 'figure out' and confer meaning upon the financial uncertainties they are tasked with predicting.

For this project I used rating reports as compendia of technical specifications and as 'figuring' documents, i.e. *documents that offer a key perspective on the processes of risk assessment and reality construction that underwrite any rating process*. Weaving together various threads of meaning and context, rating reports are conducive to my empirical effort to reconstitute the bundle of cognitive, legal, and political uncertainties which, together, explain how rating inconsistencies played out in the unfolding Greek sovereign debt crisis. In doing so, I claim that social scientists should study anticipatory knowledge not only for its predictive purpose (whether it produces accurate or inaccurate predictions about the future likelihood of specific events), but also for its 'constitutive purpose' (Mallard and Lakoff 2011). As figuring documents, rating reports present rating practices as retaining considerable amount of vagueness. Vagueness is not in itself problematic. Russell famously professed '[l]ogical words, like the rest, when used by human beings, share the vagueness of all other words' (Russell 1923, 88). A sociological investigation of rating reports allows contemplating the articulation of rating principles with practical contingencies. With the notion of figuring, I aim to show that accuracy and vagueness are inseparable. With the notion of figuring, I also challenge social scientists' widespread use of the analytical yardstick of 'accuracy' in their description and analysis of mechanisms of sovereign risk valuation. The distinctive features of the sovereign rating process require that we depart from an approach rooted in accuracy—i.e. whether a rating is (was) right or wrong—to embrace a more realistic approach rooted in the 'veracity' or 'plausibility' of a sovereign rating.[10]

Outline

The remainder of this chapter proceeds in four acts. First, I cover CRAs' views on the Greek economy between 2002 and October 2009. During the months following the collapse of Lehman Brothers, I show that Moody's affirmed the plausibility of their investment-grade rating. Far from inaccurate, Moody's ratings instead reflected a highly plausible risk scenario among other equally plausible scenarios. Second, as the Greek crisis amplified between October and December 2009, Moody's became embarked in a process by which they sought to minimize the uncertainties which the European sovereign debt crisis posed to their valuation of risk while maximizing the continuity between ratings and thereby appease concerns about their credibility. By resorting to 'backward reasoning', Moody's simultaneously made sense of Greece's developing threats and 'constituted' the list of events to which they assigned probabilities. Third, focusing on the period of January through June 2010, I investigate how ECB's (European Central Bank) reliance on ratings for regulatory purposes changed the market reception of ratings and forced Moody's to anticipate the potentially destabilizing consequences that further downgrades would have on Greece's borrowing costs. This reactive dynamic greatly affected the rating process and contributed strongly to the valuation problem described above. Overall, each section demonstrates the 'figuring' nature of sovereign rating practices during unsettled market times. The final section concludes.

Greece's Weakening Financial Prospects and Rating Plausibility

Moody's' Five Pillars

My examination of Moody's' rating reports (Moody's 2002, 2007, 2008) published between 2002 (Greece's admission into the European Monetary Union) and October 2009 suggests five persistent and complementary views supporting Moody's initial 'A' investment-grade rating for Greek government bonds (see Figure 3.2).

Macroeconomic fundamentals and prospects: Moody's emphasize the potentially destabilizing effect of Greece's poor economic performance, weakening competitiveness, and growing debt levels in both the public and private sectors. At the same time, however, they note their intention to monitor deteriorating fundamentals and financial prospects in relation to other risk factors, including government resolve at the domestic level and external support at the European level.

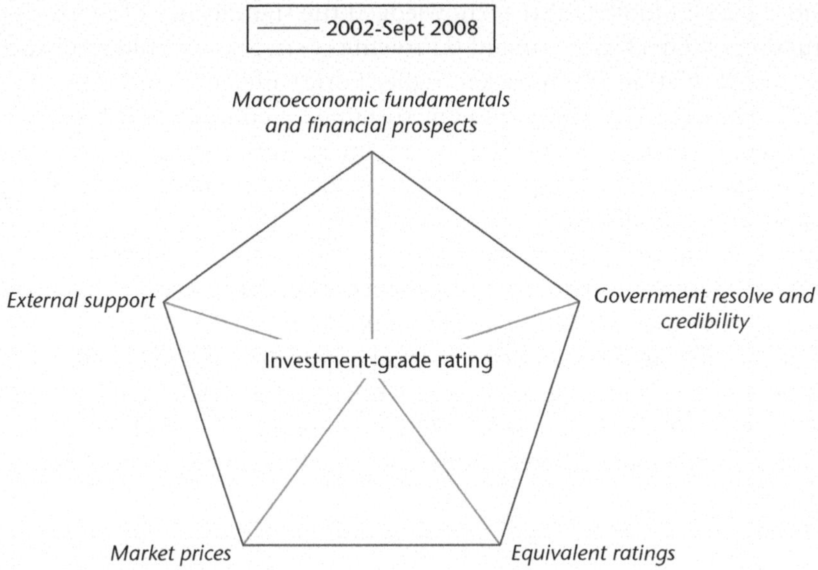

Figure 3.2. Moody's' initial investment-grade rating of Greek sovereign bonds (2002–2008)

Government resolve and credibility: At the national level, Moody's state their plan to assess the Greek government's resolve to shore up creditworthiness, as well as its margin for manoeuvre and capacity to implement efficient reform.

External support: The prospect of a sovereign debt crisis involving a Eurozone member had little precedent and did not lend itself to easy calculation. A member of the European currency zone, Greece did not control exchange rate or monetary policy. The ECB's decision to extend external support was thus crucial, especially given Greece's soon-to-be non-existent access to capital markets. Since the legal rules and procedures contained in the revised collateral framework policy of 2006 had made external support from the ECB conditional (see section 'Reactivity and Rating Standoff'), Moody's had to issue a judgement about the Greek government's willingness to repay its debt on time and in full, but they also had to imagine and evaluate the probability of another element in this scenario: the willingness of the ECB to assume its role of lender of last resort, should Greece need them to do so. For CRAs and specifically Moody's, the prevailing belief that the ECB would not let a member default made the prospect of a Greek default highly unlikely. According to Moody's rationale, liquidity risk could only materialize if the ECB refused to approve external support for a Eurozone member, a possibility Moody's considered extremely unlikely.

Market prices: Moody's also acknowledged the significance of market price fluctuation on Greek government borrowing costs. Moody's did not expect a direct causal relationship between higher borrowing costs and liquidity crisis, as long as the Greek government sustained credibility and foreign support remained plausible. This is why, despite soaring spreads and increasing risk fears expressed in CDS spreads, Moody's did not immediately downgrade Greek sovereign bonds in the autumn of 2008.

Equivalent ratings: Finally, rating all sixteen country members of the Eurozone, Moody's sought to contextualize the Greek economic situation relative to countries with comparable fundamentals. They did so for the purpose of commensuration, in order to ensure that they applied similar ratings to equivalent levels of trustworthiness. Until October 2009, Moody's justified its 'A' investment-grade rating for Greece by arguing that its financial situation was not materially different from that faced by other equivalent European countries.

Rating Affirmation

After the collapse of Lehman Brothers in September 2008, fears that the American financial meltdown would spill over into Europe began to damage market perceptions of Greek economic trustworthiness. Although sovereign CDS and bond spreads were on the rise, CRAs did not change their ratings of Greek government bonds until the end of 2009, with the exception of S&P, who downgraded Greek bonds by one notch in January 2009. For instance, Moody's maintained its 'A1' rating for Greece from November 2002 until December 2009.

Moody's did not revise their hypotheses about Greece's ability to repay its debts until December 2009. In February 2009, Moody's reaffirmed its aggregated scenario for Greece by changing their rating outlook from 'positive' to 'stable' (Moody's 2009a). As aggregate, Moody's' rating was predicated on a group of five interrelated observations, as explained above. Beginning in September 2008 Greece began to experience slower GDP growth. But Greece's deteriorating economy (first pillar) did not undermine the principles underlying the combination of the five interrelated factors that Moody's projected to assess in reviewing Greece's trustworthiness. Lower GDP output was not compounded by weakening government resolve and credibility (second pillar), or external support (third pillar). Nor was Greece's lower economic prospect unique: by early 2009, all A-rated Western economies had begun to feel the turmoil of the US market collapse (fifth pillar). Overall, the early stages of the crisis contaminated Greece only unevenly. Although cracks appeared in the first rating pillar,

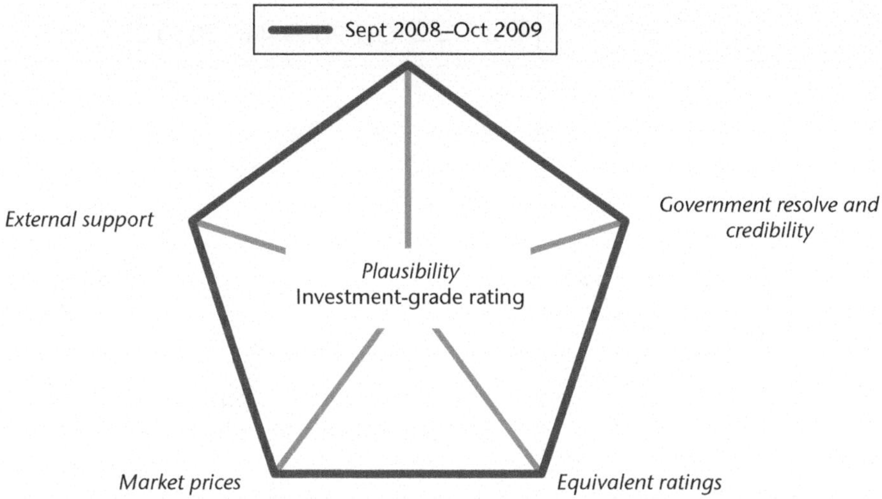

Figure 3.3. Plausibility and Moody's' affirmation of investment-grade rating (September 2008–October 2009)

the system of relationships linking together the different rating components remained highly predictable.

At the aggregate level, the situation prevailing during most of 2009 did not warrant a substantial revision of Moody's' scenario for Greece. Moody's' projected scenario was eminently plausible and, in fact, accurate: by October 2009, market fears had eased and Greek borrowing costs and CDS spreads (fourth pillar) declined to almost pre-crisis levels, thus confirming the relatively optimistic scenarios CRAs had predicted (see Figure 3.3).

Backward Reasoning and Rating Inertia

Scenario Fragmentation

However, Greece's unexpected revision of its 2009 deficit projection from 3.7 per cent of GDP to 12.5 per cent on 20 October stunned markets and significantly damaged the country's credibility in data reporting. As a result, Greek sovereign CDS and government bond spreads begun to widen again in October 2009, signalling deteriorating perceptions of Greece's creditworthiness (see timeline in appendix). By December, markets were already pricing Greek sovereign bonds in the speculative-grade debt category and Greek sovereign CDS spreads had risen well above those of Ireland, Portugal, and Spain (Gaillard 2012).

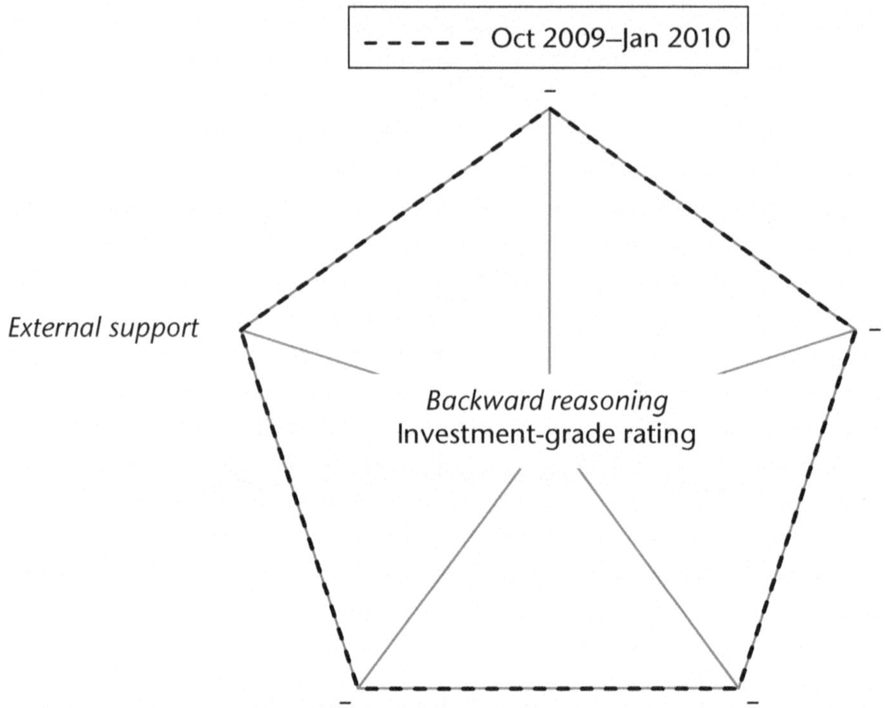

Figure 3.4. Backward reasoning (October 2009–January 2010)

This time, the deficit revision significantly undermined the plausibility of the risk scenario that Moody's had for Greece. By the end of October, only one item of Moody's rationale (external support, fifth pillar) could be said to remain unchanged (see Figure 3.4). Moody's' investment-grade scenario, therefore, critically hinged on the ECB's willingness to provide external support. In spite of these developments, and the fragmentation of their scenario, Moody's did not downgrade Greek government bonds. The deteriorating Greek economic situation also coincided with growing disagreements within Moody's. In an interview,[11] a senior sovereign rating analyst at Moody's mentioned that the rating gap forming between Moody's on the one hand and S&P and Fitch on the other (see timeline in appendix) was a constant source of frictions between her and Pierre Cailleteau, then chief sovereign officer. These frictions about Greek sovereign ratings were nothing new: a 'heated debate' had already broken out in 2001, she reminded, about the projected upgrade of Greece's sovereign debt (Moody's 2002). Since then, she explained, Cailleteau's risk views prevailed and 'Moody's substituted to macroeconomic analysis of

Greek fundamentals a more political and institutional analysis of solvency, a risk Moody's deemed inexistent.' This view prevailed from 2002 to 2009, even after it was reported that the government of Greece had issued wrong budget statements.

After 2009, Moody's deep-seated expectation of ECB support predicated their valuation of Greece's new risks. Rating reports show how Moody's continued to use their existing rationale for investment-grade rating to make sense of the uncertainties arising from increasingly negative perceptions of Greek sovereign risk. In the rest of this section I show how they did so, even as the limits of plausibility of their investment-grade rating were being tested from October 2009 onward.

Backward Reasoning

Backward reasoning is a non-linear process by which a producer of anticipatory knowledge infers the meaning of new information in a way that vindicates former views, which are themselves embedded in the producer's present anticipations of a future outcome (Mallard and Pénet 2013). The notion of backward reasoning shows how, under high uncertainty, CRAs may substitute their own 'agency time', embodied in agency perceptions, for real 'market time', represented by changing market quotations and prices. I suggest that Moody's employed backward reasoning as an adaptive strategy, on the one hand, to minimize the political uncertainties that emerged from the valuation of new risk threats in the Eurozone sovereign debt market, and, on the other, to maximize stability between ratings in order to maintain their overall rating credibility.

Moody's' rating reports published after the Greek budget revision between October and December 2009 (Moody's 2009b, 2009c, 2009d) justify (albeit somewhat warily) an investment-rating for Greece. In those Moody's refute market fears that Greece's deteriorating economic situation could materialize in a significant liquidity risk. Notably, in December, in the press release, 'Investor Fears of Liquidity Risks in Greece are Overdone', Moody's reaffirm their prevailing confidence in the ECB and calls the prospect of a Greek default 'extremely unlikely' (Moody's 2009c). Only in the highly remote case that Greek government debt became ineligible as collateral, Moody's claim, would liquidity risk become a possibility.

Moody's deep-seated expectation of ECB support constituted their valuation of Greece's new risks. Beginning in October 2009, Moody's relied on this expectation as a cognitive antecedent that conferred meaning on any new risk information pertaining to Greece's deteriorating economic situation. Thus, despite Greek government's weakening fundamentals, declining financial manoeuvre, lowered credibility, and borrowing costs that had risen above those of any other European country they had previously deemed comparable, Moody's reaffirmed its investment-grade rating. The single-notch downgrade issued by Moody's on 22 December still maintained Greece in the 'A' investment-grade range and was widely viewed by market actors as 'softer' than expected.[12]

Moody's decision to maintain its investment-grade rating for Greece even when its initial rationale was no longer (as a whole) valid has several implications. First, by calling investor fears over Greek government liquidity 'misplaced' and 'exaggerated', Moody's seemed to hope it could once again shape investors' perceptions about the Greek government's ability to repay its debt and encourage market parties to bring about the conditions that would justify an 'A' investment-grade scenario. After all, between January and October 2009, CRAs' (and most specifically Moody's') affirmation of the plausibility of their ratings seemed to have achieved precisely that goal, with CDS and sovereign bond spreads returning to their pre-crisis levels after a temporary surge in the autumn of 2008. Until 2009, the initial gap between Moody's reaffirmed perceptions of Greece's trustworthiness and the more conservative views embedded in market prices essentially expressed a conflict between *equally plausible* risk scenarios that had been resolved in favour of Moody's.

Second, after Greece's October deficit revision announcement, and its destabilizing consequences for the Greek government's fundamentals, borrowing costs, and overall credibility, Moody's rationale for its investment-grade became significantly more contrarian and the possibility that market actors would bring their predictions to pass more remote. That Moody's refrained from downgrading Greece to the 'B' range suggests a path dependency of ratings I interpret as a manifestation of backward reasoning. Moody's consistently made constitutive use of the prospect of external ECB support to restrict the range of meaning that information could acquire, even under markedly different conditions. Moody's was embroiled in a dynamic cognitive process whereby constitutive use of rating models created diminishing informational returns for every piece of new information collected. Thus, rating inertia appears to be the path-dependent outcome of a non-linear process of knowledge production and credibility assurance: so long as CRAs can use existing risk rationales, in whole or in part, to make sense of new risk information, CRAs have an incentive to uphold ratings.[13]

Therefore, non-linear rating practices and backward reasoning create an interesting paradox where the predictive capacity of a rating decreases its overall accuracy. My hypothesis is as follows:

(1) The *predictive capacity* of a rating—as measured by the number of informational components composing the rating and the number of ties linking

these components together at the aggregate level—increases the inherent *vagueness* of the rating process—as measured by the number of plausible scenarios that a CRA can compute on the basis of this information.

(2) *Vagueness*, in turn, increases the potential *inertia mass* of a rating—inertia resulting from a CRA's inclination to affirm the scenario that is closer to its former views (even though other rating scenarios may appear more plausible) in order to maximize rating stability and alleviate credibility concerns.

(3) Ultimately, rating *inertia* creates *diminishing informational returns* for each rating component, and ultimately decreases the overall *accuracy* of ratings.

Moody's expectation that the ECB—or, for that matter, the Eurozone stakeholders—would assume of the responsibilities of lender of last resort was considerably challenged in January. This political decision brought about the considerable amount of uncertainty to which I turn in the following section.

Reactivity and Rating Standoff

Since the 1990s it has become common practice for market regulators to rely on ratings' forecasting capacities to carry out their tasks of market surveillance and monitoring (Partnoy 1999, 2002; Estrella 2000).[14] When regulators appeal to ratings for 'governmentality' purposes (Foucault 2009), they inevitably alter the rules governing the market reception of ratings. When they are extended legal influence, ratings cease simply to be fluctuating opinions about the future. Instead, they function as fixed market rules, and the mechanisms governing their reception become no longer deliberative but legally binding because investors and other financial parties must comply with the enforceable standards which regulators have developed in reference to ratings.

Since the creation of the Committee of European Banking Supervisors in 2004, European financial institutions have routinely used ratings to define the risk weight of their financial exposure. Under the Capital Requirement Directive of 2006, the ECB applies a rating threshold to define the acceptable quality of collateral for refinancing purposes. In October 2008, the ECB lowered the normal 'A3/A–' threshold to a more relaxed 'Baa3/BBB–' to enhance provisions of liquidity to the Eurozone (see timeline in appendix). However, the ECB announced that they would revert to their usual, tighter collateral framework in January 2011. As

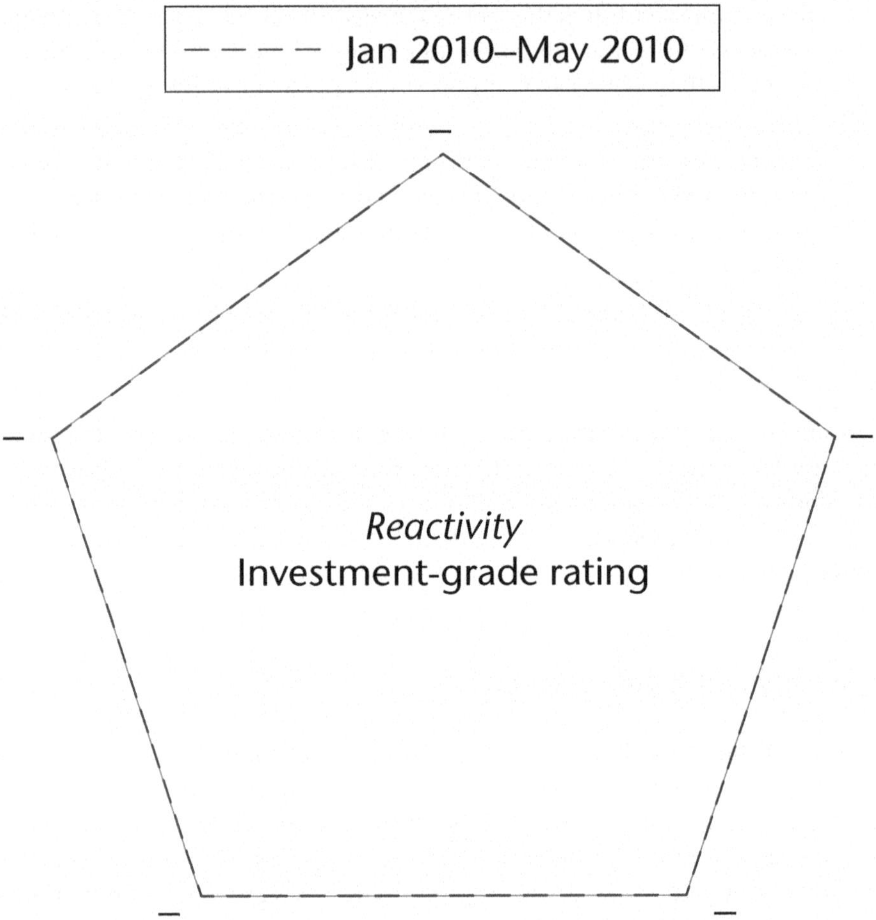

Figure 3.5. Reactivity and rating standoff (January–June 2010)

explained above, financial parties (most notably CRAs) expected the ECB to provide strong institutional commitment and to agree to step in as lender of last resort, should the need arise. Therefore, financial parties, and especially Moody's, anticipated further amendments to the ECB's collateral framework rating threshold, to accommodate the rapidly changing Greek economic situation. Instead, the contrary happened: on 14 January 2010, ECB President Jean-Claude Trichet reaffirmed his intention to let its 'Baa3/BBB–' threshold expire in January 2011.[15] This decision increased fears that liquidity risk could materialize if CRAs kept lowering ratings, which would bring Greek bonds closer to ineligibility for refunding purposes. Indeed, having faced prohibitive borrowing costs since January 2010, the Greek government was left with little means to propose a financial support package of its own and was effectively squeezed out of capital markets. It was therefore critical to Greece's ability to fund itself that its sovereign bonds remain eligible as collateral in exchange for low-interest loans from the ECB.

Representing Moody's, Cailleteau called the decision 'hard to believe' and 'not credible' and further wondered: 'why the ECB would have lowered the bar to help the banks and then raise it again at the price of creating a pretty significant European crisis?' He finally concluded: 'It's kind of a game theory.... In this story we've shown a lot of composure.'[16] The ECB's reliance on ratings in defining its threshold for collateral eligibility produced a rating standoff in which a downgrade was as undesirable for Moody's as it was for Greece (see Figure 3.5). Fitch and S&P issued multi-notch downgrades in March and April 2010 respectively, with S&P relegating Greece to junk-bond status on 22 April. With its rating well anchored in the investment-grade category, Moody's remained the only strong holdout, effectively serving with Fitch as a buffer against the prospect of Greek speculative status. Because the ECB determines the eligibility of collateral by applying the higher of the lowest two ratings,[17] the ECB thus used Fitch's 'BBB–' rating, the lowest within the investment-grade category, only because Moody's were still rating Greece in the investment-grade category (see timeline in appendix).

A 'chink' appeared in the ECB's inflexible stance, as evidenced in the complaint expressed by Ewald Nowotny, head of Austria's central bank: '[t]he fate of Greece, and if you are going to be more dramatic, the fate of Europe, depends on the judgment of one rating agency. That is an unacceptable situation.'[18] The ECB's decision thus changed the meaning that further downgrades would have on Greece's ability to borrow. It also changed the relationship between Moody's' ratings and 'reality': ratings no longer functioned as a scenario of the future, but rather, as a fiction which for many real market actors was preventing disaster.[19]

Moody's was operating under a strong and ever-increasing incentive not to translate its pessimism about Greece's financial future into a downgraded rating. After Trichet's (dramatic) decision not to further amend the rating threshold, Moody's had to take into account the potentially destabilizing consequences of its own downgrade on Greek finances: had it matched S&P's speculative rating by downgrading Greece into the junk status, Moody's would have almost certainly catalysed a significant liquidity crisis by rendering Greek government bonds ineligible as ECB collateral, which, in turn, would have forced Moody's—and other CRAs—to issue another downgrade.

The ECB/CRA standoff thus undermined the possibility that CRAs could be 'right'. Like a receding horizon, rating accuracy became moved ever-more out of reach; no matter what considerations Moody's took, the prospect of downgrading Greek sovereign bonds in an orderly fashion was no longer a possibility.

The ECB's announcement on 3 May to suspend its minimum credit rating threshold for Greece (ECB 2010b) was widely interpreted as a strategic attempt to diffuse the risk of a potential Moody's downgrade. Crucially and ironically, however, the decision also removed the incentive for Moody's not to downgrade (Gaillard 2012, 185). A month later on 14 June, Moody's issued the most severe downgrade of sovereign bonds in recent history, knocking it down four notches, to speculative status. The four-notch downgrade is puzzling for several reasons. The rating action was at the time of issuance the sharpest downgrade Moody's had ever issued on a sovereign issuer. Interestingly, Moody's' dramatic rating action was not motivated by any significant change in Greek fundamentals. Paradoxically, the downgrade even occurred when Greece's prospects had improved significantly, following the ECB's decision to suspend its minimum rating threshold. Finally, the downgrade followed by less than a month Cailleteau's departure (effective 17 May) from Moody's, a coincidence that was mentioned by my interviewee as a possible factor explaining the severity of the downgrade. In light of these inconsistencies, observers widely interpreted Moody's' rating action as 'inevitable' and merely corrective.[20] The decision 'could not be described as unexpected' said Poul Thomsen, deputy director of the IMF's European Department: 'all Moody's did was bring its own rating into line with those of other agencies, which had lowered their ratings before the government unveiled its economic program'.[21] The downgrade meant Moody's was 'only catching up to the reality markets were trading on weeks ago'.[22]

The downgrade effectively resorbed Moody's' whopping three- and four-notch gap with S&P and Fitch, respectively. Crucially, the timing of the decision—following the ECB's suspension of its minimum threshold for Greece—ensured the downgrade would have 'minimal' effect.[23] Effectively, the day of the downgrade, the euro advanced nearly 1 per cent against the dollar. The historical magnitude of the downgrade and its specific timing suggest the ECB's modification of its collateral framework essentially 'liberated' Moody's to downgrade Greece's government without jeopardizing the country's ability to qualify for low-interest loans.[24] Past studies have concluded that regulatory reliance on ratings favours high ratings (Gaillard 2012). I propose that this is the case because high ratings create incentives for ratings inertia. They can only do so temporarily, however, ultimately giving way to more dramatic patterns of rating change.

Conclusion

This chapter yields several findings. First, I challenge the common view that CRAs merely 'misread' the Greek crisis. My examination of rating reports shows that Moody's' rationale for its investment-grade rating of Greece was accurate until October 2009: in the early stages of the Greek sovereign debt crisis, ratings functioned as *plausible* scenarios. After the collapse of Lehman Brothers, CRAs assessed the plausibility of their rating scenario in relation to Greece's deteriorating economic prospects. Although cracks appeared in some risk components, the changing economic situation during most of 2009 did not undermine the perceived strength of the system of relations that CRAs assumed linked these components together at the aggregated rating level. In other words, the overall plausibility of the investment-grade scenario that CRAs had for Greece remained intact. Acting upon the plausibility of their scenario, Moody's reaffirmed their A-range rating until autumn 2009.

Second, this chapter suggests a more complex vision of how CRAs articulate the past, present, and future. Most studies of risk valuation adhere to a conventional—linear—framework in which time flows from the past to the future. From this perspective, CRAs analyse past and present information in order to assign a single distribution of probabilities to future outcomes. Departing from this linear narrative, this investigation of the Greek sovereign debt crisis shows how, beginning in October 2009 Moody's adapted strategically to cognitive inconsistencies and credibility concerns by using ratings they have already assigned to constitute the new threats they were tasked with predicting. In doing so, Moody's used a technique I term 'backward reasoning'. This appeal to the future to make sense of present threats guaranteed that new risk threats acquired meaning in ways that vindicated their previous views, because the terms of meaning were generated by their own previously assigned ratings. As such, backward reasoning helped CRAs maintain continuity between ratings, thereby preserving the consistency of opinion that marks CRAs as credible producers of valid anticipatory knowledge.[25] However, while their non-linear technique of rating production mitigated their most immediate concerns about uncertainty and credibility, this study shows that it also resulted in rating path-dependency and informational diminishing returns, two inconsistencies which are highlighted in Moody's' unusual pattern of rating migration. Overall, non-linear rating practices and backward reasoning create a dilemma for CRAs: the predictive capacities and accuracy of a rating are inversely correlated. This study of Greek sovereign ratings shows that, over time, the *predictive capacities* of rating scenarios increase the overall *potential inertia mass* of a rating, which, in turn, creates *diminishing informational returns* for each rating component, and ultimately decreases the overall *accuracy* of ratings.

Third, I show how CRAs may have had to anticipate the likely consequences of their predictions as they were *used* in the financial world, especially by market regulators. In the last section, I reintroduced governance mechanisms and legal reasoning in order to show that Moody's rating inertia in winter 2010—what analysts label as a 'rating failure' (Reinhart 2002) to anticipate sovereign risk events—was in fact the purposeful result of Moody's intention to avoid legal frictions arising from regulatory reliance on ratings. I indicate that the ECB's reliance on ratings in defining market regulations also greatly affected the rating process by forcing CRAs to anticipate the potentially destabilizing consequences that further downgrades would have on Greece's borrowing costs—a recursive process that comes close to what Espeland and Sauder (2007) defined as 'reactivity'. With specific reference to Moody's, this chapter shows that CRAs did account for the potentially destabilizing consequences of their predictions on issuers when assessing new threats. In light of this evidence, I argue that regulatory reliance on ratings can strongly influence the rating process, as evidenced by Moody's' inertia during the Greek debt crisis.

Finally, this chapter also demonstrates the usefulness of rating reports as 'figuring' documents in examining the non-linear dimensions of risk valuation practices. Rating reports show CRAs embarked in a dynamic process whereby they elaborate on, and figure out what they perceive is the most adequate scenario for future risks. This study of the Greek sovereign debt crisis points to a non-linear, complex web of cognitive, legal, and political transactions that complicate previous understandings of the market infusion of ratings, most notably those produced by theories of performativity. This chapter also shows that it is inaccurate to claim that CRAs simply 'missed' the crisis. Most criticisms of CRAs, specifically of Moody's, have been written with the benefit of hindsight. As Robert Solow pointed out, 'the proper choice of a model depends on the institutional context' (Solow 1985). My approach has been to examine the production of sovereign ratings from the point of view of how CRAs *see* sovereign uncertainties. From this viewpoint, the elaboration and active maintenance of rating scenarios by CRAs cannot be understood in abstraction from political and legal processes.

Appendix: Greek Sovereign Debt Crisis Timeline (June 2008–July 2010)

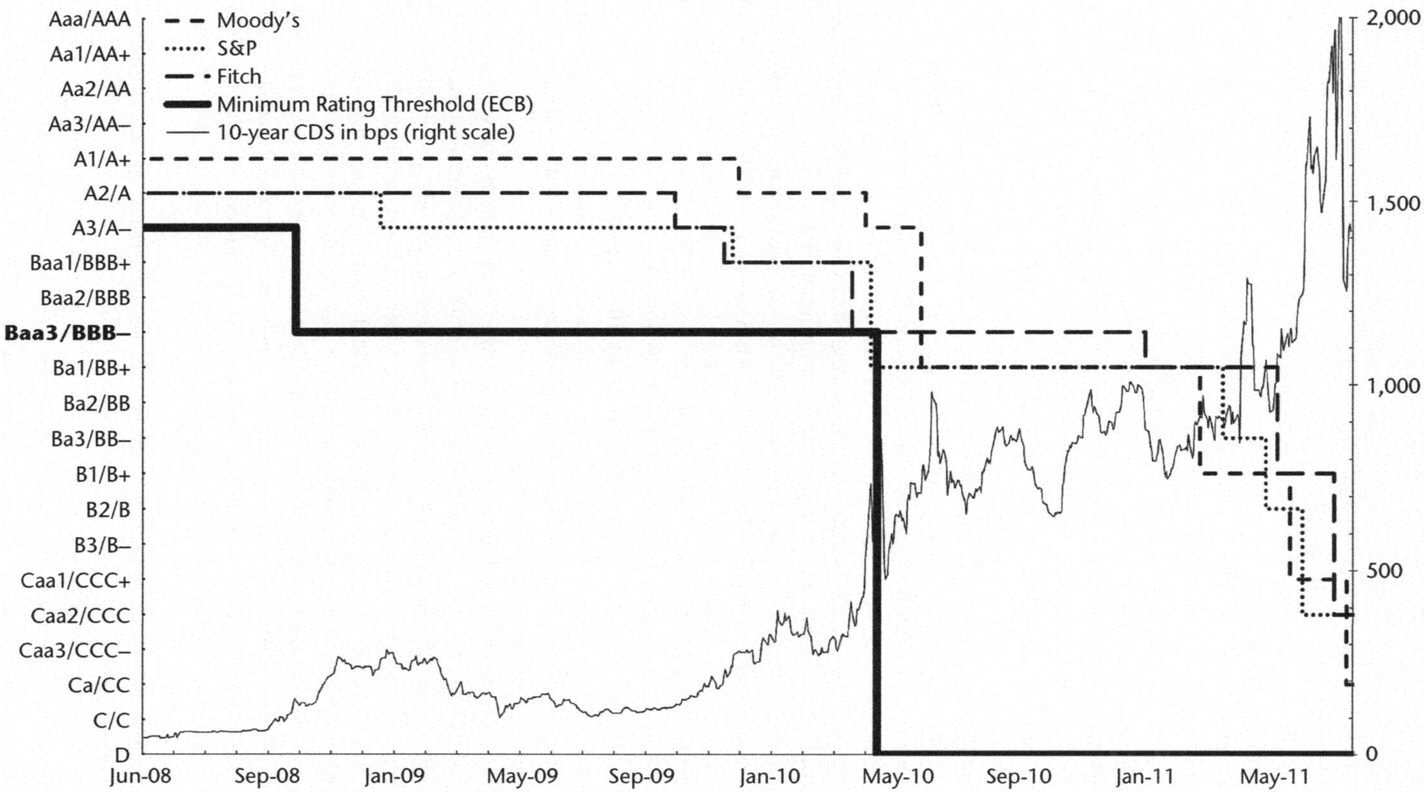

Notes

1. Credit ratings are commonly defined as systems of gradation of debt issues according to their investment quality.
2. I wish to gratefully acknowledge the support of MACROHIST, a Marie Curie Initial Training Action.
3. For instance, no rated Western countries defaulted until 1997.
4. In financial markets, as in any market environment, competing and often contradictory forms of knowledge circulate. In global credit markets, risk knowledge essentially comes from two sources: (1) market-based risk information embedded in market prices (yields, spreads), that provides an aggregated snapshot of the millions of risk pricing transactions at any given time; and (2) expert judgement in standardized (ratings, rankings), written (reports, policy briefs), or oral (press conferences) form, which reflects the particular risk views of their originators, whether governmental organizations, private agencies, or international institutions.
5. Converting CDSs into CDS-implied ratings (CDS-IRs), Gaillard (2012) finds that investors had already begun to price Greek and Portuguese government debt in the speculative-grade category as early as December 2009 and April 2010, respectively, well before CRAs aggressively downgraded Greek and Portuguese government bonds to junk status after months of rating inertia.
6. Later in 2010, Moody's would issue a five-notch downgrade on Irish sovereign bonds, the most severe downgrade Moody's has issued up to date. Overall, Moody's knocked Irish bonds down seven notches in just seven months between December 2010 and July 2011.
7. The same observation applies to S&P and Fitch sovereign ratings. Because of space limitations, these data are not reproduced in this chapter.
8. This distinction between 'normal times' and 'times of crisis' has already been used before in social theory, notably to operationalize contextual differences in models of cultural influence (Swidler 1986).
9. ABS-CDOs (asset-backed securities/collateralized debt obligations) were a new class of risky credit derivatives resulting from a securitization process. Rating ABS-CDOs required the computation of correlation values to encode the probability that different issuers within a diversified pool of assets would default simultaneously. Unable to compute such correlations of default from existing information, CRAs borrowed the techniques of calculation they used to rate corporate CDOs.
10. I here build on Bernard Williams' classic distinction between (objective) 'truth' and (socially constructed) 'truthfulness'. I also draw on MacKenzie's claim that accuracy does not exist *in abstracto* and has to be 'invented' (MacKenzie 1993)
11. The interview was conducted under condition of anonymity in Paris in summer 2013.
12. *The Financial Times*, 'Moody's gives Greece breathing space on debts', 23 December 2009.
13. This claim of path-dependency is in line with MacKenzie's findings. In his 2011 study of rating of structured financial instruments and the central computational problem of correlation values (see the section 'The Constitution of Financial

Uncertainties during the Greek Sovereign Debt Crisis'), he concluded that 'consistency with previous organizational practice [is] a criterion that shaped the original choice of correlation parameters' (MacKenzie 2011, 1805).

14. Rating-based regulations can take many other forms. First, regulators typically use ratings as prudential thresholds to restrict the amounts of types of investments of financial institutions. Regulators also employ rating-based formulae in the computing of differential disclosure requirements. In structured finance, regulators may impose rating eligibility conditions on the issuance of complex instruments. Finally, rating-implied formulas also regularly appear in capital reserve requirements. In private contracts reliance on ratings as 'triggers' is also an important development (Carruthers 2010). See Cantor et al. (2007) and Bank for International Settlements (2009) for an overview.
15. 'We will not change our collateral framework for the sake of any particular country. Our collateral framework applies to all countries concerned. And that has been said already by the Vice-President, by me and by colleagues. That is crystal clear' ECB (2010a).
16. *The Globe and Mail*, Joanna Slater, 'The search for villains is on; Banks, hedge funds, currency traders and ratings agencies are all under fire', 4 March 2010.
17. See Committee of European Banking Supervisors (2006).
18. *The Financial Times*, 'Greece to unveil new austerity plan', 3 March 2010.
19. The fictitious nature of rating scenarios and their replacement by loan contracts as the coordinating principle of Greek sovereign risk after 2010 is the subject of Pénet and Mallard (2014).
20. *The Wall Street Journal*, 'Greece downgrade ripples only mildly in markets', 14 June 2010.
21. *Toronto Star*, 'IMF says not concerned by Moody's Greece downgrade', 15 June 2010.
22. Dow Jones Capital Markets Report, 14 June 2010 (22:31 GMT).
23. Dow Jones Capital Markets Report, 14 June 2010 (23:03 GMT).
24. I am cautious to not overstate this finding. While this claim is consistent with my primary data, evidently, however, no definitive proof or testimony exists that could provide univocal confirmation. Additional research is needed on the nature of the interface between rating practices and regulatory interventions.
25. This focus on the constitutive purpose of ratings builds upon pioneering studies in cultural history by Reinhart Koselleck (2004) and François Hartog (2003), who focus on various *régimes d'historicité* (i.e. articulations between past, present, and future that they read in fictional and non-fictional forms of writing).

References

Bank for International Settlements. 2009. 'Stocktaking on the Use of Credit Ratings' ed. Basel Committee on Banking Supervision. The Joint Forum.

Beunza, D. and D. Stark. 2004. 'Tools of the Trade: The Socio-Technology of Arbitrage in a Wall Street Trading Room'. *Industrial and Corporate Change* 13(2): 369–400.

Bhatia, A. V. 2002. *Sovereign Credit Ratings Methodology: An Evaluation*. Washington, DC: International Monetary Fund.
Borraz, O. and J. Besançon. 2008. 'Uncertainties in Regulating Food Safety in France'. In *Uncertain Risks Regulated*, ed. M. Everson and E. Vos. Abingdon: Routledge, 49–68.
Callon, M. 1998. 'Introduction: The Embededdness of Economic Markets in Economics'. In *The Laws of the Markets*, ed. M. Callon. Oxford: Blackwell, 1–57.
Callon, M. and F. Muniesa. 2005. 'Peripheral Vision: Economic Markets as Calculative Collective Devices'. *Organization Studies* 26(8): 1229–50.
Cantor, R., F. Packer, and Federal Reserve Bank of New York. 1996. *Determinants and Impacts of Sovereign Credit Ratings*. New York: Public Information Dept., Federal Reserve Bank of New York.
Cantor, R., O. A. P. Gwilym, and S. H. Thomas. 2007. 'The Use of Credit Ratings in Investment Management in the US and Europe'. *Journal of Fixed Income* 17(2): 13–26.
Carruthers, B. G. 2010. 'Knowledge and Liquidity: Institutional and Cognitive Foundations of the subprime Crisis'. In *Markets on Trial: The Economic Sociology of the US Financial Crisis, Part A*, ed. M. Lounsbury and P. Hirsch. Bingley, UK: Emerald, 157–82.
Committee of European Banking Supervisors. 2006. 'Guidelines on the Recognition of External Credit Assessment Institutions'.
Dalmedico, A. and H. Guillemot. 2008. 'Climate Change: Scientific Dynamics, Expertise and Geopolitical Challenges'. In *Global Science and National Sovereignty: Studies in Historical Sociology of Science*, ed. G. Mallard, C. Paradeise, and A. Peerbaye. New York: Routledge, 195–221.
ECB. 2010a. Press Conference, Introductory statement with Q&A, 14 January 2010.
ECB. 2010b. Press Release, 'ECB Announces Change in Eligibility of Debt Instruments Issued or Guaranteed by the Greek Government', 3 May.
Espeland, W. N. and M. Sauder. 2007. 'Rankings and Reactivity: How Public Measures Recreate Social Worlds'. *American Journal of Sociology* 113(1): 1–40.
Estrella, A. 2000. 'Credit Ratings and Complementary Sources of Credit Quality Information'. *Basel Committee on Banking Supervision Working Papers* 3.
Ferri, G., L. G. Liu, and J. E. Stiglitz. 1999. 'The Procyclical Role of Rating Agencies: Evidence from the East Asian Crisis'. *Economic Notes* 28(3): 335–55.
Foucault, M. 2009. *Security, Territory, Population: Lectures at the Collège de France 1977–1978*. New York: Picador.
Gaillard, N. 2012. 'The Limits of Sovereign Ratings in Light of the Greek Debt Crisis of 2009–2010'. In Gaillard, *A Century of Sovereign Ratings*. New York: Springer, 171–85.
Hartog, F. 2003. *Régimes d'historicité*. Paris: Seuil.
Knorr Cetina, K. 2011. 'Financial Analysis: Epistemic Profile of an Evaluative Science'. In *Social Knowledge in the Making*, ed. C. Camic, N. Gross, and M. Lamont. Chicago: University of Chicago Press, 405–42.
Koselleck, R. 2004. *Futures Past: On the Semantics of Historical Time*. New York: Columbia University Press.
MacKenzie, D. A. 1993. *Inventing Accuracy: A Historical Sociology of Nuclear Missile Guidance*. Cambridge, MA: MIT Press.
MacKenzie, D. A. 2006. *An Engine, Not a Camera: How Financial Models Shape Markets*. Cambridge, MA: MIT Press.

MacKenzie, D. A. 2011. 'The Credit Crisis as a Problem in the Sociology of Knowledge'. *American Journal of Sociology* 116(6): 1778–1841.

MacKenzie, D. A., F. Muniesa, and L. Siu (eds.). 2007. *Do Economists Make Markets? On the Performativity of Economics*. Princeton: Princeton University Press.

Mallard, G. and A. Lakoff. 2011. 'How Claims to Know the Future Are Used to Understand the Present'. In *Social Knowledge in the Making*, ed. C. Camic, N. Gross, and M. Lamont. Chicago: University of Chicago Press, 339–78.

Mallard, G. and P. Pénet. 2013. 'Seeing Like a Credit Rating Agency: The Constitution of Financial Uncertainties during the Greek Sovereign Debt Crisis'. In *Financial Crises: Identification, Forecasting and Effects on Transition Economies*, ed. C. Hawthorne. New York: Nova Publishers, 164–74.

Mennicken, A., P. Miller, and R. Samiolo. 2008. 'Accounting for Economic Sociology'. *Economic Sociology: The European Electronic Newsletter*.

Miller, D. 2002. 'Turning Callon the Right Way Up'. *Economy and Society* 31(2): 218–33.

Miller, P. 2008a. 'Calculating Economic Life'. *Journal of Cultural Economy* 1(1): 51–64.

Miller, P. 2008b. 'Figuring out Organizations'. In *Nobel Symposium on 'Foundations of Organization'*. Saltsjöbaden, Sweden.

Millo, Y. and D. MacKenzie. 2009. 'The Usefulness of Inaccurate Models: Towards an Understanding of the Emergence of Financial Risk Management'. *Accounting, Organizations and Society* 34(5): 638–53.

Moody's. 2002. 'Moody's Upgrades Greece to A1 from A2'. Rating Action, 4 November: Moody's Investors Service.

Moody's. 2007. 'Moody's Changes Outlook on Greece's A1 Bond Ratings to Positive'. Rating Action, 11 January: Moody's Investors Service.

Moody's. 2008. 'Greece's Political Unrest Exposes Constraints Reflected in A1 Rating'. Press Release, 17 December: Moody's Investors Service.

Moody's. 2009a. 'Moody's Changes the Outlook for Greece's A1 Rating to Stable'. Rating Action, 25 February: Moody's Investors Service.

Moody's. 2009b. 'Moody's Places Greece's Ratings on Review for Possible Downgrade'. Rating Action, 29 October: Moody's Investors Service.

Moody's. 2009c. 'Investor Fears of Liquidity Crisis in Greece are Overdone'. Press Release, 2 December: Moody's Investors Service.

Moody's. 2009d. 'Moody's downgrades Greece to A2 from A1'. Rating Action, 22 December: Moody's Investors Service.

Muniesa, F. and M. Callon. 2007. 'Economic Experiments and the Construction of Markets'. In *Do Economists Make Markets? On the Performativity of Economics*, ed. D. A. MacKenzie, F. Muniesa, and L. Siu. Princeton: Princeton University Press, 163–89.

Partnoy, F. 1999. 'The Siskel and Ebert of Financial Markets: Two Thumbs Down for the Credit Rating Agencies'. *Washington University Law Quarterly* 77: 619–712.

Partnoy, F. 2002. 'The Paradox of Credit Ratings'. In *Ratings, Rating Agencies and the Global Financial System*, ed. R. M. Levich, G. Majnoni, and C. Reinhart. Dordrecht: Kluwer, 65–84.

Pénet, P. and G. Mallard. 2014. 'From Risk Models to Risk Contracts: Austerity as the Continuation of Calculation by Other Means'. *Journal of Critical Globalisation Studies* 7: 4–47.

Perrow, C. 1984. *Normal Accidents: Living with High Risk Systems*. New York: Basic Books.

Reinhart, C. M. 2002. 'Default, Currency Crises, and Sovereign Credit Ratings'. *The World Bank Economic Review* 16(2): 151–70.

Reinhart, C. M. and K. S Rogoff. 2009. *This Time is Different: Eight Centuries of Financial Folly*. Princeton: Princeton University Press.

Rona-Tas, A. and S. Hiss. 2011. 'Forecast as Valuation: The Role of Ratings and Predictions in the Subprime Mortgage Crisis in the US'. In *The Worth of Goods: Valuation and Pricing in the Economy*, ed. J. Becker, and P. Aspers. Oxford: Oxford University Press, 223–46.

Russell, B. 1923. 'Vagueness'. *Australasian Journal of Psychology and Philosophy* 1(2): 84–92.

Solow, R. M. 1985. 'Economic History and Economics'. *American Economic Review* 75(2): 328–31.

Stark, D. 2009. *The Sense of Dissonance: Accounts of Worth in Economic Life*. Princeton: Princeton University Press.

Swidler, A. 1986. 'Culture in Action: Symbols and Strategies'. *American Sociological Review* 51(2): 273–86.

Vaughan, D. 1996. The Challenger Launch Decision: Risky Technology, Culture, and Deviance at NASA. Chicago: University of Chicago Press.

4

Subitizing Practices and Market Decisions

The Role of Simple Graphs in Business Valuations

Neil Pollock and Gian Marco Campagnolo

The Capture of Business by the 2x2 Matrix

> The 2x2 matrix represents the most notable analytical tool ever to emerge in business management.
>
> (Lowy and Hood 2011, xiii)

Whether or not one agrees with the above statement there can be little doubt that the 2x2 matrix (hereafter the matrix) has become one of, if not the most important form of valuation tool used in business settings. One only has to think of the 'Cost Benefit matrix', the 'Product and Market matrix', the 'BCG Product Portfolio matrix' to name but a few (Lowy and Hood 2011). Today it is hard to imagine a business meeting that does not revolve around this (or some variation of this) format; the business report is not considered complete unless it includes such diagrams; and a great deal of business education involves generating and communicating ideas through these figurations. Yet despite its prominence, the matrix remains the unexplained 'success' of the business world. Scholars have but a rather vague sense of how to theorize the matrix's rise to prominence or the influence of this mode of decision-making on business settings. Whilst there has been some focus on its 'interactional' (Pels 2003) features, or how the matrix might 'frame' complex organizational problem solving (Morrison and Wensley 1991, 112), the common response has been to ignore or, worse still, dismiss the matrix as a 'simplification' (Lissack and Richardson 2003), albeit a 'powerful oversimplification' (Ghemawat 2002). Some go so far—because it is seen to reduce and hide complexity—as to describe it as 'unethical' (Lissack and Richardson 2003).

This is an understandable but unsatisfactory response. More difficult still is to take this figuration seriously and to analyse the kind of valuation that it provides. There is more to these devices than just reducing information to manageable dimensions; the notion of a simplification fails to appreciate its important transformational practices and characteristics.

Espeland and Stevens (1998, 423) argue that every professional community has its own unique kinds of 'numerical pictures'. The business community is no different in this respect. Ghemawat (2002) has discussed how, towards the latter part of the twentieth century, there was a profusion of figurations attempting to depict complex strategic and managerial decisions in relatively straightforward ways. Writing about the most famous of these, the 'Boston Box', Morrison and Wensley (1991, 114) note how the benefits of this device are that the 'reader is informed *at a glance* of what may take several paragraphs to explain'. Whilst the potential to foster insights 'at a glance' is not confined to business graphs (see Coopmans 2014), it would seem a particularly appreciated feature in these contexts. What we attempt in this chapter, through exploring this characteristic of the matrix, is to develop Espeland and Stevens' (1998) point. That is, to investigate whether matrices provide for unique kinds of valuation in business settings, as compared to the formats used by professional communities elsewhere.

To help in this endeavour we draw inspiration from recent discussions from disciplines as diverse as science and technology studies, the sociology of finance, and economic sociology on 'calculative agency' (Callon and Muniesa 2005). We attempt to supplement the discussion of calculative agency with a much-needed focus on 'temporality'. For this, we work up the term, drawn from early research on visual calculation 'subitizing'. The notion of subitizing is developed with material stemming from a long-term ethnographic study of the production and use of a well-known matrix from the information technology realm.

The Role of Devices in Fostering Calculation in Markets

There is a growing interest in how artefacts constitute markets and market actors. The idea of 'calculative agency' was developed to capture how calculations were never performed by individuals alone but, rather, how people were always propped up and aided by various kinds of material artefact (Callon and Muniesa 2005). In this view, artefacts, and not only people, are seen to have 'agency', as they produce specific kinds of effects. In terms of who or what makes someone—or something—an agent, Latour (2005, 71) argues that: 'anything that [can] modify a state of affairs by making a difference is an actor'. The notion of calculative agency has been defined broadly. A calculation may need not necessarily be mathematical or numerical; it 'starts by establishing distinctions between things or states of the world' (Callon and Muniesa 2005, 1231). Callon and Muniesa describe calculation as a process of 'framing', 'disentanglement', and 'overflowing' where devices help mark the boundary between entities and information relevant to a decision-making process and that which is not. To give one example of how this work has been applied empirically, Preda (2006) discusses how the stock market 'price ticker' was, when it was first introduced at the beginning of the last century, an agent in leading to different forms of decision-making in the trading of stocks. The price ticker produced a constant flow of prices that meant the market could be, from then on, visualized and framed in new ways. The technology constituted stockbrokers' practices such that they switched from being 'observers of the market' to 'observers of the tape' (Akrich and Latour 1992, 232).

In studying the devices undergirding markets, Miller (2008) reminds us that we require a simultaneous investigation into the ideas behind these objects. There is a 'parcel of thought' behind even the most mundane object, he argues. Thus scholars have flagged how various 'market devices' (Callon et al. 2007) not only create a *market* or *economic* point of view but stem from theoretical ideas and assumptions about the economy (Callon 1998). There are parallels here with work from accountancy, where 'mediating instruments' (Miller and O'Leary 2007) are seen to create—but are also born out of—an *accounting* view of the world. Similarly MacKenzie (2009) has discussed the 'intellectual equipment' (the theories or models) that are seen to facilitate processes of *financial* calculation within stock markets. We find this work stimulating for our own discussion of business graphs. It begs the question: what is the parcel of thought behind the matrix?

Subitizing Practices

We offer the notion of *subitizing* or *subitizing practice* to help throw light on the set of ideas that sit behind or are fostered by simple graphs in business communities. Kaufman et al. (1949) define *subitizing* as the human skill to immediately make rapid, accurate, and confident judgements about small numbers. The term derives from the Latin adjective *subitus*, meaning *sudden* and the medieval Latin verb *subitare*, meaning *to arrive suddenly* (*OED*). It is based on psychological experiments from the late nineteenth century where it was shown that a fundamental law of visual counting was that the reaction time necessary to recognize a small number of entities was dramatically different from those required to identify entities above 7 or 8 (Cattel 1886 in Dehaene 2010). During these experiments, participants were shown dots on a screen and the time taken to recognize the actual number of dots was recorded. Kaufman et al. (1949, 500) argued that a 'small number of things, from 1 to 7 or 8, are discriminated in one way and larger numbers are discriminated in another way'. There are different ideas about where the point of discontinuity lay (Kaufman et al. (1949) say it is 7 or 8; Trick and Pylyshyn (1994) suggest 4; whilst Cattel (1886) and Dehaene (2010) say it lies near 3). However, the specific number is not relevant for our argument. What is of interest is that there is a 'point of discontinuity' between small and large numbers. Whilst small numbers are treated by human perception as a single picture, larger numbers apparently require a sequential algorithm (i.e. we start to 'count'). According to Kaufman et al. (1949), participants were not counting, but nor were they guessing. Kaufman et al. (1949, 520) argued that a new term was needed to capture the way people could immediately apprend small quantities: 'We wish to avoid terms now in use, having other meanings, and terms with the misleading connotations of estimating, counting, or grasping by intuition.' They identified the ability of people to immediately apprehend small numbers as a process of what they called 'subitizing' and numbers that could be treated this way fell within the 'subitizing range'. They write '[s]ubitizing is, on average, more accurate and more rapid than estimating, and it is done with more confidence' (Kaufman et al. 1949, 520).

What does the notion of subitizing offer our analysis of the matrix? We deploy the findings from this early experiment on subitizing for analytical purposes only. It provides, to quote Garfinkel (1967), an 'aid to the sluggish imagination'. We attempt to strip the notion of its existing psychological overtones and refer to the more sociological issues of how different groups of people coordinate their practices through graphs and how figurations, in turn, come to constitute evaluation practices. Findings from early research on visual calculations are important for the sociological understanding of business graphs, we argue, because they challenge the idea that all graphs operate on a common textual surface. The concept suggests that distinctions are important. In particular it highlights a *point of discontinuity* between complex and simple graphs. Complex figurations create one kind of sensemaking and simple graphs another. In terms of our analysis, the distinction between complex and simple refers not to different things, insofar as they all are the work of 'calculation' (cf. Callon and Muniesa 2005), but the discontinuity relates to the value these figurations hold or are seen to provide to the reader. Here we suggest that these devices are deliberately constructed to channel and define the evaluation practices of readers (Lamont 2012). The value they hold therefore is that they allow readers to arrive easily at certain conclusions or decisions. In the remainder, we pursue the concept of subitizing with illustrations deriving from the work of industry analysts.

The Case of Industry Analyst Research

The bulk of our fieldwork was carried out on the industry analyst firm Gartner Inc. (though towards the latter years of our research we also conducted interviews with and observations of rival firms, IDC and Forrester, which we also briefly focus on here). Gartner, the largest industry analyst firm in the industry, was founded in 1979 by Gideon Gartner (who has long since retired). The firm employs more than 4,000 employees and has offices in over 80 countries. They operate predominantly but not exclusively in the information technology (IT) sector and their client base is said to contain up to 10,000 of the largest and most important corporations from around the world (Pollock and Williams 2010). The bulk of their activity and where most of the analysts are employed and revenues generated is in the production of 'research'. In relation to this, there is no more important piece of research than the 'Magic Quadrant' (hereafter the MQ), which is widely described as the firm's 'signature research' (Pollock and Williams 2009). The MQ rates the competence and performance of IT vendors. It is predominantly used by technology adopters when procuring new hardware or software (see Figure 4.1). There are over 150 MQs produced each year for different technologies/markets. This number changes as Gartner are continually creating new ones and 'retiring' older ones. They come with a five-page 'research note' attached and cost over

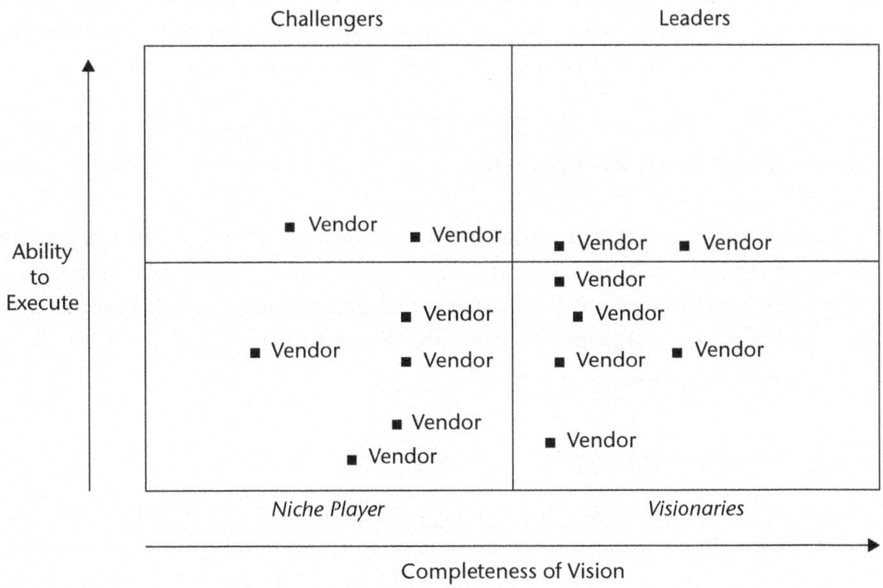

Figure 4.1. The Magic Quadrant (MQ)

£2,000 to buy (but can be found easily for free on the internet). The MQ has its own distinct ontology (e.g. it contains its own unique presuppositions about what 'good' performance consists of; Pollock and Williams 2009). It is also very much a 'dividing object' (Pollock and Williams 2009). By this we mean that it has a dramatically different significance and importance for people: it has been described as '[o]ne of the most influential pieces of business research in any industry' with the 'power to make or break a technology' (Violino and Levin 1997); at the same time, it has also been widely described as 'flawed' and 'overly simple' due to the narrow range of criteria that it assesses (Pollock and Williams 2009).

Fieldwork

In terms of the fieldwork conducted, we have studied the MQ for nearly ten years. Initially, we came across how people were influenced by the MQ as part of an Economic and Social Research Council (ESRC) study on the implementation of enterprise resource planning systems (Pollock and Williams 2009). We were later funded by the ESRC to investigate how the graph was constructed (Pollock and D'Adderio 2012). This fieldwork on the MQ is still ongoing as we have now become interested in how new groups of experts—influencer relations professionals—attempt to work with and influence its shape. In studying the format we have deployed a variety of methods to collect data: from conventional semi-structured interviews, periods of participant observation, and archival research, through to photo-elicitation techniques, etc.

Empirical Story: Three Episodes

We present our empirical material in three episodes. The first reports on the value that these simple visual graphs provide for the people who use them. The second revolves around the agency of graphs and how the subitizing range contributes to shaping IT markets. The third develops an account of how the subitizing range is achieved.

Episode 1: People Build Immediate Choices on It

The main purpose of the MQ is to support adopter firms in attempting to procure large-scale software systems or hardware. Procurement is a complex, multi-step process. It is complex because adopters have to make a decision on hard-to-assess technologies. There are not only many possible offerings available but adopters are rarely able to directly inspect these products directly.

The aim of a procurement therefore is to whittle down the many possible vendors to a shortlist. Shortlisted solutions will be given more intense scrutiny. The difficulties arising during this process are manifold. One common issue is that Chief Information Officers (CIOs) often lack the necessary technical expertise or market knowledge. Thus, in terms of what information the MQ provides, according to an analyst, these charts help clients 'position or understand their particular vendors... where those ones are in the *landscape*' (interview, IDC analyst). 'What the [MQs] say', we are told by a software vendor and former analyst, is 'this is the *battlefield*' (interview, vendor a). As reported by an independent industry analyst, the MQ therefore provides a useful guide for CIOs to help them construct a shortlist: 'If you put yourself in a CIO position, if you do not really know about the market and you want to figure out *really fast* who are the top companies and what you want to put in your shortlist, the MQ is an excellent tool to do that.'[1] Not only do they help the CIO but they can be used to communicate a decision to others in the adopting organization. For instance, as one of our informants puts it: 'These are very simple tools to communicate to executive management. For example if a CIO wants to buy a new ERP or CRM... this is a very simple tool to *defend* or make a *quick evaluation*' (interview, vendor a).

The MQ comes in the form of a box with an X- and Y-axis (labelled 'completeness of vision' and 'ability to execute') dimensioning a two-by-two matrix, with four segments. Each segment is individually labelled (niche player, challenger, visionary, and leader). Those placed further to the right are seen to have more 'complete vision', whilst those placed towards the top an elevated ability 'to execute' on that vision. One unwritten rule of good procurement, our informant explains, is that those procuring 'should have 1 or 2 or 15% of these guys [pointing to the top right quadrant] in their evaluation list and invite them to a tender' (interview, vendor a). The MQ serves here as a shared frame of reference or 'powerful totem', as another of our informants put it (interview, vendor b). It has the capacity to 'rubber stamp' decisions (interview, IDC analyst) such that the old adage about buying IBM has been replaced. Today it is 'nobody ever got fired for using a [MQ]' (interview, IDC analyst). Another feature of the MQ is its seemingly intuitive format, which facilitates communication across roles: 'Imagine'—our informant continues—'a CIO wants to buy a new CRM system for a large organization costing... £15m and then he makes a decision, and he has to justify this decision in front of the board where... the CEO has no idea about IT' (interview, vendor b).

A downside of the MQ, according to some of the analysts we talked to, is that it has become 'too good' in imparting information. What is meant by this? There are two aspects to this. On the one hand this appears a positive comment and relates to how they require very little time to decode. There is no need to 'sit down and discuss in detail these charts' (interview, adopter),

Figure 4.2. Clients photographing a newly released MQ at a Gartner event

says one adopter. People find them 'easy to read'. Apparently they can be read and understood in the time it takes to point a camera (see Figure 4.2).

They are (too) effective because people have become familiar with and know how to read the format:

> The success [of MQ] is because of the repeatability. People have learned how to use it. It's predictable. It's the same each time, so it's easy to go back to it and not have to *figure out* what the analyst is trying to convey. (Interview, Gartner analyst, JL)

On the other hand there is also a downside to the MQ in that they seemingly encourage *quick* decisions. As one analyst put it, they invite people to jump to conclusions 'too fast'. Why is this problematic? The analysts seemingly attempt to warn clients against taking procurement decisions by only looking at the MQ: 'Our clients tell us... things that we find scary, like we've just narrowed our shortlist down to anyone who's in the latest quadrant. We say: "don't do that"' (interview, Gartner analyst, JL). The analysts also complain that even though the MQ comes with a detailed research note that provides further detail and caveats, this document is seldom read. They attempt to encourage their clients to talk more fully with the analysts who compiled the MQ in the first place. These experts have much more information and detail on the vendors but surprisingly, they point out, this is rarely required. An analyst describes how 'most users don't care. They want to know that the vendor is in the top 10 biggest revenues and this is enough' (interview, Gartner analyst, ET). Another analyst notes how:

> it would be very worrying if the user were simply to take one MQ or one Marketscape... and say, because this is there on that picture I am only going to go with this solution, or only look at these three. They'd need to do a lot more due diligence, including interrogating the analyst... reading all the research material from probably Gartner, Forrester and IDC, especially when making the big decisions, and including going around talking to some of the vendors' customers and talking to some mates in the industry. So the amount of value and the amount of importance that can be attached to a graph has I think not to be overestimated. (Interview, IDC analyst)

Others we interviewed also echoed this point about due diligence and taking time. For them the MQ was only a small part of the process: 'When a major decision like that is being made it would mainly be a cross-party, cross-group decision so that we tend to be fairly slow about selecting things but then we would do more research' (interview, adopter).

Figure 4.3 captures the range of views found concerning the usefulness of the MQ and similar matrices. What we want to flag is the point of discontinuity between: (a) those who thought the tools encouraged people to 'jump to

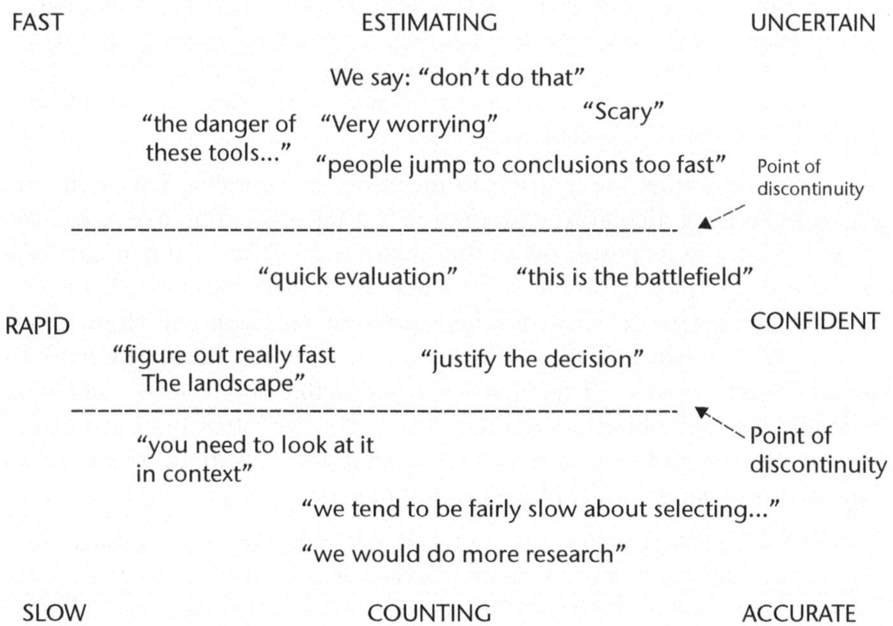

Figure 4.3. Subitizing range applied to empirical material from episode 1

conclusions too fast'; (b) those who would look at tools like the matrix but would take more time over the process and do more research; and (c) those who thought the tools give them 'just enough' information to understand the 'landscape' (e.g. to help begin the process of taking of a decision). In other words, the first episode demonstrated how, for certain groups of people, the matrix is easy to understand and familiar. It establishes a certain confidence in the reader that she or he has grasped the situation and — importantly—that it has all happened rapidly. However, it might be argued that these features can be found within any simple graph. What is specific about the matrix described here?

Episode 2: The Magic Quadrant is *the Marketplace*

What we want to show in this second episode is that its producers are trying to achieve a figuration that is neither too simple nor too complex for the reader. They are attempting to create what we are calling (building on Kaufman et al. 1949) the *subitizing range*. One aspect of this argument can be found in the words of this analyst:

> In all these kind of graphics you have to be careful that you *don't introduce complexity or something that's counter-intuitive*, that's the first thing. You want something that is simple and that follows people's understanding. If we started introducing different shapes, something that went against a 'quick glance kind of view' then the amount of time spent in interpreting it for users to understand, and users interpreting it to get buy impacts when they're looking for budget from CIOs. You've got to factor that in, a lot of these people are very busy and they want something that can be assimilated in a fairly 'quick glance', certainly at that kind of level. (Interview, IDC analyst)

The analyst flags how the matrix can never be too complex. The subitizing range applies in particular to temporality. If it takes too long to decode, the matrix would lose its power over other measures. But again this might be a feature of any graphical format. What makes the matrix distinctive? The next example demonstrates clearly the crucial point of our argument. The achievement of the subitizing range is not just about simplification. The work of subitization also involves a very particular rationalization process. Achieving the required range sometimes requires *adding* entities rather than just taking away. In the excerpt below, for instance, an analyst talks about how the goal of the MQ is to get all of the players onto one space:

> I think the interesting issue is, it's a way of getting all the main players in a market on one piece of paper in an interesting way you can talk about it. That both the buyer and the analyst and the vendor can all talk about things. They may disagree about where the dots are but they can all talk about it. (Interview, Gartner analyst, ET)

No matter how numerous (or scant—as we will see below), if the players are to be pictured on a piece of paper, then they should total a certain amount: 'Gartner [MQs] are designed to deliberately limit it to a *specific* number of vendors, not an *exact* number, you don't have a [MQ] with 100 on, you don't have a [MQ] with 2' (interview, Gartner analyst, ET). Our informant discusses the extremes of the range, where complexification does not work but neither does straightforward simplification:

> graphically, you can't—you can, we've done it, you can have a 100 dots on the chart—but it is unreadable. It is just garbage. It is just a bunch of dots [...] And likewise when there is 3 dots on it, it is meaningless. What's the point of having a [MQ] with 3 dots? (Interview, Gartner analyst, ET)

He gives a concrete example where the situation had become too simple and as a result the clients had lost interest in the particular MQ:

> we used to do things like operating systems [but] when Microsoft started dominating operating systems on... desktop applications it was pointless having 4 dots on a chart... and the colleagues all turn around and go 'what was the point in that?' The clients don't read them anymore, they are not so interesting... their value is very, very low. The dots hardly move. And nobody is very interested. (Interview, Gartner analyst, ET)

Finding the right range keeps the analysts 'in the game' (e.g. their clients will still come to them and—importantly—*purchase* their advice). Strikingly, the different analysts we spoke to seemed to converge on what they thought the right range was:

> So, while it is in that sort of state between about 25 down to maybe 10 vendors, there is a choice, there's a multiple different dimensions to it, and different ways of evaluating, how you write each vendor up. There is complexity in it, and therefore there is a game for us to play. (Interview, Gartner analyst, ET)

Another analyst similarly reports:

> It all depend on how you define that market. [...] When it settles down to a market where you have anywhere between, anywhere between 8 and maybe 25 vendors, something like that. And you can define a nice box around that. And there are competing relatively similarly. And there is a whole lot of discussion about what is a market. (Interview, Gartner Analyst, PM)

When analysts provide graphs that are within the range it means that their research potentially has value for the client. If it is outside the range then it is likely that it won't be read. But if it is inside the clients will find them useful. An analyst talks about the value of the MQ for readers:

> from the PR, corporate and marketing side they value them [the MQ] very highly. They know that they get a lot of hits. The list of the top ten most read documents

> on any given month, 4 or 5 of them will be [MQs]. They get long repeat hits which is good for Gartner. Readership is a key element to it. Retaining membership. It directly correlates with our retention of clients, so there is a financial incentive up to a point. (Interview, Gartner analyst, ET)

Not only did we find the search for the subitizing range to be a common feature across analyst firms, but most strikingly, that if the subitizing range failed to emerge 'naturally', then the analyst firms had various strategies to go out and create it. For instance, an analyst from a competitor firm to Gartner, and creator of the Forrester Wave, describes how: 'in general we try to be clutter cutting and we don't want more than 10 to 12 vendors cluttering up a Wave, right. We've seen quadrants where you have 40 and they are all blasted on there and your eyes start to glaze over. Our job is to *prioritize*' (meeting transcript). What does 'to prioritize' mean in this context? An analyst describes how these firms will intentionally leave large numbers of players *out* of the graphs in order to obtain what they perceive to be the correct range:

> Gartner's [MQ] will exclude people, exclude companies, organizations that don't have a certain size or don't have presence in more than X or Y countries, so it leaves the small guys out, or the local guys out and again that can be very misleading. Indeed, even if it has a local player in they may be very much dismissed. BT on the global stage will be very much overlooked in comparison with AT&T. (Interview, IDC analyst)

Creation of the subitizing range is far from neutral and can lead to contestation. We observed one meeting between analyst relations professionals working for IT vendors and a Forrester analyst, for instance, where a participant voiced his concerns in relation to the narrow perspective taken by those producing the matrices:

> I guess it is quite *arrogant* in some ways to define, to try and define the market based on the number of dots you can put on a graphic... Specifically, when you look at the number of hardware players. You can limit the Wave to 10. I am cool with that. When you look at business consulting it becomes, not only irrelevant, but almost risible in some ways. (Meeting transcript)

In Figure 4.4 we depict how there is a point of discontinuity between: (a) those graphs that were too simple, such that they were 'meaningless' for the client and thus in all likelihood wouldn't be read; (b) those where there were too many dots such that the client couldn't easily and (importantly) rapidly make sense of the situation; and (c) the situation where they had seemingly found the delicate balance between too much and too little information such that reading and making sense of the graph required neither extensive nor fleeting periods of time or effort. This takes us to the final empirical episode. How did the analysts come up with this format? Is it just an accident (or

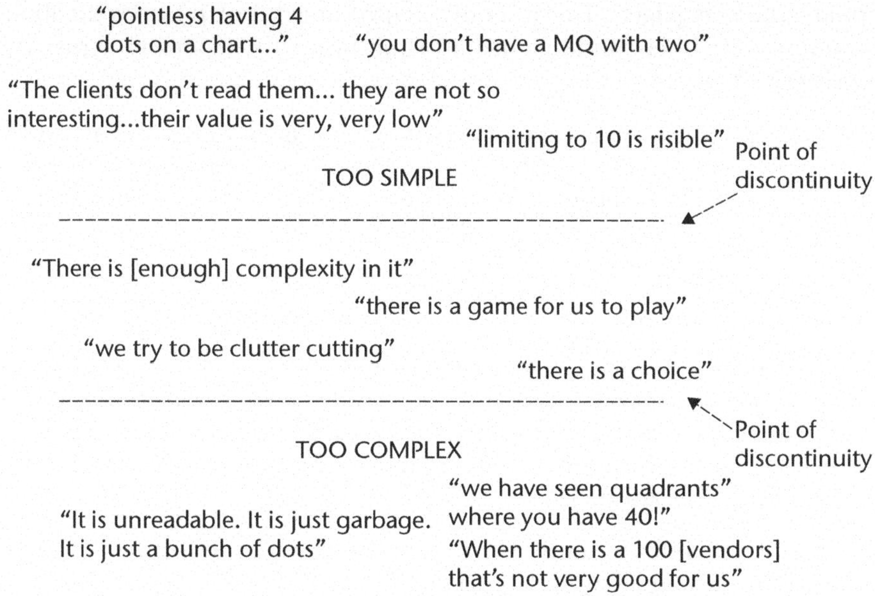

Figure 4.4. Gartner creates the subitizing range

'arrogance') or was there method in what they were doing? Moreover, what does the analysts' research process looks like?

Episode 3: Format not an Accident!

With this last episode we take a more historical lens to the rise of the matrix and subitizing range in this firm and across the industry. Our empirical material here mainly derives from interviews with Gartner's founder Gideon Gartner and from analysis of his blog. The temporal component of these graphs was a key feature discussed in previous episodes. We saw how graphs were designed with assumptions about how much time was required for readers to 'get' the picture. We continue this theme since timeliness was also an important component in how the MQ was constructed. There was a constant push within Gartner for analysts to be 'productive'. There was a correct *range* also for time spent in producing the graphs. To understand this, we first need to briefly look at the origins of the MQ.

When Gideon Gartner first entered the industry analysis business he found that all the existing analyst firms were producing and selling 'lengthy' research reports. These not only took, in his view, an inordinate amount of time for executives to read but also for the analysts to produce. His immediate reaction therefore, upon setting up Gartner, was to introduce an alternative format—the 'one pager'. This not only shaped how his own firm went about communicating their findings but also the norm for reporting across the industry:

> We had reports, but I decided to do very brief reports instead of long reports, which everybody was doing in those days, which is really getting into issues and perhaps some of the companies. I wanted the notes to be very brief so I designed a one-page format which everybody had to adhere to. (Interview, G. Gartner)

The key aspect of the 'research note' was its design. This was to encourage simplicity and (importantly) speed in reading and writing:

> designed to provide what I considered to be 'incremental' information, broken into user-friendly categories, while being sufficiently brief to be completed within 1–2 hours (which would lead to attractive analyst productivity). Of course, we produced medium-size reports as well, but the one-pagers were quite appreciated by our clients. (G.Gartner, blog)[2]

The MQ directly builds on these earlier moves when it was introduced internally within Gartner a few years later:

> around 1987/88 I... happened to introduce the 'stalking horse' graphic as one technique which our analysts could occasionally use when presenting at research meetings to support a conclusion. This initiative was meant to be for internal discussion only, because the method seemed an oversimplification (yet an interesting starting point for certain confrontations which would be challenging and educational at our meetings). (G. Gartner, blog)[3]

Within a short period of time the 'MQ feature grew to be a major deliverable' (G. Gartner, blog). Gideon Gartner's early concern was to maximize research productivity. He describes how in the initial days of the firm Gartner enjoyed low variable costs but suffered from high fixed costs. Therefore, not only did much work go into the production of the MQ, but there was also a push to bring down the effort required to create and publish each MQ. For instance, when asked to give us an estimate of how long the research process took to produce a MQ today, an analyst responded:

> An average analyst might do... about 330, 350 enquiries a year. So that is 300 conversations. And then face to face like we are doing here, that might be another 150, 200 conversations like that a year. So, 700 face to face conversations at between 20 minutes up to an hour. That is a lot of data in just one area. (Interview, Gartner analyst, ET)

Gideon Gartner described himself as 'neurotic' about the productivity of research staff (G. Gartner, blog). Any improvements in the productivity of analysts would therefore be significant. The skill required was the ability to 'find the right mix', 'getting it about right', 'nailing it'. In what follows one analyst tries to define the exact range of effort that takes to recognize a pattern:

> [You] could then have another 100 conversations, it won't change [what] you have learnt already. Somewhere between 10 and 15 [conversations] you have pretty much... as long as you have got the right people... *you have nailed it.* (Interview, Gartner analyst, ET)

Having the right people means finding the right mix between informants: user, vendor, and financial or academic. Getting in touch with the right mix of people gives analysis an 'element of truth', as mentioned below:

> at the heart of it there is a sort of *truth element* to it. In other words, [vendors] are lying to me and there is an assumption, I mean I was told when I started that I should get 70 per cent of my information from users, 20 per cent from vendors, and 10 per cent from financial or academic. That should be the kind of mix. And that is about right. And most of us trust what the users say to . (Interview, Gartner analyst, ET)

Interestingly, this 'subjective' form of research is criticized internally by the more quantitative Gartner researchers. In response, analysts point out that by being in constant interaction with market players, they are 'more on the button':

> our primary research guys are always very sarcastic about the way we do our research, this qualitative type research. Now we point out that we are always ahead of you, we are always *more on the button* about what is going on in our area. But we are doing it all through rather subjective enquiries. (Interview, Gartner analyst, ET)

To summarize this final section, what we show is the range of views on the research process behind the MQ. There were those (a) who thought it unnecessarily protracted and could be improved (e.g. speeded up). In the view of the founder of Gartner, for instance, analysts took too much time to produce the necessary picture. There were (b) those, by contrast, who that thought the exercise should be longer still and include research on even more actors. And (c) there was the situation where a seasoned analyst could recognize a pattern and put together a picture ('nail it') in a relatively short period of time.

Discussion

Our argument is that specific forms of action and processes of decision-making have become possible in the late twentieth century through the production and use of simple graphs. Scholars have taken a rather reductive lens to study the way these figurations have taken hold in business settings and have thus only partially captured their influence. 'Graphical representations', writes

Quattrone (2009, 109) 'are always so partial and simplified that they essentially contain very little; they have little truth in them; for, if it ever existed, it has been lost in the process of diagrammatic representation which has sacrificed details and context for the sake of clarity'. Quattrone argues that it is only through a process of simplification that graphs can 'effectively communicate and engage the user in a performative exercise' (2009, 109). We agree with this point but would argue that the success of the matrix is only in part about simplification. It is also about what we are calling 'subitization'. Subitizing is different from simplification because it is not just about sacrificing detail and reducing features for the sake of clarity and visual manageability. Those producing matrices can *increase* as well as decrease the information portrayed. Our findings resonate with the view of Lynch (1985, 43) who argues that visual displays do more than simplify because they also *add* features not found in the original knowledge. While Lynch addresses the 'device of the dot' in scientific settings, our argument wants to be specific about the amount of dots needed for a figuration to be meaningful in business settings (see also Pollock and D'Adderio 2012).

The work of subitization also involves the deployment of an alternative set of conventions and tools. To appreciate these points we need to supplement our understanding of these graphs for it turns out that even the most apparently simple graphs have their 'rules'. There is a specific rationalization processes associated with them. We have shown that those who produce matrices have dedicated and methodic practices for finding or 'creating' the delicate balance between too much and too little information.

Their aim is to produce figurations that encourage readings that are neither prolonged nor fleeting. Subitized business graphs are those which can be portrayed and communicated instantly (often in the time span necessary to point a camera—see Figure 4.2). Subitizers hope to identify a clear point (or 'range') to allow people to apprehend the situation straight away. Understanding subitized knowledge should not be time consuming or protracted; there should be no need to 'sit down and discuss in detail these charts', to paraphrase one informant. But, at the same time, just as these graphs shouldn't be overly complex, neither should they encourage a guess or conjecture. There should be enough information for the reader to understand the situation ('the battlefield', 'the landscape') and to be able to act with confidence as a result.

The notion of subitizing helps throw light on a number of connected issues related to the 'temporality of calculation'. What do we mean by the temporality of calculation? As Preda (2006, 757) has argued, once we accept that devices have agency, we have to treat them as having their own 'temporal structures'. This means they do not reproduce existing time structures but generate their own. Figurations that offer a complex picture will elicit a different response than those that offer a simple one. A matrix that presents

100 possible choices will differ from one that offers 25 or 4 for that matter. The graph that is 'cluttered' will be read differently from the one where the information has been 'prioritized'. This challenges the assumption—implicit in much of the writing about business graphs—that all figurations operate on a common textual plane or that there is a continuum from the complex to the simple.

In terms of how this chapter relates to the overall theme of the book, subitizing meets Lamont's call for further study of some of the 'constraints' placed on valuation practices. Subitizing is the study of how valuation practices are structured through what Lamont (2012) might call a 'technology of evaluation'. Matrices create or afford particular kinds of decision-making or decision-maker. The matrix, if designed in the subitizing range, can help modify the decision of the client. The agential significance of subitizing is in enabling predictable and conscribed business decision-making within and across heterogeneous contexts. It both transforms and at the same time frames the decision. How do buyers draw up shortlists when there are so many vendors and their products appear so similar? In this respect, the matrix plays a role. From the many possible options available it offers the buyer a ready solution—choose not between an infinite number but between these selected few! In the discussion above, we were struck by how precisely informants could identify this range (for the MQ is it is between 10 and 25 and the Forrester Wave between 10 and 12). These numbers are clearly not arbitrary. The selection of this range is, on the one hand, aimed at providing value to the client, because, to paraphrase Karpik (2010), the matrix is 'consumer oriented' and 'commercial'. It is also, on the other hand, created to provide value to the analyst firm. To quote from Karpik: it is 'committed to the conquest and the keeping of customers' (2010, 52).

Conclusion

The notion of subitizing draws on but also attempts to supplement Callon and Muniesa's (2005) definition of 'calculative agency'. Calculative agency is concerned with the creation of 'calculative spaces' whereas the notion of subitizing attempts to adds a more temporal dimension to this. Callon and Muniesa (2005, 1231) write: '[i]t is important to take the variety of such calculative spaces into consideration. An invoice, a grid, a factory, a trading screen, a trading room, a spreadsheet, a clearing-house, a computer memory, a shopping cart—all these spaces can be analysed as calculative spaces, but all will provide different forms of calculation.' We would add to this list the matrix and look to foreground the particular forms of calculation afforded by this device. For Callon and Muniesa (2005, 1238), the power of a calculation depends on the number of entities that can be portrayed and sorted in a single space: for them this is a 'long, yet finite list of diverse entities'. This contrasts with the matrix where the information to be included is clearly bounded to create immediate forms of sense-making. Whereas Callon and Muniesa (2005) are interested in what entities are included we focus on 'how much' information is required to foster a decision. What makes the matrix powerful is that an identifiable limit is drawn around what needs to be considered. This recognizable limit (the 'range') then acts as a shared coordination mechanism for the business community (Millo and MacKenzie 2009).

In his recent critique of the upsurge in interest in how economics performs the economy, Miller (2008) has argued that we need to be wary of assuming that all modes of calculation are a direct derivative of economics. He suggests that different disciplines, such as accounting and finance amongst other things, will constitute markets in different ways (though he doesn't say how exactly!). His point, of course, raises the question as to whether there are further forms of calculation—perhaps those that stem from business settings themselves—that we might need to consider. Indeed scholars have noted the distinctive, hybrid characteristics of the business domain and how it is influenced and constituted by lots of disciplines—not just economics or accounting but also, going back a century, engineering, psychology, and sociology (Khurana 2007). Indeed, Miller (2008, 59) argues, it is exactly the 'hybridization of practices' that occurs over time that shapes economic life. In this respect, this invites the conjecture as to whether the hybrid processes we have tried to capture here through the notion of subitization might feature as a mode of calculation that has evolved out of business and which continues to exert enormous influence in this domain today.

Notes

1. <http://wikibon.org/blog/new-gartner-magic-quadrant-signals-an-end-to-traditional-storage-arrays/>, accessed 15 August 2014.
2. <http://gideongartner.com/2010/04/gartner-innovation-during-its-formative-years/>, accessed 26 July 2014.
3. <http://gideongartner.com/2011/02/gartners-original-research-processes-part-2-including-mqs/>, accessed 26 July 2014.

References

Akrich, M. and B. Latour. 1992. 'A Summary of a Convenient Vocabulary for the Semiotics of Human and Nonhuman Assemblies'. In *Shaping Technology, Building Society: Studies in Sociotechnical Change*, ed. W. Bijker and J. Law. Cambridge, MA: MIT Press, 259–65.

Callon, M. (ed.). 1998. *The Laws of the Markets*. Oxford: Blackwell.

Callon, M. and F. Muniesa. 2005. 'Economic Markets as Calculative Collective Devices'. *Organization Studies* 26(8): 1229–50.

Callon, M., Y. Millo, and F. Muniesa (eds.). 2007. *Market Devices*. Oxford: Blackwell.

Cattel, J. M. 1886. 'The Time Taken Up By Cerebral Operations'. *Mind* 11: 377–92.

Coopmans, C. 2014. 'Visual Analytics as Artful Revelation'. In *Representation in Scientific Practice Revisited*, ed. C. Coopmans, J. Vertesi, M. E. Lynch, and S. Woolgar. Cambridge, MA: MIT Press, 37–60.

Dehaene, S. 2010. *Reading in the Brain*. New York: Penguin.

Espeland, W. and M. Stevens. 1998. 'Commensuration as a Social Process'. *Annual Review of Sociology* 24(1): 313–43.

Garfinkel, H. 1967. *Studies in Ethnomethodology*. Englewood Cliffs: Prentice-Hall.

Ghemawat, P. 2002. 'Competition and business Strategy in Historical Perspective'. *Business History Review* 76(1): 37–74.

Karpik L. 2010. *Valuing the Unique: The Economics of Singularity*. Princeton: Princeton University Press.

Kaufman, E. L., M. W. Lord, T. W. Reese, and J. Volkmann. 1949. 'The Discrimination of Visual Number'. *American Journal of Psychology* 62(4): 498–525.

Khurana, R. 2007. *From Higher Aims to Hired Hands: The Social Transformation of American Business Schools and the Unfulfilled Promise of Management as a Profession*. Princeton: Princeton University Press.

Lamont, M. 2012. 'Toward a Comparative Sociology of Valuation and Evaluation'. *Sociology* 38(1): 201–21.

Latour, B. 2005. *Reassembling the Social: An Introduction to Actor-Network-Theory*. Oxford: Oxford University Press.

Lissack, M. and K. A. Richardson. 2003. 'Models without Morals: Toward the Ethical Use of Business Models'. *Emergence* 5(2): 72–102.

Lowy, A. and P. Hood. 2011. *The Power of the 2x2 Matrix: Using 2x2 Thinking to Solve Business Problems and Make Better Decisions*. San Francisco: Jossey-Bass.

Lynch, M. 1985. 'Discipline and the Material Form of Images'. *Social Studies of Science* 15(1): 37–66.

MacKenzie, D. 2009. *Material Markets: How Economic Agents are Constructed*. Oxford: Oxford University Press.

Miller, P. 2008. 'Calculating Economic Life'. *Journal of Cultural Economy* 1(1): 51–64.

Miller, P. and T. O'Leary. 2007. 'Mediating Instruments and Making Markets: Capital Budgeting, Science and the Economy'. *Accounting, Organizations and Society* 32 (7–8): 701–34.

Millo, Y. and D. MacKenzie. 2009. 'The Usefulness of Inaccurate Models: Towards an Understanding of the Emergence of Financial Risk Management'. *Accounting, Organizations and Society* 34(5): 638–53.

Morrison, A. and R. Wensley. 1991. 'Boxing Up or Boxed In? A Short History of the Boston Consulting Group Share/Growth Matrix'. *Journal of Marketing Management* 7(2): 105–29.

Pels, D. 2003. *Unhastening Science: Autonomy and Reflexivity in the Social Theory of Knowledge*. Liverpool: Liverpool University Press.

Pollock, N. and R. Williams. 2009. 'The Sociology of a Market Analysis Tool: How Industry Analysts Sort Vendors and Organize Markets'. *Information and Organization* 19(2): 129–51.

Pollock, N. and R. Williams. 2010. 'The Business of Expectations: How Promissory Organizations Shape Technology & Innovation'. *Social Studies of Science* 40(4): 525–48.

Pollock, N. and L. D'Adderio. 2012. 'Give Me a Two-by-Two Matrix and I Will Create the Market: Rankings, Graphic Visualisations and Sociomateriality'. *Accounting, Organizations and Society* 37(8): 565–86.

Preda, A. 2006. 'Socio-Technical Agency in Financial Markets: The Case of the Stock Ticker'. *Social Studies of Science* 36(5): 753–82.

Quattrone, P. 2009. 'Books to be Practiced: Memory, the Power of the Visual, and the Success of Accounting'. *Accounting, Organizations and Society* 34(1): 85–118.

Trick, L. M. and Z. W. Pylyshyn. 1994. 'Why are Small and Large Numbers Enumerated Differently? A Limited-Capacity Preattentive Stage in Vision'. *Psychological Review* 101(1): 80–102.

Violino, B. and R. Levin. 1997. 'Analyzing the Analysts'. *Information Week* (17 November): 38–56.

5

Capitalization Devices

Business Models and the Renewal of Markets

Liliana Doganova and Fabian Muniesa

Introduction

Robert is an academic entrepreneur.[1] During his PhD at a French public research organization specialized in computer science, he took part in the development of a technology based upon an algorithm that allows processing data incoming from vehicles in order to compute predicted travel times. He would like now to bring this technology to the market. He has just founded a start-up company with a senior researcher from his research team. The technology seems to be working well. And the travel times that it produces can be put to many uses—a bit like the weather forecast, Robert explains. There are applications for individual drivers who wish to estimate their travel time, but also for business clients, such as truck fleet managers, who wish to optimize their logistics. But the entrepreneurs are having a hard time convincing venture capitalists to invest in their start-up: the whole problem, Robert laments, 'is about the business model of this thing'.[2]

What is this 'problem', and how does 'the business model' provide a solution to it? We could start by saying that the problem is to make the travel times computing technology *valuable*. But there are many ways in which something may be made valuable (Stark 2009; Aspers and Beckert 2011; Berthoin Antal et al. 2015). That may be the case, for example, when a technology is shown to have an application, or, to put it in marketing terms, to meet the unsatisfied needs of a set of users. In this respect, Robert's technology definitely is valuable, and all the more so as it has many applications. But the existence of applications is not enough to solve this 'problem' that the entrepreneurs seem to be struggling with. There is something else at stake here, another form of valuation going on. To grasp it, we need to move beyond the entrepreneurs' viewpoint and look at the investors whom they are trying to convince.

Bernard is a venture capitalist. Meeting entrepreneurs like Robert and their technologies with numerous and certainly valuable applications is his daily routine. But applications are not what he is looking for. He recalls the case of one of his most successful investments. The start-up's founders contacted him, praising the merits of the software they had developed—a technology that large organizations, ranging from banks through insurance companies to hospitals, could use in order to search within their voluminous dispersed databases. At first, the venture capitalists said no 'because selling software tools to people is both difficult and of little ambition', adding with a bit of dismay that 'there are tons of people who invent software tools every morning' and that 'it does not mean that you can make a firm with that'. Their argument was also about the figures: 'We may be able to sell it a first time for 100,000 euros, a second time for 50,000, a third time for 10,000, and then we will have a firm that will make a turnover of one million over twenty years'.

The advice Bernard gave to this start-up was to go for a 'new business model': use their technology to make a search engine that would allow internet users to find the best price for a product and hence allow online merchants to attract these willing-to-buy customers in exchange for a small contribution paid to the search engine for each relevant click. The start-up followed the advice, and Bernard's venture capital firm made the investment. A few years later, the search engine proudly showed millions of clicking and buying users and was sold to an internet giant for no less than 475 million euros.

What we are interested in here is not a Google-like fabulous success story, but the kind of *problem* that the *new business model* allowed to solve. That problem, we argue, lies in transforming a technology into an *asset* that has the power to generate a steady stream of future cash flows, that is, into *capital*. What is at stake here is a peculiar way of making things valuable. The chapter discusses how the business model instruments such a mode of valuation, which we call *capitalization*. In order to do so, we characterize the particular kind of *encounter* that this mode of valuation requires between someone like Robert and someone like Bernard, that is, an entrepreneur and an investor.

The chapter proceeds as follows. We start by documenting the rise of business models, emphasizing their focus on the notion of value and the controversies that they have triggered among management scholars. The chapter then introduces recent approaches to business models, which shed light on the performative role that they can play, and explains the approach adopted here, which examines business models as *valuation devices* (Doganova 2011) and, more narrowly, as *capitalization devices*. An empirical section follows which investigates how business models work by focusing on two moments of business model innovation related to the birth of new industries (internet and biotechnology). The chapter concludes on capitalization as a singular mode of valuation instrumented by business models.

The Rise of Business Models

The business model is a recent invention. Ghaziani and Ventresca (2005) trace its first appearances back to the mid-1970s. The term then referred to computer-based models of business practices. Concomitantly to the advent of the 'Digital Economy', the mid-1990s marked a strong shift in the use of business models. In the ABI Inform database which the authors searched, the incidence of the term grew from less than ten articles per year until the early 1990s, to 600 articles in 2000. A more recent study using the EBSCO host database confirms this trend, with the number of publications reaching more than 1,000 per year in 2010 (Zott et al. 2011).

The rise in numbers, Ghaziani and Ventresca (2005) argue, goes hand in hand with a shift in the 'frames' to which the keyword 'business model' has been associated. Within its original frame (which the authors call 'computer/systems modelling'), the business model was a software model of an existing business, a simplified representation of an already functioning organization—similar to the scale model of a plane for example. Since the mid-1990s, the predominant frame of business models has been that of 'value creation', which the authors illustrate with the following excerpt from an article published in the *Journal of Business Strategy* in 2000: 'The key to reconfiguring business models for the knowledge economy lies in understanding the new currencies of value' (Ghaziani and Ventresca 2005, 538, citing abstract from Allee 2000). The change is blatant: business models no longer deal with depicting existing practices and organizations, but with finding new sources of 'value'. In a similar vein, Zott et al. (2011) observe the centrality of the notion of value in current conceptualizations of the business model, encompassing both the 'creation' and the 'capture' of value.

Ghaziani and Ventresca (2005) analyse the rise in numbers and the shift in frames as an instance of 'cultural change'. We argue that the change in question reaches beyond the domain of ideologies and beliefs, for the business model is not only a 'keyword' (or merely a 'buzzword', as some would say): it is a device that instruments new forms of valuation, to the advent of which its expansion has contributed. A clear sign of the magnitude of change is the virulent reaction that the rise of business models triggered among strategy scholars. For example, Michael Porter—an eminent strategy scholar, who has also been an outspoken critic of business models—wrote:

> Instead of talking in terms of strategy and competitive advantage, dot-coms and other Internet players talk about 'business models'. This seemingly innocuous shift in terminology speaks volumes. The definition of a business model is murky at best. Most often, it seems to refer to a loose conception of how a company does business and generates revenue. [...] The business model approach to management becomes an invitation for faulty thinking and self-delusion. (Porter 2001, 72–3)

The quote from Porter captures quite well the main lines of criticism addressed to the business model in the management literature. They can be summed up into three key problems: the problem of definition, the problem of reference, and the problem of (in/dis)utility. First, scholars have pointed out, the business model is *untruthful to itself*, because it does not have a stable definition. It remains, as Porter puts it, 'murky at best', in spite of academics' and practitioners' continuous attempts to find the essence of the business model and fix it in a correct and clear definition. Second, the business model is *untruthful to its external reference*, that is, the enterprise that it is supposed to describe. It is no more than a 'loose conception of how a company does business'. It fails to fulfil its predictions—some have even denounced it as serving the purposive concealment of charlatan-entrepreneurs' real intentions. Third, the business model is not *useful*. Modelling, several studies have shown, does not help entrepreneurs in their planning endeavours, does not improve the performance of new ventures, and even harms it, by inducing managers into what Porter describes as 'faulty thinking and self-delusion'.

The harsh criticism that business models have received in the academic literature stands in sharp contrast to their widespread use by practitioners. Recent studies have suggested that this discrepancy may be due to the failure of prevalent theoretical approaches to account for what business models are and what they do (Doganova and Eyquem-Renault 2009; Baden-Fuller and Morgan 2010; Perkmann and Spicer 2010), a failure due to the essentialist or functionalist perspectives that these approaches tend to adopt. An essentialist perspective searches for the essence of the business model, trying to provide a clear, precise, unambiguous definition of an object that seems to inevitably escape such attempts. A functionalist perspective assigns a presupposed function to the business model and tries to assess its efficiency accordingly. In so doing, prevalent theoretical approaches make two strong assumptions. The first is that the lack of a stable definition impedes the working of business models. The second is that the function of business models, known a priori, is to describe, faithfully represent, or accurately predict the characteristics of the external entity—a present or future enterprise—to which it refers.

However, as demonstrated elsewhere (Doganova and Eyquem-Renault 2009; Eyquem-Renault 2011), it is precisely the plasticity of the business model—its ability to take on different shapes and meanings—which enables it to circulate among various actors (entrepreneurs, investors, customers, technology partners, and so forth), act as a boundary object (Star and Griesemer 1989), and instrument collective exploration activities (Doganova 2013). The narratives and numbers of which it is made do not merely depict an external entity; they are addressed to a public which they attempt to enrol. Rather than as a description, the business model thus functions as a *demonstration*—an exercise 'situated on the crossroads of a probationary approach [...] and of ostentatious conduct' (Rosental 2007, 35). This suggests that the usefulness of business models does not lie in their ability to accurately represent the firm, but in their ability to circulate and enrol allies. Such an approach to business models shifts attention from their representational efficiency to the performative role that they might play in the construction of new businesses and markets.

Performativity and Valuation Devices

While there are different, and sometimes contradictory, dimensions of the idea of performativity (Muniesa 2014), three of them seem particularly relevant for business models. The first one has to do with *performance*. As the analogy with demonstrations suggests, the business model is not only a statement, but an act—an act of exhibiting something, presenting it to an audience, putting it on stage. The something in question may be a PowerPoint presentation projected at a start-up competition, a business plan submitted to investors, or the entrepreneur herself making her 'pitch' in front of someone to convince. In this respect, business models' most salient working mode is that of 'narratives that convince' (Perkmann and Spicer 2010).

Imagine Bill Gross, the founder of GoTo.com, speaking at a TED conference in 1998 about the idea of a web search engine that would rank results not according to their relevance but according to the price paid for them—an idea that gave rise to the 'sponsored search' or 'pay per click' business model which later made Google's commercial success (Battelle 2005; Levy 2011). Gross had to counter numerous objections coming from the audience, reminding his public about the Yellow Pages, where those who pay for the largest insert get the most calls, and underlining the transparency of the system he envisaged, which would display the prices that advertisers were willing to pay for each click. As noted by Stark and Paravel (2008) in their discussion of PowerPoint presentations, public demonstrations may be a perilous exercise, for they nurture counter-demonstrations. This is something that many entrepreneurs experience, as the publics whom they seek to enrol take hold of their model, and start criticizing and reshaping it.

This brings us to a second dimension of business models' performativity, which has to do with them acting as 'scale models'—small representations of a future enterprise that can be played with, as children play with a train model for example, but also, and more importantly, experimented with, as when developers gather around the prototype of a new product to assess its technical and market feasibility (Wheelwright and Clark 1992), when economists manipulate the models they have built to inquire into them (Morgan 2012), or when architects scale models up and down to get to know the buildings they are designing and gradually bring them into existence (Yaneva 2005). Comparing business models to the mathematical models used in economics and to the model organisms used in biology, Baden-Fuller and Morgan (2010) emphasize a central quality of models: they are objects that can be manipulated, experimented with. As such, business models can be used to produce knowledge about existing businesses (with exemplar cases like McDonald's or Dell being taught and discussed over and over again), change existing organizations (see, for example, Sosna et al. 2010), or build new ventures.

It is certainly in this latter case, when business models are used to build new ventures, that their performative role as scale models that can be manipulated and circulated is the most salient. The business model then describes a future enterprise—states what its activities will be, what customers it will serve and what alliances it will establish, etc.—and, in so doing, it helps bring this future enterprise into existence, because it helps enrol necessary partners, such as investors (Doganova and Eyquem-Renault, 2009). In other words, as a scale model, the business model is performative insofar it describes a set of relationships and, by circulating, it gradually builds the relationships it has postulated. The following quote from Steve Blank, a Silicon Valley entrepreneurship practitioner and author, illustrates the business model as a tool that draws links and makes links:

> A business model is actually a single slide. That's all it is. It's a single slide, a diagram, that shows all of the flows between your company and your customers. It's a single PowerPoint slide that you could put up and say: 'Here's our business model'. And in that one slide you have your material costs, you have your distribution channel, you have your customer acquisition cost. You have everything: your revenue, your expenses. And someone looking at that goes: 'I get it. I disagree with this line and with this line and with this line, but I get it.' (Transcribed from video footage of Cleantech Open 2009)[3]

Business models have the capacity to travel—not only within the entrepreneurial collective that emerges as a new venture is built, but also in the broader time and space of industries and management science. Baden-Fuller and Morgan (2010) analyse business models as 'role models', maintained by management scholars' labelling and classifying activities, and as 'recipes', lying between general principles and exact templates. As such, business models lend themselves to replication, and this is where a third dimension of their performativity is to be found. Business models that have proved to 'work' in the past are reproduced in press articles, textbooks, and the practitioners' and academic literature. They are working examples that entrepreneurs can copy and that investors can use as benchmarks to assess the propositions submitted to them. By associating themselves with a particular *type* and placing themselves in a particular category, firms gain legitimacy (Perkmann and Spicer 2010). They also spare modelling efforts.

Business models are thus performative in (at least) three ways: as performances, when the model is exhibited and put on stage; as scale models, which draw and build relationships, and hence help bring into existence that which they purport to describe; as role models, that are followed and imitated by new ventures. One question remains though: if business models are performative, what do they perform? That is, what worlds do they carry? And what do the new ventures that are built with them look like? We would like to address these questions by taking on board the observation of Ghaziani and Ventresca (2005) and Zott et al. (2011) that business models are intimately associated with the notion of value, and terms such as 'value creation' and 'value capture'. The very notion of 'value creation' (i.e. the generation of revenue) appears indeed as a crucial marker of the investment imagination (Ortiz 2013, 2014) of the business model. So what kind of value is this valuation device meant to prompt, and what difference does this make?

Business Models for the Generation of New Markets

Google

It is no coincidence that the rise of business models was concomitant to that of the digital economy. A key challenge that the internet entrepreneurs of the 1990s were facing was how to generate revenues for their start-ups, given that services were expected to be provided for free. Take Google, for example (see Battelle 2005; Levy 2011). We often think of the PageRank algorithm as Google's greatest invention. Indeed, the technology that the start-up's founders developed in the late 1990s while studying at Stanford represented a dramatic improvement in comparison with existing search engines, e.g. AltaVista. The latter ordered webpages by reading their content and relying on keywords. Taking inspiration from the citation mechanism in the academic literature, the PageRank algorithm ordered webpages according to the number of links pointing at them, which greatly enhanced the relevance of search results. While Google's technology attracted users, investors, and public attention almost immediately, it took the start-up two years to find a business model for its search engine. The invention of this business model—known as AdWords at Google, 'pay per click', or 'sponsored search'—was no less important for the development of the company than the PageRank algorithm.

The business model that made Google's success was invented in 1998 by a start-up called GoTo.com (later renamed Overture). At that time, the predominant business model in the industry followed classic advertising methods. Internet start-ups provided their users with free services and made money (if they did) by displaying ads on their websites—ads that visitors were faced with and on which they were likely to click if interested. The key metric here was that of traffic: the more traffic a website (e.g. Yahoo's portal) had, the higher price it could require from advertisers willing to display themselves on the website in the hope to redirect some of the traffic that it drew onto their own websites. The intuition of GoTo.com was the following: it was not only traffic—the numbers of visitors coming to a website—that had value, but the ways in which these visitors were behaving, and more precisely the words that they were typing. These words had potentially commercial value, for they expressed the—potentially buying—intentions of the visitor. To put it in marketing terms, visitors with a 'purchase intention' had much greater value for the online merchants to which they could be matched, and a lower 'cost of acquisition' than that incurred by placing an ad in front of numerous but undifferentiated internet users who were most likely uninterested, and sometime even irritated, by the ads that they were forced to see.

How can value be put on the words typed by a visitor in a search engine? GoTo.com's idea was to sell these words to online merchants. How can a price be put on them? GoTo.com made online merchants bid for the keywords they wanted to be associated with, and was paid for every click that led a visitor from its search engine to a merchant's website—hence the name 'pay per click' for this business model. The idea was controversial: instead of ranking webpages according to their content, as search engines did at that time, or according to the links that pointed at them, as Google did, GoTo.com was ranking webpages according to the price that those who produced them were willing to pay. The most 'relevant' results were neither the most similar in terms of content, nor the most popular on the web, but the ones that led to the highest bidder. And yet, it worked: by 1999, GoTo.com had attracted thousands of merchants and millions of searches. Two years later, Google introduced AdWords, and started displaying the results of 'sponsored' search (i.e. results displayed because merchants had paid to be associated with a given keyword) next to those brought about by the 'natural' search instrumented by the PageRank algorithm. AdWords sold keywords through a combination of bidding and pay per click—an imitation for which it was sued by GoTo.com—while adding its own flavour in the ranking of results by taking into account the popularity of commercial links (i.e. the numbers of times they had been clicked on) when ordering them.

In his reflections on the performativity of networks, Healy (2011) analyses Google's PageRank algorithm as perfomative, insofar as it was built upon a network-based theory of relevance where citations indicate the relative importance of an object (be it an academic article or a webpage); assumed a certain network structure where some nodes are more important than others for they are more central, and at the same time helped reproduce this structure by reinforcing the centrality of the webpages that it ranked highest; was adopted by many internet users in their practice and understanding of what web search is; and was manipulated by some internet websites that played on the algorithm's assumptions to improve their ranking (giving rise to a new industry called 'search engine optimization'). This line of analysis may be extended to the other major invention of Google. AdWords, and the sponsored search/pay per click business model that it copied and popularized, helped establish an internet market whose survival was still highly uncertain in the late 1990s and seriously threatened by the 2000 crash. It served as a 'role model' for new start-ups entering the market, and for the investors who funded them, both copying a template that had proved its economic viability. By allowing to target potential customers and hence to decrease their 'cost of acquisition', it also unleashed markets for many small online shops which could not afford to buy advertising space on central internet locations such as the Yahoo portal.

If the PageRank algorithm embeds citation-based definitions of relevance and network imageries, the AdWords business model carries a peculiar theory of valuation. Instead of lying in present size (e.g. the overall number of visitors that an online portal reports, as indicated by 'traffic' or 'audience' metrics), here value is derived from the *future flow* of singular transactions, each of which consists in a click that a particular user, driven by a 'purchase intention', makes to reach a certain product and, thereby, the merchant who happens to offer that product and rank well. In such a model, valuation both occurs in 'real time'—the time of users clicking on links and merchants bidding for keywords—and deploys in the future, as the search engine gets a grasp on the transactions to come and 'monetizes' them. The model thus enables both the creation of economic value, by turning the words that someone types in a search engine into a commodity that can be sold and bid for, and the capture of the value thus created, by means of a complex technology of tracing clicks and visualizing transactions.

Genentech

In his study of the 'science business' of biotech, Pisano (2006b) identifies the birth of the biotechnology industry with the founding of Genentech, the first biotechnology start-up. Genentech was founded by scientist Herbert Boyer and venture capitalist Robert Swanson in 1976. Three years earlier, Boyer and colleagues had introduced a new technique of genetic engineering called recombinant DNA (rDNA). The technique was a breakthrough because it enabled producing therapeutic proteins, such as insulin (until then, proteins could not be synthesized through traditional chemical methods because of their large size; a few proteins could be obtained from natural sources, such as pig pancreases for insulin). Swanson, the story goes, heard about this and contacted several scientists, among whom Boyer, who agreed to talk to him for ten minutes. At the end of a three-hour meeting, the two decided to create a firm that would exploit the possibilities offered by recombinant DNA in view of developing new drugs, namely insulin.

Drug development is a very lengthy, costly, and uncertain process. While Google's founders could put together the first demo of their search engine with materials at hand, Genentech would have needed years of time and millions of investment to master the rDNA technique and go through the phases of discovering, developing, and commercializing a new drug. As noted by Pisano, the pharmaceutical industry had huge barriers to entry, and had not seen any successful entries since 1944. As in the case of Google, the innovation that Genentech made was twofold: not only did it introduce a new technology for drug development, but it also invented a new business model that was then copied and adapted by the hundreds of biotech start-ups founded in its wake. It gave rise to an industry that, for thirty years, has attracted more than $300 billion in capital (Pisano 2006a). What was that business model?

The model proposed by Genentech relied on alliances drawn with universities, venture capital firms, and incumbent pharmaceutical companies. The biotech start-up would focus on research, in collaboration with universities. In the case of Genentech, Boyer retained his position at the university and only consulted for the company he had co-founded; the company began life as a 'virtual enterprise' with no labs and research conducted through contracts with universities. In the absence of revenues, the start-up's research would be funded by venture capital for a few years. At a certain stage of the drug development process, the start-up would enter into an R&D (research and development) partnership with a large pharmaceutical company that would fund the remaining development of the drug in exchange of the rights to commercialize it. Thus, Genentech and Eli Lilly signed an agreement for recombinant insulin in 1978 (the resulting drug, Humulin, was the first approved biotechnology drug). For Pisano (2006b, 85–6), this agreement pioneered 'an entirely new business model for entrants into the pharmaceutical industry'; it was 'a critical business innovation' which 'created a template' and 'provided a proof of feasibility of R&D collaboration as a mode of funding'.

The invention of this business model was critical for the emergence of the biotechnology market—a market in which promises of future drugs are being bought and sold. It enabled the transformation of scientific or technological entities—such as recombinant DNA in the case of Genentech, a new molecule, or knowledge about a biological mechanism of action—into economically valuable assets that have the capacity to generate streams of future cash flows. The profile of this stream is quite different from the one that we examined above: instead of the series of almost continuous but very small amounts of money generated by the pay per click model, only a few inflows, but of a high magnitude, occur here. Typically, a start-up would raise several rounds of venture capital investment; then, when establishing a partnership with a pharmaceutical company, receive research funding and milestone payments on different stages of drug development, as well as royalties if a drug reaches the market; finally, sell itself to the capital markets or to a larger company, with the money going back to the start-up's founders and investors. For example, Genentech was sold to Roche in 2009 for 43 billion dollars. This, of course, is quite an exceptional case in the history of the biotechnology market. Still, the amounts of money that flow between start-ups, investors, and pharmaceutical companies are often counted in millions of dollars. A significant portion of these flows end up sinking, as the probabilities that a development succeeds and a new drug reaches the market are very small, and the chances that a start-up continues attracting the funding it needs until it finds a buyer for its products or for itself are not high.

While Genentech's business model was copied by many start-ups entering the biotechnology market that emerged from it, the development of the industry gave rise to new business models (Mangematin et al. 2003 ; DiVito 2012). Nevertheless, this model left an enduring imprint, serving not only as a template, but also as a foundational myth for the biotechnology community whose members still regularly evoke that 1976 meeting between a Nobel prize-winning scientist and a visionary venture capitalist (Pina Stranger 2011). It epitomizes the surprising capacity of business models to orchestrate encounters and, in so doing, to transform a priori non-economic entities (such as a genetic engineering technology) into assets that generate streams of future revenues, that is, into capital.

Business Models and the Crafts of Capitalization

The business model is a device that performs a singular mode of valuation through which a variety of things—keywords, online behaviour, a genetic engineering technology—are transformed into 'assets' that have the power to generate streams of future revenues. Valuation revolves around this *asset-becoming* process: a process through which something becomes an object of investment and, therefore, an object that is considered primarily from the angle of capitalization, that is, as a vehicle for return on investment. In other words, the business model makes things valuable by capitalizing them. The device carries its own theory of valuation, so to say. And this embedded theory is that value does not come from just considering things as objects you can buy and sell in a market. It comes from considering the thing from the viewpoint of its 'earning power' (Muniesa 2011, 2014, 104 ; Doganova 2014), that is, in its capacity to ensure a stable stream of future revenues to the investor. It is in this very particular sense, we claim, that the object of a business model *becomes business*.

The cases of Google and Genentech stand as authoritative exemplars of the powers of business models to create new markets, new business opportunities, and new economic realities. They also illustrate two critical traits of the configuration a capitalization device sets in motion. Which are those? We refer, first, to the orchestration of a scene in which an entrepreneur and an investor encounter and stimulate each other and, second, to the resolution of this encounter through the actualization of a future revenue in the form of discounted value.

Let us focus on the first trait: that of the role of the business model in propelling an *encounter* between an entrepreneurial venture and a capitalistic investment. The business model stands, primarily, as a proposition involving two *dramatis personae*: the entrepreneur, who delivers the 'value' proposition, and the investor, who receives and assesses it. It does not matter if those two anthropomorphic actors correspond in reality to employees in bureaucratic organizations (e.g. a firm, a bank). What counts is their impersonation in an actual physical encounter between two characters: two persons, or rather personalities, that in the case of Genentech, for example, achieve an almost legendary status. The choreography of the historical meeting between Boyer and Swanson has been told and remembered again and again. A quick net search for images of the encounter provides astonishing evidence of the iconic, near-mythical character of this event.[4] And this is not a detail of folklore. The actual event of the encounter is a crucial step in the valuation configuration. The business model is rehearsed and presented. It is a demonstration of value, an exercising of the valuating self in which the entrepreneur and the investor need to simulate each other in order to stimulate each other (Muniesa 2011, 28), the purpose being the attainment of a mutually beneficial state of capitalization.

We talk about 'orchestration' and 'choreography' because the configuration of these types of business model encounters does actually require the establishment of a whole industry of business *matching, pairing*, and *partnering* (Doganova 2012). In the biotech industry, consultant firms and dedicated service providers specialize in the construction, maintenance, and commercialization of databases that operate as the informational ferment for the pairing of start-ups and venture capitalists. Other firms provide this industry with a suite of 'partnering conferences' that have become requisite hubs for the achievement of capitalization encounters.

Once this encounter has been set up and figured, there enters the second noteworthy trait of the business model considered as a capitalization device: that of shifting valuation from present products to future relationships. 'Future' is indeed the word that most evidently resonates in the proposition that the entrepreneur addresses to the investor, and in what the latter asks to hear. The investor, the motto goes, does not look at what the start-up is and has got in the present, but at what it can become in the future. The business model rarely goes very deep into the nitty-gritty of the underlying technology; making sense of the business model is less about assessing the technical verisimilitude of a technology than about envisioning the concatenation of prospective business links. In this respect, the operation instrumented by the business model consists in detaching value from objects in the present and attaching it to connections in the future. This observation resonates with McGrath's (2010) analysis of business model thinking as a shift away from classic strategy paradigms, which place value in organizations' present positions or resources—as in Porter's five-forces model or in the resource-based view of the firm.

It is not surprising that business models gained prominence with the 'internet revolution', as a major concern then was to transform technologies that were obviously valuable to their users (e.g. a search algorithm) into technologies that were also valuable to investors, for they could be capitalized upon. Google 'had value' because words typed by users in search queries could be thought of as 'having value'—value for users, but also for Google and for Google's financiers. But, as this value becomes prospective, a number of precautions apply in order to protect and reward the investor in time. As a capitalization device, the business model is hence entwined with *discount* methodologies in capital investment (Doganova 2011, 2014). The enormous money flows that Google's AdWords business narrative entailed were not a reflection of the actual price of keywords in a spot market, but the very outcome of this compound of capitalization.

Conclusion

It is emblematic that the study of business models in the management literature increasingly focuses on the issue of business model innovation (Chesbrough 2010), and the invention of 'social business models' in particular

(Thompson and MacMillan 2010; Yunus et al. 2010). Envisaging the business model as a device for capitalization—whose valuation principle consists in transforming things into future flows of revenue, by detaching value from present objects and attaching it to future relationships—helps us understand why it developed first within the contexts of the biotech and internet business 'revolutions', and how it managed to move beyond these particular settings to incorporate other valuation themes, such as social entrepreneurship.

This capacity of business models to *colonize* not only the future, but also spheres of activity which had hitherto remained out of the scope of capitalization reveals them as a particularly efficient instrument within the trend of what Leyshon and Thrift (2007) have called the 'capitalization of almost everything'. Financial capitalism, they argue, 'is dependent on the constant searching out, or construction of, new asset streams' (Leyshon and Thrift 2007, 98). Such kinds of analyses usually concentrate on the financial arena proper, i.e. on processes of securitization, speculation, and financialization. But, as instances of the wider problem of the logic of *the investor*, they meet our observations on business models as performative instruments for the production of 'asset streams'. The realities explored here thus fall within the scope of what Horacio Ortiz has aptly called 'the limits of financial imagination' (Ortiz 2011, 2014).

Should this be a source of concern? The performative capacities of business models, and the key role they play in the financing of innovation, can of course be praised for their contribution to the augmentation and improvement of economic reality (and of society at large)—although one can rightly ask whether this means the obliteration or not of other ways in which collective decisions about the improvement of economic reality could or should be taken (Ortiz 2014, 46). We do not explore this question further here. This chapter is, first and foremost, an attempt at signalling the remarkable features of the business model considered as an instrument for 'making things valuable'.

An instrument for 'making things valuable', the business model is also an instrument for 'making things'. Recall Bernard's story evoked in the introduction of this chapter: the venture capitalist shaped the business model of the start-up turning it from a software provider into a web search engine. The enrolment of investors, conditioned upon the application of business models that have the capacity to generate steady streams of future revenues, thus has consequences for the characteristics of the products and services that populate markets. Entrepreneurs profile their technologies for capitalization, in anticipation, or as a consequence, of the investor's gaze. Venture capitalists, faced with a range of investment proposals from which they need to pick one or two, select the technologies that they will help move to the market. This is both complicated and consequential. It is complicated, but it becomes simpler when technologies become comparable once they have been pushed through the mechanism of the business model and transformed into streams of cash flows which can then be capitalized and summed up to a unique number: e.g. the investment's net present value or its rate of return. This (and here comes the consequentiality) inevitably gives priority to projects that score highest. As capitalization devices, thus, business models certainly propel innovation—although they do not do it in a very innovative way.

Notes

1. The work on which this chapter is based was partly supported by the European Research Council (ERC Starting Grant 263529). We thank Horacio Ortiz, Alvaro Pina-Stranger, Martin Kornberger, Lise Justesen, Anders Koed-Madsen, and Jan Mouritsen for comments and suggestions on an earlier draft. We also thank participants in the workshop 'Unpacking performativity processes in organizations' in May 2014 at MINES ParisTech and in the symposium 'Theories of performativity and the performativity of theories' at the Academy of Management Meeting in Philadelphia, where this chapter was presented.
2. The illustrations in the introduction are taken from Doganova (2012). The quotes are excerpts from the author's interviews with Robert and Bernard (for confidentiality reasons, these are fictitious names).
3. Steve Blank's presentation at the 2009 edition of the Cleantech Open (an important business fair) is available online from YouTube: <http://www.youtube.com/watch?v=CSDXxkSLBzw>, accessed 20 June 2014.
4. An iconic reportage is available from the website of the Life Science Foundation: <http://www.lifesciencesfoundation.org/events-Genentech_Inc.html>, accessed 20 June 2014.

References

Allee, V. 2000. 'Reconfiguring the Value Network'. *Journal of Business Strategy* 21(4): 36–9.

Aspers, P. and J. Beckert (eds.). 2011. *The Worth of Goods: Valuation and Pricing in Markets*. Oxford: Oxford University Press.

Baden-Fuller, C. and M. S. Morgan. 2010. 'Business Models as Models'. *Long Range Planning* 43(2–3): 156–71.

Battelle, J. 2005. *The Search: How Google and Its Rivals Rewrote the Rules of Business and Transformed Our Culture*. New York: Penguin.

Berthoin Antal, A., M. Hutter, and D. Stark (eds.). 2015. *Moments of Valuation: Exploring Sites of Dissonance*. Oxford: Oxford University Press.

Chesbrough, H. 2010. 'Business Model Innovation: Opportunities and Barriers'. *Long Range Planning* 43(2–3): 354–63.

DiVito, L. 2012. 'Institutional Entrepreneurship in Constructing Alternative Paths: A Comparison of Biotech Hybrids'. *Research Policy* 41(5): 884–96.

Doganova, L. 2011. 'Necessarily Untrue: On the Use of the Discounted Cash Flow Formula in Valuation of Exploratory Projects'. Paper presented at the 7th Critical Management Studies Conference, Naples, Italy.

Doganova, L. 2012. *Valoriser la science. Les partenariats des start-ups technologiques*. Paris: Presses des Mines.

Doganova, L. 2013. 'Transfer and Exploration: Two Models of Science–Industry Intermediation'. *Science and Public Policy* 40(4): 442–52.

Doganova, L. 2014. 'Décompter le futur. La formule des flux actualisés et le manager-investisseur'. *Sociétés Contemporaines* 93: 67–87.

Doganova, L. and M. Eyquem-Renault. 2009. 'What Do Business Models Do? Innovation Devices in Technology Entrepreneurship'. *Research Policy* 38(10): 1559–70.

Eyquem-Renault, M. 2011. 'Analyse pragmatique du business model et performations de marché dans l'entrepreneuriat technologique'. PhD, Ecole des Mines de Paris.

Ghaziani, A. and M. Ventresca. 2005. 'Keywords and Cultural Change: Frame Analysis of Business Model Public Talk, 1975–2000'. *Sociological Forum* 20(4): 523–59.

Healy, K. 2011. 'The Performativity of Networks'. Working paper.

Levy, S. 2011. *In The Plex: How Google Thinks, Works, and Shapes Our Lives*. New York: Simon & Schuster.

Leyshon, A. and N. Thrift. 2007. 'The Capitalization of Almost Everything: The Future of Finance and Capitalism'. *Theory, Culture & Society* 24(7–8): 97–115.

McGrath, R. G. 2010. 'Business Models: A Discovery Driven Approach'. *Long Range Planning* 43(2–3): 247–61.

Mangematin, V., S. Lemarié, J.-P. Boissin, D. Catherine, F. Corolleur, R. Coronini, and M. Trommetter. 2003. 'Development of SMEs and Heterogeneity of Trajectories: The Case of Biotechnology in France'. *Research Policy* 32(4): 621–38.

Morgan, M. S. 2012. *The World in the Model: How Economists Work and Think*. Cambridge: Cambridge University Press.

Muniesa, F. 2011. 'A Flank Movement in the Understanding of Valuation'. *Sociological Review* 59(special iss. 2): 24–38.

Muniesa, F. 2014. *The Provoked Economy: Economic Reality and the Performative Turn*. Abingdon: Routledge.

Ortiz, H. 2011. 'Marchés efficients, investisseurs libres et Etats garants. Trames du politique dans les pratiques financières professionnelles'. *Politix* 95: 155–80.

Ortiz, H. 2013. 'Financial Value: Economic, Moral, Political, Global'. *HAU: Journal of Ethnographic Theory* 3(1): 64–79.

Ortiz, H. 2014. 'The Limits of Financial Innovation: Free Investors, Efficient Markets, and Crisis'. *American Anthropologist* 116(1): 38–50.

Perkmann, M. and A. Spicer. 2010. 'What Are Business Models? Developing a Theory of Performative Representations'. In *Technology and Organization: Essays in Honour of Joan Woodward*, ed. N. Phillips, G. Sewell, and D. Griffiths. Bingley: Emerald Group, 265–75.

Pina Stranger, A. 2011. 'Apprentissage collectif à l'échelle inter-organisationnelle. Le cas des entrepreneurs en biotechnologie'. PhD, Université Paris-Dauphine.

Pisano, G. 2006a. 'Can Science be a Business? Lessons from Biotech'. *Harvard Business Review* 84(10): 114–25.
Pisano, G. 2006b. *Science Business: The Promise, the Reality, and the Future of Biotech*. Boston: Harvard Business School Press.
Porter, M. E. 2001. 'Strategy and the Internet'. *Harvard Business Review* 79(3): 62–78.
Rosental, C. 2007. *Les capitalistes de la science. Enquête sur les démonstrateurs de la Silicon Valley et de la NASA*. Paris: CNRS Editions.
Sosna, M., R. N. Trevinyo-Rodríguez, and S. R. Velamuri. 2010. 'Business Model Innovation through Trial-and-Error Learning: The Naturhouse Case'. *Long Range Planning* 43(2–3): 383–407.
Star, S. L. and J. R. Griesemer. 1989. 'Institutional Ecology, "Translations" and Boundary Objects: Amateurs and Professionals in Berkeley's Museum of Vertebrate Zoology, 1907–39'. *Social Studies of Science* 19(3): 387–420.
Stark, D. 2009. *The Sense of Dissonance: Accounts of Worth in Economic Life*. Princeton: Princeton University Press.
Stark, D. and V. Paravel. 2008. 'PowerPoint in Public: Digital Technologies and the New Morphology of Demonstration'. *Theory, Culture & Society* 25(5): 30–55.
Thompson, J. D. and I. C. MacMillan. 2010. Business Models: Creating New Markets and Societal Wealth'. *Long Range Planning* 43(2–3): 291–307.
Wheelwright, S. and K. B. Clark. 1992. *Revolutionizing Product Development: Quantum Leaps in Speed, Efficiency, and Quality*. New York: Free Press.
Yaneva, A. 2005. 'Scaling Up and Down: Extraction Trials in Architectural Design'. *Social Studies of Science* 35(6): 867–94.
Yunus, M., B. Moingeon, and L. Lehmann-Ortega. 2010. 'Building Social Business Models: Lessons from the Grameen Experience'. *Long Range Planning* 43(2–3): 308–25.
Zott, C., R. Amit, and L. Massa. 2011. 'The Business Model: Recent Developments and Future Research'. *Journal of Management* 37(4): 1019–42.

6

Valuable Assemblages—Or Assembling Values

Trine Pallesen

This chapter addresses a specific expression of value, namely a price. And though it may be a somewhat distinctive price, i.e. an administered price, it is a price which collapses and unfolds a range of values, and involves ongoing controversies. One such controversy targets the administered price itself, qualified as a 'non-market' price.

The object of the valuation to be followed in the present is wind power. Wind power has, since its early days in the 1970s, been associated with—and to a great extent premised on—different societal values. In the 1970s, wind power was framed as a response to the oil crises, and thus the dependence on fossil fuel owners, and national concerns of security of supply (Jensen 2003). Three decades later, wind power is seen as part of the solution to climate change, and decreasing fossil fuel resources. As such, wind power has for decades been closely connected to larger matters of concern, albeit these concerns have changed considerably.

Meanwhile, for wind power to become an electricity of value, the turbines must be connected to the electrical grid; i.e. the electricity produced needs to be transported from the (often) remote locations of its production, to the sites of consumption. Whereas the grid moderates this crucial aspect of the modern electricity system, dating back to the 'war' between direct and alternate currents (Hughes 1983), it also introduces commensurability of electricity produced from different technologies. In other words, wind power becomes arranged within the grid, a 'single space' (Callon and Muniesa 2005), which also include nuclear power, fossil fuel generated electricity, not to mention their production modalities (i.e. base-load production, responsive production, etc.). Accordingly, the cost of wind power generation is made comparable to, for example, the costs of nuclear power production; a comparison which generally concludes wind power to be highly expensive—and thus not competitive under market-like conditions.

As an acknowledgement of, on the one hand the potential of wind power to contribute to the reduction of greenhouse gases, and on the other hand, the lacking 'maturity' of the technology, different policy instruments or governance systems have been developed, in order to support the introduction of wind power into the electricity system. One prominent example hereof is the feed-in tariff. The feed-in tariff was designed in the US in 1978 as a policy instrument to accelerate investments in renewable energy technologies, most notably wind power. This is achieved through long-term contracts between wind power producers and utilities (for onshore wind power, it is often fifteen years) at a set price, or as a fixed premium added to the market price (Couture et al. 2010). The distinct design of the feed-in tariff may differ, but the feed-in tariff generally entails a guaranteed access to the grid (Couture et al. 2010).

The most common alternatives to the feed-in tariff as governance devices are tendering and green certificates (though the latter remain more popular in theory, than in practice). Whereas the feed-in tariff may be described as an administered price, tendering and certificates are sometimes referred to as instruments for administered quantities of wind power added to the system (Hvelplund 2001a). Whether to introduce the 'administrative' (or political) element on the quantities or the price, has often sparked debates on the 'market-likeness' of the devices, often touting administered quantities as more 'market-like' than administered prices (e.g. Hvelplund 2001b).

The price-making presented in the following was part of the adoption and definition of the feed-in tariff for onshore wind power in France in 2000/2001. Before the adoption of the feed-in tariff, France had developed a tendering programme, EOLE 2005, at the time expected to trigger the development of French wind power capacity from close to zero in 1996, when it was introduced, to reach a target of 250–500 MW in 2005 (Laali and Benard 1999). However, following four rounds of calls to tender, only 70 MW were issued (though submission and selection rounds accepted up to 324 MW) (Cochet 2000; Nadaï 2007; Szarka 2007), a result later referred to as 'the invention of virtual wind power' (Cochet 2000). The adoption of the feed-in tariff as governance system, and the ensuing definition of the distinct tariff (8.38c€/kWh) sparked a range of controversies, including the existence of the governance model itself. Characterizing the feed-in tariff as an administered price—a distinct opposition to a 'market price'—and not least the different modalities of value these prices seemed to expose, are central in the controversies surrounding the 8.38c€/kWh.

The price, put only slightly polemically, is the economists' preferred representation of value. This chapter draws on recent contributions to new economic sociology, inspired by pragmatism, and stresses *valuation* as multi-dimensional and the outcome of collective action (e.g. Geiger in Kjellberg and Mallard 2013). It illustrates the many, often opposing dimensions attempted or enrolled in the valuation process—a process which is above all destined to result in the expression of a single metric. During the process, numerous values are enrolled, qualified, and disqualified, examples being the costs of air pollution (sourced to specific energy technologies), the surplus cost of the guaranteed price, potential of industrial development, the renewability of energy technologies, 'fairness' and 'efficiency' of prices, the 'quality' of landscapes, etc. So, the valuation process is not a linear movement, from many value*s* to a single metric, but includes numerous prices, and values not easily translated into singularized expressions.

Drawing on these insights, following the controversial valuations of wind power demonstrates valuation as the work of assembling different unlike entities—and the main argument is that only via these assemblages is wind power made qualifiable and eventually valuable. And the disqualifications of the individual valuation proposals may be described as the act of cutting associations between the entities of counter-proposals—and re-knitting new assemblages, including the introduction of new entities.

Price and Value(s)

Weber describes the price system as the result of a market struggle (between men); a result of conflicts and compromises.[1] This is not an inaccurate description of the definition of the French feed-in tariff. However, this price is not determined in the market, per se, i.e. the outcome of supply meeting demand. Rather, the price of wind power is defined on the fringe of the market. A similar struggle to that described by Weber is unfolded in the description to follow, and one central controversy is the fact that the price is not 'made in the market'.

Marion Fourcade addresses *pricing* inside and outside markets, by pointing to the different roles and tools of economists in these processes of valuation (Fourcade 2011).[2] Economists, she says, have for some time now, moved in to the valuation of goods outside the market sphere, operating '*as if*' goods outside the market sphere were priceable; i.e. '*as if*' they were traded on markets (Fourcade 2011). Fourcade's distinction between two prevalent modes of valuation/pricing (inside and outside of markets) is also a comment on the so-called Parsonian Pact (see Stark 2009); a pact made between Talcott Parsons, as a sociologist, and the economists at Harvard, according to which economists would appropriate the study of *value*, and the sociologists the study of *values* (Stark 2009). According to Fourcade, this pact is long gone: from the point of view of economists, values may be collapsed into value, as all objects may be subjected to an economic valuation process (Fourcade 2011). Whereas a critique of this 'economization' process of all domains of human existence is ongoing (e.g. Ackerman and Heinzerling 2004), a more nuanced picture emerges from the study presented here. Though the tariff may be expressed as value, in the singular, the process of defining this value is a process in which values, in the plural, are mobilized, created, debated, and aligned—in other words; rather than being a straightforward process of economists peacefully defining the price of wind power (collapsing values into value), outside or on the fringe of the market, the process includes qualifications and disqualifications of wind power, its value(s), not to mention greenhouse gas emissions and their sources.

A range of techniques are involved in the valuation of wind power, e.g. the internal rate of return and profitability index method (PIM). Stressing these 'valuation devices' (see Doganova and Muniesa, this volume) is central to shifting attention from value, as a subjective or objective property of the subject matter, towards valuation as a process (or an action). This shift in attention corresponds to the recently renewed interest in valuation as viewed by pragmatism, and in particular valuation in the work of Dewey (e.g. Muniesa 2007, 2011; Stark 2009), stressing the distinction between value and valuation:

> Value can be understood as something that something has by virtue of how people consider it (how they personally like it, in particular), but also as something that something has as a result of its own condition and of its relation to other things (for instance, in relation to work or to money, or to any sort of standard metric). Valuation, in turn, refers to something that happens to something, and this happening can be a matter of consideration or of relation, or both at the same time. (Muniesa 2011, 26)

Centring attention on valuation, rather than value, involves a simultaneous attention to action, because valuation is premised on the costly and irregular activities which bring value about (Muniesa 2011). In the present study, a great proportion of these activities include controversies regarding commensuration, i.e. the transformation of differences (or qualities) into quantity that share a metric (Espeland and Stevens 1998, 2008). Commensuration implies classification in such a way that things become comparable, by creating new and obscuring existing relations among entities (Espeland and Sauder 2007). As such, commensuration shapes our attention, pointing to the ways in which things are connected—and not least, how sameness and differences are expressed. Being fundamental to measurement, commensuration is often expected (and assumed) to stabilize things such as university rankings or international figure skating judgement systems for measurement to be brought about (e.g. Espeland and Lom, this volume); however, in the case studied here, commensuration remains a contested and open question, and yet value in the form of a price is assigned.

Valuation as Assemblage

In the following, three proposals regarding the definition of the feed-in tariff are discussed. The description of the three proposals draw on fieldwork conducted in France between 2007 and 2008. The fieldwork was driven by an interest in unfolding the administered price, i.e. the feed-in tariff of 8.38c€/kWh, a price sometimes referred to as a political number, and at other times a carefully calculated price. Inquiring into the fabric of the tariff implied following associations as they were made into assemblages, by a number of protagonists, each allowing a distinct valuation to be brought about, and eventually to be translated into a single numeric expression, i.e. a price. The three valuations organize entities, such as developers, energy technologies, CO_2 emissions, valuation tools and methods, efficiency and fairness, and not least markets and the state, into well-knit assemblages. Meanwhile, each contribution places emphasis on distinct aspects of the assemblage; the first contribution sets the frame for valuation, by drawing together country-specific statistics, and making the case for an adoption of the feed-in governance instrument. Secondly, a valuation tool called the Profitability Index Method is developed and introduced, stressing the qualifications of 'fairness' and 'efficiency', but eventually allowing a price to be brought about. Thirdly, a counter-calculation is presented, stressing the reorganization of associations between CO_2 emissions, wind power and nuclear power, and not least the introduction of emission-free, rather than renewability, as valuable qualification. In other words, the three contributions represent the overall frame-setting, a reinforcement/specification of the frame, and an attempt at overthrowing and replacing the frame.

The three valuation proposals each have key protagonists, but as valuations they are larger assemblages drawing together multiple tools and methods, statistics, reports, etc. Together, they not only sum up the major arguments for and against the introduction of wind power in the French energy system, but they have left durable traces in reports and articles as well as among wind power developers and other actors involved in the field.

Valuation 1: Setting the Frame for Valuation

The feed-in tariff as a means of governing French wind power production was officially introduced in a report by Yves Cochet in 2000. Cochet was at the time vice-president of the National Assembly (member of the Green Party), and in 2001 he became Minister of Environment and Regional Planning. In 2000, Yves Cochet was responsible for drawing up an account of the renewable energy situation in France, and make recommendations for the government in order to continue the implementation of the EU Electricity Directive (Cochet 2000). The report stressed the growing 'maturity' of renewable energy technologies, and in particular wind power. This increasing success of wind power was explained by the technology's compatibility with the energy system and recent industrial and societal developments, accompanied by the 'birth of a true market' (Cochet 2000). However, the crux of this positive development, the report stressed, was the choice of appropriate governance system to organize these renewable energies. In France, the EOLE 2005 programme had first and foremost led to the invention of 'virtual wind power' as mentioned above (Cochet 2000). Therefore, to attain an objective of 10,000 MW wind power in the electricity system by 2010, the choice of governance system was crucial. Only a support mechanism including guaranteed purchase, as well as 'reasonable tariff levels' would accomplish such an ambitious goal, the report argued.

From the more general proposal of the feed-in tariff as governance system, to a more elaborate design of the device, the report proposes to model the French system on the German feed-in tariff. In other words, it is suggested to shift from a bidding system, in which the amount of wind power is controlled by EDF (Electricity of France)—on behalf of the French state—to a tariff system, in which the price is administered. But this proposal met firm opposition from various quarters:

> These were the issues... we can say both ideological and technical at the same time; of people from the CRE [French Energy Regulation Commission], people from RTE [French transmission system operator], people from EDF, even people from the DGEMP [agency for energy and raw materials], or people behind minister Christian Pierret; they said 'Look, we already have too much nuclear electricity in France, we even sell our electricity [to neighbouring countries], why are the environmentalists going to annoy us with buying much more expensive renewable electricity, when we have the cheapest nuclear power in Europe... and we will be forced to buy more expensive electricity from the environmentalists, with their 'shitty' wind turbines... its madness!'... There was this techno-ideological blockage, saying 'we are the best in the world at nuclear electricity' which is true, we are the best in the world! (Cochet, interview, my translation)

To Cochet, it was a rather hostile environment into which the feed-in tariff was introduced. And though the opposition could very well have its source in a nuclear techno-ideology (or 'technopolitical' regime, see Hecht 1998), the counter-arguments predominantly stressed the price of electricity: nuclear energy is cheap, wind power is expensive.

Introducing wind power into the electrical grid detached the good from its producer, allowing its circulation outside the site of production, but simultaneously performed a qualification by which wind power became simply electricity. In other words, the detachment performed via the connection to the grid was not simply a detachment from the producer, but also from the technology of production. And thus 'arranged in a single space' (Callon and Muniesa 2005), wind power and nuclear power were made commensurable. The opposition referred to above retains price as the only difference; and difference, in this case, was reduced to difference in price.

With the report, the merits of nuclear power were (indirectly) questioned, and it resisted the idea that prices alone should settle controversies between technologies; rather, the source of energy was paramount. Instead, multiple values were introduced: nuclear waste, renewability, and the creation of new industries. Wind power was connected to different values and defied the 'economist's act' of collapsing values into value—unlike the opposition, which argued along a single value, namely that of price. The introduction of the feed-in tariff became the pivotal centre around which these opposing arguments collided.

The argument for abandoning the tendering governance system was based upon the system's lack of success in sparking French wind power development (Cochet 2000). To illustrate the inefficiency of the tendering system and the success of the feed-in tariff system, the report presented statistics demonstrating the relation between governance instruments, the price, and the number of MW wind power realized in a number of European countries: Germany, Denmark, and Spain who all had opted for feed-in tariffs had each realized between 264 MW and 793 MW wind power connected to the grid in 1998. Holland, Ireland, and Great Britain, on the other hand, had chosen either tendering or green certificates and developed between a humble 9 MW and 42 MV wind power in 1998.

The statistics, it was argued, demonstrated the strong causality between governance system, and the development of wind power, measured in number of MW connected to the grid. The price mediated this effect. Whereas tendering systems have often been vented as the most 'market-like' governance system (see, for example, Hvelplund 2001b), the report mobilized the statistics mentioned above as a 'proof of efficiency'. In other words, economists may have concluded on the suitability of the tendering system in a market economy—in vitro—but the report made the in vivo demonstration of the efficiency of the feed-in tariff system.

In other words, the value (here a price) put on wind power, and the device, i.e. the feed-in tariff, were entangled. Achieving a high construction rate became a criterion of success in its own right, and the choice of a tariff rather than a tendering system was seen as a commitment to developing wind power. Nonetheless, the qualification of the governance systems according to 'market-likeness' remained an active component in the negotiations:

> Normally, the spontaneous market device is bidding, because in principle, it does not distort the market. Now we've distorted the market with guaranteed tariffs—it's a protected market in a way. Obviously, what we told Jospin and Pierret and the people of DGEMP was that 'this is normal for a new emerging technology in which France could become a champion because we have good engineers in France—it is normal to help it initially'. Me, I always take the example of nuclear power in France, how much was a nuclear kilowatt-hour in France worth in 1950? It was very expensive! (Cochet, interview, my translation)

Stressing a temporal dimension, i.e. the investment in a future industry, points to a required shift in 'regime of worth' (Boltanski and Thévenot 2006). Referring to the early days of developing nuclear power—and its development in price—enabled a confrontation between criteria of justification; from one of the market arrangement to one of accepting the time required to develop new industries (Boltanski and Thévenot 2006).

The disqualification of the market as an instrument for developing new energy technologies, was polemically discussed referring to the so-called virtues of competition:

> The proponents of calls to tender generally stress the ability to accelerate the lowering of the price of the production, thanks to competition, which is for the occasion dressed in all its virtues, and as proof they cite that the contractual prices of the EOLE 2005 as the lowest in Europe. In doing so, however, they confuse the notion of costs with the notion of price: if the latter reflect, as everyone knows, the strength relation in a commercial negotiation between a buyer and a seller, in time T, it is not automatically related to the real costs, undertaken by one or the other part. (Cochet 2000, 40, my translation)

Drawing the relation between costs and price, and thus unfolding the 'merits of competition' (including tendering schemes), the report stressed that even though competition may drive down prices, someone is still to pay for the development of new technologies, i.e. undertake the costs. In other words, costs are real, prices are constructs! And constructions that may—or may not—reflect the realities of costs. As a consequence, the developers would end up carrying the costs of developing renewable energy, serving a public interest. But despite the pitfalls of a belief in competition as driver of optimization, arguments from the market sphere remained central to the discourse presented to the Prime Minister and others:

> We convinced them with arguments on the one hand ecological, but also with market arguments by saying... when we have an emergent market, we need a market instrument which is a price signal to guarantee that the investors, the

> private investors, the capitalists who wants to invest in wind parks are guaranteed that their market will be sustained, but for a certain period of time, and in a way that, after 15 years, they'll be competing with the nuclear... so it was partly ecologist arguments, *and* market arguments that convinced Jospin and his counsellors. (Cochet, interview, my translation)

Though the argument drew on a different regime of worth, making a strong relation between wind power and the market remained crucial. The feed-in tariff would not exclude competition between wind power and nuclear power in the future.

Having made the case for an adoption of a feed-in tariff system, the next step was suggesting a specific price. The report, however, simply recommended copying the German tariff. Arguing that the German tariff had proven its worth (Cochet interview), the design (a tiered system) and the tariff-level should simply be replicated.

Instead, the tariff served as a way of allowing matters of concern to surface, and become framed, if not directly then indirectly, into the exchange of electricity. In other words, discussing the eventuality of a single price allowed other values to be made visible and become part of the emerging assemblage, and the new governance system thus served as a politicization of the French energy system in general; e.g. associating the first kWh of nuclear power, and a kWh of wind power in France in 2000, prompted the question: Who is to pay for emerging technologies? Whereas the Eole 2005 tender instrument had led to individual prices for each project, they were assumed to reflect the costs of the proposed project. But because the specific costs were framed within the individual bid, they remained concealed. On the other hand, making a single price had as effect that matters of concern emerged. As such, it was the translation into a single price (rather than the individual project-related prices of the bidding system) that allowed different values in the plural to emerge and become mobilized.

With the report, wind power was positioned in an assemblage with diminishing natural resources, and an urgent need for mitigating CO_2 emissions. However, the frame of valuation for wind power, i.e. the definition of a single price, opened a space within which controversies would be played out and other values emerge. In brief, it set a frame necessitating a one-dimensional translation into a price—all the while suggesting an assemblage demonstrating the incommensurability of wind power and non-renewable energies.

Valuation 2: Making Things Calculable—Fairness and Efficiency

An important contribution to the forum described above came from the French Environment and Energy Agency (ADEME). Participating in an official working group charged with the definition of the feed-in tariff, ADEME was represented by economist and senior consultant Bernard Chabot. In particular, ADEME contributed with a distinct method for defining feed-in tariffs, and Chabot published a number of articles on the calculation of the tariff (Chabot 2001a, 2001b; Chabot et al. 2002).

Chabot, and many of his colleagues at ADEME, warmly welcomed the adoption of a feed-in tariff system. But given this specific frame for valuation, attention was directed at the 'accurate' definition of the price. Thus, the method developed by ADEME to be presented in the following primarily aimed at translating the frame, described above, into a specific figure. In doing so, however, the method was also a response to the 'hostile environment' described by Yves Cochet; making 'fairness' and 'efficiency' calculable properties of the tariff.

The method, called the 'Profitability Index Method' (PIM), is described as a simple and powerful method to define 'fair and efficient' tariffs (Chabot 2001a; Chabot et al. 2002). The method 'is simply the ratio between the net present value (NPV) and the required initial investment (I): PI = NPV / I' (Chabot et al. 2002, 1). As such, the heart of the PIM is a classic discounted cash flow analysis: an analysis of future cash flows discounted into a so-called 'net present value' (based on the principle of 'time-value' of money according to which a cent is worth more today than a cent tomorrow). As future cash flows of a wind power project benefiting from a feed-in tariff are a function of the production of the number kWh and the tariff itself, these are in turn set in relation to the costs of constructing the wind power project. The PIM is therefore based on a very well-known and used project valuation tool, familiar to most project developers and policy-makers. Furthermore, the weight put on the description of the method is substantial; the legitimacy of the tariff definition is entirely bound up with the method, and it creates strong links to a variety of additional valuation methods such as discounted payback time, internal rate of return, and benefit–cost ratio.

At the heart of the PIM is the potential for assessing the profitability of wind power projects. This emphasis addresses the crux of the critique raised against the feed-in tariff; the absence of competition means that there is no means of safeguarding against 'undue' rents gained by the project developers. The notion of 'undue' rents refers to the gap between cost and price discussed by Yves Cochet. To address this challenge, the PIM enrols the profitability level of other energy technologies as part of the calculation by stating that throughout *liberalized* electricity markets, the 'minimum margin' on cost for coal power plants is approximately 10 per cent—and that this margin, to a modern coal fired plant, corresponds to a profitability index of 0.3 (Chabot et al. 2002). In other words, the coal-fired plant *and* liberalized electricity markets are enrolled and made reference points in terms of the acceptable level of profits to be made by wind power producers.

Later, the 'fairness' of a PI of 0.3 was questioned, amongst others by Chabot's colleagues at ADEME, who suspected that an 'extra' margin was included to sustain the further development of the technology. Chabot's reply to the critique, in which he retained the PI of 0.3, referred to historical data: all tariffs leading to successful wind power histories (in Denmark, Germany, and Spain), just 'happened' to have PIs superior or equal to 0.3 (Chabot, interview). Though the main argument for tariffs of a PI of 0.3 remained vested in the PIM method, Denmark, Germany, and Spain continued to be enrolled as models to follow.

According to the above, what is entailed in the PIM is a calculation guaranteeing 'fairness' and 'efficiency', respectively. To illustrate the 'fairness', Chabot (2001a) and Chabot and Saulnier (2001) calculate the profitability index determined by the number of hours of operation at rated power per year.

They illustrate the fairness of the tariff; the profitability rarely exceeds the proposed value of the PI, i.e. 0.3. To actually achieve a PI of 0.3 requires between 2,600 and 2,800 hours at rated power annually. This characteristic of the device implies, it is argued, that developers are granted incentives to use good wind sites, and choosing turbines with high productivity—both of which are likely to increase costs of the project (Chabot 2001a, 4). Therefore, the profitability of any project is an effect of the developers' skills, primarily in terms of choosing sites and turbines—and even for developers possessing these skills, the PI will not exceed 0.3. Fairness, in the sense presented here, is premised on profitability levels not exceeding what is seen for competing technologies, and rewarding the skilful.

The PIM, and the calculation of the French tariff were made widely accessible through articles and conferences, in which 'fairness' and 'efficiency' are stressed constantly as the main concerns related to the construction of the tariff. And the PIM illustrates how exactly to ensure this 'fair and efficient price', by making fairness as well as efficiency calculable. Though the feed-in tariff may be seen as a 'disturbance' of the market, the PIM is justified by the (positive) association between wind power and the fight against climate change. Instead, the PIM suggests a replacement of the resource allocation optimum allegedly produced through a free market by ensuring fairness and efficiency via calculation. The PIM folds these qualities as calculable qualities of the tariff, and thereby offers a direct response to the protagonists of competition and tendering. The assemblage suggested to be built up around the PIM draws skilful developers, competing energy technologies, and additional valuation tools together, to eventually allow the production of a number, qualified as both fair and efficient. However, whether such qualifications may be calculated remained controversial, as will be discussed next.

Valuation 3: Counter-Calculations as Dissociation and Displacement

The overall frame of valuation as well as the tariff itself outlined above were not, as indicated earlier, uniformly accepted. One major opponent to the framing of the device was CRE, the French Energy Regulation Commission.

For the present purpose, CRE's publication of a so-called notice on the feed-in tariff in 2001 is discussed. CRE's general conclusion was clear: Abandon the tariff system which provides undue rents to the developers—and return to a competitive tendering system (CRE 2001a, 2001b; see also CRE 2006). The arguments articulated in the notice, repeated and extended later in a significant report made on behalf of the French Parliament (Poignant 2003), could be grouped around two problematizations. Firstly, the relation between renewable energy technologies, such as wind power, and greenhouse gas emissions is questioned. Secondly, the level of the feed-in tariff is critiqued and (re)calculated (CRE 2001a).

Addressing the possible contribution of the feed-in tariff towards the fight against the greenhouse effects, the most common energy technologies in France were translated into their costs of production and their costs of pollution. Nuclear power, providing close to 80 per cent of French electricity, was reported to entail the following costs (CRE 2001a):

- Overall costs of production 30 €/MWh
- Fixed costs 21 €/MWh
- Variable costs: 9 €/MWh
- Value of CO_2 emissions: 0 €/MWh
- Value of air pollution: 0.3–2.5 €/MWh

As these numbers demonstrate, nuclear power has low variable costs, hardly any air pollution, and no CO_2 emissions.

Then, drawing a distinction between two categories of energy technologies, namely those providing a 'guaranteed production' (e.g. nuclear), and those of 'non-guaranteed' production (e.g. wind and solar), CRE concluded that increases in the latter category do not allow the reduction of the number of centrals providing guaranteed production. In other words, wind and solar power cannot substitute any of the technologies with a guaranteed production, because their volatility conflicts with requirements of planning and managing the energy system (this relation between fluctuating technologies, production planning, and grid management remained controversial; for example, see EWEA 2005). Instead, CRE and others argued, since these fluctuating technologies cannot decrease the number of conventional centrals (they could eventually require an increase in conventional energy technologies to compensate for fluctuations), any possible avoided cost of production would thus be limited to variable costs, primarily of fuel (CRE 2001a). And given that nuclear power has low variable cost, no greenhouse gas emissions, and hardly any air pollution, the contribution of wind and solar power is close to none in continental France (CRE 2001a). Readdressing the successes of developing wind power in countries such as Denmark, Germany, and Spain (e.g. Cochet 2000) in developing renewable energy, it is argued that these countries benefit from renewable technologies *because* of their distinctive energy system configurations, with extensive use of fossil fuels. As such, the association between wind power and greenhouse gas emission reductions was cut, even though the dissociation remained contingent; i.e. the contribution of wind power to the fight against climate change depends on the energy system configuration in which it is introduced.

This (dis)qualification of wind power was a concurrent qualification of nuclear power. Rather than 'renewability', 'emission-free' emerged as the dominant category to value. Furthermore, the replacement of category suggested a commensuration between wind power and nuclear power, allowing valuation along new dimensions; namely value as the relation between (variable) costs and costs of emissions. As such, the assumed causality of the feed-in tariff device was questioned by problematizing the association between fluctuating technologies and the reduction of CO_2 emissions in an energy system dominated by nuclear power. In other words, the positive association between wind power and reductions in CO_2 emissions was wrong.

Having concluded that increases of wind power (and solar power) were unlikely to contribute positively to the fight against greenhouse effects, the valuation put forward with the feed-in tariff was discarded. Yet, the feed-in tariff remained a hot topic in terms of its organizational effects, and its distinct level.

The profitability of wind power projects benefiting from the tariff has been an overarching concern amongst opponents to guaranteed prices, and CRE attempted to illustrate the gap between the average tariff and the (real) cost of wind power production. As input to these calculations, CRE presented the results of their hearings among 'concerned actors' (CRE 2001a) specifying investment costs between 838 €/kW and 1,143 €/kW, and annual operating costs as an approximation of 2–3.5 per cent of the costs of investments (CRE 2001a).

To demonstrate the potential gains of the wind power producers, CRE developed an alternative method to the PIM described above, based on 'value couples'. These 'value couples' were representing the *actual* costs of wind power projects, split into investment costs and operating costs, and defined a 'cost-range' between 915 €/kW and 23 €/kW (investment costs/operations costs), and 1067 €/kW and 38 €/kW.[3] Comparing the two 'value couples' to a feed-in tariff of 8.38c€/kWh, CRE produced the graph in Figure 6.1.

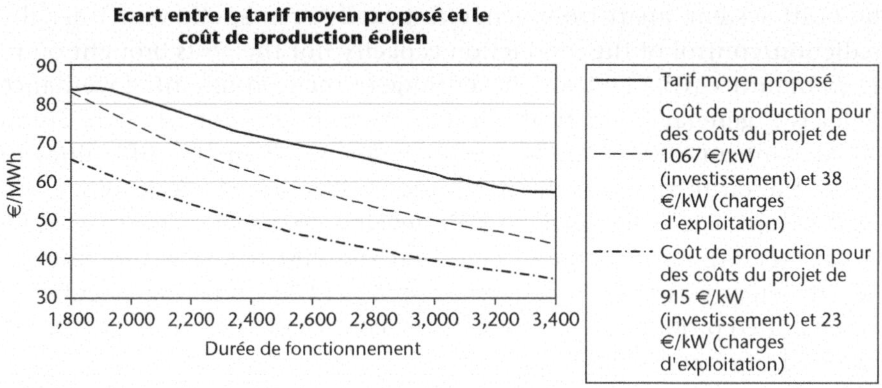

Figure 6.1. Gap between feed-in tariff and cost of production
Source: CRE (2001a: 8).

With the X-axis representing hours of operation of a given installation, the upper curve illustrates the gains based on the tariff, and the two lower curves represent the costs associated with the two 'value couples'. The graph, CRE concluded, demonstrated clearly that '[t]he proposed tariff is evidently superior to the cost price of the sector, regardless of the assumptions made' (CRE 2001a, 9, my translation).

Having thus illustrated a substantial gap between a tariff of 8.38c€/kWh, and the costs of constructing and running wind power projects, the profitability of the projects was fleshed out: the annual return as a function of site quality (i.e. wind qualities). Calculating the return, CRE could demonstrate annual after-tax returns of 20 per cent at 2,600 hours of production per year, corresponding to a 'correctly winded' site (CRE 2001a).

Yet again, the EOLE 2005 programme was mobilized as a disqualification of the tariff, as the last call resulted in an average price of 48 €/MWh for the twenty-four retained projects, operating 2,900 hours per year. According to CRE's calculations, replacing the EOLE 2005 by a feed-in tariff of 8.38c€/kWh would lead to global over-costs of €170 million over fifteen years (CRE 2001a). Summing up, CRE stated:

> Given all the above elements, the CRE considers that the proposed tariff causes undue rents for the wind power producers that will result in a significant increase in electricity prices in France, and represents an excessively costly means for the community to achieve the objective of developing the industry set by the government. CRE, therefore, emits an unfavourable opinion on the ruling. (CRE 2001a, 14, my translation)

Instead, CRE pleaded for a return to tendering (such as EOLE 2005) because of the properties of the tariff device and the tendering device, respectively.

The tariff system, apart from generating undue rents, allows neither the prediction/control of the production capacity nor the costs brought on to the community (CRE 2001a). This critique of the feed-in tariff governance model is a general theoretical critique raised by economists (e.g. Finon and Menanteau 2004). The argument is anchored in the difficulties of getting the tariff 'right': if the fixed price is too low, the technology will not develop; if it is too high, it will develop above the objectives (CRE 2001a). ADEME and Chabot's claim that the PIM would ensure fairness and efficiency was thus directly contested; CRE's competing calculation demonstrated profitability levels of 20 per cent—not 10 per cent as ADEME suggested through the PIM.

The idea that such a thing as the 'right' price could exist, however, was revived. But competition alone should be granted the power to determine what's right. Furthermore, advantages of governance through tendering implies control of production capacity, and of the geographical location of the production unit(s), allowing centralized decision power over other quality criteria of the projects; 'The substitution of market mechanisms (such as tendering or markets for green certificates) to an administered price mechanism is a safeguard for the community to achieve the desired objectives at the minimum cost' (CRE 2001a, 1, my translation).

The categorization of tendering (together with green certificates) as 'market mechanisms', allowed a disqualification of feed-tariffs from this realm. The dissociation of tariffs from market mechanisms echoes a discussion within environmental economics in which price models (with fixed prices) are deemed less market-like than quota models (fixed quotas) (e.g. Hvelplund 2001a), according to which competition among bidders is supposed to drive prices down and thus reveal the 'real' price:

> To achieve the objectives of wind power development that the government has set, the CRE recommends the use of tenders, which reveal the true prices and allow the adjustment of the location and the volume of production, all the while avoiding the creation of unjustified rents. (CRE 2001b, 1, my translation)

This quote is a rather precise example of what Cochet (above) referred to as confusion between cost and price. To CRE, market mechanisms (i.e. tendering and green certificates) reveal real prices, as well as upholding the control over the development of wind power (keeping control in the hands of centralized institutions).

This last valuation proposal thus problematized the frame for valuation of wind power, and its translation into a specific price. By dissociating the relation between wind power and reductions in CO_2 emissions, and (re)qualifying nuclear technology as 'emission-free' allowed questioning whether increases in wind power would have any positive effect on CO_2 emissions. Furthermore, the feed-in tariff blurred 'true' prices, and would eventually raise electricity prices in France. In other words, the objective of the feed-in tariff (sparking wind power development) as well as its realization (into a specific price) was made controversial. Meanwhile, the (re)valuation of wind power proposed by CRE was a simultaneous re-qualification of nuclear power: Displacing the category of 'renewability' by 'emission-free' along which to value energy technologies, nuclear power and wind power were made commensurable.

Valuation in this counter-calculation is brought about through an assemblage, which not only repositions entities, but also introduces new ones; nuclear power, a 'cheap' and 'emission-free' energy, energy system management, and alternative calculations, are reorganized. Distinctions are drawn between investments and variable costs, and costs and prices are associated in new ways. Market-likeness of the governance system is made a qualification, a guarantee against undue rents, and over-costs. However, the assemblage is also one which excludes certain entities; nuclear waste disposal, risk of accidents, and diminishing uranium resources are never introduced in this counter-valuation.

Discussion

Accepting the premise that goods do not possess value a priori, and not least that goods may experience changes of status (Calışkan and Callon 2009), encourages a view of valuation which departs from visualizations or identifications of an 'inherent' value of the object. And even though the pivotal theme throughout the three valuations above is the demonstration of wind power's value, in fact, at no point is the 'intrinsic' value of wind power discussed—deprived of its relations to other technologies, production and circulation modalities, governance systems, cleanness, etc. In other words, the valuation processes unfold as entities; calculations, governance systems, and categories are assembled. Nonetheless, the valuation proposals all eventually translate these assemblages into a fixed price (e.g. 8.38c€/kWh) which stands alone, cut off from the associations (and values) feeding into its production.

In all three valuations, value is at least partly related to the feed-in tariff, either as an arena for demonstrating the 'real worth' of wind power, or as an instrument that distorts everything 'objective' about price-making. As such, the feed-in tariff becomes more than a simple instrument for bridging political objectives with the order of market exchange; it is entirely entangled with the construction of value for wind power. Instead, it draws attention to the actions underlying the valuation of wind power, and the various forms it takes; the shift in governance system, from tendering to a guaranteed price in the form of a feed-in tariff, is justified due to the important role the device has had for all successful national initiatives of wind power development. The exact number is less central in the first valuation proposal—and at first, the German tariff level is suggested copied into French regulation. Instead, it is argued, the choice of governance system demonstrates a 'commitment' on behalf of the French government to support the long-term development of wind power—and thus creating the stability for developers to be willing to invest. Calculating the price, on the other hand, is pivotal to the development of the PIM; developing a method that allows the calculation of 'fairness' and 'efficiency' creates the legitimization of the price. As such, the PIM counters the common critique of the feed-in tariff regarding over-pricing electricity through guaranteed prices, allowing developers to gain undue profits. The method's proposed 'fairness' and 'efficiency' targets the distinct price which will enable the (politically) desired development, all the while safeguarding against undue profits—in other words, calculations replace the expected optimum as the outcome of markets. Finally, the third valuation not only disqualifies wind power's contribution to the mitigation of greenhouse gases, but also the level of the tariff. The counter-calculations demonstrate profitability levels well beyond those suggested by the PIM. However, rather than suggesting a lower tariff, CRE urge the abolishment of the device. In other words, the calculations are used as demonstration of the unlikely/improbable incident of 'getting the tariff right'.

As such, the governance system, i.e. the feed-in tariff, is itself placed at the centre of the controversies in a larger quest for what kind of (energy) economic approaches should dominate the design and adoption of distinct devices, including their relation between costs and prices, and eventually questions regarding responsibilities for developing new energy technologies. Also, the feed-in tariff is mobilized in controversies of what energy system management is—and should be—e.g. centralized or decentralized, or what should fuel it, e.g. uranium or renewables. These controversies often unfold around dichotomies: centralized versus decentralized electricity production, renewable versus sustainable energy, stable versus fluctuating energy, cheap versus expensive electricity, market price versus political/administered price, etc. Yet, these dichotomies suggest underlying controversies regarding similarities and differences between different electricity technologies, as well as between policy instruments. Meanwhile, the exact proposals come about, not as well-articulated arguments for distinct approaches to either economics or energy system management, but rather as assemblages of various entities of a much more mundane character, which eventually allows a translation into euros.

Valuation, as illustrated above, is premised on the activity of meticulously assembling energy technologies, categories, grids, statistics illustrating national developments of wind power, calculative devices, etc. Each of these is made part of elaborations aiming at the stabilization of a value, eventually to be expressed in euros. But to arrive at the conclusion, i.e. a specific price, they are tied together in likely—and occasionally unlikely—assemblages. The first valuation establishes strong associations between wind power development, price, and the distinct governance system. In the report authored by Cochet, wind power statistics relating governance system and increase in wind power capacity, mediated through the realized price, is made a powerful claim for the feed-in tariff. It mobilizes the 'great success stories' of wind power development, namely Germany, Denmark, and Spain, to demonstrate causality between governance model and increases in installations of turbines. Furthermore, the category 'renewable energy' is clearly distinguished from versions of 'sustainable energy', thus attempting to cut any commensurability between wind and nuclear power. Meanwhile, as a response to articulations of price divergences between wind and nuclear power, a temporal perspective is introduced; comparing prices should take into account the maturity of the technology. In other words, wind power prices in 2001 should be compared to the nuclear power prices of its early days.

To a large extent, the second valuation proposal is an elaboration of the first assemblage, adding with the PIM an *economization* of the frame set with the feed-in tariff; whereas some proponents of the feed-in tariff (e.g. Cochet) 'admits' the 'market distorting' properties of guaranteed prices, the PIM performs the 'fairness' and 'efficiency' of the feed-in tariff, otherwise assumed to be guaranteed by the market. Commensurability in this proposal is framed as the calculated representations of 'fairness' and 'efficiency'. Enrolling the profitability levels of more mature energy technologies, and translating these into profitability indexes allow the conclusion that wind power as a technology is no more privileged than other energy technologies, in terms of the economic returns to be gained from feed-in tariffs. Sameness in the sense suggested here is transposed to profitability levels, rather than the price itself.

Finally, the third valuation attempts to unmake most of the suggested associations between wind power, governance system, mitigation of greenhouse gas emissions, and the existence of 'fair' and 'efficient' tariffs. Firstly, replacing the category of value, i.e. 'sustainability' rather than 'renewability', nuclear power and wind power may be directly compared along dimensions such as costs. Though wind and nuclear power has been made commensurable through their coexistence in the grid, and made quantifiable in kWh as well as euros, sameness and difference remain unsettled issues. Though quantified along the same dimensions, the two energy technologies connect to quite different values: predominantly emission-free, renewability, and controllability. Instead, introducing the distinction between guaranteed and non-guaranteed electricity production suggests yet a new dimension along which to discuss the sameness of electricity sources. CRE argues, that combining the system balance ability of the energy technologies, and their CO_2 emission profiles, additional balancing capacity will be required in case of high increases in wind power (to compensate for the unpredictable fluctuations in production). This argument was later expanded to predict an *increase* in CO_2 emissions with substantial increases of wind power in the energy system (e.g. Poignant 2003). This last valuation proposal suggests an assemblage according to which the larger 'societal' value of wind power is negligible. Its valuation, it is argued, should be premised on competitive bidding in the form of tendering. In other words, only bids given under competition will drive down the price of wind power—towards its costs—to eventually 'reveal' its 'true' value.

Conclusion

At no point in the three proposals described above is valuation addressed as an 'assessment' (Vatin 2013) of wind power's value. However, the final price, 8.38c€/kWh, when eventually detached from the controversies around its definition, remains a numeric representation of wind power's value. But defining a value for wind power implies knitting together different assemblages from a range of heterogeneous entities, which allows the different actors to put forward opposing value proposals. These assemblages suggest different associations of energy systems, the production profiles of the individual energy technologies, the economic methods and instruments to apply in the valuation process, fairness, and eventually ideals of the future, such as sustainably versus renewably driven societies. In other words, the assemblages create or cut associations between wind power and larger societal values, all the while the value of the electricity remains unaddressed.

Though the feed-in tariff was eventually settled, the issue of commensurability remained (and still does) open and contested. In other words, even though wind power became organized in the same grid, using the same metrics, and ultimately indistinguishable from electricity generated from other technologies, sameness and differences were continuously debated along multiple dimensions. Whether wind power could or should be compared to nuclear power for instance, kept sparking new questions, such as: comparing at what point in time, comparing costs or prices, or the profits to be gained, etc. The introduction of the feed-in tariff as governance instrument was at the centre of these controversies, either as justification necessitating calculations of fairness or as a distortion of the market; in other words, the valuation of wind remained indistinguishable from the qualifications of the feed-in tariff. Eventually, the actual object of valuation seemed to shift, within and across the three valuations, from wind power's relation to CO_2 mitigation, profitability levels, or the feed-in tariff instrument, depending on the configuration of the distinct assemblage put forward.

Notes

1. Weber described prices and the price system as 'a struggle of man against man; and prices are expressions of this struggle; they are instruments of calculation only as estimated quantifications of relative chances in this struggle of interests' (Weber 1978, p. 108).
2. Fourcade pays particular attention to situations in which economists, with tools such as cost–benefit analyses, contingent valuation, etc. make price(s) happen, and to 'a focus on economic valuation processes, where the value problem is much more general and encompasses everything that people care about (or are believed and made to care about)' (Fourcade 2011, 46). Therefore, the distinction is more of a distinction in practices of the economists undertaking pricing/valuation, as well as the situations in which they occur; e.g. in cases where markets do not exist, and sometimes are not sought to exist.
3. The 'value couple' of 1,067 €/kW and 38 €/kW was an approximate average to the prices defined through EOLE 2005 (CRE 2001a). In other words, the preceding tendering programme was mobilized as an indication of 'true' prices, notwithstanding that this governance system had failed to spark the development of wind power in France.

References

Ackerman, F. and L. Heinzerling. 2004. *Priceless: On Knowing the Price of Everything and the Value of Nothing*. London: New Press.

Boltanski, L. and L. Thévenot. 2006. *On Justification: Economies of Worth*. Princeton: Princeton University Press.

Calışkan, K. and M. Callon. 2009. 'Economization, Part 1: Shifting Attention from the Economy towards Processes of Economization'. *Economy and Society* 38(3): 369–98.

Callon, M. and F. Muniesa. 2005. 'Economic Markets as Calculative Collective Devices'. *Organization Studies* 26(8): 1229–50.

Chabot, B. 2001a. 'Fair and Efficient Tariffs for Wind Energy: Principles, Method, Proposal, Data and Potential Consequences in France'. Paper presented at the 2001 European Wind Energy Conference—Wind Energy for the New Millennium, Copenhagen, 2–6 July.

Chabot, B. 2001b. 'La nouvelle tarification de l'énergie éolienne: genèse, description et première analyse'. *Revue de l'Énergie* 528: 390–6.

Chabot, B. and B. Saulnier. 2001. 'Fair and Efficient Rates for Large Scale Development of Wind Power: The New French Solution'. Paper presented at the CanWEA 2001 Seminar and Conference, Ottawa, 29–31 October.

Chabot, B., P. Kellet, and B. Saulnier. 2002. 'Defining Advanced Wind Energy Tariffs Systems to Specific Locations and Applications: Lessons from the French Tariff System and Examples'. Paper presented at the Global Wind Power Conference, Paris, 2–5 April.

Cochet, Y. 2000. *Stratégies et moyens de développement de l'efficacité énergétique et des sources d'énergie renouvelables*. Paris: Documentation française.

Couture, T. D., K. Cory, C. Kreychik, and E. Williams. 2010. *The Policy Maker's Guide to Feed-in Tariff Policy Design*. Golden, CO: National Renewable Energy Laboratory.

CRE. 2001a. 'Avis de la Commission de régulation de l'électricité en date du 5 juin 2001 sur l'arrêté fixant les conditions d'achat de l'électricité produite par les installations utilisant l'énergie mécanique du vent'. <http://www.cre.fr/documents/deliberations/avis/arrete-fixant-les-conditions-d-achat-de-l-electricite-produite-par-les-installations-utilisant-l-energie-mecanique-du-vent>, accessed 16 December 2014.

CRE. 2001b. 'La CRE a émis un avis négatif sur le tarif de reprise de l'électricité d'origine éolienne'. Press statement, 22 June. <http://www.cre.fr/documents/presse/communiques-de-presse/la-cre-a-emis-un-avis-negatif-sur-le-tarif-de-reprise-de-l-electricite-d-origine-eolienne>, accessed 16 December 2014.

CRE. 2006. 'Avis sur le projet d'arrêté fixant les conditions d'achat de l'électricité produite par les installations utilisant l'énergie du vent'. *Journal Officiel* (27 July). <http://www.cre.fr/imgAdmin/1154108653140.pdf>, accessed 20 October 2006.

Espeland, W. N. and M. Sauder. 2007. 'Rankings and Reactivity: How Public Measures Recreate Social Worlds'. *American Journal of Sociology* 113(1): 1–40.

Espeland, W. N. and M. L. Stevens. 1998. 'Commensuration as a Social Process'. *Annual Review of Sociology* 24: 313–43.

Espeland, W. N. and M. L. Stevens. 2008. 'A Sociology of Quantification'. *European Journal of Sociology* 49(3): 401–36.

EWEA. 2005. 'Large Scale Integration of Wind Energy in the European Power Supply: Analysis, Issues and Recommendations'. <http://www.ewea.org/fileadmin/ewea_documents/documents/publications/grid/051215_Grid_report.pdf>.

Finon, D. and P. Menanteau. 2003. 'The Static and Dynamic Efficiency of Instruments of Promotion of Renewables'. *Energy Studies Review* 12(1): 53–83.

Finon, D. and P. Menanteau. 2004. 'La promotion des énergies renouvelables dans les nouveaux marchés électriques concurrentiels', Working Paper 2004-6, published in the *Annales des Mines-Réalités Industrielles*, August.

Fourcade, M. 2011. 'Price and Prejudice: On Economics, and the Enchantment/Disenchantment of Nature'. In *The Worth of Goods*, ed. J. Beckert and P. Aspers. Oxford: Oxford University Press, 41–63.

Hecht, G. 1998. *The Radiance of France: Nuclear Power and National Identity after World War II*. Cambridge, MA: MIT Press.

Hughes, T. P. 1983. *Networks of Power: Electrification in Western Society, 1880–1930*. Baltimore and London: Johns Hopkins University Press.

Hvelplund, F. 2001a. *Renewable Energy Governance Systems: A Comparison of the 'Political Price-/Amount Market' Model with the 'Political Quota-/Certificate Price Market' System (The German and Danish Cases)*. Ålborg: Ålborg University, Institute for Development and Planning.

Hvelplund, F. 2001b. 'Political Prices or Political Quantities? A Comparison of Renewable Energy Support Systems'. *New Energy* 5: 18–23.

Jensen, I. K. 2003. *Mænd i modvind*. Copenhagen: Børsens Forlag.

Kjellberg, H. and A. Mallard. 2013. 'Valuation Studies? Our Collective Two Cents'. *Valuation Studies* 1(1): 11–30.

Laali, A. R. and M. Benard. 1999. 'French Wind Power Generation Programme EOLE 2005: Results of the First Call for Tenders'. *Energy Policy* 30(10): 839–48.

Muniesa, F. 2007. 'Market Technologies and the Pragmatics of Prices'. *Economy and Society* 36(3): 377–95.

Muniesa, F. 2011. 'A Flank Movement in the Understanding of Valuation'. *Sociological Review* 59(2): 24–38.

Nadaï, A. 2007. 'Planning, Siting and the Local Acceptance of Wind Power: Some Lessons from the French Case'. *Energy Policy* 35(5): 2715–26.

Poignant, S. 2003. *Rapport 2160 pour la commission des affaires économiques, de l'environnement et du territoire sur le projet de loi modifié par le sénat*. Assemblée Nationale (1669).

Stark, D. 2009. *The Sense of Dissonance: Accounts of Worth in Economic Life*. Princeton: Princeton University Press.

Szarka, J. 2007. 'Why is There No Wind Rush in France?' *European Environment* 17(5): 321–33.

Vatin, F. 2013. 'Valuation as Evaluating and Valorizing'. *Valuation Studies* 1(1): 31–50.

Weber, M. 1978 [1922]. *Economy and Society: An Outline of Interpretive Sociology*, vol. 1. Berkeley: University of California Press.

7

Valuation Devices' Orientation to Each Other

Imitation and Differentiation among Devices Valuing Companies' Social and Environmental Performance

Sabina Du Rietz

The present study investigates the orientation of valuation devices in a particular field relative to each other. The study observes a situation in which several similar, although slightly differently composed, valuation devices coexist. A difference in composition, one could argue, may be due to differences in the task at hand, just as a similarity could be due to the similarity in tasks. Conversely, as Czarniawska and Joerges (1996) remark, the inventor of the camera hardly did so to solve the problem of taking pictures. Furthermore, explaining the difference in composition with the difference in what is being valued assumes that we know enough about what is being valued independently of our methods for valuing it. In contrast to simply capturing the value of the object, authors such as Kalthoff (2002) have observed that devices for valuing, in a sense, constitute what they value by representing and/or describing it in certain terms. Particularly in cases where what is valued is something unknown and variable, such as performance, it is hard to argue that the designers are only oriented towards this unknown object when composing its valuation.

If we cannot simply explain valuation devices' composition by referring to what is being valued, then how do we explain their composition? Imitation has been described as a characteristic response to uncertainty in decision-making (Cyert and March 1963). In neo-institutionalist theory, decision-makers imitate peers, especially peers who are perceived to be successful and legitimate, to minimize search costs and to avoid the costs of experimentation (DiMaggio and Powell 1983). When we do not know how to compose a valuation device, looking to the composition of successful peers, orientation in the form of imitation is a possible course of action. However, once adopters have an experience of their own, they may choose to abandon the imitated device. In this vein, Rao et al. (2001) find that when one's own experience reveals the value of the adopted course of action, it alters the institutionalization dynamics. In such cases, circles of adoption, disappointment, and abandonment may occur. In relation to this literature, Beunza and Garud (2007) observe that imitation involves calculation; market actors adopt the calculative frames employed by successful peers. In addition, the authors observe a great deal of variation. Hence, Beunza and Garud (2007) stress that imitation does not fully account for the observed activity. They introduce the notion of frame-making, which emphasizes the strong incentives that exist for analysts to produce original work. They suggest that the notion of frame-making explains how and why analysts deviate from the consensus of their peers. In this way, previous literature suggests that actors are oriented towards each other and each other's devices when designing or adopting a valuation device. Imitation of devices is one reoccurring strategy, but Beunza and Garud (2007) also find that the actors seek originality. Building on this insight and to further explain the composition of valuation devices in a field, the present study investigates: *how are the different valuation devices oriented to each other?*

In this vein, this study analyses valuation devices' orientation towards each other in terms of concurrent imitation and differentiation. It does so informed by Czarniawska and Joerges' (1996) work on the materialization and travel of ideas. Czarniawska and Joerges' (1996) concept of the materialization of ideas underlines that ideas are embedded in devices and may be connected to other ideas occurring at other moments in time. In this way, their account serves to explain valuation devices as oriented towards each other. The analysis is based on empirical examples from a larger study of Nordic investor analysts and their devices for assessing companies' social and environmental work.

Studies of Valuation Devices

Valuation devices can be viewed as models for valuing[1] in a material form or, in the words of Kalthoff (2005), theory-loaded instruments of representation. As such, a valuation device constitutes the object it values by, for example, determining its qualities. If the value models or theories are only incorporated into the heads of economic actors, they may have a precarious status. However, when these theories are incorporated into material devices, they can take on a life of their own. The theory, or 'idea', may in this sense 'travel' (Czarniawska and Joerges 1996). When incorporated into procedures, routines, and material devices, the models or theories can have effects, even if those who use them are sceptical of the model's virtues, unaware of its details, or even ignorant of the underlying idea's very existence (MacKenzie 2006). Pinch (2008, 467) calls it 'the embedding or freezing of choices' when social choices are so deeply embedded in technologies that they appear to have vanished. These ideas and their choices, embedded into material devices, produce effects because social action is mediated by materiality. We put agency into devices and the devices assert agency in constraining our action. When the incorporated choices and assumptions appear to have vanished or appear invisible, then these have become powerful institutions (Pinch 2008).

Valuation devices also shape what they value. By visualizing, valuation devices may be used to conceive of organizations in specific terms with the purpose of intervention (Hopwood 1992). In fact, many times a device is introduced with the belief that 'what gets measured gets done'. However, the visualization a valuation device brings may have unintended effects such that the making visible starts to change that which was rendered transparent (Roberts 2009). Valuation devices may induce reactivity in the valued object. Valuation devices elicit responses because people are reflexive beings who monitor and interpret the world and adjust their actions accordingly (Espeland and Sauder 2007). However, valuation devices do not just visualize or induce reactivity; they also constitute what they value by representing and/or describing it in certain terms (Kalthoff 2002, 2005). Through valuation, the object's value is not just revealed. It is brought into existence.

One area where valuation devices are introduced and employed to visualize and elicit responses is the social and environmental corporate scene. In reaction to concerns about human effects on the environment, corporate social and environmental performance is calculated and assessed by a range of actors in a variety of ways. On a corporate level, there are reporting frameworks, such as the Global Reporting Initiative (GRI), that a company can adopt to conceive of its own actions and sustainability performance. A company's performance is also calculated by external actors such as non-governmental organizations (NGOs) (O'Dwyer et al. 2005), investors (Arjaliès 2010; Du Rietz 2013), and researchers (Igalens and Gond 2005). Previous work in the area has studied valuation devices such as Corporate Social Performance (CSP) employed within Socially Responsible Investment (Déjean et al. 2004), the GRI framework (Brown et al. 2009; Etzion and Ferraro 2010) for sustainability reporting, and the Carbon Disclosure Project (Kolk et al. 2008) for climate change and accounting procedures for global carbon markets (Lohmann 2009; MacKenzie 2009). These cases emphasize the role of valuation devices in the social and environmental area, such as how measurement tools influence the legitimacy of an industry (Déjean et al. 2004) or frame new agents, spaces, relations, and objects (Lohmann 2009).

Among those who, in a sense, explore the concurrent similarity and difference in valuation devices, there is Beunza and Garud's (2007) study of frame-makers. They study the reports written by security analysts about a particular object of valuation: the company Amazon. Their study highlights that the analysts deviate from the consensus of their peers; thus, there are differences in the valuation practices. The authors suggest that frame-making, the construction of the device, explains how and why. They find that there are strong incentives for analysts to produce original work and that the quickest way is to provide an original interpretation by means of a calculative frame. They also find that imitation is calculative, as actors do not simply copy others' actions but, in fact, adopt the calculative frames employed by successful peers. Beunza and Garud's (2007) study thus suggests that analysts' valuation devices are oriented to each other because they find both striking regularity and rivalry in frames, as well as imitation in terms of circulating Excel spreadsheets. The authors propose that changes in frames arise from the combined effect of information and the social context. The present study builds on these insights and further investigates orientation among devices, such as imitation and differentiation.

Explaining Differences and Similarity in Valuation Devices

Investigating differences versus similarity is a popular tradition within organizational theory. In reaction to research focused on explaining the variety in organizational structure, DiMaggio and Powell (1983) turned the focus to the startling similarity, the homogeneity, in organizational forms and practices. They argued that organizational fields display diversity at the outset, but, when established, there is an inexorable push towards homogenization in approach and form. Their account thus views homogenization as occurring over time with maturation. They use the concept isomorphism to describe the process of homogenization and identify three mechanisms through which it occurs: coercive, mimetic, and normative. Valuation devices, such as performance measures, can be understood from the perspective of institutional processes. Meyer (1994), for example, states that the spread of performance measures can be explained by institutional theory to the extent that it can be linked to external developments that force performance measures upon organizations, i.e. coercive isomorphism. Alternatively, in the absence of compulsion, institutional theory explains the spread of performance measures as imitation of one another's performance measures for the sake of legitimation, i.e. mimetic isomorphism.

To make sense of the fact that organizations simultaneously reveal striking similarities and differences, Sahlin-Andersson (1996) adds to DiMaggio and Powell (1983) and argues that we need to study how forms and practices are shaped and reshaped in the various stages of diffusion. In Czarniawska and Joerges' (1996) terms, we need to follow how ideas travel. Czarniawska and Joerges (1996) theorize change as ideas turning into action in ever new localities and local action emerging and becoming institutionalized on a more 'global' scale. Czarniawska and Joerges (1996) are thus concerned with how individual action becomes collectivized and the other way around. The present study is informed by their theorization of the materialization of ideas and imitation. In their account, ideas materialize into forms of writings and recordings. In this way, ideas of valuing corporate social and environmental performance take the material form of written-down combinations of variables and formulas.

Czarniawska and Joerges' (1996) concept of the materialization of ideas underlines the ideas embedded in devices. This view of devices is similar to Kalthoff's (2005) theory-loaded instruments. However, Czarniawska and Joerges' (1996) materialization of ideas connects the ideas embedded in devices to those occurring at other moments in time. To become public knowledge, an idea must become objectified (Czarniawska and Joerges 1996). Only then can it travel between local places and moments and, from a point of view, be seen as translocal. This way, their account helps us explain valuation devices as oriented towards each other.

Czarniawska and Joerges (1996) reject the micro–macro type of framework and instead describe a translocal pattern as consisting of connected localities. Because of their interest in how the local and translocal interact, Czarniawska and Joerges (1996) provide an interesting view of imitation. In a given time/space, some actors discover an idea, which may appear new. In fact, it is new in this particular context. When we take a translocal perspective, however, we discover patterns of imitation and reject the view of it as novel. How do we reconcile these accounts? Czarniawska and Joerges (1996) write that we recognize ideas as 'the same' or 'different' according to what our social categorization tells us to see. 'New' local action means a change in practices existing in a given place and moment, although it may recreate an old institution at another time, elsewhere. Thus, what may, from a translocal point of view, be viewed as imitation may, from a local point of view, be seen as original and new. The actors involved rarely see more than one or two stages of the entire process because they are framed by events in their local time/space. To identify this 'new' action as 'the same', as institutional isomorphism, one has to take a translocal view. According to Czarniawska and Joerges (1996), researchers typically take the translocal view, whereas actors are bound to their local time and place as their frame of reference.

This view of how actions are both individual and collective informs the following analysis. Instead of deciding what is imitation and differentiation from a researcher perspective, I here take into account the local views and actions that result in, from a translocal point of view, the imitation or travel of ideas. In particular, this perspective helps explain how orientation among devices may appear as differentiation from a translocal point of view but is perceived as 'the same' in a local perspective. Alternatively, how imitation from a translocal point of view is not perceived as such in the local perspective.

Research Site, Data Collection, and Analysis

The example used here is part of a larger study of the field of Nordic investor analysts analysing corporate social and environmental performance, conducted between December 2009 and November 2012. The example I mainly use here is an initiative and collaboration among fifteen large Swedish institutional investors[2] that sent a survey to the 100 largest Swedish listed companies to assess their social and environmental performance. This survey is one example of a valuation device in the field of Nordic investors concerned with companies' social and environmental performance. While there exist many similar valuation devices in the overall study that could have been displayed here and the analysis would, in general, apply to them as well, I have focused on the present example because the 'travel of ideas' is particularly evident with imitation between devices in two national contexts, Norway and Sweden. In addition, the devices' detailed composition over time is also available for analysis and display.

The extracts from the empirical material presented in the analysis are from interviews with the investors involved in the Swedish initiative, observations of meetings and presentations, and documents of the survey or where it is mentioned. However, to study orientation among devices, it is clearly necessary to take into account other devices, towards which the studied device is or could be oriented. Hence, while focusing on the example of the survey device, knowledge of other related devices in the field where the investors and their devices are located is necessary. As a result, the overall analysis is informed by the entirety of the field material, but the above-mentioned empirical material forms the basis for the selected example, presented in the following.

A Valuation Device in Survey Form

Of the studied investors, fifteen asset managers and asset owners active on the Swedish market are engaged in a national 'Sustainable Value Creation Initiative'. The initiative sent out a survey to the 100 largest companies listed on the NASDAQ OMX in Stockholm for the first time in 2009 and a second time in 2011. The survey aimed to assess these companies' social and environmental performance and was addressed to the chairman of each board. For some of the investors in the Swedish initiative, this survey is their sole device for assessing companies' social and environmental performance. For others, it is a complement to other similar devices that they possess and use. The survey's focus is mainly on the management of social and environmental aspects. Good performance, or a good score, is achieved if the companies work with social and environmental issues in certain ways. The survey, in the words of Power (1997), is hence a form of 'control of control'.

The survey requires company representatives to fill it in. It is thus a form of company self-assessment, albeit structured and evaluated according to rules set by the investors. The possibilities of what can be a social and environmental performance are limited. The company representatives can choose from a limited range of predetermined possible answers or boxes to check. The survey hence requires the respondents to identify with the suggested responses and, in a way, commensurate (Espeland and Stevens 1998) their answers. As a result of the survey, the investor analysts receive a seemingly comparable range of data of the companies' social and environmental performance.

The survey is composed of mainly categories and variables. In the case of the Swedish 2011 survey, the variables were organized under four categories, as shown in Figure 7.1.

These four broad categories are, in turn, composed of a number of questions. Each question further consists of one or several variables. Figure 7.2 is an example from Part One, Governing Guidelines, question number seven.

Question number seven of Part One concerns environmental guidelines and is divided into seven variables, for example, guidelines regarding climate change or emissions to air. Each of these variables can be answered with an answer from a range of five options.

Scales are frequently used in the composition of the survey. In question number seven of Part One, there is an implicit scale on which the company's answer will be located. The answer can be a 'better' answer (the guidelines are publicly available) or a worse answer (the company does not have any guidelines). In the survey, there are also more explicit forms of scales on which the company's

Aimed at the 100 biggest companies listed on the Nasadq OMX, the survey contains a total of 28 question within four main areas:

1. Governing guidelines
2. Implementation and compliance
3. Communication and reporting
4. The responsibility of the board

Figure 7.1. Swedish 2011 survey structure

PART 1 – GOVERNING GUIDELINES

7. Does your company have guidelines concerning its impact on the climate and external environment?

	Yes, publicly available	Yes, available internally	To be completed during 2011	No	Not relevant
The environment—in general	□	□	□	□	□
Climate change	□	□	□	□	□
Emissions to air	□	□	□	□	□
Emissions to water and land	□	□	□	□	□
Consumption of resources (energy, water, etc.)	□	□	□	□	□
Waste management	□	□	□	□	□
Biodiversity	□	□	□	□	□

Figure 7.2. Swedish 2011 survey, question number seven of Part One

PART 1 – GOVERNING GUIDELINES

2. Does your company work towards indentifying substantial risks in relation to sustainable value creation?

Sustainable value creation referes to value creation that takes into account the balance between financial, environmental, and social values.

You can provide examples or additional comments below.

□ Every year
□ Every other year
□ When necessary
□ Scheduled during 2011
□ No

Figure 7.3. Swedish 2011 survey, question number two of Part One

answer is located. One example is frequency; if the company answers that it does something more frequently it earns 2 points and if it does something less frequently it earns 0 points, as in the question shown in Figure 7.3.

Other questions do not include scales but, rather, are binary. The company can answer simply yes or no, with 1 or 3 points for yes and 0 points for no. In all of the survey, each answer corresponds to a certain score.

The results of these variables are added up and become the result of the question. All questions in the survey are assigned a weight by how much the answer contributes to the result of its particular survey area.[3] Hence, the results of the questions are weighted and further added up and become the performance of a particular area; in the case of the questions displayed here, the area is 'Governing Guidelines'. Every survey area is assigned a weight relative to how heavily it affects the overall results. In the present case, each of the four areas has a weight of 25 per cent. In the overall survey results, the companies' performance is represented by a score and certain companies achieve a higher score than others. Hence, their total scores are located on a numerical scale. The same valuation device is used to produce each company's score.

How the categories and variables are combined does not simply reflect what they attempt to measure, i.e. social and environmental performance, but also reflects their orientation to others of their kind, as we will see in the following section.

Diverging Accounts of Similarity

Having studied the Swedish initiative and survey for a few months, I discovered that it was related to a similar Norwegian initiative. The Norwegian initiative and survey can be seen as a forerunner to the Swedish one. Three of the Swedish investors, also active on the Norwegian market, participated in both initiatives. The Norwegian initiative sent out its first survey in 2008 and the second in 2009. In fact, the first project manager of the Swedish initiative was from a Norwegian financial institution that also participated in the Norwegian initiative. For the three investors who are active on the Norwegian and the Swedish market, the Swedish survey was, in a sense, an extension to what they had already done in the Norwegian market. Because of the link to the Norwegian survey, it is less clear whether the Swedish survey as a device is 'new' or if it is an imitation of the Norwegian one. If it is an imitation, then the Norwegian theorization and underlying ideas of what should comprise corporate social and environmental performance has 'travelled' into a new national context.

Interestingly, the view of the orientation between the Norwegian survey and the Swedish one differed between the different localities. The Swedish initiative did not refer to the Norwegian one in interviews, for example, which is why I only discovered its existence after a few months. The difference in views is mirrored in the two 2009 survey reports. This was the first year of the Swedish survey and the second year for the Norwegian one. The Swedish 2009 report only notes, at the end of the report, that the Norwegian survey is 'a model' for the Swedish one. In contrast, the Norwegian report refers to the Swedish survey as an extension of itself:

> The second aspect that is new is that this year the survey is also being carried out in Sweden with the support of major Swedish investors. That gives us the opportunity to compare ourselves with our neighbouring country.

In the Norwegian report, it appears as if the two surveys are the same device. In the Swedish context, however, there was no question that these two surveys were two separate devices. A Swedish participant, from an institution involved in both initiatives, acknowledged that the composition of the Swedish survey had been modelled on the Norwegian survey but claimed that the Swedish project members had composed at least 50 per cent of the questions. Similarly, the second project manager for the Swedish survey noted that the Swedish report did not include a ranking of the companies' performance, which the Norwegian report from the same year did.[4] In general, the Swedish initiative and its representatives thus underlined the differences between their survey and its Norwegian model. By viewing the Norwegian survey as a model, the Swedish initiative saw the two surveys as separate devices linked by some degree of imitation or inspiration.

Comparing the 2009 Swedish survey with the Norwegian one, side by side, one difference in composition is that a question clearly specific to the Norwegian market is removed from the Swedish survey. Another difference is that a question about election of board of directors is replaced by a question about the board's annual risk analysis and sustainability areas. In addition, the answers to check are adjusted in a few questions. Overall, from this point of view, the Swedish survey clearly shares striking features with the Norwegian one. The layout and almost identical formulations reinforce this appearance. Whether these two surveys are separate devices or not, the overall ideas of corporate social and environmental performance have, from the perspective of this type of comparison, travelled into a new national context and locality. From the point of view of the Norwegians, the two devices were initially the same valuation device applied on different subjects, companies based on nationality. In this sense, the ideas had not travelled. The valuation device had just extended its application.

The degree of imitation and comparability between the two devices would diminish over time. First, the Norwegian initiative did not send out the survey in parallel with the Swedish 2011 survey. Second, neither of the two surveys had stable compositions. Both the Swedish and the Norwegian surveys were re-composed and hence, not stable over time. In 2008, the Norwegian survey consisted of 20 unsorted questions, but one year later it contained 27 questions that were explicitly structured under new overarching 'active management' headlines. A question about whether six different social and environmental areas were part of the company's target management had disappeared, for example. A question about whether the company integrates sustainability in different organizational strategies (each spelled out) appeared. Likewise, the Swedish survey increased from 26 questions in 2009 to 28 questions in 2011.

In a way, the changes in composition over time among the national surveys were larger than the differences between the imitated and imitation in 2009. Despite this fact, the national devices were unquestionably viewed as 'the same', whereas the national surveys, particularly from the perspective of the Swedes, were viewed as separate devices. The Swedish 2011 survey form, slightly different from the Swedish 2009 survey, states on its first page:

> The survey is composed in the same way as in 2009; however, certain modifications have been made within the respective areas. The questions are formulated such that they can be applied to all companies, regardless of the industry or market. Nevertheless, the relevance of the questions may vary. Please use the comments fields to clarify your responses and provide more specific details applicable to your particular company.

To the Swedish initiative, it is clearly the same device used for the same purpose, although it has changed in its content (more content) and structure (dividing the survey into four parts). Apart from such changes, many of its formulations are identical. Thus, the changes are not of the type that would make the Swedish investors view it as a 'new' device.

After the 2009 Swedish survey, a new project coordinator was assigned to the project. The second project coordinator was from a Swedish asset owner and, unlike the first coordinator, not involved in the Norwegian initiative. In interviews with the new coordinator, it appeared that the device was this time foremost oriented towards its past (2009) version. Part of this orientation consisted of self-imitation, reproducing what the 2009 survey had contained, but part of it was also different from the 2009 survey. An example of the self-imitation is that the question about the board's risk analysis, which was one of the differences between the Swedish and Norwegian surveys, remained. Overall, the survey still consisted mainly of the same questions, ensuring a level of consistency and continuity. However, several answer options had disappeared or been reformulated. A few new questions appeared, for example, again in the area of the board's sustainability work. As another example of differentiation, areas in the 2009 survey where the companies scored fewer points were extended.

To summarize, the Norwegian 2009 survey and its materialized ideas could, from a translocal perspective, be viewed as orientation in the form of imitation and as having travelled into the Swedish context. Concurrently, neither of the local groups of actors viewed it exactly this way. The Norwegian initiative viewed the Swedish survey as their device being launched in the Swedish setting. The Swedes, for their part, saw their survey as mainly their own composition, although they acknowledged that the Norwegian survey was a model and that there was a degree of imitation that would allow for some useful comparability. Hence, imitation, from a translocal view, is not necessarily 'simply' imitation in the local.

Considering the 2011 Swedish survey, did the ideas that had travelled into the Swedish context last over time? Again, the local and translocal perspectives diverge. From the Swedish initiative's perspective, the 2011 survey was 'the same' survey. Comparing it to its 2009 version, however, the differences are, in a sense, larger than between the Norwegian and Swedish 2009 surveys. Thus, differences and originality do not mean, in the local, that something is new. Large similarities do not mean that it is the same or an imitation either. From the point of view of composition, the materialized ideas were modified in the 2011 survey, compared to the 2009 Swedish survey. From this perspective, the travelled ideas did not last in the form they had arrived. Despite this, in the local, the orientation between the Swedish 2009 and 2011 surveys was mainly viewed as self-imitation.

Discovering Similarity Without Imitation

While the Swedes and Norwegians held different views of the orientation between the two survey devices, the difference in views did not seem incompatible. If there was a disagreement, it was not something they expressed or about which they particularly did something. In contrast, in the Swedish setting, differing views of the device's similarity to and difference from other devices did become an issue that the initiative had to address. In particular, the Swedish companies subject to the survey viewed it as sharing important features with other valuation devices available in the field.

In their presentation of the 2009 survey results, the Swedish investors claimed that company representatives had called the survey a 'useful internal exercise'. Despite this fact, it appeared that the survey respondents did not whole-heartedly welcome the survey. In fact, most of the questions posed by the survey respondents during the survey presentation concerned whether the investors would use the information provided in the survey to make investment decisions and, if so, how it would be used in comparison to other information sources the investors already had and receive through other devices. Thus, the need for this particular device had to be defended in response to questions from company representatives during observations, in interviews and on the initiative's website. Seemingly, the survey's existence and composition in a field with what the companies perceived as similar devices was not uncontroversial.

> Yes, the Swedish companies that are a bit irritated, they wrote us a letter where they mentioned some different rating institutes, but I hardly know of these ones. I know of one of them. So that's [the ratings] nothing we use. I understand that they think it's annoying to fill in 40 surveys when you don't know what they are used for.

The ones that recognized the similarity between the initiative's valuation device and others in the field were the companies that were subject to the valuation. In response, the initiative members highlighted differences, such as a new question on board responsibility, by comparing the survey's composition to other devices. Because of the companies' claim of similarity between their device and that of others, it had to be underlined that the survey contained types of variables that the other devices did not. As one investor expressed during an interview:

> We wouldn't have posed these questions in a survey that way if we didn't feel that the type of questions... Then, there's certain questions 'Have you signed the Global Compact?', which was question number two; of course, we know this in other ways too, but many of the questions in the Sustainable Value Creation Initiative are of a character that you don't report on in the sustainability report. It's quite unusual, for example, to report on what kind of ESG indicators affect bonus outcomes and so on.

This way, the respondent acknowledged that certain content of the survey was included in other available devices as well. However, in the quote, she emphasizes content not included by certain devices, such as the sustainability reports. While the companies recognized similarities between the initiative's survey and rating devices, the investors did not particularly know these devices; thus, these rating devices did not directly affect how they composed their device. Just because the companies highlighted similarities between survey devices in the field did not mean that the investors would orient their device towards these ones. However, the investors are familiar with certain other devices in the field, such as sustainability reporting in the quote, and would orient their device towards these. Even more precise identification of which devices the initiative members recognize as similar and themselves compare with their survey is available in the FAQ on the Swedish survey initiative's website:

> Many companies already fill in other extensive surveys, for example the CDP (Carbon Disclosure Project) and the SAM/DJSI (Dow Jones Sustainability Index). The praxis is also developing, for example, the GRI (Global Reporting Initiative). Why is this survey needed and how extensive is it to fill in? CDP, SAM/DJSI and GRI are more exhaustive and detailed and include the measuring and reporting of companies' performances, while our investigation focuses on companies' governance and control systems. Many surveys are not public, with the result that we as investors do not have access to companies' responses. The project group's viewpoint is that our investigation complements the existing surveys and for most companies is less demanding in terms of resources and the time required to fill it in.

Here, the initiative identifies particular devices: CDP, SAM/DJSI, and GRI. By underlining the individual accentuation in composition, such as the focus on governance and control systems, the initiative argues that the survey device complements the other surveys rather than substitutes them, for example.

Whereas GRI is a reporting framework, both CDP and SAM/DJSI are surveys. The survey devices, in particular, share a critical feature: they require companies' time to fill in the survey. Competition for company responses and the risk of survey fatigue, possibly leading to a low response rate, motivate differentiation in the investor's device. However, all devices relying on corporate reporting compete in a sense. When a device relies on corporate reporting (which is not always the case; for example, some devices rely on media reporting or service provider data), the companies resent having to continually provide identical information.

The investors may not have been oriented towards these already available devices in the field when composing their first 2009 survey. If they had been, some of the questions they received might have been avoided and the need to defend it would have never appeared. However, when planning for the second survey, the initiative had been made aware of similarities between their device and competing devices. As an example, respondents argued in interviews that because of the survey and reporting fatigue, they waited two years after the 2009 survey before they sent out the next survey. It was also argued that this delay would also allow the companies time to progress because some changes could not be done rapidly. Another example is that the Global Compact question was reformulated from the 2009 survey to the 2011 one.

Discussion

Valuation devices can be seen as 'materialized ideas' (Czarniawska and Joerges 1996). In the present case, the valuation device contains ideas of how companies should manage their social and environmental work and how this work should be assessed. In the Swedish 2011 survey, for example, companies score higher if they have a system in place where social and environmental performance affects management's variable salary. Thus, there is an underlying assumption that such systems and effects on variable salary are desirable and hence, having a system in place contributes to a higher value of the companies' social and environmental work.

As in previous research, I find that these materialized ideas, such as that social and environmental performance should affect management's variable salary, can be seen as coming from somewhere. In fact, as studies such as that of Beunza and Garud (2007) suggest, valuation devices are oriented towards each other. By studying valuation devices as materialized ideas, we can seek to trace how the ideas travel in and between momentary spaces. Thereby, from a translocal point of view, they form the orientation patterns of imitation and differentiation. In the present case, for example, while the Norwegian survey was not sent out in 2011, large parts of its ideas of corporate social and environmental performance and how it should be assessed can be seen in the Swedish survey. What had travelled into the new Swedish context unaffected can be viewed as institutionalized. The changes to the Norwegian survey and its materialized ideas that, in the future continue to be imitated, can be seen as revitalizing the institutional order (Czarniawska and Joerges 1996).

Taking into account the actors' own view of events, the empirical story is not just a story of imitation. This way, the present work adds a perspective that is not included in some earlier work on devices and imitation (e.g. Déjean et al. 2004; Beunza and Garud 2007). Granted, the Swedish initiative referred to the Norwegian survey as a model, just the term DiMaggio and Powell (1983) use when they describe mimetic behaviour. In this sense, the diverging views concerned not so much the process, imitation in the form of modelling, as the outcome. It is clear that the Swedish 2009 survey was not perceived as imitation in the Swedish or Norwegian localities. Czarniawska and Joerges (1996) write that viewing something as 'the same' and 'different' depends on what our social categorization tells us to see. In the present case, the social categorization differed not only between the translocal and local levels but also between the two, although interconnected, localities of the Swedish and Norwegian investor communities. The Norwegians, framed by events in their local time/space, viewed the Swedish survey as an extension of their own survey, while the Swedes perceived that they had composed large parts of the survey themselves and that it was clearly a separate device. The outcome of imitation can evidently be viewed in different ways, not necessarily as similarity.

The other example of diverging accounts between the local and translocal is the self-imitation and self-differentiation between the 2009 and 2011 Swedish surveys. Again, the accounts of the process, self-imitation and self-differentiation, are not the main points of difference but the accounts of the outcomes of this process. From the local Swedish initiative's point of view, the two Swedish surveys were unquestionably 'the same'. From a translocal point of view, however, it could be seen as changed; the differences between the 2009 and 2011 surveys were more significant than those between the Norwegian and Swedish surveys. The categories of business ethics and anti-corruption, for example, were no longer joined together in questions but were now separated and treated as separate issues. From a researcher or translocal point of view, such changes can be seen as significant developments but were not recognized as such in the local.

Because of such changes, the ideas that had travelled into the Swedish context did not remain in the form in which they had arrived. In a sense, the materialized ideas did not 'remain' at all but travelled into a new time/space with the 2011 Swedish version of the survey. Some of the ideas survived, but others did not, and yet others were modified, such as separating the categories of anti-corruption and business ethics. As Czarniawska and Joerges (1996) write, using the example of a city that plans a metro, was it the same metro that emerged 50 years after its planning and was it the same city that needed the metro? In the present case, only two years had passed, but the initiative members had gained experience in those two years, some project members had changed staff, there was a new project manager, and the companies to be valued had undoubtedly changed as well. From this point of view, the survey was not the same, and the object to be valued was not the same. Through the orientation towards the 2009 Swedish survey, however, ideas incorporated in the 2009 survey travelled and materialized again in 2011, from one momentary space to another. Again, a few ideas disappeared, and others were simply adjusted in the process.

The sameness and difference between devices can also be, in some way, negotiated among interconnected localities. As shown in the examples, the companies that are subject to the valuation perceived similarities between the Swedish 2009 survey and other available devices in the field. Because the investors depend on the companies to respond to their surveys, they could not disregard their point of view of sameness between their survey and other valuation devices. Thus, sometimes the interconnected localities and their diverging views of sameness and difference encounter and interfere with each other. In this case, the similarity was not the result of a process of imitation. The investors in the initiative had not attempted to imitate the rating surveys to which the companies referred. Framed by their time/space, however, the companies recognized similarities that were not visible to the Swedish initiative. When composing the second survey, the Swedish initiative was at least conscious of the views of the companies. They had, for example, produced statements defending the composition of their survey.

Conclusion

The present work investigates how valuation devices are oriented towards each other. In this way, it underlines the existence of other types of social demands, such as the orientation of valuation devices to each other, which have effects on how we assess value. Studying valuation devices in this way emphasizes that valuation devices are not simply composed in terms of what they assess. The ideas of how something should be valued may come from elsewhere. The present work analyses the orientation between devices in terms of the classic dichotomy of imitation and differentiation. It does so informed by the work of Czarniawska and Joerges (1996) on travel and materialization of ideas. Valuation devices can, from this perspective, be seen as materialized ideas. In this vein and in contrast to some earlier studies, the present work takes into account orientation in local time/space that, from a translocal perspective, may form patterns of imitation and differentiation. Thus, in line with Czarniawska and Joerges' (1996) approach, the present work does not attempt to decide when devices are imitations or different, but to connect translocal patterns to local realities.

In line with Czarniawska and Joerges (1996), the analysis shows diverging views of when devices are 'new' or 'the same', particularly between the translocal and local perspectives. In addition, in the present case, the views also differed among different localities, such as the Swedish and Norwegian investor communities. Thus, there is not one local and one translocal view, as a micro/macro division might suggest, but several localities, possibly with conflicting views of devices' similarities and differences. Sometimes the different local views of valuation devices' orientations encounter each other and have to be reconciled or in some other way influence events. This was the case of the Swedish initiative and the companies subject to their valuation. The companies discovered and noted the similarity between existing rating devices and the investors' survey device. In response, the investors underscored any difference between their device and other devices. In this way, there were attempts to reconcile the diverging views of the devices' similarities and differences. The discovered similarity affected local events, such as the work with the next survey.

This example also illustrates when similarity in valuation devices is not a consequence of imitation. Imitating one device may result in unintended similarity with another device, from both a local and a translocal point of view. The Swedish initiative agreed that the Norwegian survey served as a model, but they had no intention of imitating the rating surveys. Imitation is, supposedly, intentional, and in this example, any similarity with the rating surveys was unintentional. As the respondent said, they were not aware of these rating surveys before the companies had brought attention to them. The companies, in a way, made the rating devices part of the initiative's locality. Without taking into account the local perspective, one might have interpreted the similarity between the devices as mimetic isomorphism. Thus, although we may identify patterns of similarities and differences, this does not necessarily mean that there is orientation in the form of imitation.

Was the similarity with the rating devices coincidental? Both devices might still, in some way, be influenced by the same ideas. However, the route of travel was not as simple as direct imitation in this case. A fruitful approach for further research, hence, may be to look at several steps of travelling ideas, as well as over longer periods of time.

Acknowledgements

I gratefully acknowledge the financial support of Jan Wallander and Tom Hedelius, as well as the Infina Foundation. An earlier version of this chapter was presented at LAEMOS 2014.

Notes

1. Valuing has been defined as measuring and comparing something according to a scale. Evaluation is related to value and refers to the classification and categorization of things to allow us to distinguish their value in relation to one another (Aspers and Beckert 2011).
2. In this case, large banks, pension funds, insurance companies, foundations, etc.
3. A picture of the weighting is not included because the document is solely in Swedish.
4. It is, in fact, not a ranking but a display of which companies are located in which range of the survey score.

References

Arjaliès, D.-L. 2010. 'Institutional Change in the Making: The Case of Socially Responsible Investment'. Essec Business School, Cergy, France.

Aspers, P. and J. Beckert. 2011. 'Value in Markets'. In *The Worth of Goods: Valuation and Pricing in Markets*, ed. J. Beckert, and P. Aspers. Oxford: Oxford University Press, 3–38.

Beunza, D. and R. Garud. 2007. 'Calculators, Lemmings or Frame-Makers? The Intermediary Role of Securities Analysts'. *Sociological Review* 55(2): 13–39.

Brown, H. S., M. de Jong, and D. L. Levy. 2009. 'Building Institutions Based on Information Disclosure: Lessons from GRI's Sustainability Reporting'. *Journal of Cleaner Production* 17(6): 571–80.

Cyert, R. M. and J. G. March. 1963. *A Behavioral Theory of the Firm*. Englewood Cliffs: Prentice-Hall.

Czarniawska, B. and B. Joerges. 1996. 'Travel of Ideas'. In *Translating Organizational Change*, ed. B. Czarniawska, and G. Sevón. Berlin: de Gruyter, 13–48.

Déjean, F., J.-P. Gond, and B. Leca. 2004. 'Measuring the Unmeasured: An Institutional Entrepreneur Strategy in an Emerging Industry'. *Human Relations* 57(6): 741–64.

DiMaggio, P. J. and W. W. Powell. 1983. 'The Iron Cage Revisited: Institutional Isomorphism and Collective Rationality in Organizational Fields'. *American Sociological Review* 48(2): 147–60.

Du Rietz, S. 2013. 'Accounting in the Field of Governance'. School of Business, Stockholm University, Stockholm.

Espeland, W. N. and M. Sauder. 2007. 'Rankings and Reactivity: How Public Measures Recreate Social Worlds'. *American Journal of Sociology* 113(1): 1–40.

Espeland, W. N. and M. L. Stevens. 1998. 'Commensuration as a Social Process'. *Annual Review of Sociology* 24(1): 313–43.

Etzion, D. and F. Ferraro. 2010. 'The Role of Analogy in the Institutionalization of Sustainability Reporting'. *Organization Science* 21(5): 1092–1107.

Hopwood, A. G. 1992. 'Accounting Calculation and the Shifting Sphere of the Economic'. *European Accounting Review* 1(1): 125–43.

Igalens, J. and J.-P. Gond. 2005. 'Measuring Corporate Social Performance in France: A Critical and Empirical Analysis of ARESE Data'. *Journal of Business Ethics* 56(2): 131–48.

Kalthoff, H. 2002. 'Figures, Writing and Calculation Thoughts on the Representation of Economic Practices'. *Economic Sociology, European Electronic Newsletter* 3(3): 28–40.

Kalthoff, H. 2005. 'Practices of Calculation'. *Theory, Culture & Society* 22(2): 69–97.

Kolk, A., D. Levy, and J. Pinkse. 2008. 'Corporate Responses in an Emerging Climate Regime: The Institutionalization and Commensuration of Carbon Disclosure'. *European Accounting Review* 17(4): 719–45.

Lohmann, L. 2009. 'Toward a Different Debate in Environmental Accounting: The Cases of Carbon and Cost–Benefit'. *Accounting, Organizations and Society* 34(3–4): 499–534.

MacKenzie, D. 2006. *An Engine, Not a Camera: How Financial Models Shape Markets*. Cambridge, MA: MIT Press.

MacKenzie, D. 2009. 'Making Things the Same: Gases, Emission Rights and the Politics of Carbon Markets'. *Accounting, Organizations and Society* 34(3–4): 440–55.

Meyer, M. W. 1994. 'Measuring Performance in Economic Organizations'. In *The Handbook of Economic Sociology*, ed. N. J. Smelser and R. Swedberg. Princeton: Princeton University Press, 556–80.

O'Dwyer, B., J. Unerman, and E. Hession. 2005. 'User Needs in Sustainability Reporting: Perspectives of Stakeholders in Ireland'. *European Accounting Review* 14(4): 759–87.

Pinch, T. 2008. 'Technology and Institutions: Living in a Material World'. *Theory and Society* 37(5): 461–83.

Power, M. 1997. *The Audit Society: Rituals of Verification*. Oxford: Clarendon Press.

Rao, H., H. R. Greve, and G. F. Davis. 2001. 'Fool's Gold: Social Proof in the Initiation and Abandonment of Coverage by Wall Street Analysts'. *Administrative Science Quarterly* 46(3): 502–26.

Roberts, J. 2009. 'No One is Perfect: The Limits of Transparency and an Ethic for "Intelligent" Accountability'. *Accounting, Organizations and Society* 34(8): 957–70.

Sahlin-Andersson, K. 1996. 'Imitating By Editing Success: The Construction of Organizational Fields'. In *Translating Organizational Change*, ed. B. Czarniawska and G. Sevón. Berlin: de Gruyter, 69–92.

8

What Is a Catastrophe Model Worth?

The (e)Valuative Practices of Cat Analysts in Insurance Companies

Laure Cabantous and Théodora Dupont-Courtade

Introduction

Hélène is a 'catastrophe risk' analyst at INSUR Group, a large European insurance company that has subsidiaries in more than fifty countries. As a 'Cat analyst' in the headquarters of INSUR Group, her job consists of estimating the level of accumulation of catastrophe risks—such as hurricanes, earthquakes, floods, or tsunamis—that INSUR Group has in its portfolio of insurance policies. Put simply, Hélène provides INSUR Group with an evaluation of its exposure to catastrophe risks. This evaluation is critical to INSUR Group activity as like any insurance company, INSUR Group is a risk-bearing entity, which can become insolvent if enormous losses, such as the ones created by catastrophe risks, occur.[1] After Hurricane Andrew hit Florida in 1992 for instance, nine insurers became insolvent as a result of the losses they incurred (Kunreuther 2005). The evaluation of the exposure to catastrophe risks (or 'view of risk') that the Cat team produces annually is thus a crucial input for several INSUR Group teams, such as the reinsurance team—which negotiates contracts with reinsurers[2]—and the team in charge of ensuring that INSUR Group meets its solvency capital requirements.

To assess INSUR Group's exposure to catastrophe risks, Hélène relies on catastrophe models developed by third-party firms. Over the last two decades, catastrophe modelling has become the standard technology to estimate the future losses from potential natural catastrophes (Clark 2002). Catastrophe models are incredibly useful as they reduce the uncertainty inherent to the evaluation of the economic consequences of natural catastrophes. Yet, the three catastrophe models that are available on the market do not necessarily give the same estimate of an insurance company's risk exposure, as each model embodies a specific set of assumptions or 'calculating frame' (Beunza and Garud 2007). If the reliance on one catastrophe model alone can reduce uncertainty, the simultaneous use of 'dissonant' models (Beunza and Stark 2012) generates further uncertainty. How do Hélène and her colleagues from the Cat team deal with this uncertainty? How do they reconcile dissonant risk estimates in order to confidently evaluate INSUR Group's exposure to catastrophe risks? In short, how do they know what a catastrophe model is worth?

In this chapter, we build on the rich body of work from economic sociology which shows the 'material reality of calculation' (Callon 1998, 5) and the importance of calculation and valuation practices in the functioning of markets (Espeland and Stevens 1998, 2008; Karpik 2000, 2011; Power 2004; Callon and Muniesa 2005; Lamont 2012; Cochoy and Dubuisson-Quellier 2013; Vatin 2013) to open the black box of catastrophe models and investigate Cat analysts' valuation practices. Empirically, we build on a three-year (2009–12) participant observation within the risk management department of a large European insurance company called INSUR Group. This period of time is of utmost interest for us as it coincides with the setting up of a new regulatory regime in the European insurance industry called Solvency II. Under this new solvency regime, insurance companies are required to have a comprehensive understanding of their catastrophe risks. The change of regulation has therefore a profound impact on Cat analysts' work practices.

Overall, our research, which depicts Cat analysts as sophisticated 'qualculators', contributes to the existing literature on valuation and calculation practice in two ways. First, despite the importance of catastrophe insurance markets in most economies and the centrality of calculation in these markets, social scientists have shown little interest in the calculative practices associated to catastrophe risk insurance (see Bougen 2003; Ericson and Doyle 2004; and Collier 2008 for noticeable exceptions). As a result, we still know little about the calculative practices that sustain the functioning of catastrophe insurance markets and the economization of natural hazards. In this study, we fill this gap by shedding light on the calculation practices of a specific group of market professionals—Cat analysts—that is central to the functioning of the market for insurance but has been overlooked so far.

Second, Callon and Muniesa (2005) have offered a broad definition of calculation that avoids the conventional distinction between pure calculation and pure judgement. Yet, more empirical research needs to be done to understand the mystery of 'qualculative' practices (Cochoy 2004, 2008). In documenting Cat analysts' practices, we provide further insights into the interplay between 'literary' (or qualification) work and 'computational work' (Cochoy and Dubuisson-Quellier 2013). In particular, our study points to the importance of reflexivity in 'qualculative' practice. Our study thus also complements existing work on the reflexive use of models (Beunza and Stark 2012).

Catastrophe Models and the Economization of Natural Hazards

Catastrophe Modelling and the Extension of the Sphere of Calculative Practice

In a book entitled *Risk Society: Towards a New Modernity* Beck (1992) has advanced the thesis that contemporary societies are characterized by the rise of a new type of large-scale risks (e.g. terror attacks, technological accidents, natural disasters), which because they exceed the calculative limits of insurers would sign the crisis of calculative rationality. Beck's 'insurability thesis' has been criticized by many authors (Campbell and Currie 2006), some of whom have shown that those supposedly 'non-insurable' risks are in fact covered by insurance policies (Bougen 2003; O'Malley 2003; Ericson and Doyle 2004).

Collier (2008) develops an original critique of Beck's thesis in arguing that Beck has missed some important developments in the insurance of catastrophe risks. Collier argues that Beck is right when he says that a new type of risk challenges the traditional knowledge upon which insurance is based—and which Collier calls 'archival-statistical knowledge'. However, Collier considers that Beck is wrong when he concludes from this fact that the entire insurance system has reached its limits and that calculative rationality *in general* is under threat. For Collier, the growing use of catastrophe models in the insurance industry shows that this industry has developed a new rational approach to assessing large-scale risks. Yet, contrary to what some students of catastrophe risk insurance have advanced (e.g. Bougen 2003), Collier considers that the new approach to understanding large-scale risks—which Collier calls the 'enactment' approach—is not more 'subjective' or less 'scientific' than the traditional archival-statistical approach. Instead, he considers that the new style of reasoning about risks that catastrophe models embed is a renewed expression of calculative rationality. Thus, catastrophe risks have not threatened calculative rationality but have renewed it and expanded its reach outside its traditional boundaries.

Collier (2008) points to the important differences that exist between the new enactment approach at play in the insurance industry and the traditional archival-statistical approach. When insurers use catastrophe-modelling technologies, they do not anymore assess the likelihood and consequences of future risks by relying on *past* (historical) events. Instead, they assess the likelihood and consequences of future catastrophic events by 'produc[ing] a complete range of potential annual aggregate and occurrence loss experience from natural catastrophes' (Clark 2002, 183). In other words, insurers assess catastrophe risks by 'enacting' (Collier 2008) a virtual world where thousands of natural catastrophe events are possible.

Inside a Catastrophe Model: Enacting Thousands of Potential Natural Disasters and Evaluating their Monetary Costs

The approach that underlies catastrophe-modelling dates back to the mid-1980, when AIR worldwide—one of the three leading risk-modelling firms in the world—introduced the first fully probabilistic catastrophe risk model[3] (Clark 2002). Catastrophe modelling, however, really took off in the mid-1990s, especially after Hurricane Andrew. In about two decades, this technology has became the standard approach to assessing catastrophe risks, and three risk-modelling firms—EQECAT, Risk Management Solutions (RMS), and AIR worldwide—dominate the market (Doherty 1997; Clark 2002; Grossi et al. 2005). Put simply, a catastrophe model is a sophisticated computerized system that embodies knowledge from various fields of studies (e.g. seismology, climatology, engineering, economics) and uses historical event information and simulation techniques in order to generate a robust set of simulated events and to provide estimates of the likelihood and consequences of future potential natural catastrophes.

Catastrophe models are composed of four modules (Grossi et al. 2005; Ericson and Cleary 2012). First, a *stochastic event module* generates a catalogue of potential future catastrophe events. Second, a *hazard module* builds on seismographic and climatologic data as well as geocoding and geospatial hazard data in order to estimate the intensity and location of each of those potential catastrophe events. A third component relies on *engineering data* about the buildings (e.g. age, type of structure) located in the areas where the natural catastrophes are likely to occur to quantify the physical impact of those catastrophe events on the properties at risk. In essence, the engineering component estimates the physical damage associated to potential natural catastrophes. Last, the model uses a *financial module*, which includes data about the replacement values of the buildings that are in the insurance company's book of business, in order to calculate the potential insured claims. This component turns the structural damage into a monetary loss and calculates the insured loss. Figure 8.1 summarizes the catastrophe model valuation process.

At the end of the evaluation process the potential peril—which has been enacted by the model—is granted the 'right' qualities and properties: it is attached to a set of economic metrics that insurers are familiar with. For instance, the catastrophe model provides insurers with an Exceedance

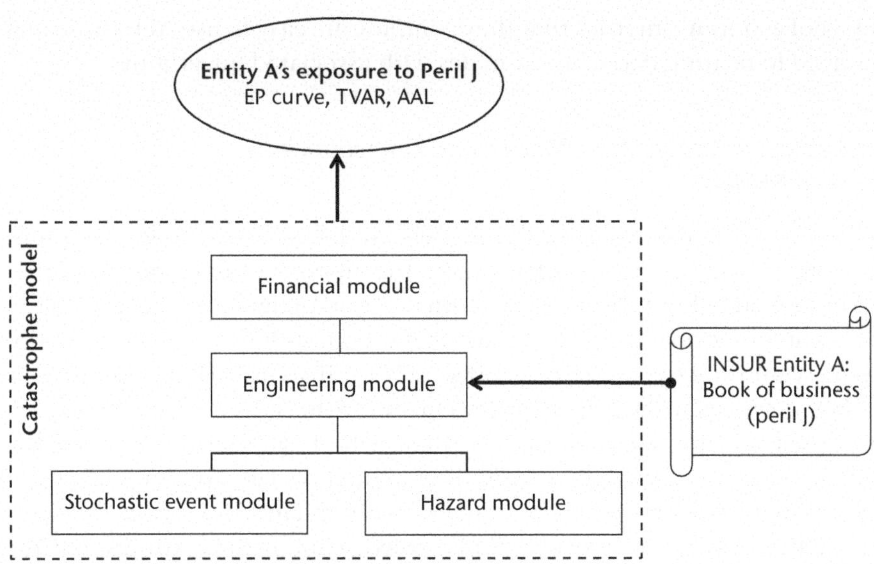

Figure 8.1. Catastrophe models' evaluation process

Probability (EP) curve—which gives the probability P(L) that losses will exceed a certain threshold L and links a loss to a probability and a return period.[4] The model also gives the Tail Value at Risk (TVAR), which complements the EP curve by giving information about the average severity of loss in the tail of the distribution, and the Average Annual Loss (AAL), which gives the entire loss distribution.

The diversity and sophistication of knowledge that is embedded in catastrophe models is impressive. It goes far beyond the knowledge base of most insurers who do not have an academic background in physical sciences or engineering. A catastrophe model thus is an artefact that piles up four modules rooted in different disciplines in order to link various professional experts—such as climatologists, seismologists, and engineers—with the world of insurance. In moving from the natural science vocabulary to the engineering vocabulary and ultimately the insurance world's vocabulary, catastrophe models perform a translation work that enables insurers to make important decisions. For instance, they use those metrics to decide on insurance premiums for property insurance policies that include natural hazard insurance coverage, to estimate their capital needs, or to negotiate their reinsurance coverage with reinsurers. The value of catastrophe modelling thus comes from the fact that it provides insurers with an evaluation of the catastrophe loss potential derived from *their* company's book of business in a language that they understand (Clark 2002). Even though catastrophe models combine an impressive amount of expert knowledge from various scientific disciplines, the set of economic metrics that they compute are easy to use. Yet, those metrics need to be understood as estimates with associated uncertainty.

Uncertainty in Catastrophe Models and Discrepancies between Models

Despite the fact that catastrophe models are based on cutting-edge physical sciences and the best available data, the amount of uncertainty in their metrics remains high. In order to estimate the damages associated to, say, a hurricane in Florida, modellers must make assumptions on ground motion intensity and the dynamics of wind speeds for instance. These assumptions are based on scientific knowledge about hurricanes; but our knowledge in this domain is limited, and modellers know that each hurricane is unique. Modellers also need to make assumptions about how the structures located in the area hit by the simulated hurricane will respond to wind. Again, engineering science provides us with sound knowledge about those things, but this knowledge suffers from limitations, which creates additional uncertainties. Last but not least, the quality of a catastrophe model's outputs depends on the quality of the input data, which varies depending on locations and types of natural catastrophe risks. Typically, information regarding hurricanes in the USA is more reliable than information regarding flood risk in a remote region of the world.

Catastrophe models thus suffer from all sorts of uncertainty, ranging from *model uncertainty* (are we using the right model to describe the dynamic of the natural disaster?), to *parameter uncertainty* (i.e. assuming we use the correct model, do we have reliable data to calibrate the model?), and to *aleatory variability* (i.e. the inherent randomness in the process). As a result of these various types of uncertainty, two catastrophe models (and even two different versions of the same model) can give different probability and loss estimates and ultimately can provide a different evaluation of the catastrophe loss potential derived from the *same* book of business. The metrics that catastrophe models provide therefore must be taken with care: an EP curve only gives an *estimate* about the probability of occurrence of an unknown event. This probability estimate is surrounded by uncertainty, as is the estimate of the monetary loss that the natural disaster is likely to generate.

The Economization of Natural Hazards: Catastrophe Models as 'Knowledge Knitting' Machines

Research on valuation practices shows that valuation processes are complex processes that rely on a series of transformation, and rest on various types of commensuration techniques. As Fourcade (2011, 1725) puts it: if the 'outcome of monetary commensuration looks flat [...] the process obviously is not'. In the case of catastrophe modelling, the economization process (Calışkan and Callon 2009) of natural hazards—i.e. the valuation process by which these 'natural' phenomena are turned into economic entities—is far from being 'flat'. This process includes several types of calculative practices rooted in different scientific disciplines and requires several steps. In a sense, the model knits several bodies of knowledge together in order to create a 'risk'. But economic valuation—strictly speaking—is only one step—the final one—in a long translation process that implies different forms of valuation and calculability. The natural catastrophe event is first 'enacted'—i.e. it is virtually brought into being through simulation techniques developed by statisticians. It is then modelled thanks to our knowledge of the underlying physics of natural hazards. Once the peril is enacted and modelled, its physical consequences are assessed by a module that embeds knowledge from structural engineering: the natural catastrophe, which was so far described using a vocabulary associated with the physical sciences of natural hazards—e.g. an earthquake is described by its epicentre and its vibrations—is now attached to a series of physical buildings and structures. Ultimately, the physical assessment is further transformed into 'economic' numbers—i.e. estimates of monetary losses—that insurers understand and can use to make decisions. At the end, what matters is being able to put a monetary value on the loss of life or property damages that the natural hazard can cause.

Reopening the Black Box of Catastrophe Modelling: How Insurers Evaluate Catastrophe Models' Metrics to Develop Their 'Own View of Risk'

In order to evaluate their exposure to catastrophe risks, most insurance companies simultaneously use several catastrophe models. At INSUR Group for instance, Cat analysts use two or three catastrophe models at the same time. As there are only three catastrophe risk models available on the market, the evaluation of risk that INSUR Group Cat team produces is thus based on all the information available. This approach to risk evaluation is consistent with the Solvency II Directive, which is a new European-level regulation in the insurance industry that requires insurance companies to have a comprehensive understanding of their catastrophe risks (Schwarz et al. 2011).[5] However, this practice, known as model blending (Calder et al. 2013a, 2013b), has a profound impact on Cat analysts' work. As the following sections will show, it requires Cat analysts to open the black box of catastrophe models. Without sound knowledge of the quality of these models, they cannot produce an estimate of their company's exposure to risks in which they are confident.

Evaluating Catastrophe Models before Solvency II: Cat Analysts' Informal Valuation Practices

When Hélène started her job as a Cat analyst in INSUR Group in 2009, the team of Cat analysts was in charge of running one, and sometimes two, catastrophe models on each of INSUR Group entity's book of business. When two models were used, John—the Cat manager—was responsible for delivering the final evaluation of the entity's exposure to catastrophe risks. In this context, Hélène's work mainly consisted in collecting raw data about the portfolio of risks of the entities she was responsible for, and running one (or two) catastrophe models on these entities' book of business for each type of peril. Once she had conducted these analyses, Hélène had to collate an Excel spreadsheet, such as the one depicted in Figure 8.2.[6] An important task was to report the catastrophe model's estimate of the EP curve in the OEP/AEP curve section.[7]

When John received a spreadsheet associated to an entity (e.g. Canada) and a certain type of catastrophe risk (e.g. windstorm), his job was to produce a final evaluation of this entity's exposure to this peril. His final judgement integrated the catastrophe models' evaluations of risk but also reflected his own view about the quality of those evaluations. Figure 8.2 shows that in order to produce a final judgement John had to give a 'weight' to each catastrophe model. Specifically, he had to report the weights that he had used in the prior year for each model (EQE, RMS, and AIR) (see the 'N-1' column), and then he had to decide which weight to attribute to each model this year (column N in Figure 8.2).

As this short description shows, the valuation practices that Hélène, John, and more generally the entire Cat team, deployed to evaluate INSUR Group entities' exposure to catastrophe risks were loosely formalized. The final assessment rested mainly on John's ability to evaluate the catastrophe models' metrics. As one of our interviewees said, 'There was no "quantitative" method. It [the aggregation or blending] was based on an expert judgement, and the experts were the CAT manager primarily together with another CAT expert from the CAT team. [...] That aggregation was clearly based on an expert judgment' (interview with a Cat analyst, 19 March 2012). Even though John had extensive knowledge of the catastrophe models used by his team, his knowledge remained tacit. Over time John had developed a good understanding of how each catastrophe model worked. Put simply, he had acquired expert knowledge about those models, which enabled him to attribute a confidence weight to their results. However, there were no clear rules about how to assess the value of a model and how to translate a subjective assessment into a number. Overall, John made up the 'blending rule' every year, and he also tended to stick to the same rule from year to year, unless he had been

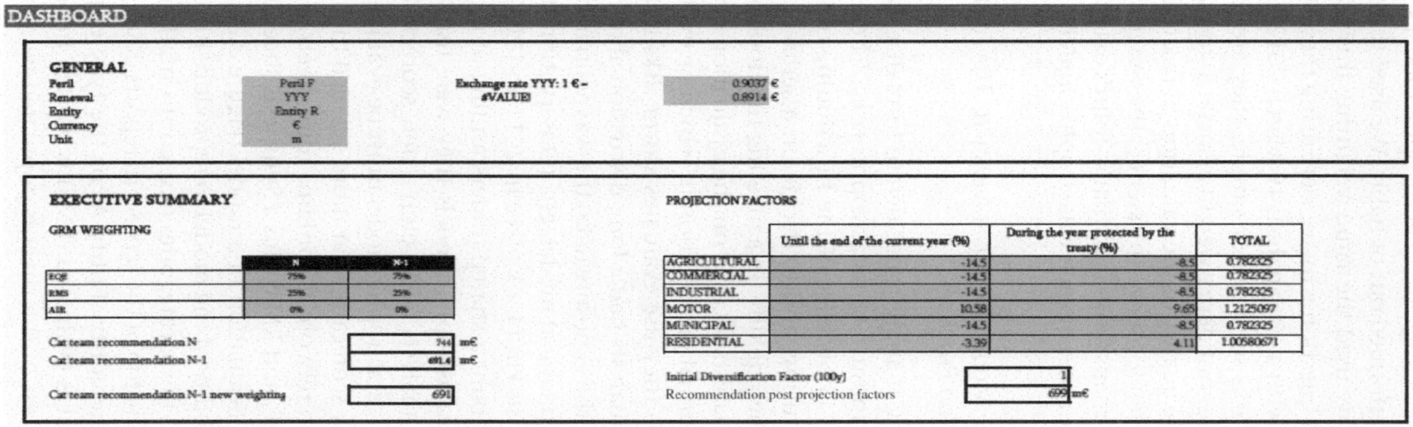

Figure 8.2. Evaluating catastrophe models before Solvency II

made aware of a major change in a catastrophe model's version: 'The risk aggregation task was performed out of habit. We used this weighting [blending rule] last year, and we used the same weighting this year and so one. We didn't ask ourselves the question why we were using these weights. It was like a tradition' (interview with a Cat analyst, 19 March 2012).

Even though these tasks seem pretty simple, they are incredibly strategic and highly complex: the confidence weight associated to a model summarizes John's assessment of the quality of the valuation of risk that this model gives for a given peril in a given location. In essence, the weight summarizes—in a numerical form that perhaps looks a bit 'flat'—John's extensive knowledge of the strengths and weaknesses of each catastrophe model.

Evaluating Catastrophe Models Under Solvency II: The Formalization of Cat Analysts' Valuation Practices

In 2011, INSUR Group Cat analysts decided to formalize the way they evaluate their company's exposure to catastrophe risks. They organized several meetings to share their knowledge of the functioning of the three catastrophe models they were using, and to decide on a series of criteria that they could use to evaluate their quality. In a meeting that took place in April 2012 for instance, the Cat analysts focused on the evaluation of storms in Europe. A Cat analyst made a formal presentation in which he explained how one of the catastrophe models they use evaluates storm risks in Europe. After this presentation, the Cat analysts had a long discussion about this model. They discussed the source of the exposure data, the way vulnerability is calculated, the functioning of the financial model, etc. (Observation, 10 April 2012).

Several meetings of this kind took place in 2011 and 2012. Thanks to these meetings, Cat analysts built a shared understanding of the functioning and overall quality of the catastrophe models they were using. These meetings ultimately helped Cat analysts to develop a new scorecard that summarizes their view about how a catastrophe model must be evaluated. As Figures 8.3a and 8.3b show, the new scorecard is far more detailed than the Excel spreadsheet that John used to rely on: it contains four sheets, one for each catastrophe model (AIR, EQE, and RMS) plus a Synthesis sheet (Figure 8.3b). Each sheet dedicated to the evaluation of a model (Figure 8.3a) contains a list of fourteen criteria (e.g. ability of the model to reproduce historical events, peril consistency...) grouped in six categories (e.g. confrontation with past experience, consistency...). The top of the scorecard reports descriptive information such as the name of the entity (Entity A) or the type of peril (Peril J). The name of the model that is evaluated (RMS) is written in bold in the middle of the document. The rest of the sheet is populated with many cells of various colours. Cells with red circles have 'to be filled out by the analyst' using

Entity	Entity A	Peril	Peril J	Country	Country Q	Year of renewal	YYY	Triggering fact.	F	Analyst	Analyst Name
External Model:	RMS									Version	9.0

	CRITERIA	CRITERIA SCORE	WEIGHT	THEME SCORE	Comments
I – Confrontation with past experience					
I.1	Ability of the model to reproduce historical events	3	3	17 / 25	Model reconciliation has been made following Krill. Inclusion of the recent historical events ir the model.
I.2	Date of the last model update	4	2		Model updated in 2008 (v8.0) following Kyrill event
II - Physical characteristics of the model					
II.1	Geographical scope	3	3	34 / 50	Basin-wide but not including Eastern Europe
II.2	Completeness of risk modeling	4	2		No specific comment
II.3	Frequency of events	4	2		High frequency events specifically accounted for
II.4	Hazard module accuracy / reliability	3	3		Hazard module is complex, associated with uncertainty at many steps of the methodology Lack of confrontation with climate data
III - Vulnerability characteristics of the model					
III.1	Refinement of risks description	4	1	10 / 15	Good refinement of risk description in general
III.2	Vulnerability curves accuracy / reliability	3	2		Doubt on quality of re-calibration following Kyrill
IV - EP Curve Analysis					
IV.1	EP Curve behavior at different return periods	4	3	12 / 15	Correct
V - Consistency					
V.1	Geographical consistency	3	2	24 / 40	Rather consistent 100y destruction rate (0,08%) compared to France (0,07%), given the concentration of exposure
V.2	Line of business consistency	3	3		Rather consistent
V.3	Peril consistency	3	1		N/A
V.4	Temporal consistency	3	2		Rather consistent
VI - Documentation					
VI.1	Completeness of documentation	2	1	2 / 5	Rather poor documentation for such a complex technical approach

GLOBAL MODEL APPRAISAL

99 / 150

➤ Performance with uncertainty

: *fields to be filled out by the alanyst*

Legend		
Score	Color code	Appraisal
>=100	●	Performance validated
[75;100[	◕	Perf. validated with uncertainty
[0;75[	◔	Low performance
NA	○	Model inexistent

Destruction rate by Line of business		
LoB	1/100 Y	1/250 Y
AGRICULTURAL		
COMMERCIAL		
INDUSTRIAL		
MOTOR		
MUNICIPAL		
RESIDENTIAL		

Figure 8.3a. Evaluating catastrophe models under Solvency II

Entity	Entity A	Peril	Peril J	Country	Country Q	Year of renewal	YYY	Triggering fact.	#REF!	Analyst	Analyst Name

SYNTHESIS

External Model	Internal score of external model	Appraisal	Weight recommendation	Expet judgment analysis	Validated CAT Model
RMS	99	**Performance with uncertainty**	35 %	**Recommended model: 35% RMS + 65% EQE + 0% AIR** *Previous model: 50 %RMS + 50 %EQE+ 0 %AIR* Expert judgment conclusion: Adjustment due to very close scores	50 % RMS + 50 % EQE + 0 % AIR
EQE	104	**Performance Validated**	65 %		
AIR	74	**Low Performance**	0 %		

Comments

The EQECat model's hazard methodology over performs the RMS one. This is balanced by a more developed vulnerability module in RMS.
The final scores obtained by the two models are considered as not significantly different (less than a 5% gap). Therefore, an equal weighting is retained.

: fields to be filled out by the alanyst

Figure 8.3b. Evaluating catastrophe models under Solvency II

a scale ranging from 1 to 5. All the other cells are prefilled and the value of these cells has been subject to discussion among the Cat team members.

Figures 8.3a and 8.3b suggest that the Cat team's valuation practices have profoundly evolved towards greater objectivity. The new scorecard is similar to a standard evaluation procedure: it lists the criteria according to which a catastrophe model should be ranked and valued and thus makes explicit the way the Cat team judges the quality of a catastrophe model. It is important to note that beyond giving a score to each criterion, Cat analysts have to justify the scores. Figure 8.3a shows that the Cat analyst who has evaluated the RMS model (for Entity A, Peril J, and Country Q) gave a score of 4 out of 5 to the 'Frequency of event' criterion (II.3) and justified this high score by explaining that 'high frequency events [are] specifically accounted for'.

However, the establishment of lists of criteria that Cat analysts must take into account only partially solves Cat analysts' problem. In order to appraise the overall quality of a model, Cat analysts also have to find a way to combine these criteria together. This implies answering questions such as: 'How important is criteria VI.I about the "completeness of documentation" in the value of a catastrophe model?'; 'Is this criterion more or less important than the "Temporal consistency" criterion (V.3), or than the "EP curve behaviour at different return periods" criterion (IV.4)?' The creation of a list of fourteen criteria thus calls for more calculation. Cat analysts have therefore also formalized the relative importance of each criterion in the global model score by pre-filling the scorecard with 'weights' ranging from 1 to 3. Figure 8.3a for instance shows that the Cat team has decided that criteria IV.1 would be given more weight—3 out of 3—than criterion V.3 and criterion I.1. As these weights are pre-filled, the scorecard can automatically compute the overall performance of the model once the Cat analyst has entered the 'criteria score'. Specifically, the spreadsheet returns a ratio, which appears in bold and in colour in the middle of the document (see the 'Global model appraisal' column), and links this ratio to a colour (red, orange, or green) to visually associate the score to a level of performance (see the legend table in the bottom left of the spread sheet).

Finally, the Cat analyst can fill the 'Synthesis sheet', which as Figure 8.3b shows, reports the model global score calculated in the previous steps (see the 'internal score of external model' column). The 'Synthesis sheet' also reports the weight recommendation for each catastrophe model that the Cat team has predefined. In Figure 8.3b, we can see that the Cat team has judged that when it comes to Entity A, Peril J, and Country Q, the EQE model gives better quality results than the RMS model. It has decided to materialize this judgment by attributing a weight of 65 per cent to EQE, 35 per cent to RMS, and 0 per cent to AIR.[8] Yet, this weight recommendation can be challenged, and the Cat analyst can give different weights to the models in the final formula.

In the case depicted in Figure 8.3b, the Cat analyst has given the same weight to the RMS and the EQE models (see the Validated Cat model column), and she has also explained the reason for this weighting in the red-circled box below the score.

Even though the two scorecards (Figures 8.2, 8.3a, 8.3b) end with the same kind of formula—a weighted average of the three models (i.e. x% RMS + y% EQE + z% AIR)—the work of Cat analysts has greatly evolved between the two periods. The new scorecard clearly shows that Cat analysts have found a way to overcome catastrophe models' complexity and have made them commensurable. Thanks to a prodigious effort of inventory, comparison, and assessment, the Cat team has produced a stabilized account of the approach they follow to judge the quality of a catastrophe model. This commensuration work, however, has required the Cat team to 'open' each catastrophe model they use in order to gain an in-depth understanding of their functioning: 'We ha[d] to read the whole user documentation related to each model. These documents have more than 500 pages each! Also, we ha[d] to consult

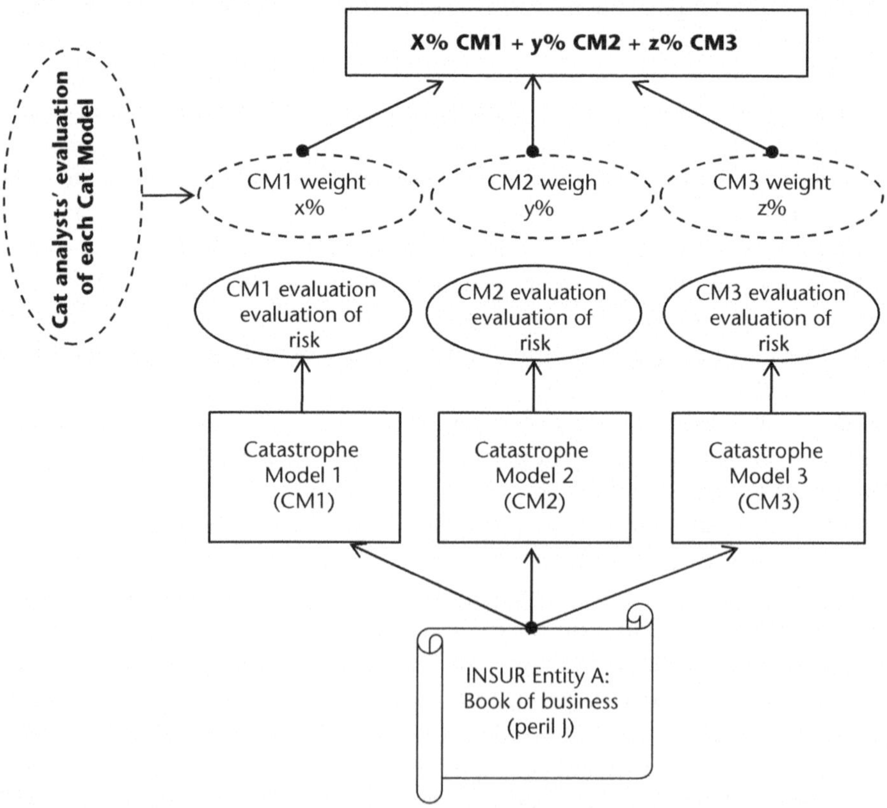

Figure 8.4. Cat analysts' evaluation of their company's exposure to catastrophe risks

other sources of information in order to be aware of any recent changes in the domain and to know whether the models are far from reality or not. [...] This takes a lot of time! Ultimately, it requires that all criteria must be the most possible accurate' (interview with a Cat analyst).

In order to evaluate INSUR Group entities' exposure to catastrophe risks, Cat analysts have to judge the quality of the valuation of risk provided by the three catastrophe models they use. The valuation process that Cat analysts follow in order to assess the quality of the catastrophe models they use is highly structured (Figure 8.4). Models have been made commensurable, and a spreadsheet has been created in order to ensure that the same criteria are used to evaluate different models. In addition, Cat analysts' final judgement over the value of a model is expressed in a numerical form: it is a weight of confidence that ranges between 0 and 100, which reinforces the impression of objectivity. Yet these weights remain the expression of a subjective judgement about the quality of each model.

Discussion and Conclusion

In this chapter, we studied the valuation practices of Cat analysts in a large European insurance company called INSUR Group. Cat analysts are experts in the management of uncertainty and the evaluation of catastrophe risks; their job consists in providing a sound evaluation of their insurance company's exposure to catastrophe risks. Our study shows that beyond being able to run catastrophe models on their company's book of business, Cat analysts have to grasp the complexity of multiple catastrophe models and to assess the uncertainty attached to their potentially divergent outputs. Qualification, contextualization, and expert judgement thus emerged as crucial ingredients in the evaluation of an insurance company's exposure to catastrophe risks. The final evaluation of an insurance company's exposure to catastrophe risks indeed not only incorporates the risk evaluations that catastrophe models produce, but it also reflects Cat analysts' informed judgement about the quality of the catastrophe models that are used.

In documenting how Cat analysts reflexively use catastrophe models in order to provide a sound evaluation of their company's exposure to catastrophe models, we aim to complement prior works on calculation and valuation practices in two ways. First, despite the importance of various forms of measurement, calculation, and valuation systems in the management of catastrophe risks, few studies have documented the material practices associated with the functioning of insurance markets. Most works on calculative practices have focused on financial markets and have documented the calculative practices of traders (MacKenzie and Millo 2003; Beunza and Garud 2007;

Poon 2009; Beunza and Stark 2012). The few studies that have focused on the insurance industry have been more concerned with the changing logic of this industry and the emergence of new insurance mechanisms (Bougen 2003; Ericson and Doyle 2004; Collier 2008) than with the concrete organizational calculative practices. Collier (2008), for instance, shows how insurers have moved away from an 'archival-based' to an 'enactment' approach to catastrophe risk appraisal. His study traces the genealogy of the enactment approach and shows how this approach, which initially developed in civil defence, has been recombined to tackle catastrophe insurance and terror risk assessment. Collier (2008), however, remains relatively silent on the calculative practices that constitute this new risk management approach. Our research therefore complements Collier's study by providing an in-depth description of the 'qualculative' practices that sustain the enactment approach to catastrophe risk insurance. Future research could systematically compare the ways in which insurance professionals operating under an archival-based approach and an enactment approach to risk management balance qualification and computational work. Such research could help better understand the extent to which different risk management logics, or cultures (Mikes 2011), foster different combinations between expert judgement and modelling. It could also shed light on the importance that regulators of financial markets give to 'qualculative' practices.

A second insight of this chapter points to 'qualculation' practices (Callon and Law 2005; Cochoy 2008) and how they dynamically sustain the interplay between qualification (or 'literary work') and calculation (or 'computational work') (Cochoy and Dubuisson-Quellier 2013). Our findings depict Cat analysts as sophisticated 'qualculators'. Cat analysts' ultimate task is to estimate their company's risk exposure. To do so, they first use catastrophe models to imagine a whole set of potential natural catastrophes, measure their impact, and evaluate their likely monetary consequences. Then, they rely on a complex 'qualculative' infrastructure to assess the quality of the numbers that the catastrophe models produce. In their work, Cat analysts thus rely on a sophisticated 'accounting' equipment—the catastrophe models—to do the indispensable computational work associated to the estimation of an insurance company's risk exposure. However, they do not blindly rely on these models to evaluate their company's exposure to risk. Instead, they perform an important 'literary work' of qualification (Cochoy and Dubuisson-Quellier 2013) in order to understand the uncertainties associated with the models' risk evaluations. This qualification work enables them to qualify the models they use, and ultimately to produce an expert evaluation of risk that reflects their judgement about the value of these models. In other words, the output of their work is neither a pure 'mechanized judgment' (Porter 1995) that a model could produce automatically, nor is it a purely subjective and idiosyncratic judgement. Rather, it is a 'quality-based rational judgment' (Cochoy 2008) of their company's exposure to catastrophe risk. In depicting Cat analysts as 'qualculators' who aim to reconcile the outputs of dissonant catastrophe models, our study ultimately suggests that the ability to reflexively use dissonant models (Beunza and Stark 2012) is a key ingredient of 'qualculative' practices. INSUR Group Cat analysts have developed a 'qualculative' infrastructure because they purposively sought model dissonance and they wanted to be able to trace back the chain of evidence and reasoning leading to dissonant risk evaluations. The scorecard is the material artefact that enables them to be reflexive about the limitations of the complex 'knowledge knitting machines' that they use. Our study thus suggests that economic actors who purposively search for model dissonance may need to develop a 'qualculative' infrastructure in order to construct their own judgement and to cope with the uncertainty generated by the use of multiple dissonant models.

Notes

1. The focus on catastrophe risks comes from the fact that these risks generate the potential for very severe losses and have a huge impact on multiple lines of business at the same time. If a hurricane hits Florida, not only homes, cars, but also businesses located in this region will be damaged at the same moment.
2. Insurers' traditional instrument to hedge catastrophic risks is reinsurance (Doherty 1997).
3. While the first catastrophe models that were developed in the 1980s were 'deterministic' in the sense that they relied on 'worst case' scenarios or historical losses, catastrophe models developed since the late 1990s are 'fully probabilistic'—i.e. they simulate hundreds of thousands of possible catastrophe events (Ericson and Cleary 2012)—before providing a financial estimate of the damages.
4. Suppose a company has fixed a threshold for a loss at $200,000, the EP curve gives the probability that the insurance company will experience a loss of $200,000 or higher in the next year. The EP curve also gives the average return time period (i.e. the estimated time interval between two events of similar size or intensity). For instance, if the return period of flood is 100 years, this means that the probability of occurrence of a flood is 1 per cent (or 1/100) in any one year: in any one year, there is a 1 per cent chance that a flood occurs regardless of when the last similar event happened. <http://www.niwa.co.nz/natural-hazards/faq/what-is-a-return-period>.
5. Changes in catastrophe models' assumptions can have a huge impact on insurers' exposure to catastrophe risks and their solvency requirements; but insurers have no control over these changes. The release of RMSv11 in February 2011 for instance 'surprised the market' (Bernews 2011) because it dramatically increased the risk profile for hurricanes in the US and for windstorms in Europe, and greatly affected

insurers' potential losses (Ellis 2012; Willis Re 2012; Artemis 2013). Through Solvency II, the European regulator thus urges insurers to maintain control over the evaluation of their exposure to catastrophe risks by using several catastrophe models and by assessing the uncertainties surrounding these models.

6. Each INSUR Group entity is associated to several such forms, one for each type of peril.
7. There are two types of EP curve: the Occurrence Exceeded Probability curve (OEP) gives the EP curve for one single event loss in a given year, whereas the Aggregate Exceedance Probability curve (AEP) gives the EP curve for more than one event loss, in a given year.
8. Note that each weight ranges between 0 per cent and 100 per cent and the sum of the three weights must be equal to 100 per cent.

References

Artemis. 2013. 'RMS Launch Hurricane Model v13, Use for MetroCat Re Risk Analysis'. 1 August. <http://www.artemis.bm/blog/2013/08/01/rms-launch-hurricane-model-v13-use-for-metrocat-re-risk-analysis>.

Beck, U. 1992. *Risk Society: Towards a New Modernity*. London: Sage.

Bernews. 2011. 'Bermuda Firms "Beginning to Embrace" Model'. 21 May. <http://bernews.com/2011/05/bermuda-firms-beginning-to-embrace-model/>.

Beunza, D. and R. Garud. 2007. 'Calculator, Lemmings, or Frame-Makers? The Intermediary Role of Securities Analysts'. *Sociological Review* 55(2): 13–39.

Beunza, D. and D. Stark. 2012. 'From Dissonnace to Resonance: Cognitive Interdependence in Quantitative Finance'. *Economy & Society* 41(3): 383–417.

Bougen, P. D. 2003. 'Catastrophe Risk'. *Economy & Society* 32(2): 253–74.

Calder, A., A. Couper, and J. Lo. 2013a. 'Catastrophe Model Blending: Practicalities'. Vignettes from the 2012 GIRO Paper. Communication at the ASTIN Colloquium, 22 May.

Calder, A., A. Couper, and J. Lo. 2013b. 'Catastrophe Model Blending: Techniques and Governance'.*The Actuarial Profession*, 13 August.

Calışkan, K. and M. Callon. 2009. 'Economization, Part 1: Shifting Attention from the Economy towards Processes of Economization'. *Economy & Society* 38(3): 369–98.

Callon, M. (ed.). 1998. *The Laws of the Markets*. Oxford: Blackwell.

Callon, M. and J. Law. 2005. 'On Qualculation, Agency, and Otherness'. *Environment and Planning D: Society and Space* 23(5): 717–33.

Callon, M. and F. Muniesa. 2005. 'Economic Markets as Calculative Collective Devices'. *Organization Studies* 26(8): 1229–50.

Campbell, S. and G. Currie. 2006. 'Against Beck: In Defence of Risk Analysis'. *Philosophy and Sociology of Science* 36(2): 149–72.

Clark, K. M. 2002. 'The Use of Computer Modeling in Estimating and Managing Future Catastrophe Losses'. *The Geneva Papers and Risk and Insurance* 27(2): 181–95.

Cochoy, F. 2004. 'Is the Modern Consumer a Buridan's Donkey? Product Packaging and Consumer Choice'. In *Elusive Consumption*, ed. K. Ekström and H. Brembeck. Oxford and New York: Berg, 205–27.

Cochoy, F. 2008. 'Calculation, Qualculation, Calqulation: Shopping Cart Arithmetic, Equipped Cognition and the Clustered Consumer'. *Marketing Theory* 8(1): 15–44.

Cochoy, F. and S. Dubuisson-Quellier 2013. 'The Sociology of Market Work'. *Economic Sociology: European Electroinc Newsletter* 15(1): 4–11.

Collier, S. J. 2008. 'Enacting Catastrophe: Preparedness, Insurance, Budgetary Rationalization'. *Economy & Society* 37(2): 224–50.

Doherty, N. A. 1997. 'Financial Innovation in the Management of Catastrophe Risk'. *Journal of Applied Corporate Finance* 10(3): 84–95.

Ellis, D. 2012. 'Catastrophe Modeling: Why All The Fuss?' <http://usa.marsh.com/NewsInsights/ThoughtLeadership/Articles/ID/27004/Catastrophe-Modeling-Why-All-the-Fuss.aspx>.

Ericson, A. and K. Cleary. 2012. 'The Actuary's Use of Catastrophe Models in ORSA'. In *Risk Metrics for Decision Making and ORSA*, e-book, 49–51.

Ericson, R. V. and A. Doyle. 2004. 'Catastrophe Risk, Insurance and Terrorism'. *Economy & Society* 33(2): 135–73.

Espeland, W. N. and M. Stevens. 1998. 'Commensuration as a Social Process'. *Annual Review of Sociology* 24(1): 313–43.

Espeland, W. N. and M. Stevens. 2008. 'A Sociology of Quantification'. *European Journal of Sociology* 49(3): 401–36.

Fourcade, M. 2011. 'Cents and Sensibility: Economic Valuation and the Nature of "Nature"'. *American Journal of Sociology* 116(6): 1721–77.

Grossi, P., H. Kunreuther, and D. Windeler. 2005. 'An Introduction to Catastrophe Models and Insurance'. In *Catastrophe Modeling: A New Approach to Managing Risks*, ed. P. Grossi and H. Kunreuther. New York: Springer, 23–41.

Karpik, L. 2000. 'Le guide rouge michelin'. *Sociologie du Travail* 42(3): 369–89.

Karpik, L. 2011. *Valuing the Unique*. Princeton: Princeton University Press.

Kunreuther, H. 2005. 'The Role of Catastrophe Modeling for Estimating Risks'. *Natural Hazards Observer* 30(1). <http://www.colorado.edu/hazards/o/archives/2005/sept05/>.

Lamont, M. 2012. 'Toward a Comparative Sociology of Valuation and Evaluation'. *Annual Review of Sociology* 38(21): 201–21.

MacKenzie, D. and Y Millo. 2003. 'Constructing a Market, Performing a Theory: The Historical Sociology of a Financial Derivatives Exchange'. *American Review of Sociology* 109(1): 107–45.

Mikes, A. 2011. 'From Counting to Making Risk Count: Boundary-Work in Risk Management'. *Accounting, Organizations and Society* 36(4–5): 226–45.

O'Malley, P. 2003. 'Governable Catastrophes: A Comment on Bougen'. *Economy & Society* 32(2): 275–9.

Poon, M. 2009. 'From New Deal Institutions to Capital Markets: Commercial Consumer Risk Scores and the Making of Subprime Mortgage Finance'. *Accounting, Organizations and Society* 34(5): 654–74.

Porter, T. M. 1995. *Trust in Numbers: The Pursuit of Objectivity in Science and Public Life*. Princeton: Princeton University Press.

Power, M. 2004. 'Counting, Control and Calculation: Reflections on Measuring and Management'. *Human Relations* 57(6): 765–83.

Schwarz, G., D. Meler, R. D'Acunto, and F. Schepers. 2011. *Solvency II Rewrites the Rules for Insurers*. Bain & Company Tower Watson. <http://www.bain.com>.

Vatin, F. 2013. 'Valuation as Evaluating and Valorizing'. *Valuation Studies* 1(1): 31–50.

Willis Re. 2012. 'Willis Re Release Report on the Impact of RMS v11 European Windstorm Catastrophe Model Changes'. *Willis Re News Release*, 14 June. <http://www.willisre.com/Media_Room/Press_Releases_(Browse_All)/2012/20120614_Willis_Re_on_RMS_v11_European_Windstorm_Catastrophe_Model_Changes/>.

9

The Enactment of Economic Things

The Objects of Insurance

José Ossandón

Insurance has not been the most attractive object of analysis for social sciences. There are, though, important exceptions. Most of the attention has been focused on: (i) understanding the place of insurance as a modern (successful or failed) technology to tame uncertainty (Ewald 1991; Beck 1996; Ericson and Doyle 2004; Collier 2008); (ii) insurance as a central dispositive in the production of liberal and neo-liberal solidarity (Knights and Vurdubakis 1993; O'Malley 1996; Baker and Simon 2002; Ewald 2002; Van Hoyweghen 2010; Lehtonen and Liukko 2012; Ossandón 2014); and (iii) the symbolic and socio-technical effort needed to stabilize insurance markets (Zelizer 1978, 1981; Chan 2009a; McFall 2009; Lehtonen and Liukko 2010; Ossandón 2012). Instead of criticizing or trying to improve any of these streams of research, this chapter follows a different approach: it defends the relevance of studying the objects of insurance.

I am aware that objects—such as buildings, advertising leaflets, and other 'market devices' (Muniesa et al. 2007) have already been introduced as characters that deserve to be followed in insurance research (McFall 2009; McFall and Dodsworth 2009). However, I am referring here to a more limited notion of object. I do not mean the material elements used to frame market encounters nor the set of tools that enable economic calculation. I am referring, instead, to those things that are sold, priced, and exchanged in insurance markets. In the terms of this book, the main goal of the chapter is to produce a conceptual base that enables studying a diverse array of valuation processes, happening at different sites and conveying their own agents and respective modes of expertise, that together work in making insurance valuable. By studying these different processes together, I expect to produce a solid, although distributed, understanding of our object of attention, in this case health insurance in Chile.

While this type of concern might be new in insurance studies, the study of economic objects has a longer history if we consider social studies of markets more broadly. There are at least two very influential streams of thought that have been working in this direction. First, the work developed by Michel Callon and colleagues has brought about the emphasis given in science studies to following the costly processes of stabilizing controversial and contested objects into economic analyses (Callon and Muniesa 2005; Callon et al. 2002). Second, there is an important amount of work done in economic anthropology which has been useful in recovering the rich supply of concepts—that go all the way to authors such as Simmel, Marx, and Mauss—that have been developed to understand the particular ontology of economic objects (Appadurai 1986; Thomas 1991; Strathern 1999). These two traditions are combined in this chapter in order to delimit a distinct research programme.

In the first part of this chapter, the article 'The Economy of Qualities' (Callon et al. 2002) is used as the main conceptual raw material. Without denying its influence, it will be argued that this work has two important shortcomings that need to be worked through in order to develop a solid conceptual base for the agenda here proposed. First, one of its main concepts—'product'—is not clearly delimited, and second, too much relevance is given to a single mode of stabilizing economic objects ('good singularization'). The work of science scholar Annemarie Mol and economic anthropologists Arjun Appadurai and Marilyn Strathern will be mobilized in order to respectively deal with these problems. With their help, the process of bringing a new economic object forth is named 'enactment', instead of 'production', and, apart from 'goods', two other types of economic objects are distinguished: 'commodity' and 'property'. The second part of the chapter illustrates the different processes connected with the enactment of each of these objects for a very particular case, private health insurance in Chile. The final section closes the chapter with a brief conclusion.

Economic Objects

In their organization of the field, Çalışkan and Callon (2010, 16) suggest that the study of economization can be divided into three main framings: calculative agencies, market encounters, and pacified goods. In all of them non-human agents play an important role: economic calculation is distributed in multiple technical devices, markets encounters are framed by walls, screens, and other materials, and pacified goods are the outcome of socio-technical networks.

However, it is only in the latter process that objects are not only enablers of something else (a market encounter or economic calculation), but the main subjects of interest too: they are what has to be explained. This specific agenda has been developed in several articles written by Callon and colleagues (Callon 1998; Callon et al. 2002; Callon and Law 2005; Callon and Muniesa 2005). In these papers, most of the attention has been paid to understanding the process of disentangling things from their original networks and their subsequent stabilization as economic objects among other objects in markets. In perhaps the most influential paper of this series, Callon et al. (2002) suggest the pair 'product and good' as a core conceptual distinction. The difference between these two notions, it is argued, is not a matter of quality but of the temporal frame of observation: a 'product' is an economic object seen from the point of view of its chain of transformations, while in a 'good' the attention is focused on one moment, when an object is made comparable to other economic objects in markets. In other words: while product denotes a process, good refers to a moment of stabilization. Without denying the centrality of this argument, as will be shown in the next sections, the conceptual pair product/good should be adjusted in order to become the base of the research programme here suggested.

Producing or Enacting?

The usage of the notion 'product' by Callon and colleagues echoes an older discussion developed by Arjun Appadurai in his famous introduction to the edited volume *The Social Life of Things* published in 1986. There, Appadurai proposes that economic objects are not only creatively transformed in their production, but also in other moments of their life, particularly in their exchange and circulation. On the other hand, Callon et al. (2002) suggest that it is not only in manufacturing, but also in a wide range of processes—including marketing, packaging, and placing—where economic objects are produced. Both authors, like Simmel (1990) long before them, share an important assumption: economic objects are not only the outcome of the action of a producer, but are made and remade in a wider chain of relations. This way these works extend the sources of agency over economic objects, by including the many agents that work in the processes of framing a good, in the case of Callon and colleagues, and by considering those that participate in bringing an object in and out of market exchange in Appadurai's text.

However, despite these similarities, different concepts are used in both texts. In fact, while Appadurai openly attacks a bias towards production as the only creative moment in the life of economic things, Callon and colleagues bring the term 'product' back to the centre. But, this difference is, in one way, misleading, because a product in the latter text does not only refer to 'production', but, in the words of the authors, to 'an economic good seen from the point of view of its production, circulation and consumption' (Callon et al. 2002, 197). A product is not only the outcome of production, but also of two other processes: 'consumption' and 'circulation'. The authors provide some support for their choice of term. The quotation continues:

> The concept (*producere*: to bring forward) shows that it consists of a sequence of actions, a series of operations that transform it, move it and cause it to change hands, to cross a series of metamorphoses that end up putting it into a form judged useful by an economic agent who pays for it. During these transformations its characteristics change. (Callon et al. 2002, 197)

However what Callon and colleagues do not explain is why they did not try to find a more abstract concept that does not risk the confusion produced by collapsing three different actions under the name of only one of them, one that already has a clear and strong meaning for the economic agents. Indeed, some candidates are already available. This is in fact what Appadurai (1986) and Kopytoff (1986) attempt with concepts such as 'social life' or 'cultural biography' of things. These notions are more abstract and also highlight the fact that economic objects are not only transformed in production. However, these are not good alternatives here because they explicitly point to a specific process: how value is created when things are brought in and out of the market exchange, which in itself is another very rich research agenda.

To be fair, it should be mentioned that even Callon himself, although this time with another co-author, has shown dissatisfaction with the notion of product. In their words: 'Extending that much the notion of production may be counterproductive and bring more confusion than analytic clarification' (Lépinay and Callon 2009, 274). In this latter text, Lépinay and Callon suggest the notion of 'derivation' as alternative. However, as discussed below, it is better to keep this term for a more specific process. My own choice is the concept of 'enactment' as used by another science and technology studies scholar, Annemarie Mol.

In her book *The Body Multiple*, Mol (2002) distinguishes 'enactment' from another important concept in recent social sciences: 'performance'. As Mol explains, this latter term—associated for instance with the work of Judith Butler and Erving Goffman—has been central in extending our understanding of the practical and constructed character of social categories such as 'gender' or the 'self'. Without questioning the importance of this specific research agenda, Mol argues that a different concept is needed to study not only how social identities are brought forth, but how 'objects' are made. Enactment is therefore suggested to name the specific process of stabilizing objects.

It is important to keep in mind that the concept of enactment has a larger history, which is also connected with the discussion developed in this chapter. In an article about the evolution of the insurance industry, a way of modelling risk that is not based on actuarial statistics but on acting out future scenarios is called 'enactment' (Collier 2008). Some years earlier, organization scholar Wanda Orlikowski suggested that technologies do not embody social structures but are part of creative interactions with other technologies, human actors, and social practices. In this context, she suggests, users do not appropriate these tools, but their uses are enacted in their interaction (Orlikowski 2000).[1] Also within organization studies, a whole tradition of thought has been developed under the notions of 'enactment' and 'sense making' as they were developed by Karl Weick (Abolafia and Kilduff 1988; Weick 2003). Finally, cognitive scientists Varela et al. (1999) refer to 'enaction' as a concept that transcends both subjectivism and realism. Objects, they argue, are not a projection of our minds nor are they out in the environment. Identities, such a table or a specific colour (like 'red'), emerge from interactions between system and environment.

Despite their differences, these different modes of using the notion 'enactment' share a relational view of things whereby objects are not pre-formed entities, but emerge from interactions. In the first case, risk is not just past information projected onto the future, but emerges together with the potential consequences of the action of different actors reacting to a particular threat. In the second, technologies are not tools that are appropriated by particular subjects, but are co-created in interactions. And in the third, identities are forged from a history of system/environment relations.

To this relational point of departure, Mol's notion of enactment adds two further aspects. First, her notion keeps the emphasis given by Callon and colleagues—and previous research on Actor-Network Theory (Latour 1993, 2000)—on the analysis of the stabilization of technical objects. Objects are not only social products but emerge out of socio-technical assemblages; are not closed but have to be closed; and, once stabilized, new sources of uncertainty can open them again.[2] Second, and finally, Mol's term strongly marks that objects are not the outcome of a single process, but can be enacted in multiple ways. Therefore, the main challenge is not only stabilization, but also coordination, or dealing with different versions of an object that can be differently enacted in multiple sites and times and the tensions that this could produce.

To sum up, the notion of enactment is abstract enough and it refers specifically to the emergence of new objects. However, it is a notion developed in a different context, and, accordingly, it does not say much about the specific process of enacting economic objects. To face this issue it is necessary to go back to the other side of the pair suggested in 'The Economy of Qualities': goods.

Singular or Multiple Economic Objects?

A second element that can be questioned in the formulation of Callon et al. (2002) is the centrality of the notion of good. This concept, as nicely put in the next quotation and according to a basic principle within Actor-Network Theory, considers stabilization of objects as a process that resembles semiotic differentiation.

> The process of singularization consists of a series of operations resulting in the calculability of the good. Profiling a product consists in establishing a calculative space in which it can be connected and compared to a finite list of other products [...] Singularizing a product also means linking it to other products in the same space or on the same list. This is a process of classifications, clustering and sorting that makes products both comparable and different. The consumer can make choices only if the goods have been endowed with properties that produce distinctions. (Callon and Muniesa 2005, 1235)

In other words, an economic object is delimited as a good when it is made comparable with other goods. Goods are goods among goods. In this sense, those different elements (such as labels, brands, supermarket shelves) that make these things both comparable and singular are studied as central factors in the process of enacting a new economic object.

This is no doubt an important point. However, it is worth asking whether good singularization is the only form of enacting an economic object? This issue has in some sense already been discussed. In an article that appeared in the same special issue as 'The Economy of Qualities', Don Slater (2002) pointed out that Thomas' (1991) notion of 'disentanglement', which is so important in Callon's (1998) original formulation, does not necessarily direct towards singularization, or more broadly calculation, but towards a different process: 'alienation'. In Slater's terms: 'Market exchange is commodity exchange. It presumes a form of property right in which a transfer of ownership ends all claims of the previous owner: the object is thoroughly alienated' (Slater 2002, 237). In other words: economic objects are not only linked 'to other products in the same space or on the same list', but they are (perhaps more fundamentally) attached to property rights and made transferable.

Thomas is part of the important renewal of property thinking within economic anthropology (Hann 2006). Particularly important here, is the reflection developed by another influential anthropologist: Marilyn Strathern (1999). In her work on controversies regarding what she has named 'potential properties' (i.e. heritage, university research, or genes), Strathern has explicitly questioned the traditional idea that property is a bundle of rights that connect pre-existing things with pre-existing people. In this sense, she follows a long tradition within anthropology that goes all the way to Mauss (1967), where it is assumed that objects and subjects of exchange are co-constituted. In other words, instead of starting from the liberal assumption of individuals as pre-existing economic subjects (Dumont 1992), attention is paid to how different types of 'collective' persons emerge out of economic relations (see also Hart 2006). However, and more importantly for the discussion in this chapter, Strathern points out that not only the subjects of ownership are delimited with property controversies, but also the objects that are traded. In the terms introduced in this chapter, economic objects are not only enacted through the singularization of goods among other goods, but also by the delimitation of ownership, a process that has been downplayed in Callon's work.

In Slater's quotation above, property is not the only concept that is strange to Callon's pair, a second one is 'commodity'. Appadurai (1986) also, like Slater and Thomas, does not talk about goods, but about commodities. Certainly, both notions share some common features, and can eventually be assimilated (Muniesa 2006).[3] In fact, Appadurai's usage of commodity does not greatly differ from Callon's understanding of goods. In his words:

> But how are we to define the commodity situation? I propose that the commodity situation in the social life of any 'thing' be defined as the situation in which its exchangeability (past, present, or future) for some other thing is its socially relevant feature. (Appadurai 1986, 13)

Nevertheless, the notion of commodity has a different conceptual history, which is not just associated with the calculability or exchangeability of economic objects (as stressed by Simmel, Appadurai, and Callon), but also with the asymmetric relation, pointed out earlier by Marx (1981; Lash 2007) between objects that are at different levels of abstraction, a process that has received increasing attention in recent finance studies.

For instance, sociologists Carruthers and Stinchcombe (1999) have shown that tradable securities are enabled by a process of abstraction that connects multiple specific things or events in further financial products. In this context, as MacKenzie and Millo's (2003) detailed historical account of financial derivatives proves, an increasingly relevant role is played by mathematical formulas that pragmatically connect underlying assets and the new products. Derivatives, in this sense, are what Vincent Lépinay has named a 'parasitic economic activity', where already available commodities are assembled into more abstract ones, creating a new layer that is both dependent on the underlying assets but that can also make them work following its own rhythm (Lépinay 2007). In more recent publications (Lépinay and Callon 2009; Lépinay 2011, 222–32), Lépinay has used anthropologist Jane Guyer's work to suggest a more general idea: 'derivation' is a process whereby new entities are built from existing ones through conversion, or what he calls 'transactional formulas'. In the terms of the research agenda here suggested, this is a third mode of stabilizing economic objects that, and in order to respect

Marx's old notion, can also be called 'commoditization' or the enactment of new commodities.

The difference between the stabilization of goods and commodities suggested here can be made clearer for those readers of this book more interested in the 'valuable' side of the title than in 'making things', if the parts played by prices in both contexts are compared. Following Muniesa (2007), a price can be understood as a sign that can work in the three different senses distinguished by Charles Sanders Peirce: as an icon, an index, and a symbol. In the case of standard goods, a price is a symbol, it does not resemble the product it represents nor does it index it to something else, but it enables the differentiation among multiple economic objects of a similar category. This is not the case of singular goods (Karpik 2010) where comparison is difficult to make (for instance among art pieces). There, prices are difficult to detach from the object they denote; actually, they communicate their quality (Velthuis 2004), working more as an icon. Finally, in the case of derivatives, prices are indexical; pricing connects the new economic object with its underlying objects, enabling, at the same time, its enactment as a new commodity.

To sum up, this section has attempted to organize a conceptual set of tools to study the stabilization of economic objects. To do that, the work of Callon and colleagues has been used as the main starting point. However, and drawing from other works, two important conceptual reparations have been introduced. First, the notion of production has been replaced with the concept of enactment to name the process of bringing new economic objects forth. Second, the excessive emphasis given to the singularization of goods has been corrected by distinguishing two other modes of enacting economic objects: the delimitation of property rights and commoditization.

The Objects of Insurance

The last section suggested that the study of the enactment of economic objects can be divided into three different processes. In the following pages these three different forms of studying economic objects are going to be illustrated with stories from a particular case, private health insurance in Chile. The empirical material presented here summarizes information that has been discussed at length elsewhere (Ossandón 2009). The main sources of information used to construct the case were multiple secondary sources (including policy reports and papers, newspaper controversies, parliamentary discussions, and other regulation documents) collected between 2005 and 2009. Complementarily, thirty in-depth interviews with managers, salespeople, regulators, and experts were carried out between December 2005 and April 2006.

There is not the space here to discuss the history of the health insurance industry in Chile. It is important to mention though that this system was created in 1981, within the context of the social reforms introduced during Pinochet's dictatorship that aimed at replacing former state-based social security with market-oriented institutions (Scarpaci 1991; Jimenez de la Jara and Bossert 1995; González-Rosseti et al., 2000). Like the Chilean private pension fund system, which was created almost simultaneously, the funding of health insurance is based on mandatory income contributions, currently 7 per cent of monthly salary. And, unlike most private health insurance in the world, private health insurance in Chile works as an alternative to the public system. Users that can afford it and pass the private insurers' screenings can choose to be covered either by the public insurance or by some of the private firms. Not without controversies, this system is still functioning today covering about a fifth of the population of the country.

Singularizing Goods

Figure 9.1 is a simplified version of the type of table included in most of the documents used to summarize the characteristics of an insurance policy in this industry. The first column lists the different types of medical events that are covered by the policy: in-patient care (*'prestaciones hospitalarias'*), ambulatory care (*'prestaciones ambulatories'*), and other events (*'otras prestaciones'*), while the second and third columns show different types of deals with medical providers: a special programme or *'oferta preferente'* for this policy with a clinic called *'Santa María'*, or 'free choice' (*'libre elección'*) in any other medical institution. The cells show the ceilings and co-payments for each combination. Each new policy, the goods of this market, corresponds to a different way of combining these elements. As some interviewees told me, the main source of 'inspiration' to plan new goods are the policies offered by other insurers. In other words, in order to keep their offer updated, insurers have to ascertain, for instance through 'fictitious consumers', what other companies are offering and they are not providing. This is a market where copying, even contracts with almost identical phrasing but a different name, is an everyday occurrence (Ossandón 2012).

This imitation dynamic, unsurprisingly, has had as a side-effect the proliferation of thousands of alternative policies, making the process of comparison and more broadly calculation very complicated. It does not help that, perhaps in order to avoid increasing costs of administration, the regulation of this industry does not allow insurance brokers. In fact, the lack, or rather excess, of information has become one of the main topics of debate among the economists and regulators interested in this case. On a more practical

Prestaciones	Libre Elección % bonificación	Libre Elección Tope bonificación	Oferta Preferente % bonificación	Oferta Preferente Tope bonificación	Prestadores Derivados
Prestaciones hospitalarias, cirugía ambulatorias y urgencia					
Día cama					
Sala cama					
Incubadora					
UTI-UCI Intermedio	90% sin tope				
Día cama transitorio			90% sin Tope, Clínica Santa María		
Exámenes de laboratorio					Clínica Dávila
Derecho pabellón					
Kinesiología, medicina sica, rehabilitación					
Procedimientos y honorarios Médicos Quirúrgicos		10 Veces AB1			
Medicamentes	90%	Sin tope			
Material Clínico		Sin tope			
Consulta médica hospitalaria		1,9UF	90%	45 UF	
Día hospital psiquiátrico	23%	Sin tope			
Prestaciones ambulatorias y urgencia		1,8 UF			
Consulta médica hospitalaria		1,5 Veces AB1			
Exámenes de laboratorio		3,10 Veces AB1	70% sin Tope		VidaIntegra, Avansalud
Derecho pabellón		7 Veces AB1			
Procedimientos y honorarios Médicos Quirúrgicos	70%	4 Veces AB1			
Kinesiología, medicinafisica, rehabilitación		3,5 Veces AB1			
Consulta, tratamiento psiquiátrico y psicológico		1,6 UF			
Otras prestaciones		1,8 Veces AB1			
Traslados	70%	1,8 UF			
Cirugía Óptica		1,8 Veces AB1			

Figure 9.1. Leaflet summarizing information for a specific insurance policy

level, it is possible to distinguish different 'market devices' that help in reducing this complexity and making these goods singular.

The first of these devices is sales agents. As McFall (2009) points out, sellers are pivotal to the success of insurance markets, and the case of health insurance in Chile is not an exception. Various interviewees conveyed that the real competition between the firms that constitute this industry takes place mainly at this level. By regulation, health policies are indefinite contracts, but they are reviewed once a year, when firms have the right to update their premium and users are able to change their policy. In this sense, competition is constantly open among current users. As an interviewee explains:

> There is a huge rotation in the Isapres [*Instituciones de Salud Previsional*, the generic name given to this particular type of health insurers in Chile] market, which has to do with the way this system has been conceived. Every year users receive a 'renewal letter' informing them of the up-dated premium and asking if they would like to maintain their policy. This mechanism makes people have to choose and look for other alternatives. On the other hand, Isapres grow because of their sales force. Each Isapre has more than 500 sellers in the street, which makes 'stealing' affiliated people a normal affair.

The sale agents to whom I spoke explained that their job mostly depends on their ability to create trust. They are continuously striving towards creating a relationship with their customers so as to make a current client recommend them and their company to the next. In this sense, sellers aim to build something like a portfolio of connections. These networks can be composed by different kinds of ties. For example, as one interviewee told me, her last sales were all connected with a particular place, a school, and they will call her every time they hire a new worker that does not yet have any health protection. Another interviewee said that he found his main path in family connections, specifically when children stop being dependent on their parents and need their own policy (the same with friends) (for a deeper analysis of the different types of social ties involving insurance sales, see Chan 2009b).

But the main question remains: What kinds of comparison do the sellers make? What is considered, at the moment of promoting a sale, in order to compare different policies and companies? The sellers who were interviewed agreed that their work is not about informing clients of all possible options, nor the ones available in the market or within their firm. What sellers do is to compare the potential client's current policy with one of the options put forth by their firm looking for ways to improve the client's current policy. At most they show two or three options. As one told me: 'for me there are always two alternatives, I don't show them many insurance policies, because otherwise my customer will get dizzy or will like all of them'.

A second device is market 'quality niches' (White 1981; Favereau et al. 2002). This industry is differentiated in socio-economic segments. In fact, everyone clearly distinguishes at least two different areas among the customers: the upper class on the one hand and the middle and lower middle class on the other. In the first context, how goods get singularized seems to not only be based on the specific characteristics of each policy, but mostly on their ability to be attached to the quality of other health actors, such as private hospitals, in-patient medical chains, and prestigious doctors. This fact is also exploited at the levels of brands, in the sense that, even though this type of integration is regulated in this industry, most of the insurers are part of wider conglomerates. In this sense, goods are not only qualified with their specific set of provisions, but they are also associated, through logos and other forms of identities, to goods of a different industry, 'medical provision' (Ossandón 2012). Similarly, if you follow the advertisement of health insurance, it is possible to see that this does not focus at all on specific policies but mostly on the qualities of the different firms. At this level, the alternatives are quite reduced. In fact, three decades after it started, this industry is highly concentrated with just five companies. Here comparison is not just about specific goods but about brands. Brands, as Celia Lury (2004) suggests, are complex objects that connect different goods under a same name or logo, representing the unity of this multiplicity.

On the other hand, for those policies targeted towards lower-income users who can still access private insurance premiums, private insurance policies are not just measured against those offered by other firms, but they are mainly compared with public insurance. For those users in the higher-income bracket the private health system is almost a given fact; however, for those with less economic resources, it is compared with its public counterpart. Different interviewees argued that what is in fact being compared is not the policy, but the qualities associated with both public and private forms of health administration. In other words, this competition is not just between private companies, but also between the companies themselves and the public system. Following Boltanski and Thévenot (2006), it is possible to argue that at this level the delimitation of the 'good' is not only about market competition, but about the critical contraposition of two different forms of attributing worth: public efficiency and market competition. However, unlike the Finnish case, discussed precisely in these terms by Lehtonen and Liukko (2010) where both logics are complementary, here public and private are in competition; in other words, actors have to be able to critically switch between different value frames when they choose (Thévenot 2002).

Delimiting and Contesting Property

The creation of the Chilean private health insurance in 1981 aimed at the introduction of private capital and competition in a previously public field. But what is 'private' in health insurance? An informant, who was the president of the board of one of the main health insurance firms and who has participated in this industry since it was created, affirmed that 'the specification that mandatory contribution [the portion of the salary compulsorily withdrawn to health insurance] is a property of each worker justified the beginning of the system'. This definition was not seriously contested until the onset of a controversy which surrounded the last health reforms that were finally approved in 2004 (for a deeper analysis of this controversy, see Ossandón 2014).

The main initiative of these reforms was the introduction of a new health plan that would guarantee coverage for fifty-one of the most relevant pathologies in the current epidemiological pattern of the population, for those covered by both public and private insurance. In order to finance it and make the reform more egalitarian, the government suggested the creation of a 'solidarity fund'. This fund was designed on the basis of a distinction between the average cost of covering these new guaranteed events and the expected cost corrected when taking into consideration some factors that correlate with health risks such as age and sex. Thus every insurer would initially receive the average cost that corresponded to each user, with the exception of those insurers whose pool of users had a lower health risk; these would have to give part of their fund back to the solidarity pool which would then be distributed between those insurers who were covering the riskier population. In practical terms, this would have implied an important circulation of resources from private insurers—that generally cover a segment of the population with lower risk—to the public system, where the riskier population is concentrated. (private insurers are allowed to screen and exclude potential users that have 'pre-existences', or previous pathologies, and premiums are higher for women of fertile age and older users. Premiums in public insurance are not risk priced, and its coverage cannot exclude previous pathologies.

The announcement of this plan generated a huge parliamentary discussion, mainly in the Senate, where the social democrat government needed the support of at least part of the conservative opposition to pass the bill. As the next quotation (taken from the Acts of Congress) shows, opposition was not only based on issues about the design and potential results of the bill, but it was claimed that creating a solidarity fund would also violate a constitutional right: the inalienability of private property.

> He [a member of the Senate] stated that their claim will be funded because of the fact that the fund is financed by health contributions, which are each user's

> property. To orientate part of them to the Compensation Fund implies creating a concealed tax, directed at a specific aim, and it constitutes a flagrant violation of each user's property right concerning their own health insurance contribution. (Senado 2004, 74)

In other words, as the informant at the beginning of this section stated, the 7 per cent that each worker has to compulsorily give to public or private insurers is a 'thing' that they own. Therefore, instituting a Compensation Fund would imply an illegitimate expropriation, an action that is against the constitutional right that guarantees private property. Finally, and in order to sanction the rest of the bill, the government found a different way to levy resources, namely increasing the Chilean VAT from 18 per cent to 19 per cent.

This controversy is interesting because it questioned one of the main elements that has been a principal component of this system from its inception: the privatization of health insurance contribution. However, the question remains, what exactly has been privatized? What was finally defended by the parliamentary opposition? To understand this issue it is pivotal to think about property and the particular characteristic of insurance. Insurance is always collective; it is based on the production of a statistically connected population (Knights and Vurdubakis 1993). However, the limits of the collective are variable. In fact, one of the main strategies in this business is to create new pools or new forms of connecting potential events and grouping users. The creation of private health insurance in Chile did not made a public good individual, but engendered new collectives: differentiating health users between those covered by public insurance and those under the shield of different private insurers. The solidarity fund implied a potential rearrangement of this order, creating a new collective which would connect, in different forms, the different pools involved. In this sense, it is possible to state that the discussion was about private and public, not about individual and public property; it was about delimiting the form and borders of different collectives. However, as Strathern has suggested, in this type of controversy it is not only the collectives and rights that are contested, but also the object that is actually exchanged. Health insurance, in other words, is not only enacted in its singularization as a good among other goods, but also in the legal delimitation of the property rights attached to it.

Commoditizing Risk

An element that is certainly essential to any insurance policy is its 'premium'. Premiums are the price of insurance. The case of the policy depicted in Figure 9.1, and in general in private health insurance in Chile, presents the particularity that the premium is not in the common Chilean currency (*pesos*), but in a financial unit indexed to inflation called UF (*Unidad de Fomento*). Also particular is that the elements that can be considered to differentiate the price of a specific policy for its different users are limited by regulation. For instance: risk pricing can be based on age and sex, but not on the previous medical history of the potential user. However, what is not regulated is how the premiums of new policies are established. This is perhaps the core moment in the enactment of any insurance, and can be understood as a process marked by a series of translations.

Figure 9.2 visualizes an encounter between a possible customer and an insurance seller who works for one of the health insurance firms in Chile. Most likely such an encounter will happen after the salesperson, interested in increasing her client portfolio, contacts a possible user who has agreed to have an introductory meeting. When they meet, the seller asks certain socio-demographic information (sex, age, number of family members, income) from which it will be possible to suggest the array of insurance policies available for the pool to which this prospective user belongs, and the premiums and coverage in each case. If the potential user is still interested, she will be asked to fill out a 'medical declaration' which, for the most part, focuses on her previous medical history. The meeting finishes here. At the next meeting, the salesperson plays a different role; now her work is informing the outcomes of the medical declaration.

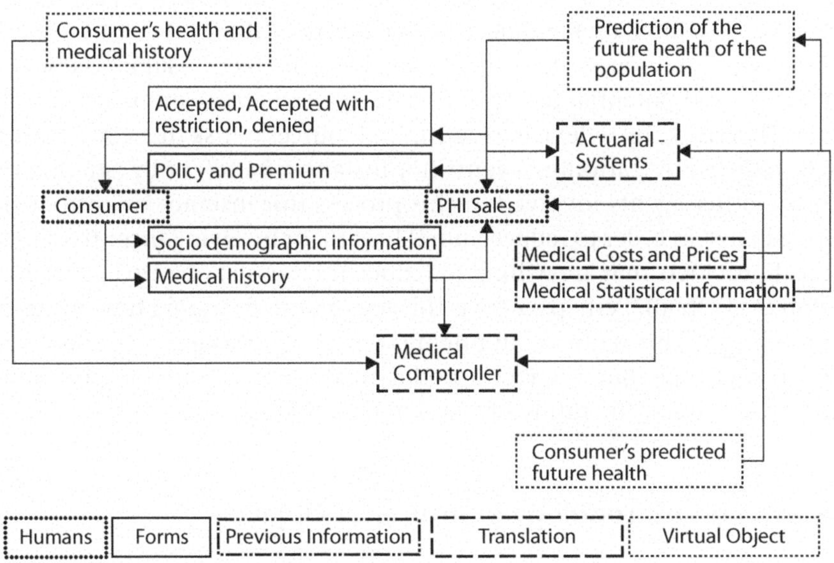

Figure 9.2. Diagram of insurance exchange

There are three main options: accepted without restrictions; accepted but with a restricted policy; or not accepted. Restrictions and rejections are connected to the user's medical history, or what is called 'pre-existences', that is, past medical events that suggest potential future medical expenses which insurers are legally allowed to not cover. In case the prospective user does not agree with the outcome of this process, it is possible to appeal, and the controversy will be solved with external medical tests.

But what has happened here? When the seller gathers socio-demographic information and proposes certain policies, she connects with an already defined process. Here the main actors are those that work at the actuarial departments. Actuaries deal with information systems that match available health statistics and the potential cost of medical provisions. Actuaries produce 'virtual objects' (Law 1996). These are virtual because they are not material (a tendency in statistical software) yet they are regarded as objects because from the moment they are produced they are assumed as real, and cause a real impact upon the next stages of the socio-technical network they help to assemble. There has been a process of visualization and signification (Van Loon 2002), that sanctions the transformation of socio-demographic information into possible future events, and valorization, when this is translated into a third element: potential monetary cost. On the other hand, the medical declaration is evaluated by those working at a different department known as 'medical comptrollers'. By using previous epidemiological information, medical comptrollers attempt to predict the future medical risk of new users, determining the existence of relevant pre-existences. Here two new virtual objects are produced: the past medical history of a potential user and her possible future health.

However, this process does not finish here. In fact, insurance does not just face a fixed potential future, but actively participates in making its own future. This works by reflexively identifying sources of risk that could eventually be reduced by patrolling events (for instance 'fraud') or by 'sharing risk' with the other agents involved in this process (for instance by introducing 'co-payments' in order to reduce 'moral hazard' or by giving incentives to the medical providers that are willing to reduce their costs) (see also Baker 2000; Ericson et al. 2000). Perhaps, here is the key to understanding how insurance commoditizes. This is not about pricing something priceless, nor about valuing existing things, but it is about producing its own commodity: risk, which in action acts upon the future of the elements that it assembles.

Towards an Anthropology of Insurance Objects

The stories presented in the last section described three different forms of enacting the objects of insurance: the first was about the process of making policies singular and the market devices that are used in this context; the second was about the limits between public, individual, and collective in private insurance; and the third was about pricing and the delimitation of a risk-based commodity. Conceptually, each of the stories can be associated with the three different ways of enacting economic objects distinguished in the first part of this chapter. In the first, objects are stabilized in opposition to other goods; in the second, stability is reached through the delimitation of what belongs to an owner and can, eventually, be traded; and in the third, an object is enacted from a process that connects a set of different things at a different level of abstraction.

In relation to the topics discussed in the other chapters of this book, it is important to stress that the stories here presented are not only different from each other, but they connect to different valuation processes. The first was about sales and brands, the second about parliament and regulation, and the third about actuaries. In conceptual terms, it could be said that insurance is not only a multiple object, in the sense given by Mol, but also 'multi-sited' (Marcus 1995). Therefore, researchers interested in grasping the enactment of an object such as insurance need to face the methodological challenge of following and learning about a varied array of economic actors (firms, consumers, sellers, actuaries, regulators), devices (pricing models, marketing, sales leaflets, parliamentary acts), and their respective modes of economic expertise.

More generally, this chapter has rehearsed a broader research agenda, namely, studying economic processes through the enactment of economic objects. Frank Cochoy has used the expression 'sociology of market-things' to name the study 'of how commercial objects, frames and tools equip consumer cognition' (Cochoy 2007, 109). Considering the influence of anthropological research within our context, the research agenda highlighted here could be more appropriately named 'anthropology of economic objects'. It will be a task for future research to study whether there are other forms of enacting economic objects that have not been distinguished here. It suffices to say that the framework here suggested does not aim at being exhaustive in this regard.

Acknowledgements

This research has been funded by Beca Presidente de la República from the government of Chile, the Central Research Fund awarded by the University of London, and the research project 'VRA-Prácticas Culturales e Identidades Sociales' from Universidad Diego Portales. This latter funding also made it possible to have the helpful assistance of Felipe González. A very early version of this work was presented at the Economic Sociology Winter Workshop, Goldsmiths, University of London, and a newer version at the Economization of Uncertainty, University of Helsinki. The author is grateful for comments received during both events, particularly the inspiring suggestions given by the discussants in each session, respectively, Daniel Beunza and Jeanne Lazarus. Comments and the criticism given by Tomás Ariztía, Keith Hart, Scott Lash, Celia Lury, David Stark, Sebastián Ureta, and the editors of this book have been also very helpful.

Notes

1. Orlikowski refers to two different dictionary definitions of 'to enact': in one of them it is defined as 'to constitute, actuate, perform' while in another as 'to represent in or translate into action' (Orlikowski 2000, 425).
2. Using M. Serres' and B. Latour's comments about the etymological connection between the words 'thing' and 'cause' (in the sense of an open not delimited procedure (Latour 1993, 83)) it could be said that 'thing' refers to an 'object' that is not yet stabilized.
3. As the *Oxford English Dictionary* explains, the term 'commodity' comes from the French word *commodité* which has its origin in the Latin *commoditas*, and it is associated with a useful or convenient object; while a 'good' corresponds to a 'desirable individual or object; a thing worth attaining'.

References

Abolafia, M. and M. Kilduff. 1988. 'Enacting Market Crisis: The Social Construction of a Speculative Bubble'. *Administrative Science Quarterly* 33(2): 177–93.

Appadurai, A. 1986. 'Introduction: Commodities and the Politics of Value'. In *The Social Life of Things: Commodities in Cultural Perspective*, ed. A. Appadurai. Cambridge: Cambridge University Press, 3–63.

Baker, T. 2000. 'Insuring Morality'. *Economy & Society* 29(4): 559–77.

Baker, T. and J. Simon. 2002. 'Embracing Risk'. In *Embracing Risk: The Changing Culture of Insurance and Responsibility*, ed. T. Baker, and J. Simon. Chicago: University of Chicago Press, 1–26.

Beck, U. 1996. 'Risk Society and Provident State'. In *Risk, Environment & Modernity: Towards a New Ecology*, ed. S. Lash, B. Szerszynski, and B. Wynne. London: Sage, 27–43.

Boltanski, L. and L. Thévenot. 2006. *On Justification: Economies of Worth*. Princeton: Princeton University Press.

Çalışkan, K. and M. Callon. 2010. 'Economization, Part 2: A Research Programme for the Study of Markets'. *Economy & Society* 39(1): 1–32.

Callon, M. 1998. 'Introduction: The Embeddedness of Economic Markets in Economics' in *The Laws of the Markets*, ed. M. Callon. Oxford: Blackwell, 1–57.

Callon, M. and J. Law. 2005. 'On Qualculation, Agency, and Otherness'. *Environment and Planning D: Society and Space* 23(5): 717–33.

Callon, M. and F. Muniesa. 2005. 'Peripheral Vision: Economic Markets as Calculative Collective Devices'. *Organization Studies* 26 (8): 1229–50.

Callon, M., C. Méadel, and V. Rabeharisoa. 2002. 'The Economy of Qualities'. *Economy & Society* 31(2): 194–217.

Carruthers, B. and A. Stinchcombe. 1999. 'The Social Structure of Liquidity: Flexibility, Markets, and States'. *Theory and Society* 28(3): 353–82.

Chan, C. 2009a. 'Creating a Market in the Presence of Cultural Resistance: The Case of Life Insurance in China'. *Theory and Society* 38(3): 271–305.

Chan, C. 2009b. 'Invigorating the Content in Social Embeddedness: An Ethnography of Life Insurance Transactions in China'. *American Journal of Sociology* 115(3): 712–54.

Cochoy, F. 2007. 'A Sociology of Market-Things: On Tending the Garden of Choices in Mass Retailing'. *Sociological Review* 55(2): 109–29.

Collier, S. J. 2008. 'Enacting Catastrophe: Preparedness, Insurance, Budgetary Rationalization'. *Economy & Society* 37(2): 224–50.

Dumont, L. 1992. *Essays on Individualism: Modern Ideology in Anthropological Perspective*. Chicago: University of Chicago Press.

Ericson, R. and A. Doyle. 2004. 'Catastrophe Risk, Insurance and Terrorism'. *Economy & Society* 33(2): 135–73.

Ericson, R., D. Barry, and A. Doyle. 2000. 'The Moral Hazards of Neo-Liberalism: Lessons from the Private Insurance Industry'. *Economy & Society* 29(4): 532–58.

Ewald, F. 1991. 'Insurance and Risks'. In *The Foucault Effect: Studies in Governmentality*, ed. G. Burchell and P. Miller. London: Harvester Wheatsheaf, 197–210.

Ewald, F. 2002. 'The Return of Descartes's Malicious Demon: An Outline of a Philosophy of Precaution'. In *Embracing Risk: The Changing Culture of Insurance and Responsibility*, ed. T. Baker, and J. Simon. Chicago: University of Chicago Press, 273–301.

Favereau, O., O. Biencourt, and F. Eymard-Duvernay. 2002. 'Where Do Markets Come From? From (Quality) Conventions!' In *Conventions and Structures in Economic Organization: Markets, Networks and Hierarchies*, ed. O. Favereau and E. Lazega. Cheltenham: Edward Elgar, 213–52.

González-Rosseti, C., T. Chuaqui, and C. Espinosa. 2000. 'Enhancing the Political Feasibility of Health Reform: The Chile Case'. <http://new.paho.org/hq/dmdocuments/2010/40-Enhancing_Political_Feasibility_Health_Reform-Chile.pdf>.

Hann, C. 2006. 'A New Double Movement? Anthropological Perspectives on Property in the Age of Neoliberalism'. *Socio-Economic Review* 5(2): 287–318.

Hart, K. 2006. 'Intellectual Property'. <http://www.thememorybank.co.uk/2006/10/20/intellectual-property/>.

Jimenez de la Jara, J. and T. Bossert. 1995. 'Chile's Health Sector Reforms: Lessons from Four Reform Periods'. *Health Policy* 32(1–3): 155–66.

Karpik, L. 2010. *Valuing the Unique: The Economics of Singularities*. Princeton: Princeton University Press.

Knights, D. and T. Vurdubakis. 1993. 'Calculations of Risk: Towards an Understanding of Insurance as a Moral and Political Technology'. *Accounting, Organizations and Society* 18(7–8): 729–64.

Kopytoff, I. 1986. 'The Cultural Biography of Things: Commoditization as Process'. In *The Social Life of Things: Commodities in Cultural Perspective*, ed. A. Appadurai. Cambridge: Cambridge University Press, 64–92.

Lash, S. 2007. 'Capitalism and Metaphysics'. *Theory, Culture & Society* 24(5): 1–26.

Latour, B. 1993. *We Have Never Been Modern*. Cambridge, MA: Harvard University Press.

Latour, B. 2000. 'When Things Strike Back: A Possible Contribution of "Science Studies" to the Social Sciences', *British Journal of Sociology* 51(1): 107–23.

Law, J. 1996. 'Organizing Accountabilities: Ontology and the Modes of Accounting'. In *Accountability: Power, and Ethos and the Technology of Managing*, ed. R. Munro and J. Mouritsen. London: International Thomsom Business Press, 283–306.

Lehtonen, T. K. and J. Liukko. 2010. 'Justifications for Commodified Security: The Promotion of Private Life Insurance in Finland 1945–90'. *Acta Sociologica* 53(4): 371–86.

Lehtonen, T. K. and J. Luikko. 2012. 'The Forms and Limits of Insurance Solidarity'. *Journal of Business Ethics* 103(1): 33–44.

Lépinay, V. 2007. 'Parasitic Formulae: The Case of Capital Guarantee Products'. *Sociological Review* 55(2): 261–83.

Lépinay, V. 2011. *Codes of Finance: Engineering Derivatives in a Global Bank*. Princeton: Princeton University Press.

Lépinay, V. and M. Callon. 2009. 'Sketch of Derivations in Wall Street and Atlantic Africa'. In *Accounting, Organizations & Institutions: Essays in Honor of Anthony Hopwood*, ed. P. Miller and A. Chapman. Oxford: Oxford University Press, 259–89.

Lury, C. 2004. *Brands: The Logos of the Global Economy*. London: Sage.

McFall, L. 2009. 'The Agencement of Industrial Branch Life Assurance'. *Journal of Cultural Economy* 2(1–2): 49–65.

McFall, L. and F. Dodsworth. 2009. 'Fabricating the Market: The Promotion of Life Assurance in the Long Nineteenth-Century'. *Journal of Historical Sociology* 22(1): 30–54.

MacKenzie, D. and Y. Millo. 2003. 'Constructing a Market, Performing Theory: The Historical Sociology of a Financial Derivative Exchange'. *American Journal of Sociology* 109(1): 107–45.

Marcus, G. 1995. 'Ethnography in/of the World System: The Emergence of Multi-Sited Ethnography'. *Annual Review of Anthropology* 24: 95–117.

Marx, K. 1981. *Capital: A Critique of Political Economy*. Harmondsworth: Penguin Books.

Mauss, M. 1967. *The Gift: Forms and Functions of Exchange in Archaic Societies*. New York: W. W. Norton.

Mol, A. 2002. *The Body Multiple. Ontology in Medical Practice*. Durham, NC: Duke University Press.

Muniesa, F. 2006. 'Good/Commodity'. In *International Encyclopaedia of Economic Sociology*, ed. J. Beckert and M. Zafirovski. London: Routledge.

Muniesa, F. 2007. 'Market Technologies and the Pragmatics of Prices'. *Economy & Society* 36(3): 377–95.

Muniesa, F., Y. Millo, and M. Callon. 2007. 'An Introduction to Market Devices'. In *Market Devices*, ed. M. Callon, Y. Millo, and F. Muniesa. Oxford: Blackwell, 1–12.

O'Malley, P. 1996. 'Risk and Responsibility'. In *Foucault and Political Reason: Liberalism, Neo-Liberalism and Rationalities of Government*, ed. A. Barry, O. Thomas, and N. Rose. London: University College of London Press, 189–208.

Orlikowski, W. 2000. 'Using Technology and Constituting Structures: A Practice Lens for Studying Technology in Organizations'. *Organization Science* 11(4): 404–28.

Ossandón, J. 2009. 'The Enactment of Private Health Insurance in Chile'. PhD thesis, Goldsmiths, University of London.

Ossandón, J. 2012. '¿Cómo se hace un mercado?... Agregue: formaciones sociales, conflictos políticos y economistas'. In *Produciendo lo social: usos de las ciencias sociales en el Chile reciente*, ed. T. Ariztía. Santiago: Ediciones Universidad Diego Portales, 285–310.

Ossandón, J. 2014. 'Reassembling and Cutting the Social with Health Insurance'. *Journal of Cultural Economy* 7(3): 291–307.

Scarpaci, J. 1991. 'Dismantling Public Health Services in Authoritarian Chile'. In *Health Services Privatization in Industrial Societies*, ed. J. Scarpaci. New Brunswick: Rutgers University Press, 219–44.

Senado. 2004. 'Informe de la Comisión de Salud, recaído en el proyecto de ley, en Segundo trámite constitucional, que establece el Régimen de Garantías en Salud'. BOLETÍN No 2.947-11.Ley No 19.966 Establece un régimen de garantías en salud (Plan AUGE). *Historia de la ley, Vol. 2007: Biblioteca del Congreso Nacional de Chile.*

Simmel, G. 1990. *The Philosophy of Money* (2nd edition). London: Routledge.

Slater, D. 2002. 'From Calculation to Alienation: Disentangling Economic Abstractions'. *Economy & Society* 31(3): 234–49.

Strathern, M. 1999. *Property, Substance, and Effect: Anthropological Essays on Persons and Things*. New Brunswick: Athlone Press.

Thomas, N. (1991), *Entangled Objects: Exchange, Material Culture, and Colonialism in the Pacific*. Cambridge, MA: Harvard University Press.

Thévenot, L. 2002. 'Conventions of Co-ordination and the Framing of Uncertainty'. In *Intersubjectivity in Economics: Agents and Structures*, ed. E. Fullbrook. London: Routledge, 181–97.

Van Hoyweghen, I. 2010. 'Taming the Wild Life of Genes by Law? Genes Reconfiguring Solidarity in Private Insurance'. *New Genetics and Society* 29(4): 431–55.

Van Loon, J. 2002. *Risk and Technological Culture*. London: Routledge.

Varela, F., E. Thompson, and E. Rosch. 1999. *The Embodied Mind: Cognitive Science and Human Experience* (7th edition). Cambridge, MA: MIT Press.

Velthuis, O. 2004. 'An Interpretive Approach to Meanings of Prices'. *Review of Austrian Economics* 17(4): 371–86.

Weick, K. 2003. 'Enacting and Environment: The Infrastructure of Organizing'. In *Debating Organization: Point–Counterpoint in Organization Studies*, ed. R. Westwood and S. Clegg. Oxford: Blackwell, 184–94.

White, H. 1981. 'Where Do Markets Come From?' *American Journal of Sociology* 87(3): 517–47.

Zelizer, V. 1978. 'Human Values and the Market: The Case of Life Insurance and Death in 19th-Century America'. *American Journal of Sociology* 84(3): 591–610.

Zelizer, V. 1981. 'The Price and Value of Children: The Case of Children's Insurance'. *American Journal of Sociology* 86(5): 1036–56.

10

The Politics of Values

A Case Study of 'Conflict-Free' Gold

Juliane Reinecke

Gold has long been seen as the ultimate measure of value. Until the fall of the Bretton Woods system in 1971, gold was the ultimate measure of currency value. The US dollar was tied to and backed up by gold, measuring paper monies against the gold standard. Gold has been humanity's oldest medium of exchange and form of wealth preservation for thousands of years. Its material properties make gold a perfect candidate for the measure and store of value. In contrast to other metals that may be poisonous such as mercury, liable to corrosion such as iron, or too hard to extract such as platinum, gold is not only scarce and readily recognizable for its bright lustre. The precious metal can be relatively easily melted yet is permanent, durable, and can be lastingly stored. But more importantly, gold is perfectly divisible and fungible. Unlike an uncut diamond, any one unit of gold can be substituted with any other unit of gold. No matter its age, origin, whether it has been newly mined or recycled from ancient jewellery, when refined to its pure form, each ounce of gold is qualitatively equal to and thus interchangeable with any other ounce of gold. Gold is endlessly recyclable and no value is lost in the process. 'Gold is gold is gold', this equation captures the premise of the global gold industry.

More recently, however, there have been attempts to qualify gold ethically and socially. Specifying gold as 'eco-friendly gold', 'green gold', 'fairmined gold', 'conflict-free gold', or in the negative, 'dirty gold', 'conflict gold', or 'blood gold' has been perceived by some as a fundamental threat to the principle of gold's perfect fungibility. Through socio-ethical qualification, a materially equivalent unit of gold is differentiated on socially defined grounds. For instance, a 'fairmined' stamp on a piece of jewellery indicates the socially 'fair' origin of gold beyond its mere material specification. Similarly, the 'No Dirty Gold' campaign encourages jewellery consumers to differentiate between 'dirty' gold and gold that is sourced in ways that do not pollute, displace native communities, infringe workers' rights, or damage delicate ecosystems. Whereas efforts to certify ethical jewellery as fairmined, green, or recycled may remain confined to a relatively small niche market, a recent legislation posed a more fundamental threat to the fungibility of gold. In parallel to non-governmental organization (NGO) campaigns, the US Congress passed a law in 2010 that requires US-listed companies to disclose whether minerals necessary to the functionality of their products contain 'conflict gold'. In response, global gold mining companies, refiners, brokers, metal traders, and industry associations have taken steps to ensure their gold to be conflict-free, seeking to protect the premise that gold is gold.

The case of gold, as the ultimate measure of value, and its more recent social qualification, opens up important questions about the relationship between value and values. On the one hand, scholars have been concerned with the quantification of value, that is, the way in which values are transformed and converted into value. The price mechanism has been typically seen as a powerful means to performing quantification, and the capitalist market system more generally as a mechanism through which 'all values [are] reduced to value' (Skeggs 2014, 1). On the other hand, sociologists and organizational theorists have focused on the influence of social, cultural, and ethical values on value, arguing that values and value are always dialogic, dependent, and co-constituting (Fourcade 2011; Skeggs 2014). Few studies, however, focus on the 'politics of values' that is, the political process of establishing and controlling what and whose values matter in defining valuation criteria and subsequent value. Rather than quantification, the focus is on the contentious process of social-ethical 'qualification' (Callon et al. 2002). This chapter examines how human rights NGOs and other civil society actors in conjunction with the state have been working to 'qualify' the precious metal by creating distinctive categories that qualitatively differentiates 'conflict gold' from 'conflict-free gold', while industry incumbents battled to prevent gold becoming subject to values through qualification by protecting the fungibility of gold.

Quantification: From Values to Value

Much scholarly attention across disciplinary boundaries has been given to the process of how values are converted to value, to a price, an exchange value or the appearance form of value. This 'value problem'—the processes through which actors assign value to goods using a common standard—is central yet not unique to the functioning of markets (Callon and Muniesa 2005; Beckert 2009). Aristotle referred to the value problem in terms of the commensurability of use-values (even though, as Marx later pointed out, Aristotle lacked the concept of value, failing to distinguish between its substance and appearance form). For goods to be exchanged, he argued, they must be commensurate:

> This is why all things that are exchanged must be somehow comparable. It is for this end that money has been introduced, and it becomes in a sense an intermediate; for it measures all things, and therefore the excess and the defect—how many shoes are equal to a house or to a given amount of food. (Aristotle 1985, Book 5)

What Aristotle suggests is that there is a need for a common standard of value against which all other values can be gauged. In the words of the anthropologist Chris Gregory (1997, 13), '[f]or a value system to operate efficiently there must be a generally accepted standard of value because valuation is essentially a comparative process by which two unlike entities—be they commodities in the market, gifts in the *kula* ring, or castes in India—are compared and judges to be the same of different with reference to this standard'. On commodity markets money has evolved as the standard measure of value. Money expresses equivalence when the multi-dimensional qualities of different goods are translated into a unified representation of their value. The strength of the market's valuation device, the price mechanism, is understood as harmonizing the will of individuals through its capacity to produce compromises out of situations of conflicting interests (Thévenot 2001). Markets have therefore been described as 'organized collective devices that calculate compromises on the values of goods' which 'make complicated calculations possible, and [...] produce practical solutions to problems that could not otherwise be solved by purely theoretical reflection' (Callon and Muniesa 2005, 1229–30). Quantification thus translates the plurality of individual value judgements and interests into a one-dimensional numerical expression. For this reason, the '[m]arket has emerged as the most politically significant institution of valuation in the world today' (Gregory 1997, 16).

For Marx, gold is the ultimate money commodity and ultimate expression of value. Gold, he explains, 'serves as an ideal measure of value'. Importantly, as gold is not the substance of value, the labour value embodied in commodities must be transformed [*verwandelt*] into exchange value, expressed by the money commodity.

> The values of... commodities are... changed into imaginary quantities of gold... magnitudes of the same denomination, gold-magnitudes. As such they are... being compared with each other and measured. (Marx 1887, 191)

Exchange value is realized only through the social process of exchange in which different kinds of human labour are equated with each other and expressed in reference to the standard of value. Value thereby gets expressed, or price fixed, in the relationship between gold and all other commodities that are equated to gold 'in imagination' and can potentially be exchanged with it (Harvey 2010).

A Marxist lens on value suggests that a process of abstraction and transformation [*Verwandlung*] in which values are detached from value is at the heart of quantification and market valuation. Value is the product of a process in which entities become detached from the context and the social relations that constitute the substance of value. Entities gain an independent, detached existence in a new space: they become commodities on the market. Commodities become autonomous so that 'persons exist for one another merely as representatives of, and, therefore as owners of, commodities' (Marx 1887, 59). Marx famously referred to this as 'commodity fetishism', describing the belief that the value of a commodity arises from a mystical property inherent to it, rather than from concrete labour-time expended upon it. In *Capital*, Marx (1887, 164–5) thus spoke about the 'metaphysical subtleties' and 'the mysterious character of the commodity form'. As human labour becomes embodied and objectified in the material form of commodities, the social relation between people assumes the 'fantastic form of a relation between things' (Marx 1887, 34). Central to this idea is the notion that the logic of capital produces an abstraction, an enigma, which conceals and mystifies the social relations so that 'a relation between people takes on the character of a thing and thus acquires a "phantom objectivity"' (Lukács 1971, 83). Through the fetishism of commodities, relationships between people are disguised as relationships between commodities. Quantification, thus, creates value in its appearance form, but at the same time, abstracts from and conceals the essence of value—which is the concrete relations of production.

Anthropologists have similarly seen alienation from social context and values as the demarcating line between gifts and commodities. Unlike in gift exchange, where objects are never completely separated from those who exchange them, 'decontextualised, dissociated and detached' commodities cut the social ties that would otherwise transcend the singular event of the market exchange, after which buyer and seller must be quits (Callon 1998, 19). Commodities 'are placed in a context in which they have exchange value and can be alienated. The alienation of a thing is its dissociation from producers, former users, or prior context' (Thomas 1991, 39). Things are made equivalent units in the process of the substitution of social relations. It is thus the detachment of social relations, memories, affections, ethics, and cultural entanglements, in short the detachment of values from value that performs quantification.

Studies of quantification have not been limited to the conversion of values into exchange value. The valuation logic of the market has permeated many other domains of social life, which have been made quantifiable and measurable. The question of quantification has been seen, more broadly, as an issue of creating comparability between unlike entities or how to express qualitative things in a common quantitative metric (Espeland and Stevens 1998). A large body of research has examined the creation of conventions of equivalence (Desrosières 2008), coding and taxonomy (Thévenot 1997), commensuration (Espeland and Stevens 1998), media ranking systems (Espeland and Sauder 2007), classification and standards (Bowker and Star 1999; Lampland and Star 2008). For instance, the Research Excellence Framework in the UK transforms different research activities into numerical expressions of research quality, using the 'timeless logic of a standardized indicator' to judge research quality on a singular scale (Strathern 2000, 317). While it is the beyond the space of this chapter to review the rich literature on quantification, what these studies have in common is a focus on the process by which plural values are reduced to a uniform expression of value.

Qualification: From Value to Values

The reverse process, the transformation of value into values has received less attention. To be sure, economic sociologists have emphasized the social and cultural 'embeddedness' of market behaviour (Granovetter 1985; Zelizer 1994). And critically, quantification is not the pure application of a numeric algorithm, but requires qualitative judgment (Callon and Muniesa 2005, 1232). In particular, 'economic valuation processes are deeply bound up with other aspects of social organization—notably law, politics, economic expertise, and environmental knowledge' (Fourcade 2011, 1724). Examining the differences in the economic valuation of nature in oil spills litigations in France and in the United States, Fourcade (2011, 1769) notes that ascribing economic value on things 'does not stand outside of society: it incorporates in its very making evaluative frames and judgments that can all be traced back to specific politico-institutional configurations and conflicts'. Also, the values relating to the social relations embodied by a thing matter for its valuation. As an extreme case of attachment in the Melanesian exchange system, items 'carry no guarantee of equivalence [...] This pig was reared by that partner, that by another' (Strathern 1992, 187). What Strathern points to is that the value of any item, such as a pig, depends on the social relations regarding cause and origin which differentiate otherwise uniform entities qualitatively. As Cochoy (2008, 17) showed, supermarket shopping trolleys redefine consumer's calculations so that they make 'quality-based rational judgements'—taking into account a range of qualitative values when making value judgements guiding their shopping choices. It is maybe as Skeggs (2014, 1) suggests, that 'values will always haunt value'.

The multiple meanings and usage of gold show how value and values are intricately related. Gold is often simultaneously used as adornment as well as storage of value, as the Indian tradition of wearing gold bangles indicates. In contrast to the persistency to quantify things, this suggests that values can also be explicitly (re-)attached to value and take on new meanings. The notion of 'qualification' is particularly helpful to understand how this may occur (Callon et al. 2002). Qualification is a socio-economic processes through which qualities are attributed to goods, stabilized, objectified, and arranged. A good is thereby seen as a bundle of characteristics, such as quality, location, time, availability, which different economic agents can shape and change in the process of qualifications-requalifications. Zelizer's (1994) notion of 'earmarking' money is a prime example of qualification, which illustrates how even the money commodity itself can become subject to qualification. Zelizer (1994, 216) shows how money in the household becomes subject to domestic standards of values through which 'people will segregate, differentiate, label, decorate, and particularize it to meet their complex social needs'. Housewives would 'earmark' money for qualitatively different purposes when labelling the tins where they kept household money: 'groceries', 'carfare', 'gas', 'laundry', 'rent', 'savings', 'miscellaneous'. This differentiation process converts a generalized quantitative standard into multiple qualitative standards. The attachment of symbolic consumer value (Lury and Moor 2010) is a another example of transforming otherwise uniform commodities into singularities, such as bottled water. Even though research has repeatedly established that bottled water is generally no safer or purer than what comes from the tap in most developed countries, a whole new set of evaluative criteria has emerged that requalified the public good by infusing it with symbolic consumer value, contributing for a burgeoning market for bottled water with a high premium for an otherwise standardized, inexpensive public good (Wilk 2006). Or, consider the case of coffee. A standardized commodity until the 1980s that was traded in bulk with generic standardized grades, coffee has rapidly changed into a sign of cultural and ethical differentiation. In a 'qualities turn', new qualities emerged that have become mainstreamed, as the case of Starbucks illustrates. Starbucks started as a specialty coffee house in 1971 in Seattle selling high quality coffee beans. More than fifteen years later it had only expanded to eight stores. Nowadays, the world's largest specialty coffee house prizes itself that you are never more than five minutes away. Today, a new class of coffee gourmets can buy high-priced coffee that has been chewed on by monkeys or digested—and then excreted (!)—by civet cats in Sumatra or elephants in Thailand. This cultural change in coffee consumption is nowhere better illustrated in Aaron Sorkin's political drama TV series *The West Wing*. In the first episodes starting in 1999, industrious White House staff are sipping non-stop from white coffee mugs filled with black, nondescript filter coffee that is readily available from large jars of office coffee makers. Soon, the white coffee mug was replaced by the Starbucks paper cup and coffee consumption becomes a cultural ceremony. The West Wing's press secretary thus gives special orders for 'her double shot, light on the soy, cinnamon-chia mochachino, no whip, sprinkles and another shot on top'.

Qualification of commodities such as coffee, water, or even money illustrates what Gregory (1997, 14) calls a 'paradox of diversity within uniformity'. The earmarking of homogenous commodities breaks with the unifying scale of exchange value and invites ethical and political judgements through an alternative valuation procedure. This resists the alienating and separating effects of monetary valuation in terms of economic utility and subjective preferences.

The Politics of Values

Neither quantifications nor qualifications arise naturally or are scientific discoveries, but are intentionally created constructs requiring heavy 'investments in forms' (Thévenot 2001), that is laborious work, political intervention and skilful administration. It takes material and social effort to produce practices that allow for 'qualculation' (Callon and Law 2005). Accordingly, commodity production 'is also a cultural and cognitive process: commodities must be not only produced materially as things, but also culturally marked as being a certain kind of thing' (Kopytoff 1986, 64). This marking, or in Zelizer's terms 'earmarking', is not a values-neutral process. It is the effect of a values judgement and produces a values judgement: 'Each standard and each category valorizes some point of view and silences another' (Bowker and Star 1999, 5).

Drawing on Appadurai (1986), I call the political process of establishing and controlling what and whose values matter in defining value, the 'politics of values'. This involves political struggles to influence and control quality judgements and value conventions that come to be the governing regimes of value, or a 'government of norms' (Thévenot 1997; Boltanski and Thévenot 2006;). The ultimate political struggle then 'is not even the struggle to appropriate value; it is the struggle to establish what value is' (Graeber 2001, 88). Value therefore, is not independent of the political process of determining what the salient values will be.

Anthropologists have discussed various 'regimes of value' (Appadurai 1986) and sociologists have described different economies or 'orders of worth' (Boltanski and Thévenot 2006), as being the 'very fabric of calculation, of rationality, of value' (Stark 2009, 4). The 'worth' of an entity is not just based on a single value dimension, such as price, but embedded in a number of different and, sometimes incompatible complex philosophical and political value systems. Each of these value systems, or orders of worth, is based on a higher common principle providing evaluative criteria and metrics (Boltanski and Thévenot 2006) for judging an idea's, object's, or person's 'worth' in different contexts (Callon and Muniesa 2005). In Boltanski and Thévenot's (2006) framework, these higher common principles include the price mechanism on the market, democratic decision-making in the civic world, hierarchical-traditional structures in the family, technical-scientific rule in the industrial world, reputation in the world of fame, divine rule in the inspired world, or sustainability in the 'green' world (Thévenot et al. 2000). Multiple economies of worth mean that valuation involves alternative, and sometimes incompatible values and principles (Boltanski and Thévenot 2006). For example, what is valued or deemed worthy, such as efficiency in the 'industrial world' and competitiveness in the 'market world', may be seen as undesirable in the 'domestic world' of family life. Valuation or determining value then is a process of 'definition' or social construction, incorporating all kinds of values and assumptions about different socially and politically structured representations of worth (Fourcade 2011). The politics of values is thus the struggle to make values matter that subvert quantification and redirect valuation along different values dimensions.

The politics of values is amply illustrated in the case of coffee, where environmentalists and fair trade activists have fought since the early 1980s to requalify coffee on ethical and environmental terms, promoting competing values of social justice, authenticity, and biodiversity. Parallel to the rise of European-style coffee house culture, a large number of not only specialty but also ethically differentiated labels have thus emerged that signify different, and sometimes conflicting aspects of sustainable coffee quality (Reinecke et al. 2012). Ethical labels and certifications interrupt the ethical uniformity of commodities and encourage consumers to make ethical, values-based, and not purely economic value judgements. Qualification thus converts commodities into what Karpik (2010) describes as 'singularities'—goods and services with unique quality-based characteristics, such as Fairtrade coffee or Fairmined gold. Fairtrade thereby not only differentiates commodities in an ethical way but also seeks to make social relations of production visible at the point of sale. The Fairtrade Minimum Price based on the cost of sustainable production actively accounts for and makes visible producers' labour as the substance of commodity value (Reinecke 2010). As a result, the social biography of a thing—production and trade—becomes part of the value of the Fairtrade labelled product. Or, borrowing Zelizer's (1994) term, Fairtrade certified coffee becomes 'earmarked'. Yet, various actors have promoted different values to qualify coffee, which ranges from fairly traded, organically or shade-grown and bird-friendly. While ethical coffee labelling started as a niche movement, in 2012/13 an estimate of 40 per cent of global coffee production was certified or verified as sustainable (even if only 12 per cent was sold under a label) (SSI 2014). Given that coffee is the second-most traded commodity in the world, this change towards ethically differentiated coffee indicates a significant trend towards qualification in what used to be a relatively homogeneous commodities market.

Gold is Gold is Gold

I have suggested so far that commodities are not only quantified, equated to a uniform standard of value and thereby detached from values, but in the reverse, commodities as homogeneous as money, gold, and to some extent water and coffee have become qualified according to multiple orders of worth. This is often a contentious process which I referred to as the politics of values. If the previous sections were concerned with the duality of value and values and the social processes of quantification and qualification, pointing to the contentiousness surrounding these, then this section is concerned with the politics of values around qualification itself. What follows is an empirical exploration of attempts by human rights activists to qualify the gold commodity and industry counter-efforts to prevent its qualification. The qualification of gold into 'conflict gold' and 'conflict-free' gold is a particularly interesting case to examine how commodities become subject to values through social-ethical qualification (Callon et al. 2002). Gold has historically been the ultimate measure of value. The gold industry is based on the assumption that 'gold is gold is gold' (WGC 2012). This reflects insistence on the commodity nature of gold, where the social and geographical provenance is irrelevant. Gold is infinitely recyclable and it becomes extremely difficult to trace its origins once it has been recycled. Yet, trade in 'conflict gold' is accused of playing a fundamental role in funding war and fuelling a humanitarian crisis in the Democratic Republic of Congo (DRC). Linking Congolese gold to the worst forms of conflict and sexual violence has challenged the mantra of 'gold is gold is gold'—denoting some gold as illegitimate 'conflict gold'.

I collected material on the legislative process leading to and following the US conflict minerals legislation, including official congressional records and documentation, the official draft versions of the evolving legal text (Dodd Frank Act), the total of 525 public comment letters, meeting notes, and transcripts in relation to the implementation of Section 1502, carried out by the US Securities and Exchange Commission (SEC), as well as reports and press releases by human rights activist groups, NGOs, and websites of affected companies and industry associations. In addition, thirty-five semi-structured, open-ended interviews were conducted between 2011 and 2013 with respondents from the US government, NGOs, and the gold and electronics industries. My research was guided by the desire to understand the significance of qualification on markets processes and the political nature of it.

Mineral Wealth Fuelling a Humanitarian Crisis in the DRC

Conflict minerals are defined as those originated in the Democratic Republic of Congo (DRC) or adjoining countries. The DRC, Africa's second-largest country, is a conflict-ridden and arguably failed state that has been subject to indiscriminate killings, mass rapes, mutilations, and forced child soldier recruitment. The country is blessed with abundant natural resources, including water and closed-canopy tropical forest, as well as large, untapped deposits of raw mineral ores, including the world's largest reserves of cobalt and significant quantities of the world's diamonds, gold, and copper as well as smaller amounts of zinc, uranium, natural gas, phosphate, petroleum, and a range of rare minerals. But rather than promoting socio-economic development, trade in minerals, even if not the root cause of the war, has been one of the main factors fuelling armed conflict in eastern DRC.

Armed conflict, instability, and sexual violence have ravaged the DRC, especially the eastern part, since the ethnic conflict between Hutus and Tutsis fuelling the 1994 Rwanda genocide spilled over to the eastern part of the DRC and created a civil war. More than 5.4 million people are estimated to have died due to violence, famine, and disease. The civil war officially ended with the country's first elections in 2006, but armed conflict continued. In 2012, the DRC was the last of the 187 countries listed on the United Nations Development Programme's (UNDP) Human Development Index. Rape, frequently described as a weapon of war, is at extraordinary high levels with estimates that almost 40 per cent of all women in the eastern DRC reported to have been exposed to sexual violence (Johnson et al. 2010). Despite a United Nations peacekeeping operation since the Lusaka Ceasefire Agreement in July 1999 with up to 19,815 troops to conduct military operations in North and South Kivu, and the recent creation of an 'intervention brigade' in March 2013, the international community has been largely ineffective in responding to political conflict in the DRC.

Gold Mining in the Democratic Republic of the Congo

It is estimated that the DRC produced 22 tonnes of gold in 2011, which represents about 0.8 per cent of newly mined gold and less than 0.3 per cent of the total supply of gold (WGC 2012). However, only a small proportion of gold produced in eastern DRC enters the formal gold supply chain and is formally exported by registered gold traders. A significant proportion of newly mined gold comes from artisanal sources. Worldwide, around 10–15 per cent of newly mined gold comes from artisanal and small-scale sources. In the DRC, it is almost 100 per cent. Most artisanal mining is in the informal sector and much of it is illegal, operating beyond government supervision, or subject to illegal and unaccounted taxes imposed by corrupt state agents (Enough 2012), and is prone to smuggling. Because mining profits are exploited by armed groups and members of the Congolese army, artisanal mining often provides few long-term benefits to local communities. It is estimated that the vast majority of eastern Congo's gold production is smuggled by armed groups across porous borders into neighbouring countries, Uganda, Rwanda and Burundi, and exported with false certificates of origin to refiners in Dubai (Enough 2012). The provenance of conflict gold is often, therefore, difficult to establish. Thus, it poses a huge challenge for companies to ascertain and verify that the product they used had been sourced ethically and is 'conflict-free'.

Qualifying Gold through 'Naming and Shaming' Legislation

While the exchange value of gold is set on global commodity exchanges like the London Bullion Market Association (LBMA), various initiatives have emerged that sought to qualify gold on ethical grounds as being fair and legitimate or 'dirty' and illegitimate. Rather than just market worth, this mobilizes other regimes of worth as appropriate categories to evaluate gold. For instance, Oxfam's and Earthwork's 'No Dirty Gold' campaign launched in 2004 seeks to create consumer awareness around the detrimental impact of gold mining on indigenous peoples, Third World economies, workers' rights, women's rights, and the local ecosystem, which suffers from pollution due to the disposal of highly toxic chemicals into open pits and waterways. 'Dirty gold' thus is attacked for its low 'civic' and 'green' worth. Similarly, Fairtrade started certifying 'Fairmined' gold in 2011. 'Fairmined' jewellery carries a Fairtrade stamp to help consumers evaluate gold products based on their ethical worth. Fairmined gold is sourced exclusively from artisanal and small-scale miners in Bolivia, Peru, and Colombia, who produced around 600 kg certified gold in 2013. Miners receive a guaranteed Fairtrade Minimum Price set at 95 per cent of the LBMA's fixing for gold plus a 10 per cent premium.

Various NGOs, like Global Witness, Oxfam, and the Enough Project had for many years fought desperately to get the international community to act. But it was when they started to focus on gold and other minerals as the root cause of the conflict that global attention was drawn to the issue. Replicating the success of making other value regimes matter in the valuation of consumer goods, such as fairly sourced coffee or sweatshop-free garments (e.g. Bartley

2007), human rights NGOs launched consumer- and brand-oriented campaigns seeking to stigmatize gold from the DRC as being tainted with conflict and sexual violence. The Enough Project most noticeably changed its strategy from targeting the international community to attacking the worthiness of conflict-stained commodities, marked by the release of the strategy paper 'Can You Hear Congo Now? Cell Phones, Conflict Minerals, and the Worst Sexual Violence in the World' in April 2009. By implying that the private sector, and Western multinational brand name companies in particular, were implicitly contributing through their purchase of consumer goods, such as jewellery, to the violence in the eastern DRC, the Enough Project's 'Raise Hope for Congo' campaign sought to create consumer demand for conflict-free products.

While these social movement-driven efforts have qualified the worthiness of gold in social and environmental terms, the imminent threat to link companies to the worst forms of conflict and sexual violence was made real by US legislation. Mandating companies to declare whether they were using 'conflict gold' shook the global gold industry. Under the Heading 'Miscellaneous' in the voluminous Dodd-Frank Wall Street Reform and Consumer Protection Act (Dodd-Frank) 2010, the US passed a provision, section 1502, which declared four minerals—gold along with cassiterite (tin ore), columbite-tantalite, or coltan (tantalum ore), and wolframite (tungsten ore)—to be 'conflict minerals'—whose trade directly or indirectly finances or benefits armed groups in the DRC and adjoining countries. The legislation reflects the US Congress' concern that trade in conflict minerals is 'helping to finance conflict characterized by extreme levels of violence in the eastern DRC, particularly sexual- and gender-based violence, and contributing to an emergency humanitarian situation therein' (Dodd-Frank Act, Section 1502). The legislation does not prevent the import of conflict gold into consumer countries, but it obliges companies to disclose whether or not they are sourcing conflict gold. This creates a de facto qualification of gold as either 'conflict' or 'conflict-free' gold—to be monitored through the naming and shaming of various human rights NGOs, like Global Witness, Oxfam, and the Enough Project.

Public disclosure was argued to 'allow consumers to make an informed choice as to purchase such goods or not'. The conflict minerals provision was thus needed to allow consumers to differentiate products based on the qualification of whether they contained conflict minerals or not, as Senator Durbin argued at a 2011 SEC Roundtable:

> We have got to alert the American business community and American consumers to the fact that our demand for products that contain these minerals could, could inadvertently be fueling this war and leading to this terrible suffering [...] For those of us who enjoy these products every day, I'd like to enjoy it with a clear conscience. (SEC 2012)

Consumers became enlisted as constituents of the politics of values. In the comment letters to the SEC a large number of consumer-citizens identified themselves as involuntary stakeholders: 'As American consumers and world citizens we were both appalled to hear that by making electronics purchases from American corporations, we could be contributing to one of the most bloody and horrific conflicts in history.' A Citizen Petition of 2,310 'concerned consumers and constituents' complained that 'Mac by Mac, Blackberry by Blackberry', they were made 'all complicit in the suffering of the people of Congo' due to lack of information about whether 'our cell phones and laptops continue to be made with blood'. Consumers called for qualification to ensure their right to 'make an informed choice in the marketplace'. This would allow them to incorporate values into purchasing decisions and '"vote" for an ethical option' in order 'to ensure that, as consumers, we no longer inadvertently funding the violence and atrocities in Congo', as a consumer commented in a letter to the SEC.

Industry Response: Preventing the Qualification of Gold

Actors from within the gold industry reported they felt 'caught in surprise' by being implicated in the seemingly remote issue of conflict gold. The conflict minerals legislation was seen to have 'slipped in the 13th hour'. While earlier campaigns by 'No Dirty Gold' or Fairmined gold were targeted at a niche market segment, the legislation radically shifted the industry's position on the issue. While before 'no one was really concerned about the issues in the gold industry', the threat to the status of gold as the ultimate, fungible commodity by a potential differentiation of gold into legitimate 'conflict-free gold' and 'illegitimate conflict gold' made the industry respond. Actors now realized that just focusing on shifts in consumer and investor demand was 'not quite the right way to look at it'. Even though conflict-free gold has 'not necessarily been to date a huge request of the consumer marketplace' and was seen to be 'not a big deal', as a respondent from the gold industry explained, it was recognized to have the potential to disrupt the market significantly. Because conflict minerals appeared in a very large number of products, albeit in very small amounts, Section 1502 could affect nearly all of the 15,000 publicly traded companies in the US—thus implicating not only jewellers, but also manufacturers using small amounts of gold for coating as well as ethical investors and institutional investors who faced increasing pressures to sign up to ESG principles in investing. Thus, industry actors worried that 'a large chunk of the gold will suddenly not be deemed good gold and that impacts the market'.

In short, the legislation had the potential to fundamentally shake up the global gold industry across multiple levels of the supply chain. Most critically, the potential stigmatization of gold represented an existential threat to the fundamental premise that 'gold is gold is gold'. While only a negligible percentage of gold that end-user manufacturing companies used originated from the DRC, even the smallest amount of illegitimate ('conflict') gold could taint the entire supply chain, due to the materiality of gold as being endlessly recyclable.

Gold market actors feared that 'there are effectively going to be lots of different tiers for gold and that's going to make the gold market function very differently'. Market actors feared that this could lead to a situation of market fragmentation with effectively different golds, as the precious metal could become segregated into 'different spheres of gold. And gold is gold is gold is no longer going to be the case', a respondent noted. This was seen as presenting significant confusion for the financial markets and a potential threat to gold markets and gold trading. This fear was expressed in a letter to the SEC commenting on the proposed draft rules. In it the World Gold Council (WGC 28 February 2011) argued that 'if all gold, regardless of country of origin, is widely stigmatized as a result of the regulations, there is a risk that gold's value as a hedging vehicle that supports the global financial economy will be compromised'.

The qualification of gold could potentially undermine the world's trust in gold as the ultimate measure of value and a store of wealth. Aram Shishmanian, the CEO of the World Gold Council stresses the status, which risked being undermined by an association (WGC 2012, 1):

> Across cultures and time, gold has been a symbol of trust. Investors trust gold to preserve wealth against the ravages of inflation. Young couples trust gold to express their love and commitment to each other. Scientists trust gold to deliver exceptional performance in a variety of technological applications.
>
> In uncertain times, the world turns to gold. So nothing could be more important than maintaining the confidence which consumers, investors, governments and producing nations place in this precious metal.

In comparison to coffee where a values differentiation could legitimately be based on 'different types of coffee and beans and different flavours coming from different places', with gold this would undermine the status of gold being 'a pure commodity'. The gold industry therefore fiercely resisted the qualification of gold. Industry strategies to preserve the uniformity of gold included direct and indirect lobbying of the SEC to minimize the social and economic fallout from this government initiative, as well as proactive responses to shape the rule. The main aim was to prevent qualification so as 'not to disrupt the gold market too much'.

Resisting Qualification

The gold industry resisted labelling all gold as a conflict mineral by default, as the SEC's Proposed Rules implementing section 1502 suggested. 'You can't use a broad brush to say any gold is a conflict mineral, that's stupid', a gold industry actor argued. Another respondent explained their lobbying efforts, 'certainly one of the things we're pressing for here in the United States is a change to the way the regulations are written, is to not define gold as a conflict mineral on a global basis but to be specific and say gold that comes from a conflict region is a conflict mineral'. Thus, in its letter to the SEC commenting on the proposed draft rules, the World Gold Council (WGC 28 February 2011) argued:

> The classification of all gold as a so-called 'conflict-mineral' in the Proposed Rules failed to acknowledge the significant difference between responsibly produced gold and gold which finances or benefits armed groups [...] To label all gold a so-called 'conflict-mineral' prior to the conclusion of the due diligence required for the Conflict Minerals Report leaves the impression that all end-users of gold are using a conflict mineral.

The industry association therefore called for using the label 'conflict gold' only for those sources that have been found to contribute to armed conflict, rather than declaring all gold as 'conflict gold' and requiring industry actors to prove the opposite. If miners, traders, and jewellers had to prove that their gold was legitimate, this might 'create two separate gold markets', one industry actor predicted. The gold market would be separated along 'legitimate' gold from non-conflict areas and 'illegitimate' gold from conflict zones.

Separating the gold market could lead to unintended consequences, as industry incumbents warned. Buyers might simply avoid buying gold from the DRC or Africa altogether, which would deprive impoverished communities from an important source of income. Thus, industry actors warned 'the Proposed Rules could stigmatize all gold being produced in the DRC Countries, as well as potentially other African countries, which could result in an effective boycott on responsibly mined gold from such countries and in turn potential adverse economic implications' (WGC 28 February 2011). This would particularly hurt artisanal miners who could not afford increased costs of labelling and certification. Artisanal miners 'probably won't benefit and they will turn to the black market' dominated by war lords, thus aggravating the problem the rule was seeking to fight.

The issue of labelling gold and other minerals escalated into a legal challenge against the SEC over the conflict minerals rule. In line with the corporate co-optation of 'free speech' that has immunized US companies in many other areas, a coalition of business interests mounted a constitutional attack against the conflict minerals rule, claiming that disclosure violated the 'First Amendment' (which protects the US constitutional right to free speech). While the legal challenge was not led by the gold industry itself but by the US Chamber of Commerce, the National Association of Manufacturers, and the Business Roundtable, the claim was initially articulated in a comment letter to the SEC by Tiffany& Co (22 February 2011). The lawyers of this high-end jeweller objected that the proposed regulations would require companies which use gold and certain other minerals to state publicly (and against their will) that their products supported human rights violations. In a letter signed by Tiffany's senior Vice President, the company objected to having to declare that products 'are not "DRC conflict free"' (SEC 2012, 29) if the company was unable to determine that they did not directly or indirectly finance of benefit armed groups:

> the most fundamental concern is that the proposed regulations would compel speech in a manner that violates the First Amendment. [...] The principal source of the irrationality is that the proposed regulations would compel disclosures by companies (like Tiffany) which have no reason to believe they use minerals originating in the DRC or adjoining countries. [...] This is not only irrational; it is a forced, false confession that should be anathema in our democratic political system.

A lawyer from an advocacy group criticized the argument that disclosure was a threat to free speech as 'a laughable sort of claim because if we agreed with that then there would be no disclosure of anything'. In the final rule, the SEC accommodated the First Amendment Challenge and changed the wording of 'not "DRC conflict free"' (SEC 2012, 29) to 'have not been found to be conflict-free', while granting a two-year transition period where products could be labelled as 'DRC conflict undeterminable'. However, less than two months after the SEC adopted the final rule on conflict minerals disclosure in August 2012, the US Chamber of Commerce, the National Association of Manufacturers, and the Business Roundtable filed suit to challenge the rule. The plaintiffs argued that the reporting obligations of Section 1502 of Dodd-Frank represented government-compelled speech in violation of the First Amendment. While the conflict minerals legislation was upheld by the DC District Court in July 2013, the Court of Appeals narrowly ruled in April 2014 that requiring companies to describe products as 'not been found to be DRC conflict free' was a violation of the First Amendment's right to free speech, while rejecting the claim that public disclosure of supply chain information was a violation under the First Amendment, thus upholding the majority of the SEC's rule to implement Section 1502. Thus companies would have to disclose without having to describe their products as DRC conflict-free or not.

Re-assuring Trust: Creating Conditions for Quasi Non-Qualification

Industry actors and associations have gone to great length to restore confidence in gold. They collaborated with each other to create responsible sourcing standards to assure market participants that formally sourced gold is de facto conflict-free. Industry associations focused on creating industry initiatives to avoid the possibility of conflict gold entering and contaminating the supply chain. For instance, the World Gold Council launched a Conflict-Free Gold Standard (WGC 2012, 2)—'a common approach by which gold producers can assess and provide assurance that their gold has been extracted in a manner that does not cause, support or benefit unlawful armed conflict or contribute to serious human rights abuses or breaches of international humanitarian law'. In March 2012, the Responsible Jewellery Council (RJC) launched a Chain-of-Custody Standard for the precious metal supply chain ensuring that sources are conflict-free as a minimum, and responsibly produced at each step of the supply chain in correspondence with the RJC Code of Practices. In 2011, the LBMA set up a Responsible Gold Guidance in order to combat serious abuses of human rights, to avoid contributing to conflict, to comply with high standards of anti-money laundering, and combating terrorist financing practice. Refiners need to adopt and show proof of compliance as a prerequisite for remaining on the LBMA Good Delivery List.

The gold industry also sought to prevent the debate from spreading to other social and environmental issues in gold mining. The industry hence tried to balance being a proactive supporter of the elimination of conflict gold while stressing the role of gold mining as a major contributor to economic growth and development:

> While working to exclude illegitimate gold from the supply chain, it is critical that mining companies and the broader international community also recognise the important role that gold mining can play in protecting the interests of countries and communities which are dependent upon legitimate gold production. (WGC 2012, 8)

The threat to non-compliances is illustrated by the following incident. Similarly to the LBMA, the Dubai Multi Commodities Center, a commodities trading authority, created the 'Responsible Market Participant' designed to stop gold mined in conflict zones from entering the global supply chain. Yet, the authority became subject to controversy when in 2014, a whistleblower who worked as an auditor for Ernst & Young reported a number of serious breaches of the rules and exposed the risk that gold refined in Dubai, a key destination for DRC minerals, may contain conflict gold. In response, the Dubai Multi Commodities Center saw itself forced to restore trust by creating a new initiative to certify the responsible sourcing of gold bars. Its CEO (DMCC 2014) commented: 'It is important for Dubai, as one of the largest physical gold trading hubs in the world, to give industry participants the assurance that they can trade with confidence knowing that upcoming refineries in the UAE and globally comply with international trade and responsible sourcing best practices.'

Qualification as Contamination: Dealing with the Non-Provenance of Gold

Social provenance is the key social qualifier that distinguishes commodities from gifts (Gregory 1997). Conversely, the key characteristic of the ultimate commodity is that it cannot be qualified based on its provenance. If 'in reference to cause and origin, no two things are qualitatively equivalent' (Strathern 1992, 187), removing the reference to cause and origin removes qualitative difference between different golds. This is what happens when gold supplies from different sources, including recycled and newly mined gold from different origins enters the refinery. At the refinery gold loses its provenance as gold from different sources is melted together refining gold into its pure periodic form, Au. In other words, qualification is lost at the refinery level. Without segregation, all traces of qualification of gold according to region, origin, or mining method get melted into a uniform, undifferentiated commodity.

The problem of non-provenance was most astute in recycled gold, or scrap, which is gold that has been previously refined. Once gold has been recycled it loses all trace of provenance. When recycled gold comes back into the refinery, industry actors claimed that there was no way of knowing where that gold had originated, whether it had been mined one or a thousand years ago. The difficulty of tracing the provenance of gold, and recycled gold in particular, posed a particular challenge to being able to claim that gold was conflict-free. This problem was described as one of contamination: qualifying gold whose provenance could not be clearly established as conflict gold could lead to all gold becoming qualified as associated with conflict: 'Any amount of DRC-sourced material will contaminate a larger batch, indeed any amount of non-provenanced material will contaminate a larger batch' (RJC 2011, 29). If recycled gold, which was estimated to account for 30–40 per cent of annual gold supply, could not be labelled 'conflict-free' then there was a significant risk that *all* or at least most gold would be contaminated with conflict.

Most actors within the gold industry considered it vital to ensure that recycled gold was inherently seen as conflict-free rather than conflict-tainted even though this 'could be labelling as "responsible" gold which has in fact been produced or obtained using the worst methods imaginable' as a gold mining company (RJC 25 February 2011, 52) commented. In an effort to shape the emergent rule on conflict minerals to be finalized by the SEC, the gold industry fought hard for being able to label recycled gold as 'conflict-free'. For instance, in a comment letter to the SEC, the World Gold Council (WGC 28 October 2011) argued that 'legitimate recycling does not finance conflict and human rights abuse, and the Commission should not hinder such efficient use of scarce resource. Legitimate recyclable material should therefore...

not be deemed to be suspect or contaminated with conflict-affected source.' Justifications were mainly based on the materiality of gold. Industry actors asserted that traceability of recycled material would be impossible to achieve given that gold was 'constantly recycled'. As an industry respondent explained, 'gold is in many ways the ultimate recyclable material because it's so valuable and so indestructible. Gold just does not disappear.'

Unlike diamonds, gold could be infinitely melted and easily lose its provenance. A physical mark could easily be removed, as a respondent explained: 'To get rid of the mark, you just melt it and it's okay, right?' In contrast, each diamond is unique so that a certification can trace it through the supply chain: 'You cut it out right, you can certify it, bang, no one is going to melt it, as you can't melt it down!' For gold, routine segregation of gold feedstocks at refineries would be required to determine its original source. To illustrate 'the general impossibility of a refiner being able to allocate countries of origin to the bars leaving its premises and entering the market', the LBMA (21 August 2012) submitted charts to the SEC depicting the range of gold-containing feedstocks from various sources and origins used by accredited gold refiners including 'industrial/electronic/jewellery scrap', 'recycled bullion', 'artisanal', and 'dore'. Each refiner used a variety of sources. Segregation of gold feedstock was not only deemed to result in substantial additional costs but would also be a potential disruption of established supply chains that could lead to a split in the gold market into 'conflict-free gold' and 'conflict-contaminated gold'.

The materiality argument was further backed by the argument that it was 'environmentally better to use this [recycled gold] than to use fresh gold from a mine'. Recycling was presented as an ecologically friendly practice that should be encouraged. While some human rights activists were concerned that recycled gold could offer a loophole for Congolese conflict gold to enter the market as 'recycled', they largely agreed that the use of recycled materials should be encouraged rather than made difficult. Incorporating these views, the SEC's final rule states that if a company's conflict minerals are derived from recycled or scrap sources, its products are considered 'DRC conflict free'.

Conclusion

I began by suggesting that much of the sociological literature concerned with value and valuation tends to concentrate on processes of quantification. In response, I have sought to extend the scope of debate towards qualification and the politics of values surrounding it as a means of also conceptualizing the dynamic relationship between value (as the domain of quantification) and values (as the domain of qualification). I have asked how new socio-economic qualifications of values come into existence, and how various interventions may be implicated in these dynamics.

The case of conflict gold illustrated the power of qualification to establish new conventions of worth, (re-)attach them to commodities and thereby allowing the social relations between human beings to reappear as part of commodities. While gold has been described as the standard of value, or the ultimate commodity, and still is seen by many as the ultimate store of value, ethical qualification meant that gold could itself become qualified through values, making visible the human conditions under which it was produced. Gold as the prefect commodity freed from the social context of its production could thereby lose its material fungibility and status expressed as 'gold is gold is gold'. Qualification by human rights NGOs, civil society, and government actors of gold as 'dirty', 'unfair', or 'conflict-tainted' as opposed to 'clean', 'fairmined', and 'conflict-free' has thus served as a powerful lever for change in the global gold industry. Given this potential to disrupt existing market arrangements, entrenched power relationships, and possibly the distribution of value on markets, I have described qualification as a political struggle to establish what and whose values count in determining the worth of entities, involving the politics of values. The focus on contentious politics is consistent with the cultural and political view of markets that has shown how actors activate values, articulate contentious issues, or mobilize collective action to create valuable categories such as sustainable forestry, grass-fed beef, or Fairtrade coffee (Bartley 2007; Weber et al. 2008; Reinecke 2010). Yet, as the case of gold revealed, what is at stake is not merely the change in and creation of new markets for novel product categories, but in fact a much wider debate about values, and the social power to define and make visible various orders of worth involved in commodity production and consumption. What was contested was not only the behaviour of market actors, but ownership over value(s) conventions underpinning market processes. To prevent ethical and social values becoming a differentiating factor on the global gold market, industry incumbents therefore resisted qualification in order to maintain gold's status as non-qualifiable by invoking their First Amendment rights and the risk of unintended consequences. But they also took steps to introduce guidelines and initiatives for responsible sourcing to prevent traces of conflict gold entering the gold supply chain and thereby contaminating conflict-free gold.

While qualification may counteract commodity fetishism, it may simultaneously be the moment when new classifications for quantification are created. There is a thin line between quantification and qualification. For instance, the creation of a Fairtrade or conflict-free gold certification may thus close down questions about other orders of worth, and establish uniformity within diversity, to paraphrase Gregory (1997). Forms of opening up new values also represent moments of closure (and vice versa). It would be therefore useful to better understand the quantification–qualification duality. The chapter invites future studies to reflect on, and finally to advance our understanding of the limits and possibilities of an enlightened politics of values.

Acknowledgements

The author acknowledges the support of an Early Career Fellowship by the Independent Social Science Research Foundation.

References

Appadurai, A. (ed.). 1986. *The Social Life of Things: Commodities in Cultural Perspective.* Cambridge: Cambridge University Press.

Aristotle. 1985. *The Nicomachean Ethics,* Indianapolis: Hackett.

Bartley, T. 2007. 'Institutional Emergence in an Era of Globalization: The Rise of Transnational Private Regulation of Labor and Environmental Conditions'. *American Journal of Sociology* 113(2): 297–351.

Beckert, J. 2009. 'The Social Order of Markets'. *Theory and Society* 38(3): 245–69.

Boltanski, L. and L. Thévenot. 2006. *On Justification: Economies of Worth.* Princeton: Princeton University Press.

Bowker, G. C. and S. L. Star. 1999. *Sorting Things Out: Classification and Its Consequences.* Cambridge, MA: MIT Press.

Callon, M. 1998. 'Introduction: The Embeddedness of Economic Markets in Economics'. In *The Laws of the Markets,* ed. M. Callon. Malden, MA: Blackwell, 1–57.

Callon, M. and J. Law. 2005. 'On Qualculation, Agency, and Otherness'. *Environment and Planning D: Society and Space* 23(5): 717–33.

Callon, M. and F. Muniesa. 2005. 'Peripheral Vision: Economic Markets as Calculative Collective Devices'. *Organization Studies* 26(8): 1229–50.

Callon, M., C. Méadel, and V. Rabeharisoa. 2002. 'The Economy of Qualities'. *Economy and Society* 31(2): 194–217.

Cochoy, F. 2008. 'Calculation, Qualculation, Calqulation: Shopping Cart Arithmetic, Equipped Cognition and the Clustered Consumer'. *Marketing Theory* 8(1): 15–44.

Desrosières, A. 2008. *L'argument Statistique. Pour une Sociologie Historique de la Quantification.* Paris: Presses des MINES.

DMCC. 2014. 'DMCC Launches New Responsible Sourcing Certification Programme for Gold'. <http://www.dmcc.ae/content-page?DMCC-launches-new-responsible-sourcing—certification-programme-for-gold&articleid=a05b0000004h26jAAA>. Accessed 15 June 2014.

Enough. 2012. 'From Child Miner to Jewelry Store: The Six Steps of Congo's Conflict Gold'. <http://www.enoughproject.org/reports/child-miner-jewelry-store-six-steps-congos-conflict-gold>. Accessed 3 January 2013.

Espeland, W. N. and M. Sauder. 2007. 'Rankings and Reactivity: How Public Measures Recreate Social Worlds'. *American Journal of Sociology* 113(1): 1–40.

Espeland, W. N. and M. L. Stevens. 1998. 'Commensuration as a Social Process'. *Annual Review of Sociology* 24(1): 313–43.

Fourcade, M. 2011. 'Cents and Sensibility: Economic Valuation and the Nature of "Nature"'. *American Journal of Sociology* 116(6): 1721–77.

Graeber, D. 2001. *Toward an Anthropological Theory of Value: The False Coin of Our Own Dreams*. New York: Palgrave Macmillan.

Granovetter, M. 1985. 'Economic Action and Social Structure: The Problem of Embeddedness'. *American Journal of Sociology* 91(3): 481–510.

Gregory, C. A. 1997. *Savage Money: The Anthropology and Politics of Commodity Exchange*. Amsterdam: Harwood Academic Publishers.

Harvey, D. 2010. *A Companion to Marx's Capital*. London: Verso.

Johnson, K., J. Scott, B. Rughita, M. Kisielewski, J. Asher, R. Ong, and L. Lawry. 2010. 'Association of Sexual Violence and Human Rights Violations with Physical and Mental Health in Territories of the Eastern Democratic Republic of the Congo'. *JAMA: The Journal of the American Medical Association* 304(5): 553–62.

Karpik, L. 2010. *Valuing the Unique: The Economics of Singularities*. Princeton: Princeton University Press.

Kopytoff, I. 1986. 'The Cultural Biography of Things: Commoditization as Process'. In *The Social Life of Things: Commodities in Cultural Perspective*, ed. A. Appadurai. Cambridge: Cambridge University Press, 64–92.

Lampland, M. and S. L. Star (eds.). 2008. *Standards and Their Stories: How Quantifying, Classifying, and Formalizing Practices Shape Everyday Life*. Ithaca: Cornell University Press.

Lukács, G. 1971. *History and Class Consciousness: Studies in Marxist Dialectics*. Cambridge, MA: MIT Press.

Lury, C. and L. Moor. 2010. 'Brand Valuation and Topological Culture'. In *Blowing Up the Brand: Critical Perspectives on Promotional Culture*, ed. M. Aronczyk and D. Powers. New York: Peter Lang, 29–52.

Marx, K. 1887. *Capital: A Critique of Political Economy* [original publication in German in 1867], vol. 1. Moscow: Progress Publishers.

Reinecke, J. 2010. 'Beyond a Subjective Theory of Value and Towards a "Fair Price": An Organizational Perspective on Fairtrade Minimum Price Setting'. *Organization* 17(5): 563–81.

Reinecke, J., S. Manning, and O. Von Hagen. 2012. 'The Emergence of a Standards Market: Multiplicity of Sustainability Standards in the Global Coffee Industry'. *Organization Studies* 33(5–6): 791–814.

RJC. 2011. 'Responsible Jewellery Council: Letter to the SEC (s74010-76) from 25 February 2011'. <https://www.sec.gov/comments/s7-40-10/s74010-76.pdf>. Accessed 16 June 2014.

SEC. 2012. 'Conflict Minerals Final Rule'. <http://www.sec.gov/rules/final/2012/34-67716.pdf>. Accessed 16 June 2014.

Skeggs, B. 2014. 'Values Beyond Value? Is Anything Beyond the Logic of Capital?' *British Journal of Sociology* 65(1): 1–20.

SSI. 2014. *The State of Sustainability Initiatives Review 2014*. International Institute for Sustainable Development. <http://www.iisd.org/pdf/2014/ssi_2014.pdf>. Accessed 3 January 2014.

Stark, D. 2009. *The Sense of Dissonance: Accounts of Worth in Economic Life*. Princeton: Princeton University Press.

Strathern, M. 1992. 'Qualified Value: The Perspective of Gift Exchange'. In *Barter, Exchange and Value: An Anthropological Approach*, ed. C. Humphrey and S. Hugh-Jones. Cambridge: Cambridge University Press, 169–91.

Strathern, M. 2000. 'The Tyranny of Transparency'. *British Educational Research Journal* 26(3): 309–21.

Thévenot, L. 1997. 'Un gouvernement par les normes. Pratiques et politiques des formats d'information'. *Raisons pratiques* 8: 205–42.

Thévenot, L. 2001. 'Organized Complexity: Conventions of Coordination and the Composition of Economic Arrangements'. *European Journal of Social Theory* 4(4): 405–25.

Thévenot, L., M. Moody, and C. Lafaye. 2000. 'Forms of Valuing Nature: Arguments and Modes of Justification in French and American Environmental Disputes'. In *Rethinking Comparative Cultural Sociology*, ed. L. Thévenot and M. J. Lamont. Cambridge: Cambridge University Press, 229–72.

Thomas, N. 1991. *Entangled Objects: Exchange, Material Culture and Colonialism in the Pacific*. Cambridge, MA: Harvard University Press.

Weber, K., K. L. Heinze, and M. DeSoucey. 2008. 'Forage for Thought: Mobilizing Codes in the Movement for Grass-Fed Meat and Dairy Products'. *Administrative Science Quarterly* 53(3): 529–67.

WGC. 2012. 'Conflict-Free Gold Standard'. World Gold Council. <http://www.gold.org/about_gold/sustainability/conflict_free_standard/>. Accessed 13 January 2013.

Wilk, R. 2006. 'Bottled Water'. *Journal of Consumer Culture* 6(3): 303–25.

Zelizer, V. A. 1994. *The Social Meaning of Money*. New York: Basic Books.

11

Notes on Objectual Valuation

Celia Lury and Noortje Marres

> The power to grasp process, to see the drama of values, is the height of the practical.
>
> Charles Horton Cooley (1912)

The idea that objects are central to social dynamics of valuation has left the laboratory, or at least, the offices of anthropologists and sociologists. The proposition can be encountered in a variety of locations beyond the university narrowly defined, including in the instruments and methods deployed in informational economies. Let us begin with some examples that suggest this. First, the public data tool Google Co-relate could be said to instantiate a type of 'object-centred valuation' that is reminiscent of anthropological understandings of objects (see Fuller and Goffey 2013; Marres and Gerlitz in press). On its data tools page, Google advertises the analytic powers of this application through a demonstration of exemplary findings, including charts for search engine query terms like 'mittens', 'bicycles', 'losing weight', and 'home for rent' (see Figure 11.1).[1] Detecting and visualizing fluctuations in the volume of these queries over time, Google could be said to give us an object—a singular entity that emerges or 'coheres' out of the aggregation of distributed indexes derived from everyday settings. Arguably, moreover, its capacity to produce this type of 'objectual effect' is critical to the 'value' proposition of data tools more generally: these tools are able to conjure patterned entities out of distributed expressions, and this objectual operation seems central to their capacity to render fluctuations of social relevance visible and predictable—'know-able' and 'valu-able'.

Furthermore, this digital deployment of objects to render explicit social dynamics of valuation is not limited to the informational economy: it arguably plays an equally significant role in informational politics. To give another

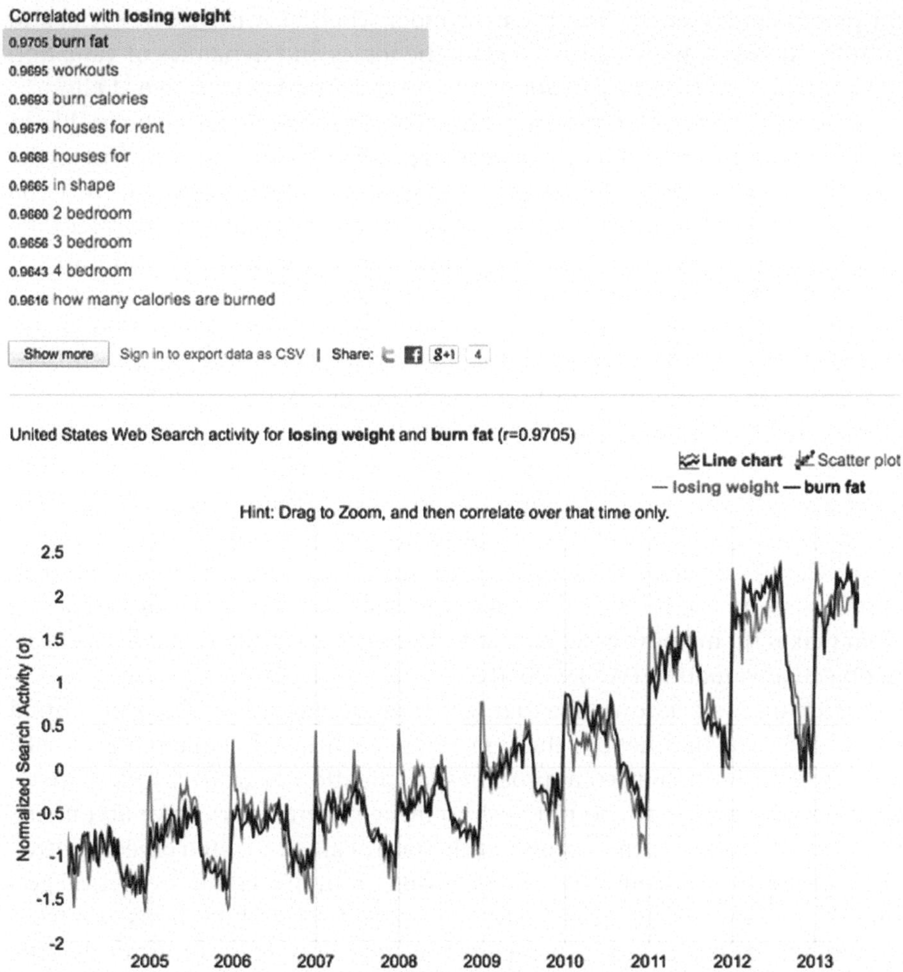

Figure 11.1. Co-related queries for 'losing weight' over time
Source: Google Co-relate (accessed 27 January 2014).

example, advocacy campaigns targeting the so-called social factories that now operate in the shadows of the 'social economy' deploy similar, seemingly mundane objects. Thus, an investigative report on the infamous 'click farms' in Southern Asia, where people are paid a minimal amount for producing a maximum number of 'likes' per hour, featured as its 'poster-object' a 'neglected courgette' on Facebook, which had achieved a counter-intuitive level of popularity, that turned out to have been accomplished by these dodgy means.[2] Of course, for the campaigners it wasn't really the courgette that was the primary object of neglect in this case, but rather the labour conditions in Bangladesh. Indeed if you consider the courgette to be an exemplary tale of misplaced concreteness, you might wonder whether it is wise of social and cultural theorists, wishing to elucidate the logics and dynamics of valuation in informational societies, to adopt an object-centred perspective at all.

While registering this concern, in this chapter we would nevertheless like to argue that attention to objects can be both productive for, and pertinent to, the social study of valuation. In doing so, we take our cue from Karin Knorr-Cetina (2001), who has proposed the concept of objectual practice, to highlight the proliferation across social life of expert arrangements, gadgets, and forms of knowledge that orient practices towards the articulation of epistemic things and their 'unfolding ontologies'. Indeed, drawing on Knorr-Cetina, we emphasize the incomplete and dynamic character of informational objects, using the term 'objectual' to highlight these characteristics: 'The defining characteristic of an epistemic object is this changing, unfolding character, or its lack of object-ivity and completeness of being... which is difficult to combine with our everyday notion of an object' (Knorr-Cetina 2001, 182). Our argument will be that it is this objectual organization of social practices in knowledge societies that helps explain the distinct capacities of 'objectual' approaches, methods, and techniques for valuation. Their incompleteness is what makes them know-able, valu-able; indeed it is -ability that is at the heart of objectual valuation (Weber 2010).

To sum up, we acknowledge that, given the proliferation of object-centred methods and techniques of valuation, it is becoming less challenging to make the case for object-centred approaches to valuation *in general*. Indeed given the examples above, we do not wish to make general, normative arguments in favour of object-centred forms of valuation at all, or to pitch object-centred over against subject-centred theories of valuation, in a grand theoretical gesture. Yet, so we would suggest, although object-centred methods and techniques may be proliferating at the present time, this does not mean that the 'object turn'—as imagined and practised in social and cultural research and theory—has been accomplished or has come full circle (Marres 2012). To the contrary, *we would like to argue that there are a number of aspects of an objectual approach to valuation that are persistently bracketed*. For us, what these aspects might be relates to how, whether, or when one might say that an object or process of objectual valuation can be said to be 'socialized' or indeed 'fully socialized'. Of course, the very notion of 'socialization' raises issues so many and various that it would be impossible for us to address them here, so our aim is merely to un-bracket some of the questions raised by the possibility that informational operations of valuation entail a socialization of objects by way of some notes (Muniesa 2011; Adkins and Lury 2011).

To elaborate these notes on objectual valuation, we draw on empirical examples from areas as diverse as branding, digital analytics, and environmental art. This choice of examples is primarily informed by our own research, but it is probably no coincidence that these three forms of expertise, method, and arrangement operate at the intersection of different fields: economy and society, data science and marketing, art and environmental awareness. As we will discuss, one of the distinctive features of devices of objectual valuation may well be their capacity for 'inter-articulation', that is, the creation of opportunities for valuation by bringing distinct fields and registers into relation. It also means that we are especially interested in valuation as a dynamic that operates across registers and thus should and can precisely *not* be limited to 'the economy' or 'ethics'.

Value is as Value Does

We find the work of the pragmatist philosopher John Dewey helpful in making these notes since he offers a starting point for interrogating objectual valuation that is somewhat different from the approaches associated with the informational logics we alluded to above. He proposes to consider valuation as a process that 'unfolds on the plane of objects' (Dewey 1939 [1908]; see on this point also Marres 2013, 9–12). Significantly for us, his work thus opens up a processual perspective on objects that is avowedly post-instrumental: he does not just jump to an instrumental understanding of objects, as 'access points' to processes of valuation, with no claim to existence above and beyond their capacity to express patterns in distributed indices.[3]

Valuation, Dewey says, is an effect that occurs as a consequence of 'a conflict of tendencies', 'a lack to be made good', 'some trouble to be done away with' that arise 'on the plane of things'; he writes:

> valuation takes place only when there is something the matter; when there is some trouble to be done away with, some need, lack or privation to be made good, some conflict of tendencies to be resolved by means of changing existing conditions. (Dewey 1939, 34)

He further proposes that valuation effects must be understood as aspects or attributes of 'objectual situations': it is in and through dynamics of conflict, privation, and trouble that occurs among and out of things and settings that particular objects and objectives come to be articulated as worthy and worth pursuing.[4] This insight[5] is further elaborated in the reformulation that the pragmatist theorist C. H. Cooley offers: 'value indicates significance in relation to some sort of crisis' (Cooley 1912, 441).[6] And here we note how the pragmatist language itself also indicates a level of open-endedness—'trouble', 'some need to be made good', 'some sort of crisis'—the wording strongly suggests that we do not necessarily know, that while it might be know-able, it is not already known, who or what participates in the happening and making of value.

Indeed Dewey locates valuation, at least in the first instance, beyond or before the realm of practical action. Valuation is not only something that is 'done'; it is something that happens, or is happening. It is of the order of the event, a process that at least partly unfolds beyond the realm of human-centred activity. His theory of valuation does not begin with an actor who 'expresses' the value of something, nor does it assume at the outset a fully formed context that would enable purposeful action (whether the end be profit or a greater good). Instead, it begins with situated, unfolding conflicts of tendency, trouble and privations, indicating constraints on action, or even its impossibility. This is also the position adopted by Cooley who says: 'the essential thing for valuation is a human organism (not necessarily a person), a situation and an object' (Cooley 2012, 442). Valuation, from this vantage point, not only does *not* imply the priority of agency, it also posits a different distribution of relevance than the one commonly associated with the realm of human or practical action. From the standpoint of 'action', relevant is what can be acted upon. The event distributes relevance differently: it includes what may affect us, quite independently of our ability to act on this, or even to know it (Fraser 2009).

For Dewey, then, action is secondary, at least insofar as valuation is concerned. Action comes into play only in relation to the happening dynamics or events of objectual valuation. But then, in this secondary way, it does matter: in Dewey's account, what marks objectual trouble, conflict, and privations as constitutive of valuation is that they can only be addressed 'by changing existing conditions'. In this secondary way, then, action or intervention is implicated in objectual valuation: valuation not only emanates from situations or environments but also involves their active modification. It may be helpful to think here of environmental events in the conventional sense of the word. Indeed, ecological disasters may be seen to provide exemplary occasions of objectual valuation: a flood, a black-out happens somewhere, somehow, beyond the immediate sphere of human action[7] and 'everything changes' in terms of what is valued and how (Tironi et al. 2014). Such disastrous events bring into focus the precarity of a whole array or tangle of infrastructural conditions in such a way as to provoke their (re-)valuation. As such, ecological events can help us to understand valuation as 'environmental occasion': they offer stark reminders both that human action 'comes second' insofar as valuation is concerned and that such occasions can only be addressed by changing existing conditions. However, while such examples may be helpful, in this chapter we approach the term 'environmental' in a more technical sense—as referring to a broad and mostly implicit set of background conditions—taken-for-granted or simply unknown, but nonetheless happening settings—in which an open-ended range of biological, material, technical, informational, and so on, entities participate in valuation.

To expand this point we can again refer to Cooley, who like Dewey accords to action a secondary—though therefore no less great—importance: 'value implies *an act of selection*; in this process a person turns one way or another under the pull of values' (Cooley 1912, 448; see on this point also Madsen 2013). Crucially, Cooley locates these selections at least partly in the environment. In addition, he further proposes that, in technological societies, environments are organized to a greater and greater extent through communication and information technologies, which not only extend the environment, but also provide for selection in relation to multiple environments, conferring on them a 'one-among-many' mode of existence. He says that communications technology 'permits [the social actor] to form his own environment by retaining what suits him from a variety of material' (Cooley 1897, 22). However, Cooley also says that the selection mechanisms that structure experience must be located beyond the individual (in the environment) and operate infrastructurally.

For Cooley then, communications provide for not only an extension, but also a possible multiplicity of environments. In this context, selection emerges as a formative, infrastructural dynamic: 'by the working of elective affinity, the man of to-day's society is offered a selection among many environments. It offers to him a proud choice of influences. [...] It renders [men] less dependent on the environments that happen to be nearest him. [...] a million environments solicit him' (Cooley 1897, 23).[8] Significantly, and again, selection is *not* understood as a voluntaristic act of the individual; instead, as Cooley emphasizes, mechanisms of selections are equally operative '*within* the environment'. They demarcate an environment of experience for their users, and they produce a situation—what we think of as an 'environmental occasion'—within which values may be accrued to objects. For Cooley, then, 'selection mechanisms' are central to processes of objectual valuation because they produce 'environments of experience' (see on these points too, Madsen 2013).

Our first note then is that objectual valuation can be understood as an 'environmental occasion'. With the help of the pragmatists, we can understand valuation as happening in a troubled context, in which an open-ended set of physical, technical, and other entities participate, in more or less motivated ways. Specifically, it involves both *problematization* and *selection*;[9] as such it requires that attention be paid both to how specific things, devices, practices participate in processes of valuation *and* how arrangements and infrastructures of selection circumscribe that participation in the articulation of problems and the sett(l)ing of objectives. However, while both problematization and selection are implicated in objectual valuation, it seems to us that their relation cannot be described in advance of any specific occasion, but is rather always in process, as each is recursively implicated in the other.[10]

Indeed, while allowing us to recognize the differences between selection and problematization analytically, adopting a pragmatist interpretation of objectual valuation—an event-ive articulation of troubling things—suspends any a priori need to decide between the two.

This suspension is not, from our point of view, a failing in the pragmatically inspired approach to objectual valuation we outline here; rather, it is helpful, enabling us to avoid the subjectual bias which suggests that since, in the operation of infrastructures, technological and epistemic logics figure prominently, it is adequate to understand their operation in terms of the theories, concepts, and methods that are deployed in their development, maintenance, and public-ization. In contrast, our approach recognizes that infrastructural arrangements—like environmental processes—operate 'in the background' as it were, and that 'we don't know' in advance which entities participate in valuation. In relation to algorithms, for example, it has been noted that no one knows how an algorithm functions, and we can add: no one knows who participates in the functioning of the algorithm (Crawford 2013). At the same time, in pointing towards both problematization *and* selection, in decoding valuation as event *and* arrangement, we also avoid the naturalistic fallacy of which some philosophies of 'mattering' are at risk.

Objectual Valuation as/in Informational Environments: Some Examples

One empirical example we offer as a way of elucidating how problematization and selection relate to each other in processes of objectual valuation is the practices associated with brand development (Lury 2004; Moor and Lury 2011; Arvidsson and Peitersen 2013). We can see brands as examples of objectual valuation in relatively straightforward ways. Take, for example, brand equity measures.[11] Although until recently it was assumed by brand managers that brand equity should be measured in terms of behavioural outcomes, for example through purchase behaviour or people's stated willingness to pay a premium for a branded version of a product it has now been proposed that brand equity may exist even in the absence of purchase (which one might think of as the most obvious indicator of 'action' from a brand development point of view), and that purchase is not an index of brand equity alone. It was also previously assumed that brand equity was a response to a firm's marketing activities, and thus could be understood in terms of market behaviour and 'marketing effects' attributable to the brand (Raggio and Leone 2009), but it is now widely accepted that its sources may lie in a wider 'information environment' that is partially independent of a firm's own marketing efforts.

One sign of this shift in measures of brand value is the rise of the measure 'propensity to recommend' (Moor and Lury 2011). In early attempts to measure consumer perceptions about brands (which is what is meant by brand equity), indices of 'customer satisfaction' gained by asking consumers how satisfied they are with a brand were used, but such indices have recently been criticized, not only as being too open to manipulation (since questions can be framed in ways that elicit a positive response) but also as inherently too subjective, in that they measure the gap between expectation and perception in ways that are open to reflexivity on the part of the subject who is being questioned. The 'propensity to recommend' model is imagined to be a more robust measure because it is held to connect feelings with observable behaviour *between* individuals; it is a measure of sociability, and as such is a measure of event and arrangement.

These measures are now routinely used in the UK by agencies such as YouGov, which conduct routine surveys of consumer perceptions of brands, asking respondents which brands they would recommend to friends or colleagues and which brands they would tell them to avoid. But 'propensity to recommend' measures are also being adopted online. Here, in part because of the potential to track actual behaviour and stated behaviour online, and by actively facilitating recommendation practices by informational means, through interactive 'like' buttons and similar features, 'propensity to recommend' is elaborated as simultaneously a property of the brand (where its 'recommend-ability' is something internal to the brand as artefact) and as a capacity of consumers (a lack to be made good, a conflict of tendencies) as well as their informational environments. And this is measured *without an a priori need on the part of brand managers to make a strict distinction between the two*: some individuals are assumed to be more likely to recommend a product than others; some individuals are assumed to have bigger or better 'networks' than others; and technologies of various kinds participate in the organization of these networks and facilitate their activation and extension. All of these dynamics are captured in propensity to recommend, producing a plane of objects (brands) in which valuation may take place.

What is measured then is the degree to which the brand is likely to be *propagated* among consumers and environments, and this is something in which both specifically equipped actors and informational settings participate: trending algorithms, user clicks, events in the news, each of these may contribute to 'bending the curves' of propensity to recommend. Furthermore, insofar as it is *this effect of propagation* that is of consequence—what matters—its successful measurement does not require any distinction to be made between selection and problematization, that is, the respective contributions of actors, devices, equipped environments, and events to facilitate the valuation of the brand.

Devices for the navigation of digital informational environments offer another empirical example to consider here, both as regards the mixing of problematization and selection and of the nature and extent of the sociability or socialization that is involved in objectual valuation. The functioning of these platforms is complex but includes a growing number of online, more or less interactive tools for data analysis and visualization, which are produced by—and with—digital platforms including Twitter, Yahoo, Google, and Facebook. While some are developed by the host companies themselves, others have been produced more independently and consequently stand in a more external relation to platforms. Online data tools offer easy-to-navigate, interactive visual interfaces with catchy names such as Google Co-relate, Twitter Trends, Yahoo Clues, Google Zeitgeist, Infomous, Mentionmapp, Twitter Streamgraph, etc. and are widely promoted as useful ways of analysing information flows in a 'generally accessible' way, by online platforms themselves and by organizations from the *Guardian* and Reuters to the United Nations and developer platforms like Scraperwiki (Marres and Weltevrede 2013; Marres and Gerlitz in press).

While they serve many functions, one of the things online data tools do is to showcase the analytic affordances of digital platforms for what we are calling 'objectual valuation'. Crucial in this respect is that the tools in question tend to deploy specific 'objectual formats' in the analysis and visualization of data. In the case of Twitter, the 'hashtag' (#) has become a particularly prominent means for identifying relevant content, on Facebook it is the 'like', and search engines like Yahoo and Google have the 'query' while a more generic, cross-platform marker of relevance is the 'hyperlink'. Online settings are closely associated with these distinctive formats, and in many ways the valuation of content with these platforms proceeds through them. Online data tools rely on these objectual formats to detect and visualize 'what is happening?' (the slogan used by Twitter until recently), as they visualize not which words are prominently used in online settings at a given time (which would be too computationally arduous) but which tags and queries and so on.

More specifically, online data tools enable the exploration of the attributes—'profiles'—of objectual entities, in terms of traceable co-relates of the type: *which users, times, locations, devices are notably associated with said object—a query, tag, URL?* For example, there are visualizations that map devices onto location, by using the Twitter's meta-data on date sources to map the type of device from which messages are sent onto geographic coordinates, showing for instance that the city of Washington, DC is topographically divided between Iphone and Android users.[12] In one of our research projects, we relied on hashtags ourselves in order to analyse and visualize the issue of 'privacy' with Twitter.[13] We chose to use co-hashtag analysis—tracing the hashtags that co-occur with the word 'privacy' on Twitter in a given period of time—as a way of exploring the 'profile' of this issue before and after the Edward Snowden scandal broke in June 2013. Figure 11.2 shows which hashtags were used in relation to 'privacy' in the days before and after

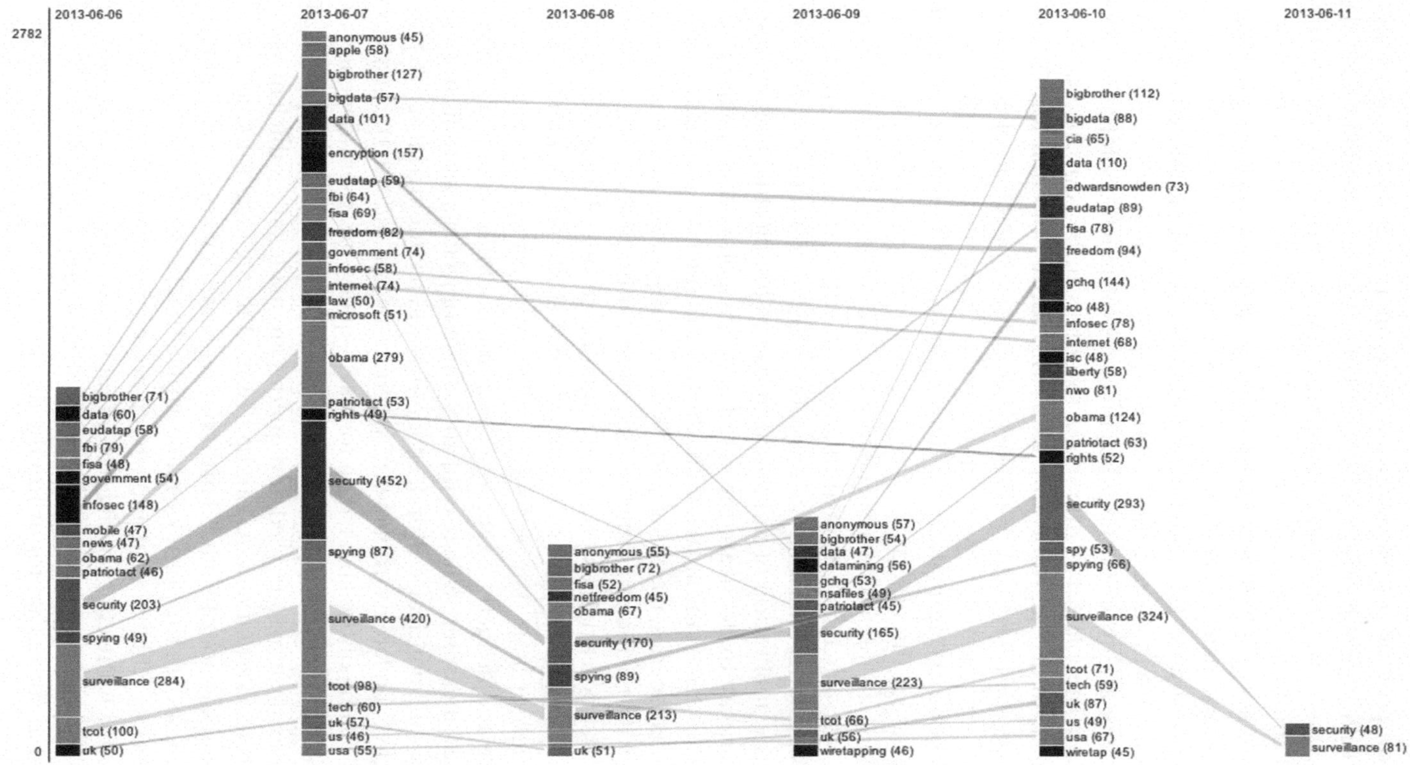

Figure 11.2. Co-hashtag profile for 'privacy' on Twitter over time: before and after Snowden
Source: produced with the Associational Profiler, DMI/CSISP (August 2014).

the mass release of NSA documents by Snowden, giving an indication of the changing 'composition' of privacy as an issue on Twitter during this time. Note that attributes like location, device, or tag differ from demographic categories like class, race, and gender which require data analysis to pass via the construct of the human as object of knowledge and arguably enable more 'subjectual' modes of valuation, in terms of demographic categories and associated behaviours, market segmentations, and so on.

Elsewhere we discuss the wider role of data tools in information economies and ecologies in more detail (Marres and Weltevrede 2013). But here we are directing attention to the 'objectual bias' of much digital analytics. The reason for this bias, it is important to note, can be construed as first of all practical. In a straightforward sense, the above objectual formatting entities—query, tag, user, device—make possible the exploration of data with digital tools, both deductively and inductively. Deductively, it is by selecting such an objectual format—query terms, tags—that a workable data set can be delineated: the objectual format allows for a provisional selection of data, making all meta-data associated with said format—time, user, location, device, etc.—available as instruments with which to explore the data. Inductively speaking, data analysis may also generate 'objectual' data selections itself: the application of numerical measures to objectual formats provides another way to delineate the set of relevant points that make up an objectual entity; for example, what are the most frequently occurring or the most connected queries, users, tags, etc.? Or the measure we used in mapping privacy on Twitter, which hashtags are the most connected?

However, the potential for objectual valuation in ditigal analytics surely cannot be *explained* by reference to the practical epistemic requirements of the exploration of large data sets—as if these would somehow 'necessitate' the inductive and deductive techniques just noted. Online data tools implement selected measures, which tend to valuate objectuals as indicators or 'captors' of social, political, cultural, economic, and technological activity, as in the Google Co-relate example with which we began. Indeed, the analytic usefulness or value of the above data formats—query, tag, user—depends to a large degree on their *currency* in informational practices themselves:[14] it is only insofar as hashtags are used and queries are made on a sufficient scale that these *these objectual formats* can be assumed to organize valuation, and may serve as indicator of such.[15] Furthermore, that they are able to do so is also a consequence of the point we made earlier, that is, that it is not possible, a priori, to specify what is event and what is arrangement: whether the trending of a hashtag is the effect of the selection processes specific to the Twitter platform or expressive of broader dynamics of relevance.

We suggested above that for us too the distinction between problematization and selection is not necessarily the important one from a sociological perspective. Indeed, it helps us to move towards a notion of the social—and socialization—that does not presume the priority or monopoly of the human. This is especially helpful given the use of the term socialization by Matthew Fuller and Andrew Goffey in their description of the objectual logics that inform contemporary digital economies. So, for example, their description emphasizes the role that object-centred programming plays in making possible the 'socialization' of computing insofar as it enables the open-ended combining of different objects, entities, relations: 'the architecture of relations between objects obviates having a program structure in which the order of actions is rigidly prescribed [...] there is an overall sense of polyphony of events and entities in dynamic relation (Fuller and Goffey 2013, 219–20). In their account, relative openness of (social or socializing or social-able) relations is *the* decisive affordance of object-centred ontologies, and of course it is also, what has more widely been deemed critical to the establishment of the 'social' relevance of information processing

However, Fuller and Goffey also note, many informational environments aren't open-ended at all, since they may equally produce and re-produce 'closed' hierarchies and asymmetries—through, for example, the iterative effects of inclusion and exclusion produced by ranking and rating operations, and less directly, through the promotion of particular information formats (of selection) over others, in the mediation of informational environments, such as the aforementioned query, citation, and score, etc.[16] It is for this reason, so we suggest, that, while there is no a priori need to distinguish between problematization and selection we need to be attentive to the manner or modes of socialization that are produced in the practices of objectual valuation.[17] This is our second note.

Multi-Valence

To consider this point further, we need to examine further how objectual valuation operates in informational environments. Crucial here is that objectual valuation *cannot* be defined as a unitary logic that is being implemented 'from above'. Rather, objectual valuation is at least in part a distributed accomplishment (Marres 2012): it is not just the methods built into dominant infrastructural services that effect objectual valuation. Data practices, formats, events, platforms, and so on equally participate in it. As mentioned, it is only because hashtags and re-tweeting are widely used—by Twitter users, in practice—'to make something trend' that it is possible and makes sense for an objectual analytics to identify trends through hashtag analysis. The usefulness or value of this method (hashtag analysis) depends on how widespread the associated social practice (hashtagging) is. And such practices of course have multiple contexts or environments. Brands, too, need to satisfy the informational requirements of each of the several environments or communities of practice they inhabit.

Indeed, both digital objectual formats like tags and queries and brands are so powerful *because* they are deemed capable of communicating or expressing multiple social environments (see on this point also Gross n.d.). Arguably, they have the potential to explicate what Alfred Schutz (1964) called the 'isohypses of relevance' that organize practices: to refer to our initial example one more time, Google demonstrated the analytic power of Google Trends through a visualization of the query 'mittens' over time, expressing a clear seasonal cycle of relevance. As we have consistently pointed out, we do not necessarily know what constitutes these environments: it is impossible to detect which entities exactly participate in the creation of the 'need' or 'relevance' emanating from social environments. The fact that we do *not* need to know this, in order to detect the particular needs or relevances belonging to a particular group, time, location, or issue, is however surely one of the distinctive characteristics of objectual valuation.

Our third note is thus to emphasize the *multi-valence* of objectual valuation. This emerges, we suggest, from the (precise and specific) indeterminacy of the processes of problematization and selection we identified as in operation earlier. In the organization of this indeterminacy, we can see the operation of a functional method in which problems to solutions can be identified in terms of multiple values, each relating in different ways to event and arrangement. And so, in what follows, we want to consider further the workings of this functional method, and consider whether and how understanding function as an interpretive category can help us analyse modes of socialization further.

First of all though, let us give an example to illustrate the point we are making about multi-valence here. The case we take is that of Klout, a proprietary measure of influence in social media (Gerlitz and Lury 2014). At the time of writing, Klout is probably the most used metric of influence in social media, a term that Klout defines as an individual's ability 'to drive action'. Like many other social media metrics, Klout takes as data records of activities pre-structured by a number of social media platforms, including tweets, retweets and replies on Twitter, comments, wall-posts and likes on Facebook, and comments, re-shares and +1s on Google+ and puts these continuously updated data points in various kinds of recursive relations with each other to calculate a Klout Score for each Klout user or participating individual. The Score—the object at issue here—is a (whole) number between 1 and 100. At the same time as acting as a tracking device, each individual Klout Score is also put in an ordered relation to other individual users' Scores, and thus facilitates a process of comparison, or ranking, in which each individual may compare their Score with those of others and/or with their own previous

Score. This proportional ranking thus simultaneously creates relations of equality and difference between social media users, connecting them to each other as influencers, whilst demarcating differences between them by locating them in relation to each other in terms of their relative position. In this regard, however, it is important to note that Klout does not only measure influence in such a way as to motivate individual users to participate more, it also deploys its measure of the influence of individuals in social media so as to drive its *own* action.

Indeed, since the launch of the company in 2008, Klout has made its users' Scores available to third parties via the Klout API: recent reports by the company indicate that their API calls have grown from 10.5 billion to 30 billion a month and that they have more than 2,000 regular 'partners'.[18] These partners deploy Klout Scores for a variety of purposes, but in one use social media clients such as Seesmic, CoTweet, or Hootsuite integrate Klout Scores into their own platforms, allowing users of social media to filter platform engagement through yet another form of mediation. In other uses, hotel chains use Klout Scores to determine upgrade rates, event organizers give individuals preferential access to parties based on their Klout, and customer relations systems such as Salesforce.com and Radian 6 deploy the Scores to decide how fast to reply to consumer requests—based on the assumption that users with a high Klout Score will influence more people when talking about a positive or negative service experience than those with a low Score. Klout Scores are also, reportedly, taken into account in the evaluation of job applications for digital economy and tech-industry positions including positions in the social media sector. In a further step, following investment in Klout by Microsoft in 2012, the company began to cooperate with the search engine Bing which now integrates Klout information into its search results for so-called 'high-profile professionals and socially active influencers'.[19]

In this way, Klout can be seen to be *inter-articulating* the spheres of marketing and everyday sociability, as the activity of multi-valent comparison generates suitable formats for information exchange that can be made to serve the purposes of varying practices (see, on the concept of inter-articulation, Callon 2009; Marres 2011; for its relevance to social media, Gerlitz 2012; Velden 2012). And the capacity for inter-articulation does not stop there: social media equally produce inter-articulations between the commercial form of marketing and the civil society form of advocacy. To provide one more example, around election time, Facebook supposedly piloted regular updates on 'who of your friends have voted', and more recently they sent mass requests for organ donation to their user base (Simonite 2012). Arguably, efforts are made (or advertised) here to inter-articulate marketing with democratic politics and social interaction. Indeed, it seems to us that inter-articulation in social media stands out for its expansive logic, branching into an ever-expanding range of domains, settings, and registers. It is striking how social media mechanisms or tactics of publicity find applications across spheres: trending as a tactic is deployed by anybody from Occupy activists to Hollywood advertisers pushing a new release. However, this expansiveness also seems to indicate that we are dealing here with a rather generic, non-distinctive mode of articulation, and as such, arguably, 'superficial' objects, or objects without volume or depth.

What such examples also reveal to us about objectual valuation is that it is not about either the brokering of equivalences in terms of sameness or the making equivalent of difference; rather it is about *multi-valence*, which may be understood as a comparative distribution of value, emerging dynamically in practices of comparison of solutions in relation to needs, lacks or privations to be made good, troubles to be done away with, as they happen in and across multiple (radically discontinuous) socialized environments. It results in practices of inter-articulation that are many and various, including *approximations*,[20] enabling exchanges—or confusions—of vocabularies, logics, or currencies across and between contexts. As the example of Klout shows, to cultivate relations with many 'friends' can now be valued in the currency of marketing. It is important to recognize however, that, as David Stark has argued,[21] the attainment of equivalence would signal the implosion of multi-valent valuation: it is precisely to the extent that friendship connections are *not* synonymous or equivalent with promotional relations that they are of value to the latter. Multi-valence, then, is a question of the differential dynamics enabled between registers of valuation.

The Politics of Objectual Valuation

Our fourth note is to point to the distinctive political significance of such dynamics. Take, for example, the problem for brand managers of how to respond to the rise in salience of ethics concerning social and environmental sustainability (Moor and Lury 2012). Measures of such ethical values are sometimes introduced into the environments that brands inhabit by agents and institutions that do not share the brand owners' interests. This movement towards 'socially sensitive accountings' such as the 'triple bottom line', the Ethical Purchasing Index, 'Social Return on Investment', and 'balanced scorecard' indicators are giving rise to new measures of value and are leading to quite different types of value metrics than those historically used in relation to brands. Such measures locate brands in relations of comparison with other entities, making them proximate along dimensions or scales that are not of their own choosing, while also potentially reducing their distinctiveness.

So how are branded organizations responding to the proliferation of these 'externally' developed forms of commensuration? One option is simply to incorporate them or comply with them. Many organizations now include some version of 'triple bottom line' accounting or 'balanced scorecard' approaches in the narrative sections of annual reports, and where such measures reflect well on brands they may even offer a source of promotional advantage. Here, values of sustainability, social responsibility, and ethical behaviour simply sit alongside a portfolio of other values to which the brand may lay claim, even if they do so somewhat uncomfortably.

Another possibility assayed by brand development managers is to try to make the brand *become* the measuring instrument in order to avoid being subject to it. This can be seen in cases where brands develop modified proprietary versions of external value systems, subsuming dimensions of those value systems within those of the brand: rather than complying with international fair trade standards on their own-label goods, for example, many UK supermarkets now operate their own fair trading schemes and codes of conduct, either with international suppliers (e.g. Waitrose's 'Fair Trade Network', which operates only for its South African citrus farmers) or UK farmers (Tesco). Similarly, in 2007 Tesco reported that it was experimenting with the idea of putting 'carbon footprint' information on all products in its stores. Here, the values propounded by external agencies are acknowledged, but incorporated into internal measurement activity. Thus one response to externally developed forms of commensuration is to internalize externally derived measures in such a way as to make the use of those measures a dimension of the brand's own distinctiveness vis-à-vis competitors. In such cases, one might argue that brands, insofar as they are organized in practices of objectual valuation, can be understood as instances of 'a thing that is also a scale' (Holbraad and Pedersen 2009, 379). In some such cases, not only is the happening of the 'environment' claimed as a dimension of the objectual valuation of the brand, but so are some aspects of the happening of 'society' via measures of social relations. And this is where we return to the significance of considering the modes of socialization.

So, for example, in the case just discussed there are issues concerning whether and how the 'happening' of society is distributed and acknowledged as (individual or collective) agency. As one commentator on Tesco's adoption of carbon labelling remarks:

> Tesco says that each sheet of its recycled toilet roll uses '1.1g of carbon' compared to 1.8g for its standard toilet roll… Let's give that some sort of context. Google declared earlier this year that each Google search generates 0.2g of CO_2. So now we know that using one sheet of recycled toilet paper has the same carbon footprint as performing five-and-a-half Google searches. We now also know that you would have to get through 200 sheets of toilet paper before you matched the carbon

> footprint of one carton of orange juice. Or 773 sheets of toiler paper before you equalled the carbon footprint of just one washload's worth of biological washing powder. We know all this because the Carbon Trust, who do the sums for Tesco, tells us so... The big question, though, is will this extra information motivate you to change your habits in any way?... What I really don't like about carbon labelling... is that is neatly passes the buck on to the consumer. (Hickman 2009)

In this case then, the internalization of a measure of carbon use as a mode of objectual valuation is done in such a way as to enhance the distinctiveness of the brand without incurring the costs of acting on the value such measures puts on the external environment(s). The capacity to act—and the costs associated with it—are allocated to the consumer.[22]

The dynamics of multi-valence then open onto multiple modes of sociability, which observation is our fourth note. Environments—in their capacity as environments (distributed, author-less, at least partly latent)—are highly vulnerable to practices of reinterpretation and redeployment to altered purposes, as when environmental responsibility becomes brand distinctiveness. Indeed, this is perhaps the most salient feature of objectual valuation in a consideration of its political effects: the potential for de-tour or re-direction.

One last example we would like to mention here to illustrate this is *Nuage Vert*, an environmental art installation produced by the English-German collective HeHe. This artwork involves the projection of a large green laser cloud onto the smoke stack of a powerplant, and was performed first in Helsinki and then in Paris (see Figure 11.3). The device can be read as a kind of critical commentary on dominant devices for the inter-articulation of energy, everyday practices, and environmental accounting.

Energy literacy projects and technologies targeting the domestic sector—such as smart energy meters—often deploy personalized forms of measurement to focus attention on domestic energy consumption as the relevant site for social and environmental change (Strengers 2013). As such, they arguably participate in a similar displacement of cost and investment onto consumers as the carbon branding devices mentioned above (Marres 2011). In this context, *Nuage Vert* operates a displacement in the opposite direction, by directing its beams back onto the factory (the powerplant) in the shape of a giant green cloud that is visible from all around, and in so doing opens up for questioning the allocation of 'emissions' as a measurable attribute of domestic energy practices.

In projecting a green cloud on the smoke stack of a powerplant, *Nuage Vert* then does not only adopt a currently prevalent vocabulary that highlights everyday living as the designated site of environmental change. It turns the factory emission cloud into the surface for this fantasy, and thereby highlights its status as precisely that (a fantasy superimposed on an industrial site). Furthermore, while curated as an in situ art intervention, *Nuage Vert* is very much the artefact of informational circulation: its projection was

Figure 11.3. *Nuage Vert* by HeHe, St Ouen, France, 2009
Source: photo by Antti Ahonen, HeHe.

captured in photographic images that travelled widely across publicity, news, online, and cultural media. As these channels were saturated at the time with sustainability promotion, *Nuage Vert* could be said to piggyback on these currents, with only the slightest re-direction of wind needed, in order to return our attention to the trouble called 'factory'/'powerplant'.

Socialization

In considering this juxtaposition of cases, we come to our fifth and final note, which is that we need to take into account how objectual valuation itself acquires value or becomes valued, not least since as we said at the beginning there are multiple environments in which such valuation takes place. Our examples suggest that if objectuals participate in the cultivation of a particular need—such as the need for influence, relevance, reputational capital, and so on—this is one way in which they themselves may become needed, relevant, endorse-able.[23] The ability of objectuals like the score, the tag, the brand, and the query—to address a variety of practices, to 'fill a space' in a broadest variety of locations—may be critical to their own success. To grasp how objectual valuation operates then we need to consider both the methods of objectual valuation that analytic tools institute *and* to produce our own valuation of—and with—these methods ourselves.[24]

Indeed, one of the key aspects of objectual valuation as we have described it is its drama. As C. H. Cooley (2012, 449) put it: 'public value is the real drama, with conflicts, crisis and denouements among values. [...] Public valuation refers to the dynamic situation, the state of play at a given time, made up of many cooperating and conflicting factors from the interworking of which the future must emerge.' 'Public drama' here can clearly not be equated with the notion of 'transparency' that is promoted by both business and government but it does perhaps denote the interplay between sites and processes beyond the singular setting that we have described here as socialization. Where Cooley speaks of the public, we have here offered the social. To do so means we can then ask: where are the interplays—the dynamics of 'cooperating and conflicting factors'—to be found in the current informational and other settings of objectual valuation?

In our discussion so far we have surmised that some of the objectual entities disclosed by the methods and instruments of the informational economy are 'socialized' and 'socializing' to a remarkable degree: the proliferation of objectual formats like search engine queries and social media hashtags makes possible a distinctly 'social' articulation of objects. Drawing on nothing but indexical expressions—queries entered, hashtags used—it becomes possible to detect patterned objectuals in aggregate data derived from distributed settings. Impressively, no operation is apparently performed other than the aggregation of 'queries', straight from the user's hands! Moreover, no efforts are made to dis-embed objectuals from the entangled settings from which queries and tags emanate—for instance by subsuming them under a homogenetic classification.[25] For these reasons we suggest that one of the most significant characteristics of contemporary objectual valuation is social-ability (Weber 2010), where the production of sociality is an -ability, a capacity that is rendered technically possible in processes of problematization and selection. This is not merely to say that objectual valuation produces or creates the social, but that the accomplishment of objectual valuation is to render sociality a structural possibility, a latent and never finished potential for processes of valuation.

But following from this, it seems to us that the socializing effects of the practices of objectual valuation that we have covered in these notes need to be recognized not only to render the social as possibility, but in doing so, as being able to equip the social with a variety of qualities. We have proposed that socia(bi)lity may be barely defined in digital analytics terms as the making of a population which operates by selection of attributes that do not require the isolation of the human actor as object of knowledge (though they do often involve the general positing of human actors). Because of this, and also because it blurs problematization and selection, this operation complicates and elaborates socia(bi)lity in ways we need to understand. One way to do so, proposed by one of us, is to specify and distinguish between different dynamics of socia(bi)lity in digital networked content, such as between proportional (frequency) and relational (co-occurrence) dynamics of relevance (Marres and Gerlitz in press). This study noted the emphasis on proportional dynamics in many commercial uses of data tools, leading us here to suggest that the objectual valuation that is produced through proportional measures comes close to establishing them as objects of a currency that—when linked with a brand name or intellectual property of some kind—is increasingly organized as a transferable property right in the capacity to make 'social' connections. However, the study also found in associationist measures the promise of an alternative valuation, one that does not so much depend on bursts in attention (mentions, links, re-tweets, and so on) to establish value, but appreciates the formation of relations across diverse spheres.

More generally, our suggestion here is that the distinctively sociological opportunity afforded by objectual valuation might be further developed if the de- and re-composition of an object from constituent parts could be made visible in terms of *how those parts and their relations encode information about the object*. Such an expanded relational analysis would drive a critical understanding of models of valuation in terms of both the qualities of objectuals and associated modes of socialization, whether this be asymmetrical exchange, ranking, reciprocity, hierarchy, or shifting associations. It would enable us to recognize the 'interested' nature of modes of valuation as 'partial' (Strathern 2004) while usefully expanding how as sociologists we can realize the value of approximations and their relation to both multi- and ambi-valence. It might also allow us to consider the changing fortunes of the total social fact, as conceived by Marcel Mauss (2000), as the power to create (metonymically) a system of reciprocity. Current practices suggest that the open-ended 'wholes' of objectual valuation are neither closed nor totalized—indeed, are rather constituted as never totalizable, raising the question of whether and how the plane of objectual valuation is capable of producing other kinds of (w)holes.[26]

Notes

1. Google Co-relate, <http://www.google.com/trends/correlate/> (accessed 27 January 2014).
2. 'Why Are Courgettes So Neglected?', *The Guardian*, 2 August 2013 <http://www.theguardian.com/technology/2013/aug/02/click-farms-appearance-online-popularity>.
3. Such an instrumental coding of an 'objectual' approach is not necessarily explicated as such in the 'about section' and blog posts introducing data tools like the co-relationist instrument with which we began, but the anti-ontological understanding of objectual methods seems to us the tendency or 'atmosphere' to be resisted. That is, we feel it is important not to go with a general 'anti-theory' sentiment associated with empirical instruments of data analysis and propose that objectual devices actually do invoke distinct ontological propositions.
4. Dewey's theory of valuation has clear similarities to his theories of public formation and knowledge making, which each in different ways develop his concept of the problematic situation. This raises the question of how valuation relates to similar but different dynamics such as politization, publicization, and issue-fication (Marres 2013). However, we do not see these broad similarities and initial lack of differentiation as a shortcoming of Dewey's work. Indeed, there may be excellent reasons why his analytic perspective does not assume a strict differentiation between functional domains to begin with, a point we will discuss in the section on multi-valence.
5. Note that given its emphasis on lack, need, and privation as precipitating valuation, one could say that Dewey's conception of valuation is a negative rather than a positive one. This is in some ways ironic, given that Dewey published his 'Theory of Valuation' in the *International Encyclopedia of Unified Science*, edited by the big names of logical positivism, Otto Neurath and Rudolf Carnap. Also more generally, pragmatist efforts to de-centre the subject, as the parlance has it, have been criticized for being 'positivist' in orientation (see for a discussion chapter 2 in Marres 2012).
6. Noortje would like to thank Anders Koed Madsen for introducing her to Cooley's work on valuation, and insisting on its relevance to understanding the politics of knowledge in contexts we characterize in this piece in terms of objectual valuation. See A. Madsen, 'Cooley's Web Vision', CSISP Online, 22 May 2012 <http://www.csisponline.net/2012/05/22/cooleys-web-vision/>.
7. We note here the existence of the insurance clause that describes such events as the 'act of God': '*An event that directly and exclusively results from the occurrence of natural causes that could not have been prevented by the exercise of foresight or caution; an inevitable accident.*' But we also note that the distinction between accident or foresight ('knowing') is one that is produced, not given and that objectual valuation is part of a paradigm in which such distinctions are not relevant, since it does not require or presume foresight.
8. Cooley argues it is the process of selection itself that requires attention, not simply the ideology that supposedly drives it.

9. See on this point also Callon and Rabeharisoa (2008), where they discuss the relation between the dynamics of problematization and those of institutionalization. If we understand them correctly, Callon and Rabeharisoa suggest there is a temporality to this cycle (as does Bruno Latour 2007), where problematization comes first, and the institutional process of the organization of the collective comes second, broadly in line with other influential conceptions of the issue cycle (Downs 1972). In our present discussion of the environmental operation of technologies of communication, we are raising the question as to whether the relation between problematization (opening up) and selection (framing?) cannot also be conceived as an 'internal' one, whereby these dynamics are mutually implicated, conditioned, and perhaps imbricated.
10. Yet at the same time, we recognize that the examples with which we start need to be contextualized within a wider historical analysis that recognizes the specificity of contemporary approaches to valuation in the settling of objects or objectives.
11. These measures tend to be developed by private providers offering services to clients and, like other measures of brand value, their use is marked by controversy and dispute.
12. E. Gundersen, 'Visualising 3 Billion Tweets', 19 June 2013, Mapbox/GNIP <https://www.mapbox.com/blog/visualizing-3-billion-tweets/> (accessed 7 June 2014).
13. N. Marres, C. Gerlitz, E. Weltevrede, and others (2013) 'Detecting the Socials: Mapping privacy with Twitter', DMI Summerschool project, University of Amsterdam, <https://wiki.digitalmethods.net/Dmi/DetectingTheSocials> (accessed 4 June 2014). Additional research conducted with David Moats (2014).
14. As we discuss below, this issue of currency—the general uptake-ability or broad contextual relevance of data formats—does not only pertain to the data practices that form the object of data analysis. It equally pertains to the contexts of use of data analysis.
15. On the other hand, this dependence also illustrates the principal danger that informational environments pose for objectual valuation: that of self-referentiality. Objectual analytics may end up detecting and valorizing objectual effects that are produced to this very end, and thus cease to operate as an 'index' of wider environmental dynamics.
16. Fuller and Goffey trace these asymmetries back to the specific forms of object-centred modelling enabled through digital architectures. Elsewhere Marres (2012) has offered a more contingent, distributive account which foregrounds mutual adjustments among formats, practices, etc.
17. The search engine is one of the notable examples here, as it combines several of the features highlighted above: it is still the device *par excellence* for the mediation of informational environments: it operates infrastructurally and its use is situationally constrained. At the same time, however, it is important to note that devices of objectual valuation are highly dynamic themselves. Thus, in a recent interview a Google representative referred to 'search's decreasing relevance in the information flow (Pascal Jürgens, Re-search Mailing list, 21 January 2014).
18. <http://corp.klout.com/blog/2012/05/more-ways-to-use-your-klout/>.

19. <http://corp.klout.com/blog/2013/03/klout-bing-instagram/>.
20. Here we note the importance of making proximate, making adjacent, bringing close to, without necessarily overlapping or merging. We might even talk about app-proximations.
21. During his comments at the 'New Social-ism' conference, University of Warwick, 12 December 2013.
22. These responses to the challenges posed by the multiplication of environments in which objectual valuation may occur are to be understood, we suggest, in the context of wider shifts in the nature of measurement. In recent years a number of authors (e.g. Barry 2002) have observed the rise of an 'entrepreneurial' approach to measurement in which a proliferation of competing metrics is not only permitted but actively encouraged.
23. Another, complementary, account would focus on the affordances of proportional measures of currency (how popular?, how influential?) in terms of scalability. They facilitate the identification of opportunities for scaling up.
24. At the same time, the proportional definition of relevance (currency; popularity) which focuses on what is most frequent, surely does in fact render digital analytics vulnerable to corruption (gaming). We are still, then, with Tocqueville, who identified 'the tyranny of reputation' as one of the principal problems resulting from the mediatization of public life in the United States in the nineteenth century.
25. Generally speaking then, online data tools enable the explication of circulating objects in ways that do patently *not* include the metaphysical, 'anti-social', trick of projecting an 'independently existing' natural object above and beyond social expressions of it.
26. Celia Lury would like to recognize the support of the ESRC, Grant no. ES/K010689/1, a Professorial Fellowship on the topic of Order and Continuity: Methods for Change in a Topological Society. Noortje Marres is grateful to the research unit Cultural Sources of Newness at the Berlin Social Science Centre (WZB) for hosting her as Visiting Fellow during the summer of 2014.

References

Adkins, L. and C. Lury. 2011. 'Introduction: Special Measures. In 'SI: Measure and Value'. *Sociological Review* 59(2): 5–23.

Arvidsson, A. and N. Peitersen. 2013. *The Ethical Economy: Rebuilding Value After the Crisis*. New York: Columbia University Press.

Barry, A. 2002. 'The Anti-Political Economy'. *Economy and Society* 32(2): 268–84.

Callon, M. 2009. 'Civilizing Markets: Carbon Trading between *in vitro* and *in vivo* Experiments'. *Accounting, Organizations and Society* 34(3–4): 535–48.

Callon, M. and V. Rabeharisoa. 2008. 'The Growing Engagement of Emergent Concerned Groups in Political and Economic Life: Lessons from the French Association of Neuromuscular Disease Patients'. *Science, Technology, & Human Values* 33(2): 230–61.

Cooley, C. H. 1897. 'The Process of Social Change'. In *Mass Communication and American Social Thought: Key Texts 1919–1968*, ed. J. D. Peters and P. Simonson. Lanham, MD: Rowman & Littlefield, 21–5.

Cooley, C. H. 1912. 'Valuation as a Social Process'. *Psychological Bulletin* 9(12): 441–50.

Crawford, K. 2013. 'Can an Algorithm be Agonistic? Ten Scenes About Living in Calculated Publics', a response to Tarleton Gillespie's essay 'The Relevance of Algorithms', delivered at the Governing Algorithms conference. <http://governingalgorithms.org/wp-content/uploads/2013/05/1-response-crawford.pdf>.

Dewey, J. 1939 [1908]. 'Theory of Valuation'. In *International Encyclopedia of Unified Science* 2(4), ed. O. Neurath, R. Carnap, and C. Morris. Chicago: University of Chicago Press.

Dewey, J. 1998 [1908]. 'Does Reality Possess Practical Character?' In *The Essential Dewey*, vol. 1: *Pragmatism, Education, Democracy*, ed. L. A. Hickman, and T. M. Alexander. Bloomington: Indiana University Press, 124–33.

Downs, A. 1972. 'Up and Down with Ecology: The Issue Attention Cycle'. *Public Interest* 28(1): 38–50.

Fraser, M. 2009. 'Experiencing Sociology'. *European Journal of Social Theory* 12(1): 63–82.

Fuller, M. and A. Goffey. 2013. 'The Unknown Objects of Object-Orientation'. In *Objects and Materials: A Routledge Companion*, ed. P. Harvey, E. Casella, G. Evans, H. Knox, C. McLean, E. Silva, N. Thoburn, and K. Woodward. London and New York: Routledge, 218–27.

Gerlitz, C. 2012. 'Brands and Continuous Economies'. Doctoral dissertation, University of London.

Gerlitz, C. and C. Lury. 2014. 'Social Media and Self-Evaluating Assemblages: On Numbers, Ordering and Values'. *Distinktion* 15(2): 174–88.

Gross, A. (n.d.). 'Marginal Details, Digital Evidence: Tracing and Signalling Persons through Search Keywords'. Manuscript, University of Warwick.

Harvey, P., M. Reeves, and E. Ruppert. 2013. 'Anticipating Failure: Transparency Devices and their Effects'. *Journal of Cultural Economy* 3(6): 294–312.

Hickman, L. 2009. 'Tesco Unravels Toilet Paper's Carbon Footprint'. *The Guardian*, 29 April. <http://www.guardian.co.uk/environment/ethicallivingblog/2>, accessed 7 December 2010.

Holbraad, M. and M. A. Pedersen. 2009. 'Planet M: The Intense Abstraction of Marilyn Strathern'. *Anthropological Theory* 9(4): 371–94.

Keller, K. L. 1993. 'Conceptualizing, Measuring, and Managing Customer-Based Brand Equity'. *Journal of Marketing* 57(1): 1–22.

Knorr-Cetina, K. 2001. 'Objectual Practice'. In *The Practice Turn in Contemporary Theory*, ed. K. Knorr-Cetina, T. Schatzki, and E. von Savigni. London and New York: Routledge, 184–97.

Latour, B. 2007. 'Turning Around Politics: A Note on Gerard de Vries' Paper'. *Social Studies of Science* 37(5): 811–20.

Lury, C. 2004. *Brands: The Logos of the Global Economy*. London: Routledge.

Madsen, A. K. 2013. 'Web-Visions: Repurposing Digital Traces to Organize Social Attention'. PhD Dissertation, Department of Organization, Copenhagen Business School.

Marres, N. 2011. 'The Costs of Public Involvement: Everyday Devices of Carbon Accounting and the Materialization of Participation'. *Economy & Society* 40(4): 510–33.

Marres, N. 2012. *Material Participation: Technology, the Environment and Everyday Publics*. Basingstoke: Palgrave Macmillan.

Marres, N. 2013. 'The Environmental Teapot and Other Loaded Household Objects: Reconnecting the Politics of Technology, Issues and Things'. In *Objects and Materials: A Routledge Companion*, ed. P. Harvey, E. Casella, G. Evans, H. Knox, C. McLean, E. Silva, N. Thoburn, and K. Woodward. London and New York: Routledge, 260–71.

Marres, N. and C. Gerlitz. in press. 'Interface Methods: Renegotiating Relations between Digital Research, STS and Sociology'. *Sociological Review*.

Marres, N. and E. Weltevrede. 2013. 'Scraping the Social? Issues in Live Social Research'. *Journal of Cultural Economy* 6(3): 313–35.

Mauss, M. 2000. *The Gift: The Form and Reason for Exchange in Archaic Societies*. London: W. W. Norton.

Moor, L. and C. Lury. 2011. 'Making and Measuring Value: Comparison, Singularity and Agency in Brand Valuation Practice'. *Journal of Cultural Economy* 4(4): 439–54.

Muniesa, F. 2011. 'A Flank Movement in the Understanding of Valuation'. *Sociological Review* 59(2): 24–38.

Power, M. 1999. *The Audit Society: Rituals of Verification*. Oxford: Oxford University Press.

Raggio, R. D. and R. P. Leone. 2009. 'Chasing Brand Value: Fully Leveraging Brand Equity to Maximise Brand Value'. *Journal of Brand Management* 16(4): 248–63.

Schutz, A. 1964. 'The Well-Informed Citizen'. In *Collected Papers II: Studies in Social Theory*. The Hague: Martinus Nijhoff, 120–34.

Simonite, T. 2012. 'What Facebook Knows'. *MIT Technology Review*. <http://www.technologyreview.com/featuredstory/428150/what-facebook-knows/>.

Strathern, M. 2004 [1991]. *Partial Connections*. Walnut Creek, CA: AltaMira Press.

Strengers, Y. 2013. *Smart Energy Technologies in Everyday Life: Smart Utopia?* Basingstoke: Palgrave Macmillan.

Tironi, M., I. Rodriguez-Giralt, and M. Guggenheim. 2014. *Disasters and Politics: Materials, Experiments, Preparedness*. Sociological Review Monograph. London: Wiley-Blackwell.

Velden, L. van der. 2012. 'Social Media Monopolies and their Alternatives'. In *Unlike Us Reader*. Institute for Network Cultures. Amsterdam: Hogeschool van Amsterdam.

Weber, S. 2010. *Benjamin's -Abilities*. Cambridge, MA: Harvard University Press.

12

Tracing Data—Paying Attention

Interpreting Digital Methods Through Valuation Studies and Gibson's Theory of Perception

Anders Koed Madsen

This chapter suggests that insights from valuation studies can be used to understand evaluative mechanisms outside the field of financial economics. It argues that methods of social enquiry can similarly be understood as valuation devices because they enable people to prioritize attention in situations where this resource is scarce. More specifically, the chapter conducts this discussion with reference to a new mode of knowledge creation—digital methods—that has begun to shape practices of social enquiry. Such methods are currently being experimented with across the public and the private sectors, and they are characterized by repurposing web-native objects (such as hits, likes, links, tags, and tweets) as social research data and turning them into dynamic visualizations of specific societal phenomena.

The rising importance of digital methods comes with a need to reflect on the epistemological characteristics of the knowledge they produce. What are the logics through which these methods make some aspects of the world visible while hiding others? How are they used to evaluate the 'attention-worthiness' of things in the world? The last five years have seen different attempts at answering these questions and this chapter will contribute to this discussion by making two claims. First, that there is a dominant narrative around the practice of digital methods that has specific ways of addressing questions about theory and representation. Second, that there is an unexplored theoretical potential in interpreting the practice of digital methods through a combination of valuation theory and James Gibson's theory of perception. More specifically, it argues that these theoretical resources can be used as a foundation for describing the visual outputs of digital methods as 'web-visions' that prioritize attention on the part of their users in different ways than those suggested by the dominant narrative.

The chapter is divided into five sections. The first connects the practice of digital methods to the field of valuation studies by arguing that the practice of tracing data is an act of valuation. The second section introduces a dominant narrative that frames digital methods as a practice that makes it possible to construct dynamic representations of the social on the basis of inductive pattern recognition of honest behavioural signals. The third section introduces Gibson's theory of perception as a foundation from which to build a theoretical vocabulary that differs from the dominant narrative. It draws upon Gibson's thoughts to conceptualize digital visualizations as 'web-visions'. The fourth section illustrates the empirical relevance of translating Gibson's vocabulary to the practice of digital methods by looking deeper into the way digital methods have recently been experimented with in the United Nations (UN). The fifth section clarifies why the suggestion to think about digital visualizations as 'web-visions' leads to a different view of their role as valuation devices than the dominant narrative.[1] Furthermore, it indicates that the suggestion to interpret digital visualizations as 'web-visions' is in line with some of the core arguments made by proponents of valuation studies in the context of financial economics.

Tracing as an Act of Valuation

The activity of tracing data is central to digital methods. In order to understand why the use of such methods can be thought of as acts of valuation, it is necessary to clarify what is meant by meant by 'tracing' and 'valuation' respectively. To start with the latter, this chapter follows the Oxford Dictionary in defining the concept of 'value' as a reference to the regard that something is held to deserve. This means that processes of valuation concern the practical work that goes into producing evaluations about the importance, worth, and usefulness of assets such as people, things, and ideas. Processes of valuation are therefore intimately connected to questions about prioritization. They produce heuristic guidelines that help people justify decisions to spend scarce resources on one asset rather than another. In other words, as soon as a process of valuation deems an asset to be of high value, it becomes reasonable and legitimate to prioritize resources on acquiring, protecting, or learning about it.

Even though such prioritizations occur in many areas of life, valuation studies have mostly been concerned with prioritizations of a specific resource—monetary capital. Valuation has primarily been thought of as the act of pricing goods and dynamics of valuation have mostly been studied with the aim of laying bare the workings of so-called 'market devices' that enable economic agents to compare goods and put price tags on them (Muniesa et al. 2007). Some studies have looked at the way stock prices are influenced by devices such as classification schemes (Zuckerman 2004) and software systems (Prato and Stark 2012). Others have looked at the way prices on loans are influenced by algorithmically generated scores of credit worthiness (Poon 2007). This shared theoretical concern with practices of pricing has led to a situation where valuation and pricing are often thought of as two sides of the same coin.

However, the concept of valuation has a long history in sociology where it has not always been as closely associated with pricing mechanisms (Dewey 1955; Cooley 1912). Recent writings have suggested a need to explore this heritage and called for valuation studies to look beyond markets and pricing mechanisms. For instance, David Stark has suggested that assets can be *made valuable* in other ways than attaching a price to them (Stark 2011). They can, for instance, be 'praised' by members in their community (as with medals of honour) or 'ranked' according to their relevance (as with websites on Google). As formulated in the editorial of the newly established journal, *Valuation Studies*: 'Valuation has many objects as well as many subjects, and is a process that takes many forms' (Helgesson and Muniesa 2013, 4). Accordingly, valuation cannot be reduced to being an act of pricing. It is rather an act of ordering that establishes a foundation for the prioritization of various kinds of scarce resources. A prioritization that can potentially have reordering effects on the aspect of the world it concerns.

The suggestion to think about the activity of tracing data as an act of valuation builds upon this broad definition of the concept. In order to make the link between tracing and valuation comprehensible it is, however, necessary to provide a few comments on what is here referred to as an act of 'tracing' in the context of digital methods. To trace something will be taken to have a double meaning. First, it refers to the act of collecting and storing native web objects such as links, tags, tweets, and log files. In digital methods this is typically done by repurposing data from powerful media platforms—such as Twitter, Google, and Facebook—that produce and own such data. Second, it refers to the activity of sketching a figure in order to delineate an empirical phenomenon and make it manageable. In digital methods this is done through the use of visualization software that turns the collected web objects into ordered depictions of specific aspects of the world. The activity of tracing data is, accordingly, seen as a combination of collecting, storing, and sketching.

The visualization in Figure 12.1 is an example of the kind of 'sketches' that can be produced by the practice of digital methods. It is made by the United Nations innovation lab, Global Pulse, and it is promoted as a new form of

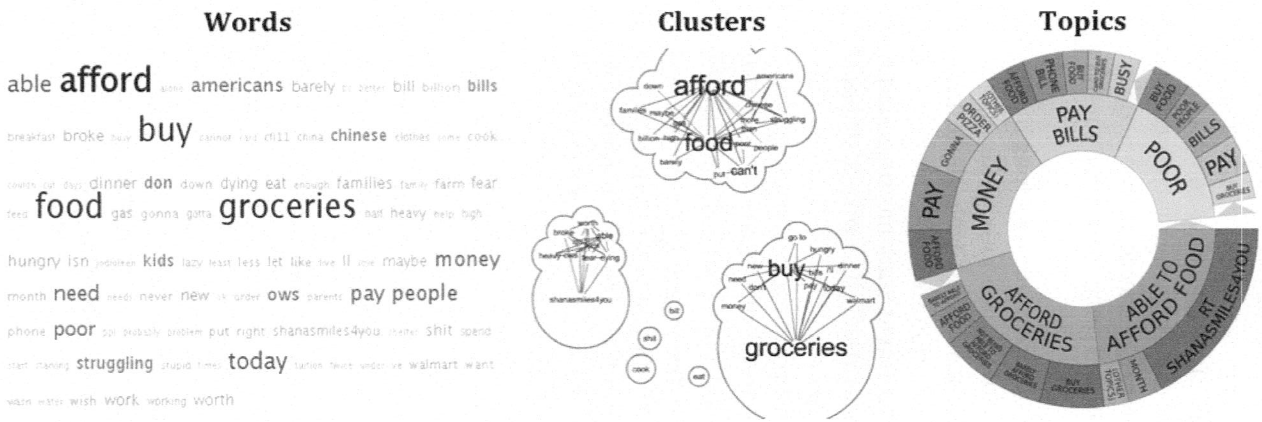

Figure 12.1. Screenshot of a 'crisis monitor' built by the UN Global Pulse that shows the semantic networks in Twitter data around the category of 'food'

crisis monitor within the UN. The visualization illustrates the relevance of attending to both of the above-mentioned meanings of 'tracing'. First, it is built by collecting words and semantic patterns in streams of Indonesian and American tweets. Secondly, it provides its users with a visual sketch of crisis-signals in Indonesia and the USA. For instance, the colours on the topic wheel to the right indicate the 'hotness' of specific crisis-related topics in the two countries. The crisis monitor is, accordingly, the outcome of an activity of tracing in the double meaning of the word. The details of its production will be returned to later in the chapter.

It follows from the arguments above that the activity of tracing can be interpreted as an act of valuation. To trace something in the context of digital methods is to produce visual tools that provide their users with a focused empirical sensitivity towards a specific aspect of the world. By highlighting some elements and connections while hiding others, such tools provide a foundation for prioritizing a limited resource, namely attention (see also Espeland and Lom, this volume). The explosion of native web objects has—just like any other new type of data—been accompanied by problems of information overload. Digital methods can be interpreted as a way to handle this resource problem. Using phrases from economics, one can say that the monitor in Figure 12.1 is a heuristic that helps identify relevant crisis-prone populations for the UN to *pay* attention to. The ascription of visibility involved in the act of tracing simply deems some aspects of the world *worthy* of attention in relation to a specific problem. Ultimately, it is a tool for deciding where to prioritize scare economic resources. The visualizations produced by digital methods are, accordingly, a kind of valuation device that is important to study in the context of the so-called attention economy.

A Dominant Narrative about Tracing and Digital Methods

The interest in debating the logic of digital methods is gaining traction across different social scientific traditions. The emerging use of these methods has been accompanied by several attempts at pinpointing how they can legitimately be used to generate knowledege about social dynamics. Roughly speaking, it is fair to say that these attempts have primarily been concerned with two themes. First, there has been a discussion concerning the role that theoretical preconceptions should play in the process of turning dynamic web objects into digital visualizations. Second, there has been a discussion about the extent to which such visualizations are productively seen as representations of the world they depict. The way these themes are approached by practitioners will arguably influence how digital methods can be used to aid decision-making. Settling the narrative about these methods is at the same time to settle how they can be used. This section argues that there is dominant narrative around these themes that has recently been influential in setting the agenda about what digital methods are and should be.

First, the debate about the role of theory has largely been dominated by works that highlight the possibility of using digital methods to generate knowledge without having to bias social enquiry with theoretical preconceptions. This inductive claim has surfaced in various forms, but it has had its most popular formulation in Chris Anderson's essay, 'The End of Theory' (2008). Anderson's core argument is that contemporary digital data flows are too big to be organized on the basis of predefined theoretical categories. Whereas previous metaphors of ordering (e.g. the filing cabinet) centred around man-made categorizations as the core sorting mechanism, Anderson suggests that the emergence of digital methods brings a need for new metaphors. Such metaphors, he argued, should take inspiration from the way a company like Google has built their success on a belief in substituting human-centred information filtering with applied mathematics when ordering information. It is this kind of inductive mindset that Anderson wants to transfer to the social sciences when he argues that, 'with enough data, the numbers speak for themselves' (Anderson 2008). In short, his argument is that digital methods should be used to guide the attention of scientists and decision-makers because they offer a possibility to bypass biased human categorizations.

Anderson's essay was written as a polemical piece in *Wired*, but elements of his argumentation are reflected in academic writings by both positivist and constructivist researchers. On the positivist side, the journal *Science* has given space to promoting the development of a 'computational social science' that also (albeit in a less confrontational manner) emphasizes the need for social scientists to let their decisions guide by algorithmically detected patterns in big data sets (Lazer et al. 2009). On the constructivist side, we can see an echo of Anderson's argument in the writings of Bruno Latour. Despite writing from a completely different ontological standpoint than both Anderson and the computational social scientists, Latour also seems to suggest that the granularity of native web objects enables social scientists to stop thinking in tired theoretical distinctions and start generating knowledge by 'following the actors' in an inductive fashion (Latour et al. 2012). In fact, Latour is explicitly referring to computational social science as a methodological movement that has the potential to revolutionize the social sciences (Latour 2010).

These arguments about the rise of an inductive empiricism are also connected to a belief in native web objects as a source of data that is more direct, unmediated, and honest than data produced through standard methods such as surveys and focus groups. Under the heading of computational social science it has, for instance, been suggested to think about these new types of data as 'honest signals' (Pentland 2008) that are derived from people's actual behaviour rather than their memory (Vinciarelli et al. 2008). Native web objects are thereby framed as having a sort of introspective capacity that can reveal people's true intentions because they are free from the kind of strategic signalling that pollute other types of data (Wu and Brynjolfsson 2009). Even though Latour has reservations concerning this line of thinking, there are nonetheless elements in his writings that bear traces of it. For instance, he has argued that native web objects open up our private worlds for scrutiny in a way that makes visible the 'precise forces that mould our subjectivities and the precise characters that furnish our imaginations' (Latour 2007).

Despite their obvious differences, it can be argued that the writers mentioned above contribute to a dominant narrative about the way digital methods can be used to guide attention towards the social. Rather than seeing the web as a phoney cyberspace, they see it as a tool for mining social realities. They build on a belief in digital interfaces—such as Google's search box or Twitter's mobile app—as infrastructures of signals that can be used to represent people's inner thoughts. This belief is ultimately connected to the extent to which they aim for digital visualizations to mirror the aspects of the world they are meant to depict. If native web objects are taken to be direct, unmediated, and honest introspections, it follows that the link between these objects and the empirical world remains relatively unproblematic. As long as the debate concerns the link between an individual consciousness and the trace it leaves, the latter is simply taken as an unpolluted index of the former that can be traced back to its origin.

The next question is how this belief affects the way the mentioned writers handle the theme concerning representation. Can a visualization that is built on an aggregation of individual traces be said to represent a social phenomenon? One popular response to this question has been to enrol the assumption that society is nothing but an aggregate of individual actions. Following this theory of 'emergence' (Johnson 2004) it becomes unproblematic to transfer claims about representation from individual data to aggregate visualizations. This is the approach to the question of representation that underpins both Anderson's writings and the movement of computational social science. However, it is evident that Latour's take on the question of representation is different. His sociological project involves an explicit critique of the tendency to see society as an aggregate of individual actions. Therefore, he refuses to see digital methods as representing the aggregate structural patterns that emerge from such actions (Latour 2005)

Latour's alternative take on representation is best explained through the concept of 'second-degree objectivity'. This concept is tied to a project entitled 'mapping controversies' that explicitly promises to use digital methods to *represent* techno-scientific controversies and make them navigable for the public (Venturini 2012). Digital methods are argued to provide 'quake-proof representations' of social dynamics as long as they are built according to two guidelines. First, their elements need to be sized according to the number of actors ascribing to them and the influence they entertain. Second, they must ensure multiplicity in the depiction of the controversy by making minority viewpoints visible. To meet these requirements, the practitioner of digital methods needs to draw a series of visualizations that are each dedicated to different aspects of the controversy in question. It is then the subsequent 'layering' of these visualizations that ensures that the whole controversy is represented in a quake-proof manner (Venturini 2012). On this account of representation it is not as important where the researcher starts his tracing. Each starting point will create a partial map, but as soon as enough maps are overlapped it will be possible to create a visualization that represents the whole controversy (Latour et al. 2012)

While the approaches of Anderson, the computational scientists, and the practitioners of controversy mapping arguably have their differences, it can nonetheless be argued that they are devising somewhat similar answers to the questions about theory and representation. They are all contributing to a specific narrative that has recently dominated the discussion about digital methods across positivist and constructivist lines of research. The core claim of this dominant narrative is that the availability of traceable web objects and powerful visualization techniques calls for new modes of social enquiry that use digital visualizations to represent social dynamics through inductive pattern recognition of honest—or at least fairly accurate—behavioural signals. To be sure, both Latour and the computational social scientists have sophisticated critical reflections about the meaning of this claim in parts of their writings,. However, it is fair to say that central parts of their work support it on one way or another. This narrative influences the way digital methods can legitimately be used in decision-making processes, because their value as tools of social enquiry becomes tied to their honesty and representativeness. The next section will introduce the perceptual theory of James Gibson and the concept of 'web visions' as the foundation of a different narrative about what digital methods are and how they can be used.

James Gibson's Theory of Perception as a Foundation for Conceptualizing Digital Visualizations as 'Web Visions'

James Gibson was a neo-pragmatic scholar of visual perception who lived from 1904 to 1979. He has not previously played any important role in the discussion of digital methods except for one mention of his work in a footnote

(Latour et al. 2012). However, Gibson's interest in the interplay between technology, materiality, and perception makes his work a promising foundation for constructing a different narrative about the logic of digital methods than the one outlined above. More specifically, Gibson's work will be used to make two suggestions. First, that digital visualizations are productively interpreted as 'visions'[2] that 'afford' specific modes of seeing though specific alignments of technological infrastructures, human intentions, and situated practices. This is different than interpreting them as products of honest signals. Second, that the heuristic value of such visions derives from the kind of 'invariants' they extract from available data streams. This is different than seeing their value as tied to that which they represent outside the data flows from which they are generated.

The first suggestion builds on a core concept in Gibson's theory of perception—that of 'affordances'. While this concept has recently been associated with functionalist theories of technology design (Norman 2000), it carries a much more complex meaning in Gibson's original writings. Here, affordances are more than a reference to functional characteristics of entities in the environment that surrounds the perceiver. Gibson explicitly intended the concept to have a dual reference to such entities as well as to the perceiving agent:

> The *affordances* of the *environment* are what it *offers* the animal, what it *provides* or *furnishes*, either for good or for ill. The verb to *afford* is found in the dictionary but the noun *affordance* is not. I have made it up. I mean by it something that refers to both the environment and the animal in a way that no existing term does. It implies the complementarity of both the animal and the environment. (Gibson 1986, 127)

When Gibson speaks about the affordances of the environment in the first part of the quote he is pointing to all the material and immaterial entities that provide a perceiving agent a potential for action and sense-making. Such entities could, for instance, take the form of 'surfaces' (a frozen lake that affords walking), 'objects' (a pencil that affords trace-making), 'persons' (a colleague that affords social interaction), or 'mediums' (air that affords the transfer of sound) (Gibson 1986, 130–7). When Gibson used the concept of 'affordances' in this way, it does indeed have the functional meaning that it has subsequently been associated with. However, the latter part of the quote clearly indicates that this is only half of what Gibson intended the concept to convey. He admittedly argued that entities in the environment condition the possibilities for perception and action, but he always emphasized the necessity of understanding such conditions in relation to the perceiving agent and the situation he or she acts within.

In short, Gibson distanced himself from functionalism and technological determinism by arguing that 'different layouts afford different behaviors for different animals' (Gibson 1986, 126). For instance, a newly frozen lake affords support for a mouse but not for an elephant and the appearance of a specific human being in the environment affords different forms of interaction for different persons depending on their previous interactions with this person. Accordingly, affordances are just as much related to the perceiving agent and the situation of perception as it is to entities in the environment. This relational focus explains why Gibson took pains to point out that the concept of 'affordances' should be read as a noun rather than a verb. He explicitly refused to think of it as a quality of either a subject or an object. He thought of it as an 'ecological object' with its own distinct ontological status—an object that emerges through the interplay between conditions set by the environment and subjective meaning making in a specific practical situation where perception or action is necessary.

For the purposes of this chapter it is interesting that Gibson also took the information that a perceiving agent needs to interact with the environment to exhibit such an ontological in-betweenness. More specifically, he argued that the information an agent uses to specify the utilities of the environment is accompanied by information to specify the characteristics of him- or herself. As Gibson formulated it: 'to perceive the world is to co-perceive oneself [...] the awareness of the world and one's complementary relations to the world are not separable' (Gibson 1986, 141). One of the simple examples that Gibson used to illustrate this point is that one must have a good sense of one's own weight in order to perceive the affordances of a newly frozen lake. Similarly, in order to correctly perceive the affordances of another person, one must have a good idea of one's relation to that person. When it came to perception and information Gibson, accordingly, took the distinction between the subjective and the objective to be utterly fruitless.

Gibson used this relational definition of 'affordances' to argue that perception and sense-making are to be seen as active achievements rather than a function of discrete anatomical parts that passively translate external stimulus to brain images (Gibson 1986, 309). In that sense, Gibson's perceptual theory represents a break with the traditional picture of perception as mental causes of external effects. In the context of this chapter, we will see how this argument around the concept of 'affordances' can be translated to a warning against seeing digital visualizations as causes of honest signals coming from outside the information infrastructure that practitioners of digital methods construct to pick them up.

Gibson's break with the established picture of perception furthermore made it problematic for him to evaluate the content of perception through criteria of correspondence. He refused to determine the epistemological value of a perception by asking whether a specific mental image is representative of the stimulus that created it. His theory of perception suggested an alternative epistemology of perception. The core element in this epistemology is the assumption that perception involves movement (Gibson 1986, 243). Being on the move was—to Gibson—the only possible way to discriminate information in an environment where information is inexhaustible, relational, and constantly flowing. He saw perception as a distributed and active system that becomes more and more elaborate through the development of practical and discriminatory skills.

Gibson's alternative to evaluating perception on criteria of correspondence and representation was to define a well-functioning perceptual system as one that enables sensitivity towards 'invariants of structure' in the environment:

> We can say that the perceiver separates the change from the non-change, notices what stays the same and what does not, or sees the continuing identity of things along with the events in which they participate. The question, of course, is how he does so. What is the information for persistence and change? The answer must be of this sort: The perceiver extracts invariants of structure from the flux of stimulation while still noticing the flux. (Gibson 1986, 247)

Gibson used the concept of 'invariants' as a reference to fixed points through which the chaos of the environment can be organized. His argument was that it is such points that structure how the perceiving agent experiences changes in the environment as well as in him- or herself. Since Gibson took such experiences to be the foundation for engaging and acting in the world, it not surprising that he took the concept of 'invariants' to be an important element of his theory of perception. In line with his theory of affordances, Gibson maintained that invariants should not be seen as something that comes as an input to a perceiving agent from the outside. Rather they are heuristics extracted from within the available data flows. The perceiving agent is not adequately understood as either a good or bad mirror of nature. He or she is rather to be understood as a 'sampling point' that is either good or bad at constantly picking up useful invariants though an active engagement with the environment (Gibson 1986, 311).

Gibson gave different examples of how such 'information pick-up' could occur. In one of his simplest examples, he asks the reader to imagine how the movement of the sun affords picking up specific types of invariants (Gibson 1986, 88–91). For instance, a shadow on a stone will move while the contours of the stone remain stable, when the sun moves from east to west. If the perceiving agent is in a situation that equips him or her to pick up this invariant, it will become a useful heuristic from which to discriminate between the empirical entities 'stone' and 'shadow'. Other examples of information pick-up concern invariants that can be extracted when the perceiving agent moves (Gibson 1986, chs. 7 and 12). For instance, the activity of walking can provide the perceiving agent with heuristics for discriminating between him- or herself and the environment. Similarly, the persistence of specific blind angles in the perceptual field while walking can enable a perceiving agent to link these blind angles to his or her physical makeup, rather than taking them to be connected to the makeup of the environment. The persistence of blind angles is, according, a useful invariant to be used for achieving a form of self-awareness that would not be possible without movement.

The epistemological conclusion that Gibson extracts from his concept of 'invariants' is that the capability to 'see' and act is coupled to discriminatory skills that are bound to be situational. They change from organism to organism and from event to event. An important point to take away from Gibson´s theory of perception is, therefore, that different perceptual systems are tuned into picking up different types of information from environments that afford very different kinds of 'information pick-up'. It is the interplay between the affordances of the environment, the perceiver, and the situation that determines the kind of invariants it is possible to extract and use to make sense of the world. Different types of interplay afford the extraction of different types of invariants and thereby different heuristics for seeing the world and discriminating between its elements. It is with reference to this interplay—rather than to any measure of correspondence—that Gibson evaluates the insights derived from this perceptual system.

Just as the concept of 'affordances' can be translated into a warning against seeing digital visualizations as causes of honest signals, we can use the concept of 'invariants' to interpret digital methods as a practice that should be evaluated by the invariants it extracts from data flows rather than on its representational achievements. Gibson's concepts of 'affordances' and 'invariants' can, in combination, be used as a foundation from which to think about digital methods as a practice that produces 'web visions' that can only be made sense of through a different narrative than the one outlined earlier. The next section will return to the crisis monitor in Figure 12.1 to illustrate the empirical relevance of interpreting digital methods through the concept of 'web-visions'.

The UN Crisis Monitor as a Web Vision That Prioritizes Attention

This section will illustrate that the crisis monitor shown in Figure 12.1 has many shared characteristics with the kind of ecological objects that Gibson referred to as affording specific modes of seeing. More specifically, it seems reasonable to interpret the monitor as a 'vision' that exists in-between conditions set by constraints in the technological environment, the intentions and assumptions on the part of its designers, and the characteristics of the situation in which it is produced. Furthermore, the section argues that it is promising to use Gibson's thoughts about invariants to make sense of the kind of empirical sensitivity that the monitor provides its users with.

If we start by looking at the crisis monitor through the concept of 'affordances', it is arguably the case that it is shaped by conditions set by the technological environment in which it is produced. One such condition is that important choices about data formatting are beyond the control of the intended users in the UN. The monitor is produced by harnessing the data that Twitter makes available to specific users (Pulse 2011). When the data comes within the reach of the UN it has already been formatted in specific ways. For instance, it comes in chunks of 140 characters and it is ordered though specific user-generated meta-data such as hashtags (#) and replies (@). Furthermore, it is produced on an interface that is not designed with the intention to produce reliable crisis-signals. To the contrary it is designed to make people communicate in specific event-driven ways that is of value to Twitter Inc. (Rogers 2013). Changes in the interface and the data formats—which will inevitably influence the visualization—are guided by concerns that are irrelevant to the crisis-related problems that they are repurposed to solve in the context of the UN.

A second condition set by the technological environment is that the flow of data is so large and fast paced, that parts of the data analysis need to be automated. A human expert cannot routinely oversee the data behind the visualization because such a check would require an excessive amount of human brainpower. As put by the project leader, the monitor needs to be a 'current enough reflection of reality to be used to respond in ways to alter the outcome' (Madsen 2012). The semantic network that visualizes the discussion about food in the middle of the monitor in Figure 12.1 is therefore the result of an algorithm that is programmed to automatically find patterns in tweets on the basis of specific assumptions about associative structures in natural language (Pulse 2011). However, even if enough brainpower were available, it would still be hard for human analysts within the UN to pin down the provenance of the tweets that serve as the basis for the visualization. Since the act of opening a Twitter account does not require any reliable act of identification, it is virtually impossible to ensure that users and accounts are equivalent. Some users have many accounts, some accounts are used by multiple people, and some accounts are run by robots (Boyd and Crawford 2011).

These are just two examples of data characteristics that are beyond the control of the people within the UN that uses the monitor to 'see' early signals of crisis. This illustrates that digital methods are a practice of knowledge creation that is conditioned by the features of the software infrastructures through which they are harnessed. Contrary to methods such as household surveys it is not possible to keep data production in-house and thereby control its provenance. In Gibson's vocabulary it can be said that Twitter's interface and data flow afford specific modes of empirical sensitivity on the part of the UN. However, it is again crucial to remember that Gibson did not use the concept of 'affordances' as a reference to features of the environment alone. A further look at the production of the crisis monitor similarly indicates that its shape is not determined by affordances of the technological environment. Rather, it is quite heavily influenced by the epistemic assumptions of its designers and the characteristics of the situation in which it is produced.

Details of this Gibsonian in-betweenness is illustrated by an enquiry into the decisions made in the process of translating the data obtained from Twitter into the final visualization (Madsen 2013b). This enquiry illustrates that such a translation is accompanied with hard epistemological and organizational trade-offs. One trade-off concerns the choice between, on the one hand, prioritizing transparency and structure in the way data is collected, and on the other hand, prioritizing the pace and adaptability of the data formats that are repurposed. Another trade-off concerns the need to choose between on the one hand, trusting and following the algorithms to reveal new aspects of the world, and on the other hand, making use of well-established metaphors that resonate with ongoing discussions in the organization (see also Madsen 2015). The interesting point to make in relation to these trade-offs is that the technological environment does not determine their answers. The way they are solved is rather influenced by epistemological assumptions on part of the project leaders as well as organizational norms within the UN.

For instance, central choices in the construction of the crisis monitor are legitimized though a reference to a statement by the UN secretary-general who argues that contemporary crises move with unprecedented speed and that traditional methods are to slow to function under these conditions (Ki-Moon 2011). This assumption about the empirical world is a reason for balancing the first trade-off in favour of dynamic and adaptable data. Similarly, the shape of the monitor reflects a choice to refrain from using purely automated pattern analysis because the visualization need to reflect the vocabulary used in the rest of the (quite bureaucratic) organization. As the director of Global Pulse puts it: 'It is not just about getting the data; it is also [...] about the organizational capacity to facture a snapshot of these types of information in the context of their on-going policy development planning' (Madsen 2012). The crisis monitor can, accordingly, be conceptualized as a 'web vision' that shares epistemological characteristics with the ecological objects Gibson refers to in his studies of visual perception. It affords a prioritization of attention that exists in-between technological conditions, epistemic assumptions, and organizational situations.

The concept of 'invariants' similarly comes out as well suited to explain how the monitor enables the UN to pay attention to certain aspects of the empirical world while ignoring others. Most importantly, the monitor is not constructed with the ambition to represent any population in the traditional sense of the word. Instead it is intended to ignite sensitivity towards empirical anomalies, which is a rather different empirical tactic. In the words of the project-leaders it is set up to spot 'something odd, some anomaly, something that looks a little unfamiliar, a little suspicious, a little concerning' (Madsen 2012). This difference between a tactic of representation and anomaly detection mirrors Gibson's distinction between representational theories of perception and his own ecological theory based on invariants. Whereas the ambition of representation is coupled with correspondence theories, it can be argued that UN's crisis monitor aims to produce useful 'visions' by building on invariants in the constant flow of data harnessed from Twitter's API.

Figure 12.2 shows a concrete visualization of such an invariant. The graph shows it to be a reoccurring phenomenon that negative sentiment about the housing economy rises around payday at the beginning of each month and declines rapidly thereafter (Pulse 2011). This invariant is extracted from within the flow of tweets but it comes to function as a baseline for interpreting future tweets on this topic in this location. It enables the user of the monitor to refrain from over-interpreting a spike in negative sentiment at the beginning of a month and instead to focus on whether it is sustained longer or shorter than is normally the case. The detected invariant can even be built into the algorithm that colours the topic wheel to the right in the figure, so that it takes more negative tweets about the economy to ignite a red colour (which indicates an emerging crisis) at the beginning of the month.

The important point to take away from this discussion of invariants is that the benchmarks for interesting findings are derived from within the stream of tweets. The interesting question is not whether the tweets represent real sentiments of a predefined population. It is rather whether they are organized in such a way as to make interesting anomalies visible that help the UN

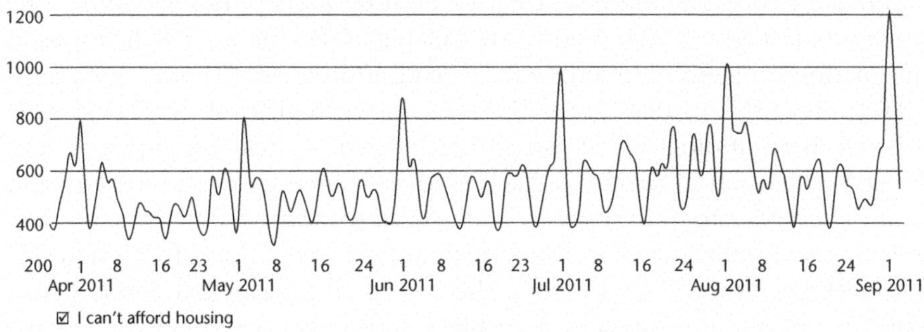

Figure 12.2. Visualization showing the number of tweets in the USA between April and September 2011 that address concerns about not being able to afford housing

to pay attention to relevant issues in a timely manner. Given the difficulty to control choices at the interface level and the difficulty to enquire into the provenance of data, this is the empirical strategy that most successfully aligns the distributed actors enrolled into the construction of the monitor. The empirical existence of such a strategy makes it sensible to follow Gibson in seeing the monitor as an ambulatory system that searches for invariants through a constant alignment of the distributed elements it is made up of.

Web Visions as a Digression from the Dominant Narrative and a Continuation of Insights from Valuation Studies

It has just been argued that the UN's crisis monitor can productively be interpreted as a 'web vision' that provides its user with sensitivity towards invariants and anomalies inside a flow of data in the Twitter infrastructure rather than a representation of a specific crisis-prone population based on honest signals about a population's well-being. This section suggests that this is an argument that points towards a quite different take on the practice of digital methods—and their potential role in guidance of attention—than the dominant narrative outlined above. Besides that it will argue that the suggestion to think about digital visualizations as 'visions' can be seen as continuing three claims made about market devices within valuation studies.

One difference to the dominant narrative is that the affordances of 'web visions' are seen as something that cannot be properly understood by attending to the characteristics of the digital technologies used to produce them. 'Web visions' are not seen as the outcome of discrete acts of data processing such as the act of leaving honest signals or the act of letting an algorithm spot correlations in an inductive fashion. They are rather to be seen as outcomes of systems with nested affordances (Gibson 1986, 205). Therefore, the potentials of 'web visions' can neither be abstracted from the contexts in which they are to be used nor the software interfaces they are built upon. Rephrasing Gibson, one can say that different 'web visions' are capable of picking up specific forms of information from environments with specific affordances (Gibson 1986, 53).

'Web visions' are therefore to be seen as 'ecological objects' that exist in-between technological infrastructures epistemological assumptions, and situated construction practices. Each of these elements set conditions that need to be understood in order to understand what digital methods are and how digital visualizations can function as devices that guide attention in specific contexts. In line with Gibson's theory it seems reasonable to say that it is only when acts are connected and aligned into a functioning whole, that a useful 'web vision' is possible. This is quite different than the way the dominant narrative has discussed the potential of digital methods on the basis of abstract descriptions of the potentials of digital data such as the possibility to break with theoretical preconceptions and the possibility to zoom in on its provenance and the context in which it is left.

This way of thinking about digital methods can be seen as a continuation of a central claim in valuation studies. Namely, that markets are not adequately understood as functions of pre-existing structures of supply and demand. To the contrary, works within valuation studies have emphasized that supply and demand only enter economic markets if there are devices that render them visible and calculable (Callon and Muniesa 2005). Therefore, it is the calculative spaces created by such devices—rather than pre-existing utility functions—that condition the way supply and demand are thought about in a market (Zuckerman 2004). Transferring this insight to the study of digital methods entails a rejection of the tendency to see native web objects—and ultimately the shape of digital visualizations—as a function of people's 'honest' behaviour. Such behaviours are only up for debate once they are made visible through specific devices with specific infrastructures. In order to understand how digital methods guide attention, one must foreground questions about software interfaces in the way suggested above.

A second difference between the concept of 'web visions' and the dominant narrative concerns the question of theory. The extent to which 'web visions' are built on theoretical assumptions cannot be reduced to a question about whether theories concerning the topic of the visualization are encoded into a software system by topical experts. The question must be broadened to include, for instance, general theories about semantics and network structures that are distributed across the chain of actors that shape the visualization. This also means that 'web visions' will ultimately assign values to assets in the world on the basis of theories with controversial assumptions. Whereas these theories may not be related to the topic visualized, it has been illustrated how the production of a visualization like the crisis monitor is filled with trade-offs about the distribution of theory. The existence of such trade-offs is a pragmatic reason for being critical towards the tendencies of thinking about digital methods as enabling an inductive empiricism.

Again, this is a take on digital methods that can be said to continue a claim made in the context of valuation studies. Namely, that the theoretical assumptions that influence market devices are distributed and multi-levelled. For instance, the so-called FICO scores that are used to evaluate the creditworthiness of potential lenders in the USA, are aggregates of a pool of data that is provided by a distributed set of actors with different theoretical preconceptions (Poon 2007). This distribution of sources entails that the FICO score is a result of an exercise in chaining together these lower-level devices (Madsen 2013a). In short, market devices rarely stand alone. They are built by chaining together various types of actors and devices that each have their own theoretical foundations. Transferring this insight about distribution to the practice of digital methods entails a problematization of the tendency to equate inductive pattern recognition with the absence of theoretical assumptions. Rather than being eliminated, theoretical assumptions can just as easily be moved elsewhere in the chain of actors.

Finally, the concept of 'web visions' entails a different take on the questions of representation than the dominant narrative. More specifically, it has been emphasized that 'web visions' should be evaluated as experimental detections of invariants produced by a perceptual system that actively aligns available objects and mediums to fixed points with reference to which the changing environment can be organized. This is a quite different epistemic strategy than either of the different strategies of representation that characterized the dominant narrative. In a data environment where it is difficult to control samples and where the provenance of data sources is often non-transparent, it seems a promising strategy to construct visualizations with the aim of detecting invariants inside the data rather than constructing them with the aim of representing something external. It leads to a different view on the ways in which they can be used as valuation devices in the attention economy.

Once again, this argument can be said to continue a claim in valuation studies. This time it is the claim that market devices perform—rather than represent—markets. For instance, MacKenzie (2006) has successfully shown how option-pricing theories can give legitimacy to specific forms of financial derivatives. Beunza and Stark (2012) have shown that security traders tend to think of their models as social cues rather than representations of reality and Quattrone (this volume) raises similar questions concerning the practice of accounting. The discussion of the representative ambitions of digital methods above mirrors these arguments. Rather than pretending to represent the mood of a predefined population, 'web visions' are built to spot anomalies inside data flowing from Twitter. It is an explicit choice to give up the idea of having external benchmarks to judge the visualization against.

Outro

The core theoretical argument put forward in this chapter is that digital methods can be interpreted as a practice that produces 'web visions'. Such visions enable their users to pay attention to specific assets in situations where attention is a scarce resource that needs to be spent wisely. They are evaluative devices because they determine the 'attention-worthiness' of specific assets on the basis of quite specific dynamics. Furthermore, the chapter argued that such dynamics of evaluation are productively understood through Gibson's concepts of 'affordances' and 'invariants'.

The suggestion to interpret digital visualizations as 'web visions' was presented as a way of understanding digital methods that sets out an alternative line of research than the dominant narrative around this emerging methodological practice. This narrative frames digital visualizations as devices that represent the social on the basis of honest (or at least fairly accurate) traces. Furthermore, it was argued that the concept of 'web visions' opens a way of interpreting digital visualizations as valuation devices that share characteristics with some of the market devices that have served as cases in financially focused valuation studies. However, a 'web vision' is an epistemological device that orders cognitive processes rather than markets and any future discussions of the concept of 'web visions' should be sensitive to this difference.

The discussion about the use of digital visualizations as evaluative tools in specific decision-making context will arguably be shaped by the way digital methods are conceptualized and understood. Whereas this chapter has shown that a visualization like UN's crisis monitor is productively made sense of as a 'web vision', it has not shown that this is true for all digital visualizations. The concept of 'web visions' may suit some cases better than others and it should be taken as a supplementary vocabulary from which to make sense of the practice of digital methods. However, with its distinct theoretical roots in pragmatic theories of valuation and perception it does allow for different questions about digital methods than the dominant paradigm. With such new questions come new suggestions concerning the uses of the exciting new epistemological devices that digitalization has provided for practitioners of social inquiry.

Notes

1. While the concept of 'web visions' does indeed provide a distinct vocabulary for approaching the practice of digital methods, it is important to emphasize its relation to existing academic works on this topic. Some of the points that the concept will be used to make in this chapter, for instance, have clear resonance with the work of writers like Noortje Marres (e.g. Marres 2012; Marres and Weltevrede 2012) and Richard Rogers (e.g. Rogers 2009). The details of the similarities and differences to these writers will not be part of this chapter, but they are thoroughly explored in the PhD dissertation that this chapter is based upon (Madsen 2013b). Furthermore, the argument of this chapter bears some similarities to work done by colleagues at the techno-anthropology research group at AAU-CPH (e.g. Birkbak 2013; Jensen et al. 2014; Munk and Jensen 2015).
2. It should be noted that Gibson rarely used the concept of 'vision' in his writings. However, he used the concept of 'perception' in a way that is equivalent to the way the concept of 'vision' is used in this chapter. Namely, as a reference to the way a person sees the world and comes to evaluate the attention-worthiness of specific assets in the empirical environment that he or she in acting within.

References

Anderson, C. 2008. 'The End of Theory'. *Wired* 16(7): 108.

Ban Ki-Moon. 2011. 'Secretary-General's Remarks at General Assembly Briefing on the Global Pulse Initiative'. 8 November. <http://www.un.org/sg/statements/?nid=5668>, accessed 11 January 2012.

Beunza, D. and D. Stark. 2012. 'From Dissonance to Resonance: Cognitive Interdependence in Quantitative Finance'. *Economy & Society* 41(3): 383–417.

Birkbak, A. 2013. 'From Networked Publics to Issue Publics: Reconsidering the Public/Private Distinction in Web Science'. *Proceedings of WebScience '13*.

Boyd, D. and K. Crawford. 2011. 'Six Provocations for Big Data'. Symposium on the Dynamics of the Internet and Society.

Callon, M. and F. Muniesa. 2005. 'Peripheral Vision: Economic Markets as Calculative Collective Devices'. *Organization Studies* 26(8): 1229–50.

Cooley, C. H. 1912. 'Valuation as a Social Process'. *Psychological Bulletin* 9(12): 441–50.

Dewey, J. 1955 [1908]. 'Theory of Valuation'. In *International Encyclopedia of Unified Science* 2(4), ed. O. Neurath, R. Carnap, and C. Morris. Chicago: University of Chicago Press.

Gibson, J. J. 1986. *The Ecological Approach to Visual Perception*. New York: Psychology Press.

Global Pulse. 2011. 'Twitter and Perceptions of crisis Related Stress'. Methodological White Paper. Homepage of Global Pulse. <http://www.unglobalpulse.org/projects/twitter-and-perceptions-crisis-related-stress>, accessed 11 January 2012.

Helgesson, C. and F. Muniesa. 2013. 'For What It's Worth: An Introduction to Valuation Studies'. *Valuation Studies* 1(1): 1–10.

Jensen, T. E., A. K. Munk, A. K. Madsen, and A. Birkbak. 2014. 'Expanding the Visual Registers of STS'. In *Visualization in the Age of Computerization*, ed. A. Carusi, A. S. Hoel, T. Webmoore, and S. Woolgar. New York: Routledge, 226–31.

Johnson, S. 2004. *Emergence: The Connected Lives of Ants, Brains, Cities, and Software*. New York: Scribner.

Latour, B. 2005. *Reassembling the social: An Introduction to Actor-Network-Theory*. New York: Oxford University Press.

Latour, B. 2007. 'Beware, Your Imagination Leaves Digital Traces', *Times Higher Literary Supplement*, 6 April.

Latour, B. 2010. 'Tarde's Idea of Quantification'. In *The Social After Gabriel Tarde: Debates and Assessments*, ed. M. Candea. New York: Routledge, 145–62.

Latour, B., P. Jensen, T. Venturini, S. Grauwin, and D. Boullier. 2012. '"The Whole is Always Smaller than its Parts": A Digital Test of Gabriel Tardes' Monads'. *British Journal of Sociology* 63(4): 590–615.

Lazer, D., A. S. Pentland, L. Adamic, S. Aral, A. L. Barabasi, D. Brewer, N. Christakis, N. Contractor, J. Fowler, and M. Gutmann. 2009. 'Life in the Network: The Coming Age of Computational Social Science'. *Science* 323(5915): 721.

MacKenzie, D. A. 2006. *An Engine, Not a Camera: How Financial Models Shape Markets*. Cambridge, MA: MIT Press.

Madsen, A. K. 2012. Interview with Robert Kirkpatrick.

Madsen, A. K. 2013a. 'Steps Towards a Conceptualisation of Digital Institutions of Knowledge', *Science, Technology & Society* 18(1): 63–74.

Madsen, A. K. 2013b. 'Web-Visions: Repurposing Digital Traces to Organize Social Attention'. PhD dissertation, Copenhagen Business School.

Madsen, A. K. 2015. 'Between Technical Features and Analytic Capabilities: Charting a Relational Affordance Space for Digital Social Analytics', *Big Data & Society,* 2(1).

Marres, N. 2012. 'The Redistribution of Methods: On Intervention in Digital Social Research, Broadly Conceived'. *Sociological Review* 60(S1): 139–65.

Marres, N. and E. Weltevrede. 2013. 'Scraping the Social? Issues in Live Social Research'. *Journal of Cultural Economy* 6(3): 313–35.

Muniesa, F., Y. Millo, and M.Callon. 2007. 'An Introduction to Market Devices'. *Sociological Review* 55(2): 1–12.

Munk, A. K and T. E. Jensen. 2014. 'Revisiting the Histories of Mapping: Is There a Future for a Cartographic Ethnology?' *Ethnologia Europaea* 44(2): 31–47.

Norman, D. A. 2000. *The Design of Everyday Things*. London: MIT Press.

Pentland, A. 2008. *Honest Signals: How They Shape Our World*. Cambridge, MA: Massachusetts Institute of Technology.

Poon, M. 2007. 'Scorecards as Devices for Consumer Credit: The Case of Fair, Isaac & Company Incorporated'. *Sociological Review* 55(2): 284–306.

Prato, M. and D. Stark. 2012. 'Attention Structures and Valuation Models: Cognitive Networks among Securities Analysts'.

Rogers, R. 2009. *The End of the Virtual: Digital Methods*. Amsterdam: Amsterdam University Press.

Rogers, R. 2013. 'Debanalizing Twitter: The Transformation of an Object of Study'. Proceedings of the 5th Annual ACM Web Science Conference.

Stark, D. 2011. 'What's Valuable?' in *The Worth of Goods: Valuation and Pricing in the Economy*, ed. P. Aspers and J. Beckert. Oxford: Oxford University Press, 319–38.

Venturini, T. 2012, 'Building on Faults: How to Represent Controversies with Digital Methods'. *Public Understanding of Science* 21(7): 796–812.

Vinciarelli, A., M. Pantic, H. Bourlard, and A. Pentland. 2008. 'Social Signals, Their Function, and Automatic Analysis: A Survey'. Proceedings of the 10th International Conference on Multimodal Interfaces, ACM.

Wu, L. and E. Brynjolfsson. 2009. 'The Future of Prediction: How Google Searches Foreshadow Housing Prices and Sales'. ICIS Proceedings. Paper 147.

Zuckerman, E. W. 2004. 'Structural Incoherence and Stock Market Activity'. *American Sociological Review* 69(3): 405–32.

Index

Index

The manufacturer's authorised representative in the EU for product safety is Oxford University Press España S.A. of El Parque Empresarial San Fernando de Henares, Avenida de Castilla, 2 - 28830 Madrid (www.oup.es/en or product.safety@oup.com). OUP España S.A. also acts as importer into Spain of products made by the manufacturer.
Printed and bound by CPI Group (UK) Ltd, Croydon, CR0 4YY
14/09/2026
02216306-0006